An Introduction to
Berkeley UNIX and ANSI C

Jack Hodges

Computer Science Department
San Francisco State University

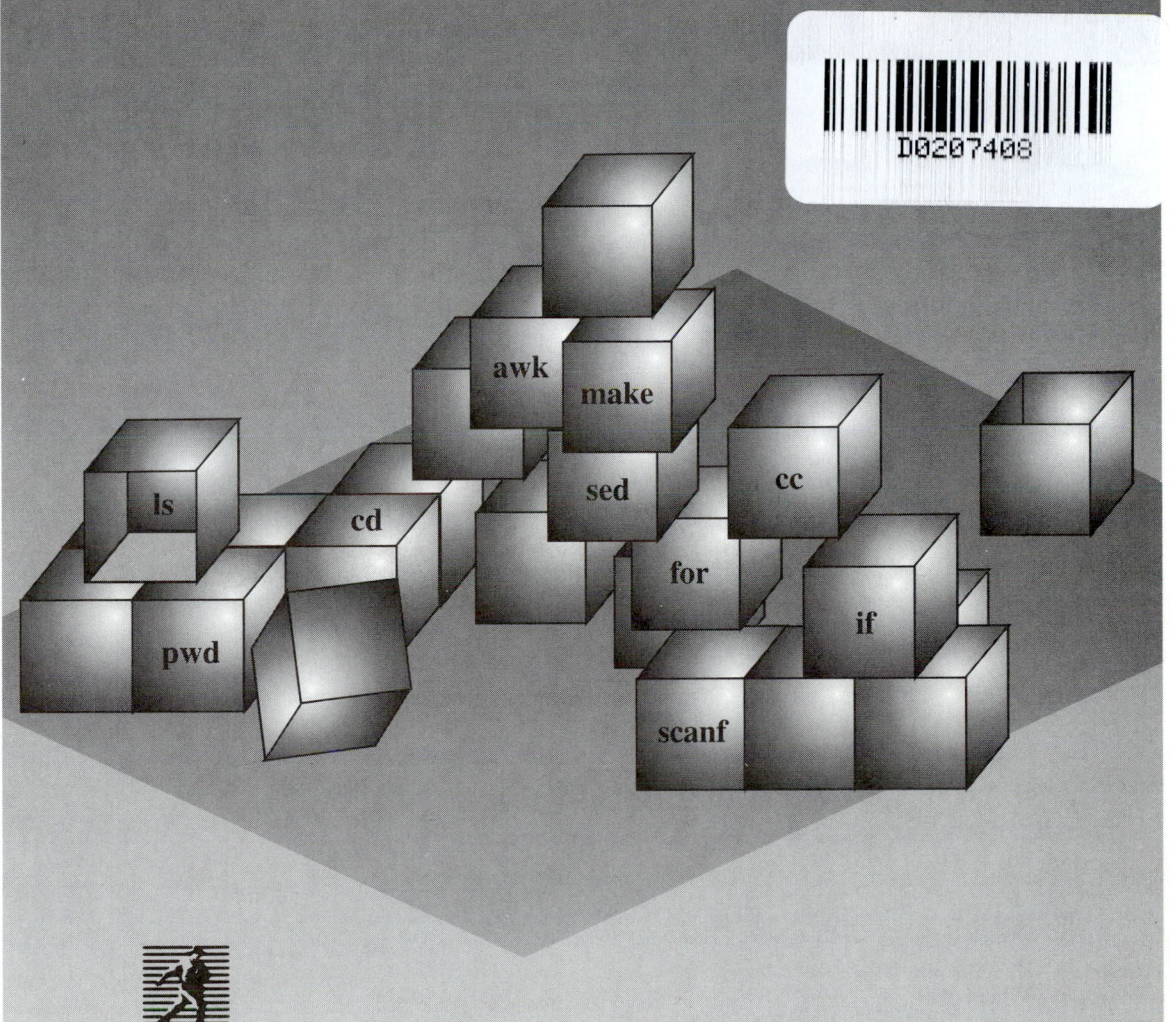

PRENTICE HALL, Englewood Cliffs, N.J. 07632

Library of Congress Cataloging-in-Publication Data

Hodges, Jack.
    An introduction to Berkeley UNIX and ANSI C / Jack Hodges.
      p. cm.
    Includes index.
    ISBN 0-13-068495-3
    1. Berkeley UNIX. 2. Operating systems (Computers) 3. C
(Computer program language)   I. Title.
QA76.76.O63H637 1995
005.4'3--dc20   94-24249
                                                                     CIP

Acquisitions editor: Bill Zobrist
Production editor: Bayani Mendoza de Leon
Copy editor: Andrea Hammer
Cover designer: Rich Dombrowski
Buyer: Lori Bulwin
Editorial assistant: Phyllis Morgan

 © 1995 by Prentice-Hall, Inc.
A Simon & Schuster Company
Englewood Cliffs, New Jersey 07632

The author and publisher of this book have used their best efforts in preparing this book. These efforts include the development, research, and testing of the theories and programs to determine their effectiveness. The author and publisher make no warranty of any kind, expressed or implied, with regard to these programs or the documentation contained in this book. The author and publisher shall not be liable in any event for incidental or consequential damages in connection with, or arising out of, the furnishing, performance, or use of these programs.

The use of trade names, trademarks, etc., even if not specially identified, should not be construed as an indication that such names are not protected by the Trade Marks and Merchandise Marks Act.

Printed in the United States of America
10 9 8 7 6 5 4 3 2 1

ISBN 0-13-068495-3

Prentice-Hall International (UK) Limited, London
Prentice-Hall of Australia Pty. Limited, Sydney
Prentice-Hall Canada Inc., Toronto
Prentice-Hall Hispanoamericana, S.A., Mexico
Prentice-Hall of India Private Limited, New Delhi
Prentice-Hall of Japan, Inc., Tokyo
Simon & Schuster Asia Pte. Ltd., Singapore
Editora Prentice-Hall do Brasil, Ltda., Rio de Janeiro

Table of Contents

6   File Formatting and Printing   173

7   Network Processing   227

Part II
Programming Languages and ANSI C

11 Programming Tools 363

Part III
UNIX Shell Programming

12 Regular Expressions and Scripts 399

13 C Shell Scripts 425

14 Bourne Shell Scripts   449

Appendices

A Answers to Sample Quiz Questions   469

B UNIX File System   495

Preface

Welcome to Berkeley UNIX! This book is intended to introduce you to a widely used version of UNIX called Berkeley System Distribution, or Berkeley UNIX. The book is intended to teach you how to understand, use, and appreciate operating systems, and, in particular, the UNIX operating system. You need not have any prior exposure to computers or to UNIX to succeed at learning this material. The intention is that you gain sufficient facility with the material that you can extend your knowledge through experience on your own. Although this material has been left to the student to learn on his or her own in the past, we have found that some guidance is extremely helpful in showing you what can be done with the UNIX operating system and how it can benefit you when using any computer. At our institution, we run this as a self-paced laboratory course and recommend the adoption of this format elsewhere.

This book is intended to accompany a one-semester introductory course in learning about and using UNIX and ANSI C. The UNIX operating system is large and diverse, so students are not expected to master it in one semester. However, they are expected to learn the *fundamentals* of the operating system, as defined by the chapter headings in this book. They are also expected to *use* the operating system. Reading alone simply doesn't work. The students' knowledge of its use will probably be examined at a fairly shallow level, but they should be expected to show expertise at that level. The book makes recommendations about how much depth should be covered in any particular topic for this course.

Students are also being introduced to a powerful programming language. They are not expected to master C, but are expected to learn the fundamentals of programming and to demonstrate the ability to program. This will include simple but correct use of syntax, programming style, debugging, and logic in simple program writing. As students read about the language and write their first programs, they should be encouraged to think about the similarities C might share with other languages, because these similarities will make the acquisition of new programming skills easier later.

To the Student

There are four basic components to any computer: (1) hardware, (2) the operating system, (3) programs, and (4) data. The **operating system** tells the hardware how and when to execute which program on what data. A **program** is a series of instructions that manipulate data according to the semantics of a programming language. Technically, an operating system is a program or a set of programs. Together, the operating system, programs, and data make up what is called **software**. This book is intended to teach you how to use and manipulate operating systems, programs, and data. The elements of programming, and the interactions that an operating system mediates between the user and the computer hardware, are generic. Thus, the concepts you learn in this book will apply to any hardware platform, operating system, language, or data file.

The prevalence of the UNIX operating system and the C programming language are widespread in academia and industry. Many operating systems being used today are UNIX derivatives (e.g., Berkeley System Distribution - BSD, Ultrix®, MACH®, A/UX®, System V®, XENIX®, and AIX®). Most of the machines that you have access to probably are or soon will be running some version of UNIX.

This course introduces you to the BSD dialect of the UNIX operating system. The UNIX dialect in which many of the examples in this book were tested is called Ultrix, which is installed at this institution on a DEC® VAX® 6420. Different UNIX dialects, particularly Berkeley UNIX and System V, have slightly different command sets, utilities, and associated mind-sets. The book is intended to introduce UNIX, and to provide a comprehensive set of tools for those learning UNIX. The examples in this book have been executed on several BSD-compatible UNIX hardware platforms, or hosts, (i.e., a computer that has a BSD-compatible operating system), so they should work for you.

The C programming language is widely used on UNIX platforms because UNIX is implemented in (i.e., written in) C. Thus, it is easier to write programs that interact with the UNIX operating system and hardware when written in C, and they are often more efficient than programs written in other languages.

This book is topically divided into three parts: (I) the UNIX operating system, (II) the C programming language, and (III) UNIX shell programming. In the following sections, the suggested organization and administration of a course that uses this book as a primary text or supplement will be presented.

HELP! — Related Materials

There are at least six sources of information for the content of an introductory course on UNIX and C.

- This book and the sample quiz questions provided with each chapter.
- UNIX reference texts: A list of references can be found at the end of selected chapters in this book.
- A UNIX directory that includes examples worked out in this text and may be helpful for experimentation and sample exercises.
- C programming reference texts: A list of references can be found at the end of selected chapters in this book.
- The UNIX online manual pages.
- Newsgroups: We have found that a dedicated newsgroup (that we call "self-paced") to be a valuable tool in disseminating information to the students taking this course on this campus. Because of the nature of such courses, a newsgroup is a valuable asset.
- Course staff: Laboratory assistants and instructor. The information about how to reach these people is generally furnished early in a course, preferably the first day.

The Book

This book is written in a modular format. Each chapter is self contained: A concept is introduced, references are cited (e.g., text page or man page), tutorial examples of how to use the concept are presented and discussed, and sample questions to test knowledge of the material are given. Answers to sample questions are provided in Appendix A. There is an index in the back of the book for finding terms too specific for the table of contents.

How to Read This Book

Each chapter in this book is broken into sections. The first section always introduces the topic and the scope of the topic on which the student should focus. The sections following introduce, discuss, and illustrate the facets of UNIX, C, and so forth associated with the topic. The examples provided are intended to be illustrative, and are not exhaustive of the scope of the chapter. Students should be expected to experiment with the commands and utilities to become proficient at the level described by the scope. At the end of many sections there will be a table of related commands or command options associated with the topic. This reference table often exceeds the minimum expertise described in the topic scope, and is presented to allow interested students to experiment more with the topic without the explicit need for a UNIX reference. The last section in a chapter is always the set of exercises and sample test problems. Answers to all of the sample test problems can be found in Appendix A.

When reading this book, references to other topics and locations will appear as (Chapter nn, Section nn, and page mm), where *nn* is the chapter or section number and *mm* is a page number or range. Text references will appear in [author year] format. Online manual references will appear as (man com) where "com" is a UNIX command name.

Book Nomenclature

Learning UNIX is best done at a keyboard, with UNIX staring back at you on a screen. To understand the responses you will see, and to understand this book, you will need to understand what we mean when we display items in different ways. Below you will find a listing of the terminology and the associated nomenclature as they are found throughout this book.

Book Nomenclature

Item		Explanation
terms	⇒	**Bolded** items are first-time definitions.
variable	⇒	**Bolded** variable names in text.
command	⇒	*Italicized courier* commands are UNIX command definitions.
command	⇒	Courier commands are later command references.
prompt	⇒	Courier system prompts.
response	⇒	**Bolded courier fonts** are user responses.
23	⇒	*Italicized* index entries refer to pages on which the UNIX command is defined or first illustrated with an example.
<Cntl-key>	⇒	Courier control characters like <Cntl-c>.
<CR>	⇒	Courier carriage returns/enter key/return key.
<ESC>	⇒	Courier escape key.
"file"	⇒	"Double quoted" items are files or directories. If taken from an example, these will be in courier font with straight quotes.
'command'	⇒	'Single quoted' courier commands items are commands or command options in text.
host	⇒	All host names will be in courier font.

Control characters are command sequences that use multiple keyboard keys simultaneously. For example, <Cntl-d> means press the "control" key, and, *while holding it down*, press the 'd' key.

Book Creation

This book has been formatted with the use of L^A^T~E~X® and FRAMEMAKER® on several platforms. Because L^A^T~E~X makes use of ASCII files and can be transmitted easily from one machine to another, I have made use of many different computers (HP®, SUN®, APPLE®, and NEXT®) to write chapters for early versions of the book. The book was originally constructed with a modified "book.-sty" documentstyle, called "module.sty." Each of the chapters was included into a command file, as described in Chapter 6. Figures have been generated from several sources. Most of the figures have been created on a MACINTOSH® and saved in POSTSCRIPT form. I wrote a T~E~X® macro that placed a figure and figure caption into the document. This macro is described in Appendix L. On the NEXT, I can even grab portions of the screen, as shown below. Many of my newer graphics have been generated on a NEXT.

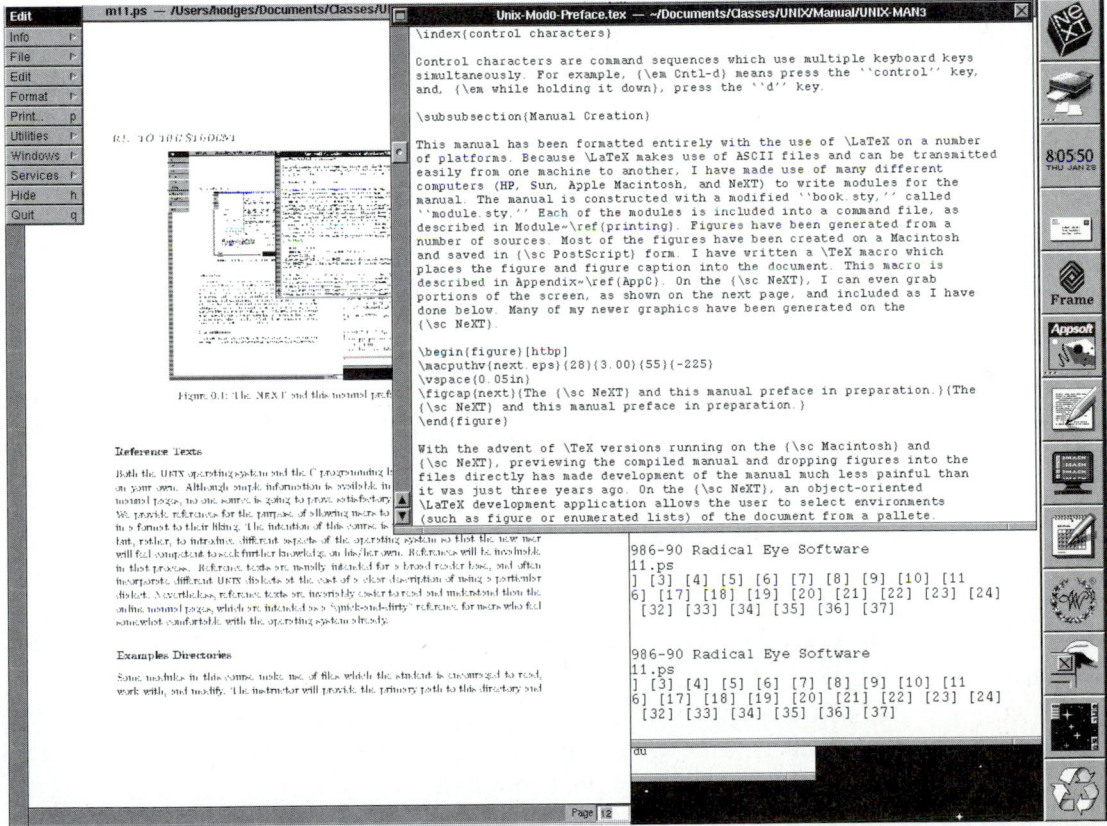

With the advent of T~E~X versions running on the MACINTOSH and NEXT, previewing the compiled book and dropping figures into the files directly has made development of the book much less painful than it was just 3 years ago. On the NEXT, an object-oriented L^A^T~E~X development application allows the user to select environments (such as figure or enumerated lists) of the document from a pallete. FRAMEMAKER has been used on the last draft of the book because of its extensive layout support. Together L^AT_EX and FRAMEMAKER provide excellent support for book construction.

Reference Texts

Both the UNIX operating system and the C programming language can be complex to learn on your own. Although ample information is available in this book, and in the online manual pages, no one source is going to prove satisfactory for any user in every situation. We provide references for the purpose of allowing users to find supplementary information in a format to their liking. The intention of this text is to introduce different aspects of the operating system so that the new user will feel competent to seek further knowledge on his or her own. It is not our intention to provide a complete reference to the UNIX operating system. References will be invaluable in that process. Reference texts are usually intended for a broad reader base, and often incorporate different UNIX dialects at the cost of a clear description of using a particular dialect. Nevertheless, reference texts are invariably easier to read and understand than the online manual pages, which are intended as a "quick-and-dirty" reference for users who already feel somewhat comfortable with the operating system.

Examples Directories

Some chapters in this course make use of files that the student is encouraged to read, work with, and modify. If used at your institution, the instructor will provide you with the path to this directory. We have found it useful to have the path integrated into the student's login environment at the beginning of the semester and to generate a symbolic link to the directory so that students have immediate read access to files pertinent to the course without the need to understand symbolic links at the onset of a course. In the appropriate sections of this book, use of these files, and their subdirectories, will be identified in text and by the icon in the left margin of this paragraph. The icon represents a directory subtree, and, in particular, one that I will refer to as UNIX. The item above the icon, here Ch6, will be a subdirectory under UNIX, and the item below the icon, here `nroff-troff`, will be a subdirectory under Ch6. It will be assumed that, wherever the directory is actually placed in the file system, the students will be given a path to expand UNIX to. We suggest that the UNIX subtree be installed in a single location.

Ch6

nroff-troff

Online Manual Pages

When this book or supplementary reference texts prove insufficient to assist you in learning a concept or command, every UNIX command available on the system is documented, online, with the manual pages. Although the man pages are terse when compared to the other documentation forms mentioned, they provide compact and accurate information. Once you learn how to invoke them (see Chapter 3, Section 3.3.1), you can use them any time you are logged on. It is important that every UNIX user become comfortable and facile with the man pages because, on a particular platform, they will be up to date, whereas books and manuals eventually become out of date. Once you feel comfortable with the man pages, your need for references will be greatly reduced, as well it should be.

In addition, you may be able to obtain course-related news on a newsgroup or bulletin board. At San Francisco State University, we use a bulletin board called "self-paced," which is where course announcements are posted. Students can also send electronic mail to course assistants, and to the instructor. The assistant's and instructor's computer IDs, and the name of the newsgroup or bulletin board for this type of course (if used at your instituion), will be provided to you by the staff.

Computer and Network Etiquette

Using a multiuser computing system comes with certain responsibilities. On a personal computer, when you erase a disk you are the only one who loses. On a computer network (i.e., computers that are connected and can interact), if you make serious mistakes that cost people their work and their time, you will be held responsible. Whether you make a simple mistake, are naive, are incompetent, negligent, or delinquent, you are responsible for what you do or say on a computer network. Throughout this book you will see the term **etiquette** in various contexts. There are generally accepted guidelines that guide our behavior on a computer network. None of these guidelines constrains your behavior beyond what is reasonable and fair. Many utilities have their own sets of rules and etiquette, and each is provided in the appropriate location in this book.

It is expected that students will want to help each other in learning how to use the tools of the UNIX operating system. If you feel frustrated at not being able to find the right command, or to get a command or command option to work, and believe you have exhausted the sources of information provided you, then you should feel comfortable asking for assistance. In the same light, you should not feel ill toward assisting someone as long as it appears that they have been trying and are simply stuck on a minor point. If you continue to ask for or give assistance to a point where learning the material is affected, then you may find it difficult to use these tools when those who help you are no longer available. Even though there will almost always be other people using a UNIX machine, you may not always find it easy to obtain assistance, so you should make it your goal to learn UNIX to a point where you feel competent enough to find new information on your own.

The use of your UNIX account will likely give you access to many people and machines. You are not simply working on an isolated personal computer; your actions may affect many other users. You will be expected to be courteous in your use of the system, as will be specified early in the book. Serious violations of proper net-etiquette are generally not tolerated and may result in the loss of your access privileges on the computer system.

An introductory course in UNIX use and appreciation offers you the potential to dramatically broaden your computing horizons. The more you experiment with and play with the UNIX operating system and its utilities, the more you will learn. You could amaze yourself with the capabilities available to you – but you are the only one that can do it. Have fun, and be courteous!

Pedagogy

This book contains some pedagogical features that help to clarify the material and provide the student with practice using it. These features include the following:

1. *Figures.* There are figures that are used to illustrate concepts when explanation alone will not suffice.

2. *Tutorial Examples.* The text is intended to be primarily tutorial, so there are many examples in how to identify and use the commands, with responses provided inline. Examples will be set off by horizontal bars, and in the left margin, away from the text, for easy access. Where appropriate, particular parts of examples are highlighted, noted, and explained in the text. Notes are always in a different font for clarity.

3. *Partial Command References.* Although the intention of this book and course is to introduce the student to UNIX, additional information on command options and how to use them is included at the end of many sections. This information should provide scope and serve as a resource for the student after a course is over. Command reference table pages are also in the index.

4. *Exercises.* At the end of every chapter, a few exercises are presented that allow the student to integrate his or her knowledge of the commands presented in the chapter and to assimilate them into the growing body of knowledge about UNIX and C. The answers to these exercises are not provided in the book but are made available to instructors who choose to augment the course with homework.

5. *Sample Quizzes.* This book is designed as a vehicle for self-learning. As such, the student needs to be able to evaluate their progress on their own. At the end of every chapter, sample quiz questions are provided that illustrate the depth and breadth of the material they are expected to learn. The answers for all sample questions are included in Appendix A.

6. *Quick Reference.* Appendices B to K provide quick reference for many of the basic tools and commands needed by the novice UNIX/C user. These provide

a general description of a utility and some key commands for using the utility, and may be adequate lookup until the user's knowledge of UNIX exceeds the basic level.

One feature of this book and course is the prevalence of material on computer and network etiquette and ethics, which have become more and more important as the UNIX community has spread into the private sector, the rest of the world and society. With the advent of services such as GOPHER, the World Wide Web, WAIS, the Serial Line Internet Protocol (SLIP), high-speed modems, and Integrated Services Digital Network (ISDN), the network is going to be moving into the home and small business to a greater and greater extent. Not only is it going to become much more important to train new users in the use of UNIX, but it will become a major issue controlling the use of the ever-expanding means of communicating with one another. Etiquette plays a major role in this educational process, and we feel that its introduction is absolutely imperative at this, beginning, stage.

Book Organization and Course Syllabi

This book is divided into three parts and fourteen chapters. Approximately one chapter per week should be covered in a semester-long self-paced course, although some students may budget their time differently. Some chapters can be completed in the span of a few minutes, whereas others will require many hours trying examples and experimenting with command argument options. The amount of time required for a chapter is not specified in the chapter, as it depends on each student, the time they allocate to the material, and the environment they work in. One thing is certain: the chapters become easier as you become more proficient with UNIX and C.

PART I: UNIX

Chapter 1 — The Login Session

Chapter 2 — Electronic Communications

Chapter 3 — The UNIX File System

Chapter 4 — File Creation and Editing

Chapter 5 — The UNIX Command Shell and Process Control

Chapter 6 — File Formatting and Printing

Chapter 7 — Network Processing

PART II: Programming Languages and ANSI C

Chapter 8 — Introduction to C Programming

Chapter 9 — Decision Making, Iteration, and Functions

Chapter 10 — Arrays, Structures, and Files

We have found that coverage of this entire book, including the C chapters, cannot be completed in a single semester. For many students, the first part of this course is sufficient for a single semester. Other students have succeeded in completing Parts I and III. Students continuing in computer science should consider Part II of the course a necessary prerequisite to later courses in computer science but may choose the route of a normal Introduction to Programming course. Part III uses some elementary notions in programming languages but does not require any in-depth or formal study for the purposes of this course. If anything, writing shell scripts may excite the user to learn more about programming.

As a recommendation to instructors, the first part of the course should be followed roughly in the order presented, with the possible exception of Chapter 6, and supplemented with Parts II and III as your curriculum and syllabus require.

Computer Accounts

This book is based on hands-on experience, so the first thing students need is a computer account on a host running Berekeley UNIX. The instructor provides you with one. You will receive two items: an account ID and a password. You will need **both** to log on to a UNIX system.

Supplementary Materials

Three types of supplements are used in this book: (1) additional software in the public domain, (2) a directory of files for the student to use in learning the material, and (3) a set of appendices that extend the scope of some of the chapters in the book.

Standard and Recommended Software

Every attempt is made in this book and course to provide alternative means for performing a task. In general, this means that the stock UNIX approach to performing a task has competition. Competition rarely surfaces unless there is a market for alternatives, and, in the utilities that are described in this book, history has shown that the alternatives can make a huge difference in how the user feels about the tasks they perform. Although most standard UNIX distributions do not contain them, it is highly recommended that the alternative utilities presented in this book be installed for courses paralleling this book, or at least that similar alternatives are presented for the sake of diversity. This section discusses my rationale for the specific alternatives presented in this book in more detail, as well as how to obtain the packages I present in the book.

- Berkeley (BSD) UNIX
- Public Domain Utilities
- Anonymous `ftp` Archives

Berkeley (BSD) UNIX

The basic Berkeley UNIX distribution is intended to support users on a wide variety of hardware platforms. It is not specifically designed to support users of particular workstations and other advanced computing environments. As a result, users who are using UNIX in a particular environment need to learn UNIX and the operating environment and its utilities *in addition* to their particular graphical user interface environment. It is important to know what limitations exist between what can and cannot be applied transparently between the two. Particularly obvious, because of their strong visual ties, are the document editors and the means whereby documents are prepared. In this book, we take the position that the UNIX environment should support the editors and document preparation methods available on *any* computational environment, regardless of whether the user has a simple terminal or a computer supporting high-resolution graphics. As a result, this book introduces and compares two editors: the stock `vi` editor and the Gnu Emacs® editor. The `vi` editor is certainly the standard UNIX full-screen editor, but most every UNIX-based computer uses an `emacs` look alike, so users who have been introduced to both will be comfortable on any UNIX platform.

Second, in an age of word processors and What-You-See-Is-What-You-Get (WYSIWYG, pronounced wizzywig) page layout applications, it is awkward to introduce the student to `nroff`, which is mostly used for formatting manual pages, or `troff`, which is a full-featured markup language but is awkward to use. The basis of text preparation is the page markup language. Regardless of what method one uses to prepare a document, each application takes the user's commands and translates them to its own peculiar markup language. When the document is saved, it can be saved in several formats: always in the application's resident (or native) format, and text, but now in device-independent interchange formats that allow an ASCII version of the document to be transmitted to other platforms and applications and edited or printed directly. As a result, we introduce L^AT_EX, one of the most versatile of non-WYSIWYG page markup languages available on a UNIX platform today. A user familiar with `nroff` and `latex` will be comfortable preparing documents on any UNIX environment.

We specifically and intentionally bypass the discussion of windowing environments (i.e., graphical user interfaces, GUIs, pronounced gooey) in this text. Although the prevalence of high-resolution computational environments is rapidly rendering standard terminals obsolete, the time has yet to arrive where there is universal agreement on a standard windowing protocol, so each windowing interface will be different. The X windows package is very popular on UNIX platforms, and the WINDOWS®, and MACINTOSH FINDER® are popular on personal computers. I am particularly enamored with the NEXTSTEP® interface, which transparently integrates UNIX with a fabulous user interface and runs on most every hardware platform. It would be an impossible task to introduce naive UNIX users to every windowing environment, so we stick to UNIX alone in this text.

Public Domain Utilities

This book introduces applications that come bundled with many UNIX platforms but are not part of the standard UNIX distribution. We strongly believe in the use of public domain software at the operating system level, because shared software and utilities stimulate cross-platform software development and exchange. The X windows project is an example of this type of exchange for graphical exchange in workstation environments.

Although MH, EMACS, and T_EX (L^AT_EX) are not standard distribution software, they are in the public domain and supported on virtually all UNIX platforms and some non-UNIX platforms. GNU EMACS is being provided on many distribution media, and all three utilities have been used by the author on many platforms. I have included a list of the current archive sites for these utilities. A casual UNIX user is probably not going to be qualified to install MH or T_EX; however, a system administrator should have no problems.

Anonymous Ftp Archives

An international archive reference service is available on the internet. The service is called `archie`, developed at McGill University in Montreal, Canada. `archie` is used to locate local `ftp` sites for shared software, and to retrieve and install that software on your platform. The use of `archie` is described in the book. Although we have provided the information herein, the GNU EMACS and T_EX archive sites can be checked in `archie` as well.

One of the RAND® mail handler (MH) archives is located at

`labrea.stanford.edu`

A GNU EMACS national archive is at

`prep.ai.mit.edu`

The T$_E$X national archive is located at

labrea.stanford.edu

in the directory "pub/tex." The use of anonymous ftp, for those unfamiliar with software archives, in discussed in Chapter 7, page 242.

Additional Materials

As previously mentioned, a directory has been constructed that includes files that may be beneficial to the student in learning the material associated with this text. Of particular merit are the files for Chapters 6, 8 to 10, and 12 to 14. The files in Chapter 6 provide working examples of how to format papers using nroff/troff and latex. Appendix L takes these examples further, by providing samples of how to format more complicated documents than those presented in the book proper.

The files in Chapters 8 to 11 are sample C programs which mirror the examples in the book, and can be accessed, compiled, and modified by the student or faculty member to assist the learning process. In a similar vein, the files in Chapters 12 to 14 mirror the shell scripts illustrated in the book, and can likewise be used and manipulated to further the student's understanding of the associated material. This directory will be made available by anonymous ftp through Prentice Hall. Talk to your sales representative for assistance.

Because this book has been designed for use in a self-paced laboratory course, no lecture slides are made available at this time. However, a set of orientation slides is available in POSTSCRIPT form and can be used as a template for organizing a course.

An online examination system has been developed at San Francisco State University for use with this material. The program is environmental, inasmuch as each student is placed into a separate directory in a file system designed by the instructor and his or her staff. The program is also progressive, inasmuch as students are asked questions of varying difficulty and the number of questions they are asked is dependent on their level of expertise. A flat passing score is used. There is a built-in UNIX interpreter that allows students to issue commands, and their responses are evaluated using a script-based technique. C programs are composed by students in vi, and then compiled with gcc (or whatever compiler the instructor desires) and executed. Shell scripts are composed in vi, and then executed in the appropriate shell environment. Both C programs and shell scripts are evaluated in the same manner as UNIX commands. The program is currently implemented in C. The questions and student administrative information are implemented in Oracle databases. The current database, which is being augmented constantly, consists of approximately five hundred questions. Based on six questions per test, there are four full test-taking opportunities per chapter. The questions are grouped in four difficulty levels, harder questions being valued greater. A student is asked a new question based on how well he or she does on the previous question. The current grading scheme provides six ways to pass each test attempt: a student can pass the test in as few as two questions and as many as six questions. There are also instructor interfaces for (1) taking questions as a student would but without the database support, (2) adding and updating information, and (3) performing statistical queries on the questions and responses. There is a full set of scripts for performing analysis of student performance during the testing process, and there is full documentation on all aspects of the program, its installation, and its administration. If you are interested in using this program, ask your Prentice Hall sales representative.

Acknowledgments

This book was originally developed and prepared for the self-paced UNIX course at San Francisco State University. Numerous people have been instrumental in producing this document. I am indebted to both Mike Dyer and Keith Holyoak at UCLA for recognizing the need for a course to teach people how to use and appreciate UNIX on a scientific network, and for choosing me for the task of developing and teaching one.

Perhaps most influential in the development of this text have been the multitude of students who have actively participated in drafts of the UCLA Cognet Manual and the SFSU UNIX Manual by ferreting out errors, making suggestions, and helping to eliminate inconsistencies.

There have been numerous other individuals who have helped to clarify the content in this text, offered constructive advice on how to add to or clarify the information, and offered support and encouragement, not the least of whom have been my editors at Prentice Hall; my academic reviewers: Henry Etlinger, Artur J. Kowalski, Matthew Treu, Fadi Deek, and Richard Newman-Wolfe; my wife Nancy; the chair of our department: Gerald Eisman; and of course my students.

The success of this book, and similar texts that evolve to assist the population in accepting and using UNIX and networked environments, will be based to a great extent on overcoming the myth that UNIX is difficult to learn. I hope that this book, having been worked over by such a large and diverse population, presents UNIX in a light that is palatable and still stimulates the experimentation that is absolutely mandatory to learn how to use an operating system.

Jack Hodges

PART I
UNIX

This first part of the book introduces the student to the concepts associated with the UNIX operating system, its utilities, and a computer network. You are not expected to become a UNIX expert, because UNIX is a huge and complex operating system. However, you *are* expected to learn how to navigate yourself around the various utilities at a level where you can use them on a day-to-day basis without further assistance, and so that you can learn more on your own. No command or utility will be presented in its entirety. Generally, a topic will be introduced that covers a broad range of situations. A few examples will be discussed that illustrate the command syntax and the interpretation of its response. Often command options will be tabulated at the end of a section, so that you can modify the examples and experiment with them. By the end of each chapter, you should have a general understanding of the concepts associated with the chapter, and a commensurate degree of skill at using the associated commands and utilities.

Chapter 1
The Login Session

1.1 Introduction and Scope

Nowadays, it is increasingly important to know something about the operating system that you use. Whether you are using a personal computer, a workstation, a minicomputer, or a mainframe, somewhere along the line you will need to interact with the system. Many operating systems these days run a UNIX derivative. Before you can use the computer running UNIX, you must first be logged on. Having an account and password are the first step, and presumably you have received these already. This chapter introduces you to the most direct methods for logging on to the system so that you can use the system to perform tasks. Specifically, the following topics will be presented:

- Terminal and console login
- The login script and logging on to a host
- Changing your password
- Logging out
- Dial-in login and terminal servers

When you complete this chapter, you should be comfortable logging on to and off of a UNIX environment, both from a terminal and from a modem. You should be able to change your password and execute a few simple commands, such as finding out who the system thinks you are.

There are two ways to log on to a computer: directly or indirectly. **Direct login** is when you are sitting at a terminal directly connected to a port on the computer, or when you are sitting at the computer's console itself. **Indirect login** is when you access the computer remotely, sometimes through what is

3

called a **terminal server** and sometimes through a network. When logging on to a system through a modem, you will generally be directed to the proper machine through a terminal server, which is basically a box that routes signals to the proper computer.

1.2 Terminal and Console Login

Terminal and console logins are the most effective way to use a system because they are directly connected to the computer. Although this login method is less convenient, there are at least three compelling reasons for using direct login rather than from a PC through a modem at home: (1) the number of access ports, (2) data transmission speed, and (3) network reliability. A remote port is connected to a computer via a modem, or set of modems, and a box, called a terminal server, which is connected to the computer. Unlike a terminal, which is part of a network, there are always a finite number of remote ports because there are always a finite number of modems. Universities rarely support massive dial-in log on, so the number of remote ports available, off campus, is limited. You may be competing with a large number of other users to log in from a modem, and may be placed in a queue. Waiting in queues can be tedious, a waste of time, and may be an unnecessary waste of money if you are paying telephone charges. Remote logins through modems are at the bottom of the data transmission performance curve. A modem's performance is traditionally associated with its **baud rate**, which is a measure of how many **bits per second** it can transfer. The transmission rate for a modem these days is typically between 1200 and 14,400 **baud**. The transmission rate of direct connection terminals is at least 19,200 baud. This means that you can get more work accomplished in the same amount of time with a direct connection. The difference in transmission rate affects the speed with which the computer will respond (usually referred to as **response time**) to your commands. Other factors in login performance are the quality of cabling, the electrical shielding of that cabling, and the length of lines between machines. These differences can affect the quality of your transmissions, as well as the speed. For example, the slower response produces a greater potential for data transmission errors because you will be logged on longer. The weather can affect your login session if the shielding on the telephone lines is inadequate, because static electricity can affect the current in the lines. Although the incidence of data loss through transmission errors has decreased over the years, the most reliable terminal connection is still direct (i.e., terminal to computer). Lastly, when you are logged in from a modem, any glitches in power or in the network could result in the loss of your signal, in which case you will be logged out. These are important motivators for doing your work on campus.

On the other hand, working in your own designated environment, whatever it happens to be, has its advantages. You can log on when you want and need not wait for someone to open a lab. You can intermix the tasks you perform on your own computer with those you can perform on the UNIX computer. There are no time limits in your own environment, whereas sometimes you have to share a terminal with other users. Often, your own environment can be much more comfortable than that of a laboratory. It might be quieter as well. In the long run, we may find ourselves being able to perform much of our work at home without any loss in speed, performance, or capability. Until then, however, you must choose for yourself depending on your needs and constraints.

1.2.1   Use of a Timesharing Terminal

Direct login is often performed on a timesharing terminal in a laboratory. **Timesharing** means that many people will be using the computer at once. The operating system determines when each task gets executed. The term **terminal** refers to a serial connection to a computer, and is often associated with a simple monitor and keyboard. This configuration is often called a *dumb* terminal. Direct login need not be relegated to a dumb terminal. A personal computer or workstation can also be connected to another computer directly, and you could connect through a network. You may find several methods to log on to a UNIX system directly!

All terminals have the same general capabilities; however, they may *appear* different and may have what are called different **terminal characteristics**. When you sit down at a terminal, you will have in front of you a monitor and a keyboard. Regardless of what type of terminal you log on from, you may need to obtain assistance to get to the point where a login script is executed. On the monitor will likely be the remains of the previous user's login session and, somewhere, a single line that looks something like the following:

```
>
```

This funny character is called a **prompt**[1] and requires a typed response from you. This particular prompt needs a specific kind of response. It requires that you try to connect to a particular computer, after which you can log on to that computer, henceforth called a **host**. If you want to log on to a host named `localhost`, then your response will look as follows:

```
> telnet localhost <CR>
```

where "`telnet`" stands for the command to connect, and "`localhost`" stands for the name of the host computer to which you wish to connect.

---

1. This discussion assumes that you have a choice of computers onto which you might log on. If you do not have a choice, then the first thing you may see is the login: prompt. If so, skip ahead to the next section. This type of prompt will likely be different at your institution.

1.3 Logging on to a Host

A log-on procedure will always look the same and consists of two steps. The host computer will prompt you for two items, one at a time: (1) your **account ID** (also **user ID**, **login ID**, or **userid**) and (2) your **password**. The account ID, usually called the userid, is what the system expects at the "login:" prompt. You must have a valid userid and password on the computer you try to log on to. Each person using the computer is called a **user**, and all users have a userid that is associated with their account. A space has been provided, below, for you to write down your account name, or userid. Write it here when you receive it or on the inside front cover of this book. Do not write down your password here, or in any place that is likely to be associated with your course.

Account Name: _____

A sample login sequence is shown, below, for a login session on sfsuvax1, a host at San Francisco State University. It begins at a terminal server prompt, indicating that this session is initiated from a modem. When I select the sf-suvax1 as the desired host, the terminal server routes my session to that computer and begins the login sequence. The first thing you will see in the login sequence is called a login prompt (login:). In this session, I have responded to the "login:" request with **jhodges**, which is my userid on the host sfsu-vax1. A user's userid is the same as their **account name**, and the name of their **home directory**. Thus, the user jhodges is the owner of the directory "jhodges." More on this in Chapter 3.

```
sfsu-annex 25: telnet sfsuvax1 <CR>
Trying...
Connected to sfsuvax1.
Escape character is '^^'.
...
login: jhodges <CR>
Password: <CR>
```

When I type jhodges at the login prompt, my response is **echoed**, meaning that the system displays my response as I type. Most commands that you type will be echoed on the monitor; however, the password is not echoed. After you enter your userid, enter a carriage return (<CR>), and the system will prompt you for your password. Your response will not be shown, so that others will not see your password. This is a security measure. Once you enter your password, an encryption scheme translates it and compares it to the one associated with the userid you entered. If they match, as mine did, then you are logged on to the machine, at which point a number of things will happen, as I will explain next. Below is remainder of the sample session started above:

```
sfsu-annex 25: telnet sfsuvax1 <CR>
Trying...
Connected to sfsuvax1.
Escape character is '^^'.

ULTRIX V4.3 (Rev. 44) (sfsuvax1.sfsu.edu)

login: jhodges
Password: <CR>
Last login: Wed Dec 29 17:36:03 from huckleberry.sfsu          ①
ULTRIX V4.3 (Rev. 44) System #32: Tue Aug 31 11:01:06 PDT 1993  ②

***************************************************************************
*                                                                         *
*    Type 'news' (updated 10/20/93) for system downtime information and    *
*    for other information.                                                *
*                                                                         *
*    Send your VAX questions or problem reports electronically to the      *
*    email address "vaxhelp@sfsu.edu".                                     *
*                                                                         *
***************************************************************************
Wed Jan  5 09:21:27 PST 1994
sfsuvax1>
```

In the session above, the first line after the password entry tells when and from where "jhodges" last logged on (at **1**). huckleberry is another host at the same institution. This means that I logged on through the network. The next line (**2**) tells about the operating system version and the date. Note the statement starting "For Downtime Information..." This block of text is called a **message of the day (motd)**. The staff that administers a host will often send messages to all the users this way, so keep an eye on them. The last line of the login procedure is the **shell prompt**, which signals that the login procedure has completed and I am now able to issue UNIX commands. Because you have now seen three different kinds of prompts, let's look more closely at what they mean and what you will see in the remainder of this manual.

1.3.1   Computer Prompts

The easiest way to inform the user where they are in the file system, or in what application, or what they should type is to provide a visual cue. A **prompt** is a symbol(s) which performs this function. Each utility on the computer has its own type of prompt. By recognizing the prompt displayed on the terminal screen, you can tell what utility you are in and act appropriately. So far you have seen a connect prompt, a login prompt, a password prompt, and a shell prompt. Some of the different prompts that you will see are shown below. It is important to remember that each prompt is associated with a specific range of actions you can take.

Table 1.1: Computer prompts

`>`	⇔	connect to a host
`login:`	⇔	log on to a host — request for userid
`password:`	⇔	log on to a host — request for password
`sfsu-annex 25:`	⇔	a specialty prompt, this one for a terminal server
`&`	⇔	UNIX mail
`C-Kermit`	⇔	kermit communications package
`ftp>`	⇔	file transfer protocol
`$`	⇔	default Bourne shell prompt
`%`	⇔	default C shell prompt
`csh>`	⇔	another common C shell prompt
`localhost>`	⇔	a customized C shell prompt, where `localhost` is the name of a computer
`localhost[3]`	⇔	another customized C shell prompt

Note that the last four prompts, above, all represent different C shell prompts. The stock C shell prompt is the first one (i.e., the percent sign — %), which is probably what many new users will receive by default. In this manual, however, examples will appear with the last two C shell prompts. There are two reasons for this. First, when you begin to log on to many hosts, it is good to keep track of which one you are logged on to, and the name of the host is part of these prompts. "`localhost`" is a placeholder for any host name, such as `huckleberry` or `sfsuvax1`. Second, when you begin to repeat the use of commands, it is easier to do so if you remember the command sequence, and the sequence number (`[3]`) is a component of the last prompt. You will learn how to customize your shell prompt in Chapter 5.

Before ending your first login session, you should issue at least two commands: (1) *whoami*, to find out who the computer thinks you are; and (2) *passwd*, to change your password. Your identity on the computer can be checked at any time with a simple command called `whoami`. When issued, as below, the system will respond with your user ID:

```
localhost> whoami <CR>
jhodges
```

You can issue a similar command, to find out a little more about who the computer thinks you are. Specifically, by typing *who am i* the computer will respond with a line that looks as follows:

```
localhost> who am i <CR>
sfsuvax1.sfsu.edu!jhodges ttyqc Jul 18 13:35 (modem13.sfsu.edu)
```

The whoami command tells you what your userid is. This could be important if you are wondering, later, about file or directory ownership. The 'who am i' command tells you your mail path, what device you logged on from, when you logged on, and from what port you logged on from. This can be important in sending mail, or for a variety of other purposes.

1.4 Changing Your Password

Once logged on to the host, two startup files are executed immediately. The first is called the .cshrc file, and the second is called the .login file. Later you will learn how to modify these files to customize your shell environment. For now, simply know that they exist in your home directory, and that they are called "dot" files. The .cshrc file is executed when your first command shell is created and is usually used to identify your terminal so that its characteristics can be set. Your .login file is executed once when you begin a login session, and is used to set your mail path, your home directory, and other things. When you first log on to a host, a **login shell** is created for you. It is called a shell because all the commands you can issue are associated with it specifically. It is in the login shell that you will issue commands to the system. When you log in, the first thing you will see is the prompt associated with your login shell:

```
localhost>
```

My prompt, localhost>, tells me what host I am logged on to. In general we will use the localhost> prompt in this manual, so that any host name will work. You can write down the name of your login host in the space provided below and in the space provided on the inside cover.

```
Local Host Name: _____
```

When you log in for the first time, you will want to change your password from that given to you by your instructor to something unique that you will be able to remember. The reason for account passwords is to guarantee the security and privacy of your account, and you should take it seriously. You would probably not feel good if someone broke into your account and destroyed your work, or worse. Here are some guidelines for selecting passwords, all of which are common sense rules to guarantee security of your account:

- Never use your first or last name: These are the first things someone will try when trying to break into your account. For that matter, avoid using any name unless you hide it with special characters.
- Do not use popular or recognizable words unless modified with special characters.
- Do not use simple alphanumeric sequences like "aaaa."
- The use of special characters and capitals is encouraged, especially when they are embedded within words that your recognize and remember. When you use numbers and special characters, place them in nonobvious locations. Avoid using numbers like zero instead of *O*, or 1 instead of *l*. These are also fairly easy to break.
- Use many characters: Shorter passwords are easier to break. Many system administrators are going to longer (8) character password lengths, so take note of the length of the password you are initially given, because it will usually coincide with the minimum length set by the system administrator.

Other than these types of general rules, you are generally free to select your own password. Remember this, though: You and you alone will know your password. If you forget your password, then you will most likely not be able to access your account for some time, because you will have to inform the system administrator, who may then require the instructor to verify your existence before issuing you a new password. Going through these steps, in both directions, can take time, certainly more than the effort to remember the password in the first place. Do not forget your password.

Only two people can change your password: someone who knows the password and someone who generates computer accounts. The system administrator generates the accounts, so he or she can modify a password. The only other person who should know your password is you, which helps to guarantee that no one gets into your account and causes problems. To help guarantee against accidents and snoopers, it is a good policy to change your password regularly. Many system administrators are starting to expire passwords on a regular schedule. If you should log in and see a message like "`your ac-`

count will expire in 6 days," don't be alarmed; just change your password in the allotted time. As for changing your password, all you need do is issue a single command, *passwd*:

```
localhost> passwd <CR>
Changing password for jhodges
Old password: <CR>
Enter new password:<CR>
Password is not different enough, unchanged.
localhost> passwd <CR>
Changing password for jhodges
Old password: <CR>
Enter new password: <CR>
Verify: <CR>
localhost>
```

At this point, the system will prompt you for the old password, which is the one you originally logged in with, and then the new password, neither of which will be echoed. When you have typed the carriage return after the new password, the system will ask you to verify the new password by typing it a second time. If you have changed your mind, or if you enter the wrong password, then the system will act as though you never issued the passwd command at all. If you have entered the same new password, then your password is changed, and the next time you log in you should enter the new password. In the first case, above, I did not change the password enough, so nothing was done.

1.5 Logging Out

When you want to terminate a login session, you need to **log out**. All you need to do is issue the *logout* command:

```
localhost> logout <CR>
session 1 - disconnected from sfsuvax1( 130.212.010.102 )...
Connection closed by foreign host.
```

You can also use the *exit* command to log out, particularly from remote shells. You will now be logged off the system. If you were at a terminal or modem, then a new ">" prompt, signaling that you are again communicating with the terminal server, would appear.

1.6 Dialup Login and Terminal Servers

Many people use a modem to connect to a computer/network. Although there are clear advantages to logging in locally, there are as many advantages for logging in remotely, from home or from a business. For example, when you are home you can get up and get coffee or take a break quite easily. You do not have to come when the building or lab is open, you do not have to wait for a turn on a terminal, you can probably choose the type of chair that you sit in, you can stay on as long as you can afford to, and you can (if you have a personal computer rather than a terminal) toggle what you are doing with other processing tasks. These are compelling reasons for remote login that often outweigh the performance advantages of direct login. If you use this method of login, you must (1) prepare your local computer with a modem and a communications package, (2) know the dialup phone numbers where you will be logging in, (3) know the command (if any) associated with the local terminal server, (4) connect to and log on to a host, and (5) log out from the computer and exit from the terminal server. A **terminal server** is a special piece of hardware that connects a bank of serial lines (e.g., from computers or modems) to a computer. It is a **switching station** or **multiplexer**. A terminal server is generally connected to many modems, and to computers and terminals. If you can log on to a computer and get a terminal server prompt, you can probably log on to any other computer it is connected to on which you have an account.

1.6.1 Getting Your Modem to Work

This manual is not set up to help you get your modem or communications software work. Because of the plethora of modems and communications packages available, not to mention the variety of computing platforms on which they can be used, most institutions will be unable to assist you in debugging your remote dialin. For that you will have to seek assistance from a friend who has similar hardware and software, or from the business where you obtained the modem or communications software. The most common problem with getting modems to work is not having the terminal characteristics set properly, having a baud rate mismatch, or having the communications protocol mixed up. Some of these problems are addressed in Chapter 5.

1.6.2 Access Numbers and Connecting to a Network

The session below is typical for a remote (dialup) login using a personal computer and a modem. Once your instructor tells you, write down the dialup telephone numbers available at your institution below.

```
1200 baud number(s): _____
2400 baud number(s): _____
4800 baud number(s): _____
9600 baud number(s): _____
14400 baud number(s): _____
```

You can generally create a telephone directory to store these numbers with your communications package, and you should also write down the numbers for your computer on the inside flap of this manual, as well as the characteristics you find to work for your communications package and the terminal type that works best.

If you are using `kermit` as a communications package, then you will have to precede the telephone number you use with a **Hayes**® command to get attention (`at`) and dial (`dt`) the telephone number. This command will work with any Hayes compatible modem:

```
atdt3382400 <CR>
```

The command above consists of an attention command, a dial telephone number command, a telephone number, and a carriage return. `kermit` and other communications packages will automatically store a telephone number list so that you do not have to remember the **Hayes** command set, but it is instructive to know a few commands in case something goes awry. For example, it is good to know the command for hanging up (`ath0`) or for testing the line (`ath1`). Generally, a modem will come with a complete listing of its command set, and it is at least instructive to look it over. When your modem makes contact with the host location, the first response you will discern is an audible squawk (if you have a speaker turned on), and then you will see a the "CONNECT" message, such as the one shown subsequently. After you see the CONNECT response, wait a moment, and, if nothing happens, type a carriage return. The remaining portion of the message will then appear.

```
CONNECT 2400/REL

                    *****************************
                    *  Welcome to SFSU FOGNet!  *
                    *****************************

    *   To connect to any host, type "telnet <host name>"    *
    *                                                         *
    *   To quit, type "hangup", "bye", or "quit"              *
    *                                                         *
    *   To get help, type "?"                                 *
    *                                                         *
    *   To break a session, press "Shift-Ctrl-6" and then,    *
    *   type "kill"                                           *
    *                                                         *
    *   To report modem problem, call 415-338-1211            *
    *                                                         *
    *               Happy Computing!                          *
    *                                                         *
    *********************************************************

sfsu-annex 25:
```

This is a sample welcome message from the network communications server here at San Francisco State University. Your welcome message will probably differ, but will likely be similar. After the "Welcome to ..." line you will see a message. This is called a **Message of the Day** (motd). It doesn't generally change every day but can contain valuable information when it does. Every machine has the potential for showing such a message, and you should at least glance at it when you log in to see if anything has changed. Often, down times and other messages from the person who administers the machine (called a **system administrator**) will be posted to all users in the motd. Note that *this* motd is not the same as the login motd. This motd is associated with the terminal server and not a particular host. Following the motd will be the connect prompt. Whenever a computer expects you to type something, it should provide you with a prompt of some sort. Depending on what you are doing, the prompt's appearance may change. By recognizing different prompts, you can avoid confusing problems (see "Computer prompts" on page 8). In this session, the prompt is "sfsu-annex 25:." This is where you will select which computer you want to log on to.

At this point, the user enters the host to connect to and proceeds with the login script, as in the direct login session above. As you can see subsequently, I have opted to log on to the SFSUVAX1. More on the naming conventions for machines and what they mean later. Notice that I use the "telnet sfsu-vax1" response. This means 'connect me to the host named sfsuvax1.' Con-

```
sfsu-annex 25: telnet sfsuvax1 <CR>
Trying...
Connected to sfsuvax1.
Escape character is '^^'.
```

necting to a machine changes from institution to institution, and can even vary widely within an institution. Please use this discussion as a general guideline for how to understand this process, and seek out assistance from your instructor on how to perform these tasks at your institution and laboratory.

Connecting does *not* mean that you are logged in. It simply means that you have selected a host and can *now* start the login script. By selecting a host and typing a carriage return, the actual login procedure is automatically initiated. See "Logging on to a Host" on page 6 for more details on the login procedure if you skipped to this section.

1.6.3 Exiting from the Terminal Server

When you have finished your work and logged off the host you were working on, you will most likely still be connected to the institution via the terminal server and will be returned to that point in the login sequence. Here you may choose to connect to another host, or you can choose to exit the terminal server by typing bye, or a suitable equivalent, as follows:

```
localhost> logout <CR>
session 1 - disconnected from sfsuvax1( 130.212.010.102 )...
Connection closed by foreign host.
sfsu-annex 25: bye <CR>
NO CARRIER
```

After you type "bye," wait until you see a "NO CARRIER" message on your screen at home before exiting from your communications package. If you then type "ath0," locally, you will manually hang up the telephone, thereby guaranteeing signal loss. The reason is that some modems are not smart enough to know when the line has been disconnected from the terminal server, and you will end up paying the telephone company for time you weren't logged in. Alternatively, you can simply pick up the telephone receiver to guarantee a disconnect.

1.7 Exercises and Sample Quiz Questions

1.7.1   Exercises

Exercise 1   Log in and out a few times without doing anything.

Exercise 2   Change your password and log out.

Exercise 3   Find out who the system thinks you are.

Exercise 4   Successfully log in from a modem (yours or a friend's).

1.7.2   Sample Quiz Questions

Problem 1   List three considerations in selecting a password.

Problem 2   When are response times the best when logged in via modem?

Problem 3   List three reasons why dial-in connections are unreliable.

Problem 4   What is the difference between a user ID and a home directory with the same name?

Problem 5   You are logged on to your `local host` by modem. You are typing away, having a great time when you realize that your commands are not working. You stop to take a look and notice that the prompt looks as below. What happened?

&

Problem 6   What is the difference between the reponses to the following commands?

- whoami
- who am i

Problem 7

- What is a computer prompt?
- How many types of prompts are you likely to see in a typical login session?
- Show what they look like and what utility they are associated with.

Problem 8   What are the two user-provided components in the login script?

Problem 9   List the steps (prompts and responses) you will provide or see when you change your password.

Problem 10   What does ATDT3381200 mean?

Chapter 2
Electronic Communications

2.1 Introduction and Scope

Most computer users have used machines set up for a single user, or machines set up to serve many users but in batch-type mode. **Batch mode** means that an entire processing task is submitted to the operating system for execution, at once, instead of interactively. Nowadays a single user on an isolated systemis becoming less and less commonplace, and the need to communicate with other users, online, is increasing. The UNIX operating system has built-in utilities that enable you to communicate with other users on your machine. More important, these same utilities provide you access to computer users throughout the world. In this chapter you learn how to use three UNIX utilities for communicating with other computer users electronically: (1) mail, (2) talk, and (3) news. Each of these utilities is intended for specific kinds of communication and has particular standards associated with its use, called **communications etiquette**. When you have completed this chapter, you should be comfortable sending and receiving mail, talking with other users, and reading/posting items to a newsgroup. More specifically, you should know how to invoke each utility, how to work with it, and how to exit the utility. You should also know when it is appropriate to use one utility over another, and what factors are involved in effective electronic communication. It is very important that you take the notion of computer etiquette very seriously with respect to electronic communications; it is as important as learning how to use these utilities.

2.1.1 Communications Etiquette

As computer users, we spend much of our time in front of a monitor and keyboard. When people are trying to reach us, or we them, it only makes sense to find a way to communicate through the medium where we are most likely to be found. In the case of electronic communications, this also turns out to be the most efficient way to communicate. The flip side of this potential benefit in communications is the potential for invasion of privacy and crank calls. As our ability to communicate electronically has improved, so has our need for a system of communicating that is considerate of other users on the system. Only by adhering to common sense guidelines can the behavior of individuals be acceptable. Unlike the open society, where you can say what you please, you do not own the network and can be restricted from access to it if you annoy enough people. As such, we will introduce some notions of network etiquette here, hoping that you will embrace them with the sensibility on which they arose, and that you will find ways to extend them in your own communications with other users.

When you send electronic mail (email) to someone, you are sending *unsolicited* comments. You are inundating the recipient with *your* opinions at their expense. Of course, a first reaction when confronted with this form of abuse is "there ought to be a law..." against this form of privacy invasion, a network etiquette that guides and protects communication between computer users. Well, there is such a "netiquette," and it consists primarily of commonsense guidelines. There are different rules depending on usage, and each is touched on in this book. The essence you are to glean from this discussion is that you should use the system as though it were a communications medium, because that is what it is. When you use a shared resource, as with a networked computer, everything you do will be scrutinized by other users, and so your attitude is important.

2.1.2 How to Communicate Electronically

The most prevalent problem with electronic communication is the decided lack of inflection, facial expression, and timing that guides our understanding of what people say. Even so, in normal conversation people constantly misinterpret comments. For example, a dry wit or a matter-of-fact statement may come off as an insult when not intended as such. When the same comments are typed at a terminal, the effect is, unfortunately, exaggerated. The result is hurt feelings, anger, and, often, return fire. This situation is compounded by the type of people using electronic mail, and by the speed at which responses can be generated and sent. When people send mail that, to others, appears unthought out or stupid, then there is likely to be some abuse coming back. The term often used for electronic abuse is **flame**. One of your goals as a network user should be to avoid giving or receiving flames. There are three general rules for communicating your thoughts electronically: (1) be clear, (2) tell someone when you are kidding, and (3) edit your messages before posting them. Being clear is much more important when you communicate electronically. Altogether too often people use sarcasm and cynicism in their normal conversations. If you are going to use these forms of speech when communicating electronically, then you have to be careful. When you are joking around, the recipient may not know you well enough to understand. It is important to give them a clue as to how to interpret what you say. The most obvious approach is to say you are joking directly, or "no offense intended," or something that makes it clear to the recipient that your comments are not intended to provoke. A **smiley face** :-) can be used (sometimes parenthetically :-) to indicate "tongue-in-cheek" comments. Smileys are a start at representing humorous comments, or comments that have double meaning that you want the receiver to interpret correctly. Their use can be abused as easily as any form of communication. As you will learn, there are many ways to type a smiley. Use them carefully. Avoiding flames can only be achieved by editing what you write. Read the message over again after you have written your reply. Think of all the recipients to the message and the ways they might interpret your response.

2.2 Sending and Receiving Electronic Mail

UNIX has a built-in command, called *mail*, for sending messages to and receiving messages from other users. You will find this to be an effective way to communicate with the course assistants or instructor when you have questions, as well as to friends. Although your use of email will be limited to begin with, for all intents and purposes there is no difference between sending mail to someone across the room or to Germany. Sending a message to someone requires five types of information.

- How to use email appropriately
- How to invoke and exit the mailer
- How to address the mail
- How to compose the message
- How to receive and manipulate messages

The first item is addressed by looking at email netiquette. The second item is required for all applications and should be the first thing you try, such as logging in and out of the computer. The third item introduces the notion of mail *path* or *address*. The fourth and fifth items introduce the mailer(s) and their use.

2.2.1   Netiquette and Email

Before you learn how to use email, there are a few guidelines to follow when using email that you should always keep in mind. The essential notion in every one of these rules is *think first*. If you do this one thing, then you will enjoy using mail without becoming frustrated or frustrating someone else.

- Never send a piece of mail to anyone who doesn't know who you are. This means that YOU are responsible for checking the carbon-copy (cc) list on incoming mail to make sure that you do not proliferate your response to the entire free world.

- Never send out any sort of solicitation. It is an invasion of privacy, and it shows extremely poor taste.

- Think before you respond. Perhaps you should compose all your responses in separate files and edit them before putting them into a mailer.

- When using electronic mail, always identify yourself and leave a return email address. The most appropriate location for the return path is in your message, at the end of your message. That way, when someone is done reading your mail, they have your return path looking at them in the face.

- Learn what a smiley face is and do not abuse its use. A smiley face is a network way of saying (just kidding : -) . There are probably hundreds of smiley faces, e.g., tongue in cheek : ^) , oh-no : -O, sad-face : - (, etc.

- Never "flame" someone. If you must clarify something sent in email, then think about what you are saying, how you are saying it, and why you are saying it. Don't send mail just to toot your own horn.

- Never do anything that might draw the attention of the postmaster (the person who administers mail on the computer). If users from other locations are sending mail to your postmaster about you, then something is very wrong.

As you can see, email netiquette does not place unreasonable restrictions on what you send. Rather, it is intended to make sure that users are considerate of one another.

2.2.2   Electronic Mail Addresses

Sending a message to someone requires an address to send the mail to. With the postal service you need a name, an address, and a zipcode. With a telephone you need a telephone number. With email, the situation is similar, except that you use the userid instead of the name. The address can be replaced with the symbolic **machine address** where the user's account is located. The machine address is associated with a uniquely numbered sequence called an **Internet Protocol** (IP) address. A machine's IP address is usually associated with one or more symbolic names. The machine's IP address can also be used to address mail, similar to a zipcode or telephone number. If you know a person's userid and machine address (symbolic or IP number), then you can send someone mail. For example, the entire symbolic address for the host `sfsuvax1` looks as follows:

```
sfsuvax1.sfsu.edu
```

In this example, both `sfsuvax1` and `"sfsuvax1.sfsu.edu"` are the machine address. Actually, both are aliases for the *real* machine address, and typically reside in a file named `"/etc/hosts"` on most systems. In `/etc/hosts`, you will find machine address entries of the form:

```
IP-address symbolic-address name1 name2 ...
```

An example is shown below:

```
localhost> more /etc/hosts <CR>
     .
     .
#
# Host Database
#
130.212.10.102 sfsuvax1.sfsu.edu sfsuvax1 vax1
127.0.0.1 localhost
     .
     .
```

The lines starting with pound signs (#) are comments. The first non commented item (i.e., `130.212.10.102`) refers to the machine's **Internet Protocol (IP)** address. The IP address comprises four numbers separated by periods. The IP address can *always* be used in internetwork communications. The next entry refers to the machine's **symbolic name address** (i.e., `sfsuvax1.sfsu.edu`), and all additional columns refer to pseudonames, or **aliases** for the machine address. Thus, `130.212.10.102`, `sfsuvax1.sfsu.edu`, `sfsuvax1`, and `vax1` all refer to the same computer. The difference between them is that the IP address is recognizable by any machine on the network, the symbolic address is recognizable by most machines on the network, and the aliases are only used locally.

A space has been provided, below, for you to write down your host's symbolic names and IP address. You should also write them on the inside cover of this manual for quicker access later.

```
Localhost Symbolic Names: _____
IP Address _____
```

The **name address** follows a convention, as follows:

HOST.INSTITUTION.INSTITUTION-TYPE

The name (symbolic) address for `sfsuvax1` in the `/etc/hosts` file above tells us that the "HOST" is `sfsuvax1`, the "INSTITUTION" is `sfsu`, and the "INSTITUTION-TYPE" is `edu`. In addition to `edu`, six other institution types are commonly used:

Table 2.1:   `mail` Institution types

.COM	⇔	Commercial organizations
.EDU	⇔	Educational organizations
.GOV	⇔	Government organizations
.MIL	⇔	Military organizations
.NET	⇔	Network organizations
.ORG	⇔	Other organizations
.UUCP	⇔	Dialup connections

The institution-type can also be a **country-code**, if the host is outside the United States. For example, the institution-type for hosts in Canada is .CA, Brittain is .UK, and Australia is .AU.

How does all this address stuff affect electronic mail? Remember, if you have a user's userid and their mail address, then you can send them mail. The standard notation for mail address is:

```
name@domain
```

where "`name`" is a person's userid, "`@`" separates the name and domain, and "`domain`" is their **mail address**. The mail address is identical to the machine address where the account is located. If `domain` does not contain any dots (.), then it it is interpreted as the name of the local (current) host. Otherwise, the message is passed to a mail host (name server) that determines how to get to the specified `domain`. For example, if your account is on the machine sfsu-vax1 and you want to send the user jhodges some mail, then you could use the userid alone, as follows:

```
jhodges
```

If, conversely, you wanted to send mail to John Q. Smith at Podunk University, whose account is on the host JSMACHINE, you would probably have to specify the entire mail address.

jqsmith@jsmachine.podunku.edu

where, according to the template provided above, "jqsmith" is the userid, and the domain breaks down to HOST.INSTITUTION.INSTITUTION-TYPE as before. In this case, the machine name "jsmachine" is the host, the school "podunku" is the institution, and because John Smith's account is at an educational institution, the institution-type is "edu." Because every userid on a particular system is unique, and because the machine address is unique, your mail address is unique.

2.3 Using the UNIX `mail` Utility

In this section, the methodology and essential commands for the standard UNIX mailer, /usr/ucb/mail is presented, and, in the next section the MH mailer is presented. Many other mailers are available, such as Emacs mail, elm, pine, and mush; however, they are similar in use to one of the mailers discussed here. You should try them if the ones presented here are insufficient for your needs.

mail is the standard, out of the crate, UNIX electronic mail utility.[1] Your mail is generally directed to a home-level directory and then accessed by whatever mail handler you use. mail is fast and accessible, but not altogether user friendly. Some of the common commands used are given below, but a full description of the mailer can be found using the manual pages (type 'man mail' as a command). What characterizes UNIX mail is its environment. When you invoke mail, alone, your prompt will change from whatever it was to the following:

```
&
```

Whenever you see this prompt, you are in the mail environment, so do not try to execute UNIX commands. The easiest way to get out of mail, without changing anything, is to type the letter 'q' as follows:

```
& q <CR>
```

2.3.1 Writing and Sending a Message

Using mail is easy. You already know that you need an address to send the mail to, so all you need now is something to send. The mail utility provides you with

---

1. Also known as a mailer or mail handler

several mechanisms for writing and manipulating the message before sending it. A simple example is illustrated below, and a list of commands follows so that you can experiment with `mail` on your own. The easiest form of email is to someone who has an account on the same machine as you. In this case, you need only know their account name. Suppose the person you wish to send mail to is John Q. Smith, who has the userid jqsmith. To send your friend Smith a message using the standard UNIX mail utility you would enter the command as follows:

```
localhost> mail jqsmith <CR>
```

the computer will respond with

```
Subject:
```

to which you enter a one-line subject of your message, for example:

```
Subject: Party this Saturday...you're invited! <CR>
```

The computer will move the cursor to the next line and wait for you to enter the **body** (content) of your message. You enter your message one line at a time, separated by carriage returns. At this point, you will not be able to edit your message other than to back space over incorrectly typed text. That is, you will not be able to move up a line and change a spelling. If you want the ability to edit your mail completely, and you know how to use an editor, then you can use your editor from within the standard `mail` utility. A brief overview is provided here, for the `vi` editor, but a complete discussion of file editing is presented in Chapter 4. In your message, on a blank line, type the following (tilde-v):

```
~v <CR>
```

and the default editor will be invoked on the your message body.[1] Once the editor is invoked, you can move the cursor around the message, character by character, with the 'j,' 'k,' 'h,' and 'l' keys on the keyboard. You can delete characters directly under the cursor using the 'x' key. You can replace a character under the cursor with 'r char,' where char is the new character. You can return to the mailer by typing two capital Zs.[2] When you are done editing, you can continue writing the message where you left off, or you can send the

---

1. See Chapter 4 for information on how to invoke and use an editor, and Chapter 5 on how to set the default editor in your mailer.
2. See Appendix G for a short description of `vi` and related commands.

message. When you have completed entering your message, type either a <Cntl-d> or a period (.) **on a line by itself**. The mailer will respond with:

```
Cc:
```

which means **carbon copy**. If you want to send the mail to anyone else (e.g., yourself), list their userid's here, separated by commas. Otherwise, press the carriage return key (<CR>). The message will automatically be sent. To abort sending a message, type <Cntl-c> (twice) before sending it.

2.3.2 Other Ways to Send Mail

An alternative for composing mail involves editing a file before invoking the mailer and then sending it. Two approaches are presented here, both of which assume that you have already composed the message with your favorite editor and named it "mesg1." In the first case, you will *include* a file into the body of the mail message. First you enter the mailer normally (i.e., with the mail command). When you get to the point where you would normally start typing the message text, type the following (tilde-r) on a blank line:

```
~r mesg1 <CR>
```

at which point the mailer will grab the file, stuff it into the current message, and return you to typing mode for the message. In this way, you can copy file segments into a mail message easily. Tilde-r is similar to the ':r' command in the vi editor (see Chapter 4), both of which have the same effect of including/merging files.

A second way to incorporate "mesg1" into a message is to use **redirection** (see Chapter 5, page 157). For the sake of continuity, the method is presented here. All you need to do is type the following at the command line:

```
localhost> mail jqsmith < mesg1 <CR>
```

The symbol < redirects where the mail utility receives the input file from. Where a utility or command normally receives input from is called the *standard input*. The standard input to the mail program typically comes from the keyboard. The redirection symbol temporarily reassigns the standard input for mail to be the file that comes after the < symbol. By using the symbol < in the example above, the entire message body will come from a file mesg1 instead of the keyboard. We will see many uses of redirection later on. The only restriction on this, batch, method is that you are not really in the mailer, so if you decide to say something in addition to what is in mesg1, then you are out of luck with this approach. You can also include a subject line using this method.

```
localhost> mail -s "subject" jqsmith < mesg1 <CR>
```

where the `mail` '-s' option includes the string that follows as the mail message subject line and whatever is between the double quotes is the subject line content.

2.3.3 Receiving and Reading Email

When you log on to the system, you may notice a message similar to the one shown below:

```
You have [new] mail
localhost>
```

The *new* part is bracketed here for a reason. If you have no new mail, but have mail that hasn't been removed (or read) from you mailbox, then you will receive this message without the [new] part. If you have new mail, then you will receive this message without the brackets. In either case, to receive mail, merely enter the `mail` command alone:

```
localhost> mail <CR>
```

If you have new or unread mail, then a list of the messages will be displayed according to the format below:

```
[STATUS] [NUMBER] [USERID] [DATE] [SIZE] [SUBJECT]
```

where each classification is described below:

Table 2.2: `mail` Message list information

STATUS	⟺	(N)ew mail, (U)nread mail, (D)eleted mail
NUMBER	⟺	The mail identification number
USERID	⟺	The userid (or mail alias) who sent the mail
DATE	⟺	The date the mail was received by the mailer
SIZE	⟺	The message size in lines/bytes
SUBJECT	⟺	The first few characters of the subject line

Using this format, consider the sample listing of messages shown below:

```
localhost> mail <CR>
Mail version 5.3 2/18/88.  Type ? for help.
"/usr/spool/mail/hodges": 92 messages 11 new 48 unread        ①
    81 preuss@sutro.SFSU.ED  Sat Jul 13 16:02  43/1625 "NeXT Campus Consul"
>N 82 vojin@omen.SFSU.EDU   Mon Jul 15 07:18  47/1937 "intrusion into my"
 N 83 eisman               Mon Jul 15 09:38  12/350  "Re: Leave of Absence"
 N 84 eisman               Mon Jul 15 09:40  14/408  "Re: address"
 N 85 eisman               Mon Jul 15 09:41  12/350  "Re: Huckleberry upgr"
 N 86 eisman               Mon Jul 15 09:45  13/426  "Re: CSc 214"
 N 87 kroll@walnut.SFSU.ED  Mon Jul 15 13:25  61/2105 "NeXT"
 N 88 kroll@walnut.SFSU.ED  Mon Jul 15 13:27  18/794  "last message"
 N 89 barbara              Mon Jul 15 15:36  29/951  "Re: Allegro Goodies "
 N 90 phoebe               Mon Jul 22 16:18  15/573  "Postscript graphs fo"
 N 91 leo@alexis.a-t.com   Mon Jul 22 22:07  37/1451                       ②
 N 92 barbara              Tue Jul 23 12:55  13/339  "test"
&
```

Notice that the first thing you will see in the listing, other than the version number and help message, is a header (at **1**) telling what your **mail path** is, which is where your mail is stored locally, how many messages are stored there, and what their general status is. The mail path in this display is /usr/spool/mail/hodges, which describes a directory in the UNIX file system. There are 92 messages in the mailbox, 11 of which are new, and 48 of which have not been read. Thus, the listing that followed only displayed a portion (messages 81 to 92) of all the mail for the user hodges on this machine.

Each of the remaining lines describes a specific mail message. The "N's" in the "status" (first) column mean that these are new messages. Message 81 has no status character, meaning it has been read. The greater than symbol (>) next to message 82 indicates this as the **current message pointer**, meaning that this is where you are "located" in the list.

If a userid is alone, in the third (userid) column, then the user account resides on the same host or subnet where the mail was received, as in the case of "eisman," "barbara," and "phoebe." When a user is on the network, the userid and symbolic mail address is used, as in "vojin@omen.SFSU.EDU."

The next four fields (columns) identify the day and time (on a 24-hour clock) that the mail was received. For example, message number 91 was recieved on Monday, July 22, at 10:07 p.m. The next field for message 91 indicates the size of the message, which, in this case was 37 lines and 1451 bytes. Notice that message 91 has no subject line. Finally, notice that when the display is complete, you are now in the mail environment, because the prompt has changed to an ampersand (&).

Suppose that you want to read one of these messages. All you need to do is type the mail ID number. For example, I decided to read message number 89, so I typed the following.

```
& 89 <CR>
Message 89:
From barbara Mon Jul 15 15:36:53 1991
Return-Path: <barbara>
Received: by toaster.SFSU.EDU (NeXT-1.0 (From Sendmail 5.52)/NeXT-1.0)
        id AA28412; Mon, 15 Jul 91 15:36:51 PDT
From: barbara (Barbara Ford)                                        ①
Message-Id: <9107152236.AA28412@toaster.SFSU.EDU>
Subject: Re: Allegro Goodies from Franz Inc.
To: hodges@toaster.SFSU.EDU (John Hodges)
Date: Mon, 15 Jul 91 15:36:50 PDT
In-Reply-To: <9107142213.AA24004@toaster.SFSU.EDU>
X-Mailer: ELM [version 2.3 PL10]
Status: R
> Barbara,
>
> At the same time we ordered the Franz upgrade we ordered some software
> upgrades for the FrameMaker application  (wordprocessing and page
> layout). Could you possibly check and see what happened to those orders
> for me?

> Thanks a lot.
>
>       Jack
I called New York Frame Technology and the upgrades for Frame Maker 3.0
for both the MacIntosh and the IBM will be shipped out this week.
I think that does it?  Does it not?
&
```

There is a *lot* of information in a mail message! Let's take a look at a template **mail header** and then you will be able to appreciate, rather than be confused, by the preceding example.

Table 2.3: `mail` **Message header information**

`Message 89:`	⟺	The mail message number
`From`	⟺	The userid who sent the message
`Return-Path:`	⟺	The userid to which a reply should be sent
`Received:`	⟺	The host that received the message
`From:`	⟺	The userid and mail alias (from finger file)
`Message-Id:`	⟺	The host identification number for the message
`Subject:`	⟺	The mail message subject line
`To:`	⟺	The mail message recipient
`Date:`	⟺	The date the message was sent
`In-Reply-To:`	⟺	The originating message subject line
`X-Mailer:`	⟺	The mailer used to compose the message
`Status:`	⟺	The status of the message from the originating sender

This is a complete header. When you read mail you may not see a complete header. Notice that the message body accompanying the header includes comments that are offset by greater than signs (>). This is a standard protocol for reminding a person of the original context of a mail message, so that the reader doesn't wonder what the sender is talking about. You can type these directly, or you can learn to automate the process.[1] In the example message above, the message easily fit into a single screen. Had the message been too long to fit, it would have scrolled past. To look at it more leisurely, you can do one of two things. First, you can specify how many lines are displayed before a display "pager" is invoked. This is accomplished with the *crt* variable in a file named ".mailrc" that resides in your home directory. You may not have such a file when you receive your account, but you can create one as long as you are careful. A value of 25 will work for most terminal screens.

---

1. You can do this by writing a script and piping mail messages through it before they are sent. Script writing and, in particular, a script that performs this type of task, is covered in Chapter 13.

```
set crt = 25
```

Alternatively, you may **save** the message to a file with the mail 's' command:

```
& s #N filename <CR>
```

where "s" stands for *save*, "#N" stands for the message number, and "filename" is the name of a new file you want to send the message to. If you omit the #N, the current message is saved. You can also use a message range, #N1-#N2. You may then quit mail with the 'q' command and read the file using your favorite editor or use the more paging utility.

The mailer will only display 20 messages at a time, so if you want to look at messages before or after the messages displayed, you need to issue the following command:

```
& f N1-N2 <CR>
```

where "f" means to take the message list lines for the following message number range and display them, "N1" is the range starting message number, and "N2" is the range ending message number.

2.3.4 Responding to Email

To respond to a message, type the following mail command:

```
& R #N <CR>
```

where "R" stands for **reply** and "#N" stands for the message number to which you are responding. The mail address of the original sender will automatically appear in the correct location, the subject of the message will be repeated, and then you will be given the opportunity to compose your message.

Replying to messages can sometimes be tricky. If someone has sent a message to you, but they have sent the same message to many other users, then it is possible that when you respond you will send your response to the other users as well. This is called *implicit* carbon-copying. This is all right as long as you are doing it intentionally. Generally, however, you should send your responses to the particular person who sent you mail in the first place. If you use the "r" instead of "R" your response will be sent to *all* the original recipients of the message. In general, you should look carefully to make sure that no other users are listed as recipients before using "r" to reply to mail.

2.3.5 Forget Those Long Mail Addresses - Mail Aliases

It is possible to create a personal distribution list, or list of **aliases**, so that you can send mail to a group of people without using their userid and mail address. Such lists can be defined by placing a line like the following in the **.mailrc** file in your home directory (if one exists):

```
alias alias-name address1,address2 ...
```

For example, suppose you have three friends who work at different businesses but you get together occasionally or share funny stories online. Instead of retyping their addresses all the time, you might want to create a mail alias called "cohorts:"

```
alias cohorts bills@widgetsrus.com,larryw@ftn500.com,sue
```

where "bills," "larryw," and "sue" are your friend's userids on their local hosts, followed by their mail addresses to which a message addressed to "cohorts" will be sent. To display the current list of such aliases, use the **alias** (a) command from within mail. Systemwide distribution lists (such as "bugs" and "help," where they exist) are defined in "/usr/lib/aliases." Contact the system administrator to be added to a systemwide mailing alias.

2.3.6 Forwarding Email to Other Users

In some circumstances, a user may have multiple accounts on a machine, or accounts on multiple machines. In such cases, it is nice if you can decide whether to read mail sent to an account, or to **forward** it to another account. This is easily done, as shown subsequently. Be careful not to produce any forwarding which might be redirected back to the original account, as this is called a **circular reference**, and will cause problems for your local postmaster. The format for producing a mail forward is to create a file named ".forward" in your home directory. In this file, you insert a line that specifies where the mail is to be sent. For example, consider the example below, which is a .forward file from the host sfsuvax1:

```
localhost> cat .forward <CR>
hodges@futon.sfsu.edu
```

In this .forward file, mail that is sent to jhodges@sfsuvax1 (the mail *receiving account*) is forwarded to the user hodges on the host futon.-sfsu.edu. The nice thing about forward files is that you can selectively decide whether to forward or not, depending on the machine and the type of traffic you receive from the machine. Also, if you edit your `.forward` files in all accounts except one to include to remaining account, then you need only log into that (remaining) account to receive all of your mail. You must be very careful, when creating `.forward` files not to type errors, because mail then sent to your userid will either be sent to the wrong person, or, worse, it will be returned as unsent to the user who sent it. This is called **mail bouncing**.

A second occasion in which you might want to forward mail is when you are unable to respond to mail for a period, e.g., if you leave town for some reason. In such cases, you may want people sending you mail to receive a message informing them that you are unable to respond for a while, to tell them how to reach you. If the `vacation` utility is supported on your host, you can modify your `.forward` file to use the vacation utility as shown below. To use the vacation utility, you must first initialize it before you change your `.forward` file:

```
localhost> vacation -I <CR>
```

This will add two files: ".vacation.dir" and ".vacation.pag" to your home directory. `vacation` will not work unless you have done this. Now you can modify your ".forward" file as shown below:

```
localhost> cat .forward <CR>
hodges, "|vacation hodges"
```

This is a different kind of `.forward` than the previous one, to show another feature, that of sending yourself mail at multiple hosts. In this file, the first item (`hodges`) makes sure that you receive a copy of the mail sent. The second item **pipes** the received mail into the `vacation` program for the user `hodges`. Piping does for commands what redirection does for files, by eliminating the need to display a command's output to the monitor (or standard output). Instead the response from one command becomes the input to the next.

When you are sent mail, the sender is sent a message whose content is defined in a file named ".vacation.msg," residing in your home directory. The message you send to people should include a mail header for them, as shown subsequently.

```
localhost> cat .vacation.msg <CR>
From: hodges@futon.sfsu.EDU (Jack Hodges)
Subject: I am showing an example of a vacation message
Delivered-by: The Vacation Program
Please bear with me, I am showing an example of the UNIX
vacation program, and will turn this off promptly

        J.B.Hodges
```

2.3.7 **mail** Commands

Table 2.4: Internal mail commands

-	⇔	Display the previous message
?	⇔	Display a brief summary of commands
!	⇔	Execute the shell command that follows
(R)eply	⇔	Reply to originator of message only
(r)eply	⇔	Reply to sender and all original recipients
(a)lias name list	⇔	With no arguments, display all currently defined aliases. With arguments defines an alias called name for addresses in list
(c)hdir DIR	⇔	Change your working directory to DIR
(co)py N1-N2 FILE	⇔	Append each message in list N1-N2 to filename FILE, but do not mark the messages for deletion
(d)elete N1-N2	⇔	Mark the message list N1-N2 as deleted
dp	⇔	Delete the current message, and display the next one
(ex)it or x	⇔	Return to the shell immediately, without modifying your mailbox
folders	⇔	List the names of folders in your mail folder directory
(fo)lder	⇔	Switch to a new mail file or folder
(f)rom N1-N2	⇔	Display the message headers for the message list N1-N2
(h)eaders	⇔	List the current range of headers; an 18-message group

Table 2.4: Internal `mail` commands (cont)

(m)ail list	⇔	Send mail to users specified in `list`
(n)ext	⇔	Display the next message in the sequence
(p)rint N1-N2	⇔	Display each message in the list `N1-N2` on the screen
(q)uit	⇔	Terminate the session, saving all undeleted messages
(s)ave N1-N2 FILE	⇔	Append each message in list `N1-N2` to filename `FILE`, and mark each message for deletion

Each of these can be typed out in full. The parentheses simply indicate the minimum characters that have to be typed for the command to be recognized; any others included are optional for the user.

I have mentioned several tilde (~) commands, ones that are used while composing a message, specifically for editing a mail message and including external files into a mail message. Below are a few additional tilde commands for mail, but this is not an exhaustive list. Remember that each of these commands must be issued on an empty line.

Table 2.5: Internal `mail` tilde commands

~!COM	⇔	Execute the UNIX command `COM`
~b USERS	⇔	Blind carbon-copy the message to userids in `USERS`
~c USERS	⇔	Carbon-copy the message to userids in `USERS`
~f N1-N2	⇔	Read the messages in `N1-N2` into this message
~m N1-N2	⇔	Same as ~f but tabs are included
~r FILE	⇔	Read contents of `FILE` into the message
~t USERS	⇔	Send the message to the userids in `USERS`
~v	⇔	Edit the message with the editor defined by the EDITOR variable in .mailrc
~w FILE	⇔	Write the message to filename `FILE`
~COM	⇔	Pipe the message through command as a filter
~~STR	⇔	Insert the string `STR` in the message, preceded by ~

2.4 MH — The RAND Mail Handler

MH is a mailer developed by the RAND Corporation to run in the UNIX command shell. Unlike the UNIX mail handler "`/usr/ucb/mail`," MH is more transparent to the user using UNIX commands. MH is not a single program that is invoked with a single command, like `mail`. MH consists of a package of programs that are executed individually rather than collectively as a separate process. Output from MH commands is normally displayed on the screen, but can be piped into other UNIX processes, and output from other UNIX processes can be piped into MH commands. This way the user can intermix mail reading/responding with other UNIX processing activities quite easily. The MH environment can be used *as is* but can also be customized by creating/editing the "**.mh_profile**" file in your home directory. This file is created the first time that you invoke MH.

2.4.1   Setting Up the MH Environment

Unlike mail, to use MH you must invoke one of its utility commands to initialize it. One way to do this is to send yourself mail and incorporate it with the MH command, *inc*. Another way is to compose a mail message with the MH command, *comp*. The initialization will be demonstrated with the former approach. If you do not have any unread mail, send yourself a dummy piece of mail with the subject line "`testmail`" and don't read it. Now you are prepared to initialize MH with the *inc* command. Type the following at the shell prompt:

```
localhost> inc <CR>
I'm going to create the standard MH path for you.
Create folder "/usr/f1/jhodges/Mail/inbox"? y <CR>                    ①
Incorporating new mail into inbox...
   1+ 01/28 To:jhodges        testmail<<>>                            ②
```

MH will now create a ".mh_profile" file, and it will ask you if you want the standard mail directory name "**Mail,**" (at item **1**). When you respond, MH will continue by incorporating new mail into your local mail folder (called "**inbox**") as shown at item (**2**), whereupon you can use MH to process mail. The "+" in this listing means that message 1 is the current message, or the one which will be displayed if the user types `show` without a message argument.

Now, if you wish, you can edit your newly-created "`.mh_profile`" to be similar to (or exactly like) the sample file provided. You can then use MH commands noted in the next section. If you want more information, please read the man entry for MH (i.e., `man mh`).

Table 2.6: Components of the MH .mh_profile

Path	Mail	⇔	directory for mail folders
Draft-Folder	drafts	⇔	directory for drafts
prompter-next	prompter	⇔	prompt for editor to use
Editor	vi	⇔	default editor
Msg-Protect	600	⇔	permissions on new articles
Folder-Protect	700	⇔	permissions on new folders
Signature	Jack Hodges	⇔	user signature for messages
anno	-inplace	⇔	directory for mail folders
dist	-annotate -inplace	⇔	form for distribution lists
forw	-annotate -inplace	⇔	form for forwarding lists
send	-verbose -alias aliases	⇔	where to look for mail recipients
scan	-form scan.size	⇔	what to do with the scan command
inc	-form scan.size	⇔	what to do with incorporated messages
ali	-alias aliases	⇔	where to find aliases
whom	-alias aliases	⇔	where to find legal mail addresses

2.4.2 MH Commands

Below is a list of *useful* MH commands. These are commands to be used with MH. Some of these aren't needed often, but have been included so that you can experiment with them. You can get by quite nicely with *comp*, *send*, *repl*, *forw*, *inc*, *next*, *scan*, *show*, *prev*, *refile*, *folder*, and *rmm*.

Table 2.7:   MH commands

`ali`	⇔	list mail aliases
`anno`	⇔	annotate messages
`comp`	⇔	compose a message
`dist`	⇔	redistribute a message to additional addresses
`folder`	⇔	set/list the current folder
`folders`	⇔	list all folders
`forw`	⇔	forward messages
`inc`	⇔	incorporate new messages (mail)
`mark`	⇔	mark messages
`mhl`	⇔	produce formatted listings of MH messages
`next`	⇔	show the next message
`packf`	⇔	compresses a folder into a single file
`pick`	⇔	what to do with incorporated messages
`prev`	⇔	show the previous message
`refile`	⇔	file messages in other folders
`repl`	⇔	reply to a message
`rmf`	⇔	remove a folder
`rmm`	⇔	remove a message range
`scan`	⇔	produce a one line per message listing
`send`	⇔	send a message
`show`	⇔	show (display) messages
`sortm`	⇔	sort messages
`whom`	⇔	report to whom a message would go
`post`	⇔	deliver a message

Message lists (or ranges) *always* take the form **mesg1-mesgn**. So if you want to remove messages 7 to 13 you would type rmm 7-13. MH commands can take zero arguments, as with comp; a message range as noted; or a folder, as with scan. Commands like scan, folder, refile, and show can change the current folder with a + sign. For example, if you are reading mail from your current folder, which is inbox, and you want to save the message just read into a folder called "mine," then you use the refile command as follows:

```
localhost> refile +mine <CR>
Create folder "/usr/f1/jhodges/Mail/mine"? y <CR>
```

Now, if you want to check to make sure that the message has been put in the folder, you can use the scan command to list the mine folder:

```
localhost> scan +mine <CR>
```

which will display a standard MH mail message list. Note that you can list mail folders with the folders command and change the current mail folder with the folder command.

2.4.3 The MH Aliases File

You can add a personal alias file to your "Mail" directory. This file contains the complete mail addresses of people that you routinely send mail to but do not wish to remember their address. The format is shown below:

```
localhost> cat ~/Mail/aliases <CR>
class:chong,manrson,adrey,goss,grenfeld,gog,chi,whirten,
      gudermon,bunns
mike:dwyer@cs.ucba.edu
test: hodges
wienrab:wienrab%oso-70@ohio-state.arpa
everyone: *
ralph:hyper@hqlabs.hq.com,hyper%hqlem@hqlabs.HQ.COM
tedc:IGRQTGC@OC.UCBA.EDU
```

The "aliases" file is organized by alias names, such as *class*. The items in the alias entry are listed, each separated by commas, and offset from the alias name by a colon (:). The alias entry is used by typing the name into the **To:** location in comp. Note the variety of e-mail addresses in this sampling. Those without full paths are IDs local on the host where the alias resides, whereas those with full paths will work from any host. In general, your alias file should use full mail paths in case you copy/move it to another host.

2.4.4   Composing a Message Using MH

A sample session using MH to write and send a message is shown below. Suppose that you want to **compose** a message to someone. The MH command to use is `comp`. When we type `comp`, depending on what editor has been selected by the user, we will get an edit window for the purpose of writing the letter. In this example, the `vi` editor is used, so the **comp** window will look as follows:

```
localhost> comp <CR>
To:
cc:
Subject:
--------
~
~
~                                                           ⟵───────  space reduced for readability
~
~
"/usr/f1/jhodges/Mail/drafts/43" 4 lines, 26 characters
```

This example normally takes up the entire screen. It has been reduced in size here to save space. In this case, you would use `vi` commands to insert the mail address for the recipient, the subject line, and the content of the message. An example is provided. To insert the recipient's mail address, you could type a '$' to get to the end of the "To" line. This would place the cursor on the colon. You could then type an 'a' to append text, and then type the address after the colon, after which you would press the <ESC> key to stop appending. To move down to the subject line, you could type a 'j' twice, one for each line. Then you could use the same procedure as for the mail address (i.e., $, a, type text, <ESC>) to type the subject, again finishing by pressing the <ESC> key. You would then type a 'j' to get onto the line of hyphens, and an 'o' to type the text of the message. When you are done composing the message, you type an <ESC> key again, and you exit `comp` by typing the standard escape key for the editor you are using. In `vi`, you would type ZZ. At this point you will see the following (what now?) message:

```
What now? h <CR>
 -h unknown. Hit <CR> for help.
```

Normally you respond with something that makes sense, like `send` or `quit`. In this example, I mistyped and then took the opportunity to list the options to "What now?" When I was done I used the `send` command to send the mail.

```
What now? <CR>
Options are:
  display [<switches>]
  edit [<editor> <switches>]
  list
[<switches>]
  push [<switches>]
  quit [-delete]
  refile [<switches>]
+folder
  send [<switches>]
  whom [<switches>]
What now? send
```

Two items of note are the "What Now? Options" and the **drafts** folder. Normally when you want to post a mail message or news posting you would reply with send, but you may also wish to review the original message using display, edit the file using edit, refile the message to a folder for future use with refile, and so on. The "drafts" folder holds copies of all messages you have composed, for future reference.

2.5 Problems Replying to Email

You should be able to give people at other institutions your email address and they should be able to send you mail. Sometimes when you try to send someone mail, or they try to send you mail, the mail will **bounce** (be returned unsent). There are different reasons for bounced mail, two common ones of which will be introduced here: unavailable service, and address problems. The bottom line is that bounced mail may not be your fault; if you find that you have the same problem repeatedly, you should speak with the postmaster or system administrator.

2.5.1   Returned Email: Service Unavailable

Occasionally systems crash. Should you be sending or receiving mail when a crash occurs, your mail should be kept in a mail spool directory on the mail gateway until the system is restored. Should you be sending mail to another site, and *its* network crashes, then you may have your mail bounced and receive a cryptic message, such as the one shown subsequently.

```
>From MAILER-D%ucsbuxa@hub.ucsb.edu
Mon Jan 30 14:09:10 1989
Return-Path· <MAILER-D%ucsbuxa@hub.ucsb.edu>
Received: from hub.ucsb.edu
(hub.ucsb.edu.ARPA) by corwyn.cognet.ucla.edu (4.12/1.3)
        id
AA06823; Mon, 30 Jan 89 14:09:01 pst
Received: from ucsbuxa.ucsb.eduby
hub.ucsb.edu (5.59/UCSB-v2)id AA18004; Mon, 30 Jan 89 14:06:25 PST
Received: from hub.ucsb.edu by ucsbuxa.ucsb.edu (3.2/SMI-3.2)
        id AB13170; Mon, 30 Jan 89
14:07:58 PST
Date: Mon, 30 Jan 89 14:07:58 PST
From: MAILER-D%ucsbuxa@hub.ucsb.edu (Mail Delivery Subsystem)
Subject: Returned mail:   ◄─────────────────────────────────── ①
Service unavailable   ◄─────────────────────────────────────── ②
Message-Id: <8901302207.AB13170@ucsbuxa.ucsb.edu>
To: <claudia@cognet.ucla.edu>
```

The message at item (**1**), the subject line, tells you that there was a problem in sending the mail. The message at item (**2**) tells you that the problem is network related. This message bounced because the remote host/system was down when it received the mail. Normally, attempts to deliver mail are made for a certain amount of time (say 3 days) before bouncing. If you should get a note like this, chances are reasonable that resending the message at another time will succeed. Otherwise you should notify the postmaster.

2.5.2   Email Address Problems

There are two common mail address problems everyone should be aware of: (1) name server problems and (2) uucp addresses. Sometimes you will receive mail and find that you cannot reply without receiving a bounced message. This may be caused by a mail server that cannot find your address (at their end), their address (at your end), or some combination in between. If this is the case, then you may be able to succeed by changing the intended recipient's mail address, on your mail, to include a machine that is very likely known. You then let that institution's name server figure it out. In such cases, apply the following rule:

replace the first @-sign with a %-sign and tack on @domain at the end

where domain is your local machine address. This will route your mail through a known machine before sending it out and usually fixes problems in mailer confusion.

Here is an example of a modified mail address:

```
jqsmith%jsmachine.podunku.edu@sfsuvax1.sfsu.edu
```

2.5.3 UUCP Mail

UNIX to UNIX System Copy (**uucp**) addresses are another primary source of bounced mail. Mail addresses that end with the UUCP Institution-type, such as the one below:

`...[host!]host!username`

are sometimes mistakenly referred to as **usenet** or **internet** addresses. `uucp` provides links to numerous sites throughout the world for the remote copying of files (see anonymous `ftp`, Chapter 7, page 242). However, `uucp` emulates a network connection and is not a direct network connection. Because of this, mail sent to or responding to `uucp` addresses may bounce. The primary cause of the bounced mail is that many `uucp` addresses are linked to a network via a modem, and messages are taken from a mail server on a network on a periodic basis. If the connection is not made within some set amount of time, then the mail cannot be delivered and it bounces. Some mailers can handle uucp-type mail addresses and will try to resend the mail. Others will simply hiccup. Below is a short list of more obscure, but valid, email addresses which show some of the combinations of notations I have mentioned.

```
DIALRA@asuacad.bitnet
74236.2754@compuserve.com
carbolz@sde.mdso.vf.ge.com
hisrov@cirrus.com
skijig@smith.risc.rockwell.com
claris!qm!Norman_Rockwell@ames.arc.nasa.gov
```

Notice that the first example is an address to an organization called **bitnet**. Bitnet is an alternative network, like uucp or internet. It should be noted that there are different networks around the world, that there are going to be new ones, and that the user should become comfortable with figuring out how to address mail rather than focusing on a specific one.

2.6 Electronic Talk

In addition to electronic mail, UNIX supports a more direct form of communication called **electronic talk**. `talk` is very similar to a telephone conversation. All you need to use it is the recipient's userid and mail address, as in email.

Unlike email, where you can send a message to many people at once, UNIX does not come stock with a means for teleconferencing using `talk`.

2.6.1   Talk Etiquette

Like email, `talk` has its own set of guidelines. Because you can "dial" any user who happens to be logged in, it is entirely possible that you could talk to someone with whom you shouldn't be talking or who doesn't want to talk with you. There are ways around this, of course, as you will see. The essential rule of etiquette is simple:

- Do not `talk` to someone unless you have sent them mail or otherwise had some introduction to them in the past.

Sometimes `talk` is not a useful way to communicate, but sometimes it is ideal. You will need to figure these things out on your own, but here are some pointers.

- Trying to `talk` a long distance is less than ideal because the signal must bounce off many machines and response times may be high.
- Trying to `talk` during peak periods could get frustrating, also because of performance.
- Trying to `talk` about personal matters can get awkward because one cannot read inflection or expression from the responder's words or face.

Other forms of etiquette apply in **talk**, probably more so because the connection is "live." In the section on email it was suggested that you edit your messages before sending them. Using `talk` you will be not be able to do any editing, so it is essential that you have a good attitude and be willing to explain what you mean by your comments. Try not to leave things out, so that the other person doesn't have to guess what you mean.

2.6.2   Invoking Talk

It is easy to `talk` to someone. You need to know (1) their userid and mail address, and (2) whether they are logged on. Two ways to find out if they are logged on are (1) **fingering** them, or (2) issuing a `who` and looking for their userid. If they are logged on, you can issue the following command:

```
localhost> talk jqsmith <CR>
```

which is the simplest form of the template

```
talk userid@domain
```

where "`domain`" is the machine address. Note that a full address may be required, and that the address could be any legal mail address. When first called, `talk` sends the message:

```
Message from TalkDaemon@domain...
      talk: connection requested by
your_name@your_machine.
      talk: respond with: talk
your_name@your_machine
```

to the user you wish to `talk` to. At this point, the recipient of the message should reply by typing:

```
talk your_userid@your_domain
```

It doesn't matter from which machine the recipient replies (i.e., they could be logged in on many machines), as long as the userid is the same and the source person's machine is appropriately noted. Once communication is established, the two parties may type simultaneously, with their output appearing in separate windows, which will look like the one below:

```
localhost> talk hodges@cognet.ucla.edu <CR>
[Your party is not logged on]

------------------------------------------------
localhost>
```

Your typing will always echo in the upper window, and that of your friend will echo in the lower window. Typing `<Cntl-l>` will cause the screen to be reprinted, while your erase, and kill characters will work in `talk` as normal. If you find that you are having awkward problems in `talk`, then the most likely problem is that the terminal's termcap is incorrect (see Chapter 5, page 143) for details on working with terminal characteristics. The most obvious problem is having a single character echoed per line.

2.6.3 Exiting Talk

To exit `talk`, just type your interrupt character `<Cntl-c>`. `talk` then moves the cursor to the bottom of the screen and restores the shell prompt.

2.6.4 Talk Protocol

Although both parties can type simultaneously, "talking" is having a dialog. You should decide on some kind of protocol for establishing the end of a comment. One such method is to continue typing until you get to where you want to pause, and then type a double carriage return. You may also decide to use a special character or phrase. It is up to you and your friend to agree, or at least for you to do something that will enable your friend to distinguish between your comments. Otherwise they will all run together and you end up with mush, especially when the screen scrolls or refreshes.

2.6.5   Talk Permissions

Permission to `talk` may be granted or denied using the *mesg* command. You can also set this in your `.cshrc` file. For example, if in general you want to receive `talk` messages, then you would set `mesg` as follows:

```
localhost> mesg y <CR>
```

Conversely, if you want to turn messages off so that you cannot be bothered, then use the same command as follows:

```
localhost> mesg n <CR>
```

These are both examples of usage at the command line. You can also put one of these commands into your `.cshrc` file, and it will become your default setting.

2.7 Electronic News

Electronic news, like email and `talk`, is a method of communicating with other computer users. Unlike email and `talk`, that single out a few users, or a single user, rn[1] broadcasts messages to a particular **newsgroup**. A newsgroup is a name associated with a forum on a particular topic. The messages associated with the newsgroup are maintained on a **blackboard**. A blackboard is a type of list whose information is available to a large number of entities. A newsgroup's messages are thus available to anyone who subscribes to the newsgroup, and anyone can post to or follow up on messages posted to the newsgroup. The messages associated with a newsgroup are maintained across the network and updated regularly. Reading news may end up being a terrific waste of time, but everyone should be introduced to its use. You have been forewarned.

News is a feature of the internet that arose from the need for governmental agencies to communicate with one another and their contractors. The use of

---

1. There are many incarnations of electronic news, of which `rn` is but one. Your institution may use `news`, `xrn`, `trn`, `rnews`, or others. In addition, there are other services which are similar to news, such as `gopher` and the `World Wide Web`, which are information servers, and `irc`, which is a multiple person talk program. Seek assistance for these services locally.

this facility has grown over the years and has led to a proliferation (type *newsgroups* sometime, but be prepared for a long wait) of newsgroups. Some of these newsgroups are extremely helpful for transmitting ideas, software, announcements, copies of papers, and so forth between institutions and individuals. Conversely, many of the newsgroups are purely social in nature, masquerading as technical bulletins. Some do not even masquerade.[1] The **.newsrc** file is a shell script for initializing news, and can be tailored to suit the user's needs just like other dot files (e.g., `.mailrc` and `.mh_profile`).

In this section some etiquette guidelines associated with news, setting up a `.newsrc` environment, invoking `rn`, reading from and posting to news will be presented. In addition, common commands for using the various news levels are presented for reference.

2.7.1   News Etiquette

News allows a computer user to express ideas to a large audience at once. Because of this feature, and because many in the audience could be people of influence or import in your field, it pays to use caution in posting and responding to newsgroups. Unfortunately, often users do not keep this in mind and find themselves *flaming* someone who could help them get a job, or into graduate school. You simply never know. There are a few guidelines that can be used to smooth your introduction to news, as presented below.

- When posting to newsgroups, never **cross post** unless you know what you are doing. Cross-posting is when a user has a message targeted toward more than one newsgroup. Because this is potentially wasteful of resources, be careful to check the newsgroups the original posting was made to before doing a follow-up. The worst-case scenario is when the postmaster is made aware that you are not using news properly, in which case you could lose news privileges.
- When posting to newsgroups, remember that the most important people in any given field are reading the newsgroup. If you make a fool of yourself, you make a fool of everyone on your network, and they will remember.

2.7.2   Invoking `rn`

Using news is quite easy. The UNIX command is *rn* (for readnews).

```
localhost> rn <CR>
```

When rn is typed for the first time, the system will present you with a (long) introduction to reading news. In this introduction, which you should

---

1. For a more complete history of the origins of email and news, add `news.announce.newusers` to your `.newsrc`.

read, is a thorough discussion of news etiquette and instructions. At the same time, the news server will present you the option of subscribing to one or more newsgroups. The list of newsgroups is *very long* and you could spend hours simply saying 'n' to every newsgroup you do *not* want to subscribe to. Suffice it to say that you can always subscribe to a newsgroup, so it is best to exit news shortly after this question/answering session begins and then later edit the .newsrc file that will be created. To exit rn, keep typing 'q' until you return to the UNIX shell prompt.

2.7.3   Reading News

rn, like mail, has its own environment and prompts. Unlike mail, rn uses multiple levels within its environment to keep track of newsgroups and messages. There are three levels in the news environment: (1) newsgroup selection level, (2) article selection level, and (3) pager selection level. Each level has its own commands and prompt, so using rn can take some getting used to. Below I have included an entire sample session using news on the host SFSUVAX1, spread across a number of examples.

```
localhost> rn <CR>
(Revising soft pointers--be patient.)
Unread news in comp.lang.lisp                         63 articles
Unread news in comp.lang.lisp.franz                    2 articles
Unread news in comp.sources.wanted                   193 articles
Unread news in rec.humor.funny                        38 articles
Unread news in rec.scuba                             159 articles
etc.
Checking active list for new newsgroups...
Newsgroup alt.allsysop not in .newsrc--subscribe? [ynYN] n
Newsgroup alt.bbs.allsysop not in .newsrc--subscribe? [ynYN] n
Newsgroup alt.binaries.pictures.d not in .newsrc--subscribe? [ynYN] N      (1)
...
```

continued...

This first portion of the session illustrates what happens when rn starts up. The first set of items (i.e., on the left) is a list of the newsgroups currently subscribed to (e.g., rec.humor.funny). The newsgroup names are organized from general to specific. For example, the newsgroup "comp.lang.lisp" is a computer science topic, the subtopic is programming languages, and the sub-subtopic is the LISP programming language. Some of the names can be difficult to understand. On the right you are told how many articles were posted since you last read a particular newsgroup. Some groups will accumulate articles at an alarming rate. Note, from the "etc." that this is only a partial listing of the active (i.e., subscribed to) groups. The next set of items are new newsgroups that have been added to the network since I last read news. It is rather long, so I used the capital 'N' response (at **1**), after responding 'n' to a few, to stop the process. The reply from `rn` is shown subsequently.

```
(I'll add all new newsgroups (unsubscribed) to the end of your .newsrc.)
(Adding misc.writing to end of your .newsrc unsubscribed)
(Adding news.members to end of your .newsrc unsubscribed)
(Adding news.software.readers to end of your .newsrc unsubscribed)
(Adding rec.games.board.ce to end of your .newsrc unsubscribed)
(Adding rec.pets.cats to end of your .newsrc unsubscribed)
(Adding rec.sport.volleyball to end of your .newsrc unsubscribed)
(Adding soc.culture.italian to end of your .newsrc unsubscribed)
(Adding vmsnet.tpu to end of your .newsrc unsubscribed)
```

continued...

This means that I will not be asked those questions anymore, but that I can subscribe to those groups in the future if I really want to. The next thing that will happen is that `rn` will start reviewing each subscribed newsgroup. Remember that the first group was "`comp.lang.lisp.`" `rn` now prompts me whether I want to read any of those articles. This is the article selection level:

```
******** 63 unread articles in comp.lang.lisp-read now? [ynq] n
```

I type 'n,' so `rn` continues on to the next group:

```
******** 2 unread articles in comp.lang.lisp.franz-read now? [ynq] n
******** 193 unread articles in comp.sources.wanted-read now? [ynq] n
******** 38 unread articles in rec.humor.funny-read now? [ynq] =
```

When the user types an equal sign (=), this tells `rn` to list the articles by a portion of their subject field (similar to `mail`'s 'f' and MH's 'scan' commands), and enters the user into the **article selection level** for the group "`rec.humor.funny.`"

```
673 stanford research
674 Forbidden Zone #121 (Relative Value Ranking)
675 Editorial Policy on Offensive Jokes -- Monthly Po
676 Ghandi and British Police
677 Proposed Improvements to World League American Fo
678 Judges, Lawyers and Whales
679 A hard thing to give up...
...
What next? [npq]
```

continued...

This partial list shows the articles by number. To read an article, type the number shown on the left. For example, we will read article number 673, hoping for a chuckle.

```
What next? [npq] 673 <CR>
Article 673 (37 more) in rec.humor.funny (moderated):
Subject: stanford research
Message-ID: <S2ae.2172@looking.on.ca>
From: elrod@ocf.berkeley.edu (Edward L. Rodriguez)
Date: 4 Jul 91 07:20:06 GMT
Keywords: topical, chuckle
Lines: 10
My first atttempt at an original joke:
How many Stanford researchers does it take to screw in a lightbulb?
Three.  One to hold the ladder, one to turn the bulb, and one to bill the
government for the house.
--
Edited by Brad Templeton.  MAIL your jokes (jokes ONLY) to funny@looking.ON.CA
If you post instead of mailing, it screws up the reply-address sometimes.
Attribute the joke's source if at all possible.  A Daemon will auto-reply.
End of article 673 (of 710) - what next? [npq] q
```

continued...

Note the portion at the bottom of the posting ("`Edited by ...`"). This means that this newsgroup is **moderated**, and all postings are screened by the moderator. Many newsgroups are unmoderated, and posting a message is discretionary. When `rn` has gone through all the newsgroups you have subscribed to, you will see the following message:

```
******** End of newsgroups- what next? [npq] q
localhost>
```

at which point you will be returned to the command shell.

2.7.4   Posting to a Newsgroup

Posting to a newsgroup means to submit an article to the newsgroup. The procedure is simple. You can edit a file or write one "on the fly" (sometimes a dangerous tactic). The command for posting to a newsgroup is *Pnews*. To use the *Pnews* command, type the following line:

```
localhost> Pnews newsgroup <CR>
```

where "`newsgroup`" is the newsgroup you wish to post to. The system will then interrogate you for a few minutes to determine how to set up the posting for distribution, will ask for an editor to use, and will then ask for a file to use. These all have defaults (in parentheses) and this is straightforward enough. When you are done, the system asks you "What now?" just as in MH (see page 35). When you eventually reply with send, the message or news posting speeds along its merry way. A short list of news commands is included below.

2.7.5   Setting Up the News Environment

The first time rn is invoked it will create a file named **.newsrc** in your home directory which instructs rn how to maintain your newsgroups. If you want to modify the .newsrc file, then you can edit it with your favorite editor. If you want to unsubscribe to a newsgroup, then simply replace the colon (:) before the message number list with an exclamation point (!). To resubscribe, simply reverse this procedure. To see the effect of the .newsrc file on the execution of rn, the rn startup procedure shown below is executed whenever you invoke rn:

- rn will look for your .newsrc file, which is your list of subscribed-to newsgroups. If rn doesn't find a .newsrc, it will create one. If it does find one, it will back it up under the name .oldnewsrc.

- rn will input your .newsrc file, listing out the first several newsgroups with unread news.

- rn will perform certain consistency checks on your .newsrc. If your .newsrc is out of date in any of several ways, rn will warn you and patch it up for you, but you may have to wait a little longer for it to start up (this could be a lot longer).

- rn will next check to see if any new newsgroups have been created, and give you the opportunity to add them to your .newsrc.

- rn goes into the top prompt level – the newsgroup selection level.

2.7.6   News Command Reference — Abridged

An abridged set of commands for each of the three news levels is provided below. Use them to set up and read news on your own. The commands for rn are divided into four sections: startup, newsgroup selection, article selection, and pager selection.

Newsgroup Selection Level

In this section the words "next" and "previous" refer to the ordering of the newsgroups in your .newsrc file. At the newsgroup selection level, the prompt looks like this:

```
******** 63 unread articles in comp.lang.lisp-read now? [ynq]
```

The following commands can be used at the newsgroup selection level:

Table 2.8: `rn` **Newsgroup selection commands**

`y, or space`	⇔	Do this newsgroup now
`=`	⇔	Do this newsgroup now, but list subjects before displaying articles
`n`	⇔	Do not do this newsgroup now, go to the next newsgroup
`P`	⇔	Do not do this newsgroup now, go to the previous newsgoup
`1`	⇔	Do not do this newsgroup now, go to the first newsgroup
`$`	⇔	Do not do this newsgroup now, go to the end of the newsgroups list
`g newsgroup`	⇔	Go to newsgroup; if you aren't a subscriber, you will be asked if you want to subscribe and how you want the newsgroup placed
`/pattern`	⇔	Scan forward for a newsgroup matching pattern, e.g., use ? to match a single character, * to match any sequence of characters
`?pattern`	⇔	Same as `/pattern`, but search backward
`u`	⇔	Unsubscribe from current newsgroup
`c`	⇔	Catch up — mark all unread articles in this newsgroup as read
`q`	⇔	Quit
`x`	⇔	Quit, restoring `.newsrc` to its state at start of `rn`; the `.newsrc` you would have had if you had exited with 'q' will be called `.newnewsrc`, in case you didn't really want to type 'x.'

Article Selection Level

On the article selection level you are not asked whether you want to read an article before the article is displayed; the normal article selection prompt comes at the END of the article. The prompt at the end of an article looks like the following:

```
End of article 673 (of 710)-what next? [npq]
```

The following are the available commands in the article selection level:

Table 2.9: `rn` **Article selection level commands**

`n, space`	⇔	Scan forward for the next unread article
`N`	⇔	Go to the next article
`p`	⇔	Scan backward for the previous unread article; stay here if there isn't a previous unread article
`P`	⇔	Go to the previous article
`<Cntl-l>`	⇔	Refresh the screen
`<Cntl-x>`	⇔	Restart the current article, and decrypt as a rot13 message
`X`	⇔	Refresh the screen, and decrypt as rot13 message
`number`	⇔	Go to the numbered article
`pattern`	⇔	Scan forward for article containing pattern
`?pattern`	⇔	Scan backward for article containing pattern
`r`	⇔	Reply through net mail
`R`	⇔	Reply, including the current article in the header file generated
`f`	⇔	Submit a follow-up article
`F`	⇔	Submit a follow-up article and include the old article with lines prefixed either by ">" or by the arguments to a "-F" switch
`c`	⇔	Catch up in this newsgroup; i.e., mark all articles as read
`u`	⇔	Unsubscribe to this newsgroup
`s destination`	⇔	Save to a filename or pipe using `sh`
`=`	⇔	List subject of unread articles

It should probably be noted that the `<Cntl-x>` and `X` commands are used to encrypt and decrypt (i.e., un-encrypt) messages that are posted that may be sensitive or offensive to certain groups. Although this may seem odd, there is no means established for maintaining the content of news postings. It is left to the postmasters at each institution to maintain control of and peace among their users. The encryption schemes are meant to inform readers that they may not *want* to read postings, in order to avoid being offended. Those who decrypt the messages have no real complaint because they were warned . . . at least, that is the intent of the mechanism.

Pager Selection Level

At the pager level (within an article), the prompt looks like the following:

```
-MORE-(17%)
```

where the percentage (here 17%) means that this is how much of the article has been displayed so far.[1] The commands available at page selection level are

Table 2.10: `rn` **Pager selection level commands**

x	⇔	Display next page and decrypt a rot13 message
<CR>	⇔	Display one more line
q	⇔	Go to the end of the current article (don't mark it either as read or unread)
j	⇔	Junk the current article; mark it read, and go to the end of the article
<Cntl-l>	⇔	Refresh the screen
x	⇔	Refresh the screen and un-decrypts rot13 message

2.8 Exercises and Sample Quiz Questions

2.8.1 Exercises

Exercise 1   Send mail to yourself as a test. Create a file and send this to yourself or a friend using redirection.

Exercise 2   Your instructor will tell you the name of an account where you can send questions about programming assignments and UNIX. Send a question to this account.

Exercise 3   Find out the address of someone on another machine and send them electronic mail. First try the userid alone, then try it with the full path.

---

1. See Section 3.5.6 , page 90 for information on `more`.

Exercise 4   Use `talk` with someone you know. Establish a consistent set of rules for separating ideas, for telling someone when they can respond, etc. For example, when you finish a comment, you might hit two carriage returns, or . . . and a carriage return, or some special sequence of characters. It is important that both of you know what each of your "end of line" will look like.

Exercise 5   Use read news (`rn`) to get information about some favorite topic. Read the introduction carefully regarding news usage. Modify your .newsrc to unsubscribe to uninteresting newsgroups. Resubscribe later. Make sure that you know the primary commands for topic search, junk, catch-up, as well as how to move from level to level within news.

2.8.2   Sample Quiz Questions

Problem 1   List two advantages and two disadvantages to electronic communications.

Problem 2   What knowledge must you possess to use electronic mail (or any application for that matter).

Problem 3   Answer the questions below:

- What is the > symbol used for in `mail` message lists?
- What is the MH equivalent to the >?
- Provide an example of how **each** would appear in a message list:

Problem 4   Provide the MH commands to do the following:

- Get new messages into MH:
- List all messages in your working mail folder:
- Respond to message number 32:
- Put message number 32 into your "Personal" mail folder:
- Exit MH:

Problem 5   What is the proper `rn` command used to catch up on unread news? To search for a specific piece of information in news articles?

Problem 6   List three types of problems posed by electronic communications that do not occur in normal dialogs between people. For each, describe why this is a problem.

Problem 7   Define 'flame.' List two practices to avoid giving or receiving flames?

Problem 8   Answer the following questions about `rn`

- What rn command is used to list the numbers and subject line of news articles within a particular newsgroup?
- What command is used to add a newsgroup?
- What command is used to follow up to a newsgroup posting?

Problem 9   Describe the name address convention, and give three examples of institution types commonly used. What is the origin of a message from someone with the following address: `irisa.irisa.fr`?

Problem 10   Name the file that contains the following line. Explain the meaning of each term in the line.

```
130.212.10.102 sfsuvax1.sfsu.edu sfsuvax1 vax1
```

Chapter 3
The UNIX File System

3.1 Introduction and Scope

From a user's viewpoint, an operating system consists of different programs that are executed to perform specific tasks. Programs that perform system-related user instructions are called **commands**. Commands are distinguished from applications and user-defined programs, which perform non–system-related tasks. All of the programs and data that reside on the system make up the UNIX **file system**, and each must be organized in a consistent manner so that it can be used when needed. This chapter presents the organization and manipulation of programs and data in the UNIX operating system. The topics covered in this chapter are listed below:

- File system components: directories and files
- UNIX commands
- Directories and directory manipulation
- Files and file manipulation
- File system security

The UNIX file system is an organization of files and directories that enable UNIX to perform its function. Knowing how the UNIX file system is organized is important in knowing how to use it. When you have completed this chapter, you should understand how the UNIX file system is organized, and how to move around within it. You should be able to manipulate the contents of the file system in different ways. For example, you should be able to *list the contents* of a directory anywhere in the file system, regardless of where you are currently *located* in the file system. You should be able to *change your loca-*

tion to anywhere in the file system, and you should be able to *manipulate the contents* of the file system: to create, move, rename, or execute them. In general, a file system can reside on any type of storage device. For example, a disk drive, a diskette drive, an optical drive, and a tape drive can all have file systems on them. By **mounting** a device, its file system can be made visible to the UNIX file system and its users. The mounting of file systems is beyond the intended scope of this course and is mentioned for clarification purposes. File system mounting can only be performed by administrative personnel. Beginning with this chapter, I will cease to print a <CR> at the end of every example. It will be assumed that, when a command name and arguments are invoked, they are followed by a carriage return.

3.2 File System Components

In UNIX, there are essentially two types of structures: **directories** and **files**. A file is a meaningful sequence of information that has a name that can be referenced. Programs and data are types of files. Files are organized in directories, so a directory can be thought of as a folder or organizer. A directory can organize other directories as well as files. Files cannot organize anything except information; neither directories nor other files.

The file system describes the organization of directories and files. Most directories can organize and be organized by other directories. There is one directory, called the **root directory**, which cannot be organized by (contained in) another directory. The root directory is often visualized as the top of a tree's root system or the branches of an inverted tree. The directories which the root directory organizes can be thought of as branch points to different parts of the root system (see Fig. 3.1). Every directory and file originates from the root directory, and every branch point actually describes a mini root system or subtree. Every directory of the file system eventually terminates with a file or a directory that doesn't organize anything, called an empty directory. A terminating file is often called a node of the file system, or a *leaf* of the tree, because nothing can emanate from it.

Figure 3.1:   The UNIX file system is comprised of directories and files

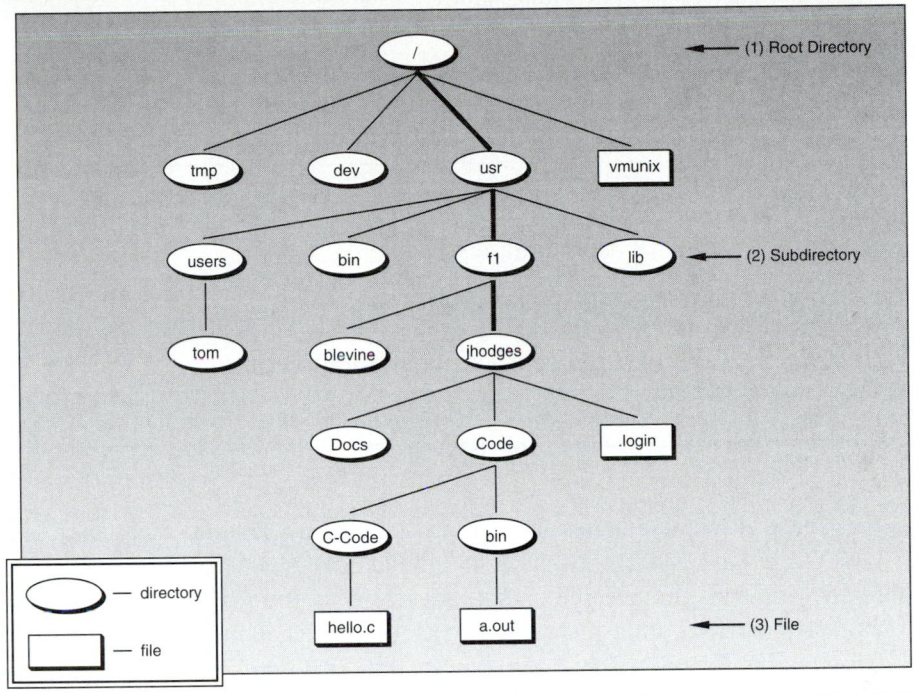

Directories and files are organized by function. The root directory contains a number of primary **subdirectories**. For example, all of the users' directories are contained in a directory called "usr." Many of the system commands are found in the directories "bin" and "etc." Other system directories are listed below:

```
localhost> ls -F /
backups/      genvmunix*    pak_admin/    sys/          vmb.exe*
bin/          lib/          pcs750.bin*   tmp/          vmunix*
dba/          lost+found/   public/       ultrixboot
dev/          mnt/          quotas        usr/
etc/          opr/          secure/       var/
```

This example is a listing of a root directory, which is denoted by a single slash (/). Whereas most directories have a name, root does not. Any directory 'below' the root directory is called a **subdirectory**. The contents of the root directory can be directories and files. For example, the item "vmunix," above, is a file. Note that "vmunix" is followed by an asterisk (*). This is the notation for an executable file,[1] meaning that it is a program.[2] Directories are denoted by a slash after their name. Thus the directory "lib" is listed as "lib/" in this listing. Below is a partial description of the contents of some of the major sub-directories. The contents of these directories changes slightly from one UNIX implementation and platform to another.

Table 3.1:   Standard UNIX top-level directories

/bin	⇔	System binaries and many of the system commands
/usr	⇔	Manual pages, user directories, applications
/lib	⇔	System libraries
/etc	⇔	System commands
/dev	⇔	Hardware device configuration files
/tmp	⇔	Temporary storage (publically read/writable)

These directory names and their contents are an important part of the UNIX operating system, because they have been standardized across the different platforms that use the operating system. If you get an account on a network somewhere other than where your current account is, and you want to know where the contributed software is, then if it was placed in "/usr/lo-cal/bin" or "/usr/contrib" on your old system, that would be the first place to look on the new system. To find out just what software is on your system, you are simply going to have to go looking around, and you are encouraged to do so. This is the best way to learn about the commands for manipulating the file system, and it is the only way to find those little jewel programs that aren't publicized but are available nonetheless.

3.2.1   Naming Conventions and Paths

Each directory and file in the file system is associated with a **path**. An item's path is a concatenation of directory names, separated by slashes (/), starting with the root directory and ending with the directory in which the item resides. The root directory is designated by a lone slash (/).

/

Any path that begins with the root directory (/) is called an **absolute** or **full path**. A full path is a path that starts at the root directory. Any file or directory can be referenced with a full path, although it is rarely necessary to

1. See Section 3.4.1, page 69 for details on this nomenclature.
2. This is not necessarily true. See Section 3.6.2 for details.

write the entire path out in full. All other full paths start with a slash to denote that every path originates with the root directory. For example, the directory belonging to the user "jhodges" resides in the "f1" subdirectory under "/usr," which is a subdirectory off root. So my directory, jhodges, resides three levels below root.[1] The path for the files and directories belonging to jhodges is denoted as follows (see bold line in Fig. 3.1):

```
/usr/f1/jhodges
```

Ch3

The root directory has no name, and all other names specify subdirectories. The path is our means of finding and executing programs in the UNIX file system. To use the path effectively, it is important to understand the syntax associated with UNIX commands and to know how to obtain information about UNIX commands. For the remainder of this chapter, and in general throughout this manual, examples will be provided from the "UNIX/Ch3" directory. It should be noted that any modifications to a directory require write permission to the directory (covered in Section 3.6.2 of this chapter). You will not be able to make modifications to either of these directories, or, in general, to anyone else's directory except your own. You are encouraged to perform the same or similar commands you are reading here in your own directory, and even to experiment and see which commands will work in directories not owned by you. You are welcome to look at the "UNIX" directory to compare what you do to what you see in the manual. They should be similar, if not identical.[2]

3.3 UNIX Commands

When users log on, the first thing they see is a shell prompt. More is explained about what happens to produce the prompt in Chapter 5, and how these events can be manipulated. For now, it is important to look at the prompt with respect to the file system. Consider the prompt below.

```
localhost>
```

When you see this prompt you are in a **command shell**. A shell is a command interpreter. This means that you can issue UNIX commands or run programs and they are evaluated and executed **now**.[3] Each UNIX command is is-

---

1. f1 is actually a mounted file system of its own, and looks like a subdirectory in the local UNIX file system.
2. The "jhodges" directory is provided as a template to illustrate the use of commands and to show a variety of responses that are not clearly shown in a simple directory such as "UNIX."
3. As opposed to a batch job, which is submitted altogether and run later according to priority ranking.

sued with the following syntax:

```
command-name [command-options][command-arguments]
```

where **command-options** (often called keys) are single or multiple characters which are used to specialize how the command response is displayed, and **command-arguments** are the user-provided items that the command operates on. Some command options or arguments may be optional, and will appear in square brackets in the command template. In general these will generally be noted in the text. In UNIX, most every command argument will be a directory, a file, or a path to same, so you, as a user, will have to know what it is you want to do (what command you wish to execute, its options, and its required arguments) before you can *do* anything. Let's say that you successfully changed your password in the first chapter of this manual. Then you correctly issued the passwd command:

```
localhost> passwd
```

passwd is a good *first* command because it performs a necessary task of providing security for your account, and because it requires no options or arguments. Many file system commands can be used in this way. Others are more complicated. What do you do when you do not know the name, options, or arguments of a command, even though you know what it is that you want to do?

3.3.1 Getting Help about Commands: Online Manual Pages

When learning about *any* operating system, it is perfectly normal not to understand the use of particular commands until you need them. This is awkward because, without knowing what it is that you need help on, or what command it is that you need to execute, you will not know where to look for the answer. The UNIX operating system is so large that no one person can remember *all* of its nuances. So there is an online version of the manual that you can call on to find out syntax and usage of any UNIX command. What is more, you will not have to know, a priori, what the name of the command is. The drawback is that the manual pages are written as a reference and not as a tutorial. They are compact to save space, and have only the information needed by someone to refresh their memory of how to execute the command. Often this is all that is necessary, but you need to know how to read the man page or you will be as confused as before you began. There are three things you need to know to use the man pages: (1) how to invoke them, (2) their general format, and (3) how to search for what you are looking for.

Invoking the Man Page

Using the online manual is simple. The command is *man*, which you type at the shell prompt. The general usage is shown below:

```
man [subsection] command-name
```

where "man" is the command name, "subsection" is an optional (as noted by the square brackets) subdirectory name, and "command-name" is the name of some command you wish information about. For example, if you type:

```
localhost> man man
```

```
                                                                  man(1)

Name
    man - displays manual pages online
Syntax
    man -k keyword...
    man -f page_title...
    man [ options ] [ -roff_options ]... [ section ] page_title...
    man [ options ] [ section page_title... ]...
    /usr/bin/man [ option ] [ section ] page_title...
    /usr/bin/man [ options ] [ section page_title... ]...
Description
    There are two man commands: /usr/ucb/man, and /usr/bin/man.  For
    most users, /usr/ucb/man is the default man command.  The command
        which man
    shows you which man command is the default.  The recommended
    default is /usr/ucb/man.
...
```

subsection

the system displays a "manual" page, or **man page** describing the online manuals. This is actually a condensed version of the full system command reference manuals that are available for the computer. The 'subsection' command argument is optional because the system has a set of *default* locations in which to look for manual pages.[1] The 'subsection' when provided, overrides the search. Notice in the listing that 'man(1)' has been labeled. The '1' refers to a subdirectory in the man library where this command's man page resides.

If you know what sort of task you want to find out about, but not the commands associated with the task, then there is a modification of the man command you can use. The modification makes use of what is called a **command option** or **key**.

---

1. Many command'sarguments have default values, which are normally identified by a value in square brackets. If a value isn't provided for an argument, then the default value is used. This could be confused with a command's optional arguments which are also shown in square brackets.

```
localhost> man -k manual
```

where the '-k' is a man command option. Virtually every UNIX command has options. The argument "manual" is called a **string**. The '-k' man option means "do a search through all the man pages for a string equivalent to 'manual,' and return a list of the man pages that pass the test." Thus, after the command issued above, the listing shown below is displayed. There are three pieces of information in the listing below: (1) command name, (2) man library subsection for the command, and (3) the subject header for the command.

```
localhost> man -k manual
catman (8)      - create the cat files for the manual
man (1)         - displays manual pages online
route (8c)      - manually manipulate the routing tables
trman (1)       - translate version 6 manual macros to version 7 macros
whereis (1)     - locate source, binary, and or manual for program
```

The items on the far left are command names, so you can then issue a man command with one of these items as the argument. There are a number of places a man page might be found. Many manual pages are located in the directory "/usr/man." The numbers in parentheses next to the command name designate a subdirectory where the man command should look to find the man page file. For example, items with a (1) after them can be found in the "man1" subdirectory under the standard man directory. The items on the right constitute the "NAME" line in the man page that describes the command on the left. This item will contain the string you were looking for. This provides the context of the string in the man page. For example, after issuing the man command, above, one of the items on the left is "man (1)." To the right of this item is the line "displays manual pages online." If you go back and look at the name line for the man man page, you will see that it is the same. There is no difference between executing the 'man 1 man' command and executing the 'man man' command. However, this is because Section 1 of the manual pages is in a default manpage directory. If the man page was in Section 8, as is the catman page, then the only way to read the manual page is to issue the command:

```
localhost> man 8 catman
```

Another name, or **alias**, for the command 'man -k' is *apropos*. You can issue the **apropos** command just as you would the 'man -k' command.[1]

---

1. You will read more about aliases and how to create your own in Chapter 5.

```
localhost> apropos manual
```

Man Page Display Format

Understanding a man page requires some 'inside' information. If you know what to expect, and what order to expect it in, then finding that information becomes a palatable task. Otherwise, it will seem impossible. Every man page adheres to a similar format, as shown below. Not every field will be found in every man page, and not always in the same order; however, Table 3.2 shows the standard man page headings and their contents.

Table 3.2:   Manual page entry headings

NAME	⇔	The command name and a short description of its function
SYNTAX	⇔	The command's legal arguments and their order of appearance
DESCRIPTION	⇔	A discussion of the command, its usage, and its history
OPTIONS	⇔	A discussion of each of the command's options and their usage
RESTRICTIONS	⇔	Special instructions and caveats
EXAMPLES	⇔	A couple illustrations of comman options application
FILES	⇔	A listing of related files, such as libraries
BUGS	⇔	Generally system specific, with notes from system programmers
SEE ALSO	⇔	Related commands and information references

Locating Information in Manual Pages

When a man command is issued, the system displays the man page using the more paging utility. more is a command that displays a file one screen page at a time. A page is displayed, and, at the bottom of the page, a highlighted box with a percentage and the word "more" is displayed. The percentage refers to the amount of the file you have already seen. If you desire to see more of the file, then hit the space bar. If you want to quit, then type the letter 'q.' To find a particular heading or string in a man page, type a slash, the string, and a carriage return. For example, if you want to find the "Examples" heading in the man man page, then after you have invoked the 'man man' command type the characters that follow, which will appear where the word "more" is displayed.

```
/Examples
```

---

where the slash ('/') is a called a **search command** and "Examples" is the string (or pattern) to search for. Note that UNIX is case sensitive, so when you type "/examples," or "/EXAMPLES," you will see different results. Below is the response to this search in the man command manpage:

```
localhost> man man
  .
  .  ◀─────────────────────────────────────────────────
  .
/Examples
  .

  .
 .skipping
      catman(8) command.
   Examples
      /usr/ucb/man Examples
     The following examples all assume the use of the default command:
     /usr/ucb/man.
    The following example shows how to locate reference pages containing
the
     keyword 'graph':
          % man -k graph
     The following example shows how to display the graph(1g) reference
page:
          % man 1g graph
     The following example shows how to display plot reference pages:
          % man 1 plot 3 plot
--More--(79%)
```

Display of first screen of man page here

The search only succeeds if the search key (i.e., "Examples") is not on the current display page. If it succeeds, the search will place the key (in this case, the word "Examples," close to the top of the screen. In this example, it is displayed at (1), which is three lines from the top of the display. If you want to search to the next occurrence of Examples in the file, you will either have to retype "/Examples," or you can type an 'n' for the *next* occurrence of the current string. You can type a question mark while in more to get a listing of additional options.

3.4 Directories and Directory Manipulation

Assuming that you have successfully logged into `localhost` at least once, that you have changed your password, and that you are familiar with a few things about the file system, then you are ready to explore the file system for yourself. As previously mentioned, this is the best way to build confidence in your ability to navigate around the file system, and it is the best way to find out what goodies are out there. In this section you learn how to navigate and manipulate UNIX directories. When you log on to a system, you are placed in your home directory,[1] so that is a good place to begin. Directories are the locations of the files which we execute or use as data. As users, we must (1) know where we are currently positioned in the file system, so that we can find and use other files, (2) be able to list the contents of a directory to see if it contains what we seek, (3) be able to move our present location in the file system so that we are in the same directory where the files we wish to work with are located, and (4) be able to create, rename, move or destroy directories. Each of these topics will be covered in the sections below.

- Current directory
- Directory contents
- Change directory
- Directory creation
- Directory renaming
- Directory relocation
- Directory removal

3.4.1   The Current/Working Directory

When users log on to a computer running UNIX, they are placed in what is called their **home directory**. Your home directory is the directory which is *owned* by your user ID. In general, your user ID and your home directory will have the same name. A user's files and directories generally reside "in," or "below," their home directory, meaning that you potentially have your own subtree in the file system. You will be able to move around the file system mostly unfettered, and look at directories and files where you go, but your ability to write (create, modify, or destroy) files and directories is generally[2] limited to your home directory. As a result, when a user successfully creates a new directory or file, it can generally be found somewhere under their home directory.[3]

---

1. This is a metaphor, of course. It is easier to speak of the home directory as a location and other directories as places to go. I will frequently use the location metaphor when referring to directories.
2. All this talk of "generally" is meant only to suggest that, at times, you will be able to write in places other than your own directory, but it is an exception rather than a rule.
3. Any user can create files and directories in the temporary directory called "/tmp," but these are deleted on a regular basis by the system administrator or when the system is rebooted.

Wherever the user happens to be located is called the **current** or **working directory**. When you log on to the system, your current/working directory and your home directory are one and the same. The working directory is important because, in general, UNIX commands assume the reference to files and directories are being made with respect to the current/working directory. For example, if you issue a command to print a file, then UNIX will assume that the file resides in the current/working directory unless you specify another path for the file's location which it can use to find the file. Because of this, it is often necessary to remind yourself of what directory you are currently located in. This can be accomplished with the command for printing (i.e., displaying) the working directory, `pwd`.

Printing/Displaying the Working Directory

Probably one of the most important UNIX commands is *pwd*, because this command will tell you where you are located in the file system. Without such a command, you might be able to get around, even create files or directories, but you would never know where you are working from. Because UNIX requires a reference point or path to every command, program, or data file, `pwd` provides a reference point. `pwd` is simple to use, as shown below:

```
localhost> pwd
```

It is not necessary to use `pwd` on the first command of a session, because when you log in the system automatically places you in your own home directory. Nevertheless, I had issued the command right after logging on, the system would respond as follows:

```
/usr/f1/jhodges
```

As mentioned previously, this is the notation that the system uses to denote the location of a directory in the file system, its path; in this case the path to the directory owned by the user jhodges. When the `pwd` command is issued, the response that is displayed will be the full path, thus the `pwd` command is an excellent way to navigate in the system. In this example, the first slash (/), as always, references the root directory, "`usr`" is a first-level subdirectory, and both "`f1`" and "`jhodges`" are other subdirectories. Directories are always separated by slashes, so it is easy to see that the "`jhodges`" subdirectory is three levels 'down' in the file system.

There are two shorthand notations for your home directory that are very useful. One is **HOME**, which is called an **environment variable**, and is set to the full path of your home directory when you log in. **HOME**, if echoed, as below, will return the same as above.[1] Notice that in referring to the **HOME**

```
localhost> echo $HOME
/usr/f1/jhodges
```

environment variable, we precede its name with a dollar sign ($). You find that this is the **reference operator** for all variable in the UNIX command environment/interpreter.

A second shorthand for your home directory is tilde (~). Any time you need to refer to your home directory you can use either of these shorthands without having to type the entire path which they represent.

```
localhost> echo ~
/usr/f1/jhodges
```

Listing Directory Contents

Knowing *where* you are in the file system is very important. Knowing the *contents* of a directory is equally important in being able to access and use the files located there. To list (i.e., display) the contents of a directory you will use the *ls* command. 1s means list the contents of a directory, meaning that the command expects a directory as an argument. When invoked without an argument; however, the *ls* command assumes that the directory is the current/working directory. If an argument is given, then the contents of that directory will be listed. If a nondirectory is given as argument, it will be echoed. For example, consider the listing of the home directory of jhodges below:[2]

```
localhost> ls
F90               csc212          mail-probs
Mail              cshrc-cognet    new-net
Manual-in-LaTeX   dead.letter     new-topics
News              fe              stud212
README.TeX3.0     filterfile      test1.c
TeX3.0            foo2            texput.log
Texmacros         forward         tmac
bin               ftp.list        widget
core              mail-elsewhere
```

Notice that the listing is in columns, and that it is alphabetical, starting with capitals. The 1s command, issued without options, provides this form of listing. However, a listing such as this is not extremely informative. Suppose you

---

1. HOME and home are equivalent for the purposes of the current discussion.
2. Typing 1s $HOME or 1s ~ would produce the same result.

have forgotten what directory you are in, or if this is not your home directory, you may not know what **type** of items (i.e. their **status**) are being listed. The `ls` command has a number of options that make directory listings more useful. For example, the '-F' option lists the contents of the directory, but adds a character that tells what the item type is. A directory is followed by a slash (/), an executable file is followed by an asterisk (*), and a link is followed by an at sign (@). Items without something after them are none of the above, and probably represent readable files. For example, if the '-F' option is used on the same directory as above, the result changes:

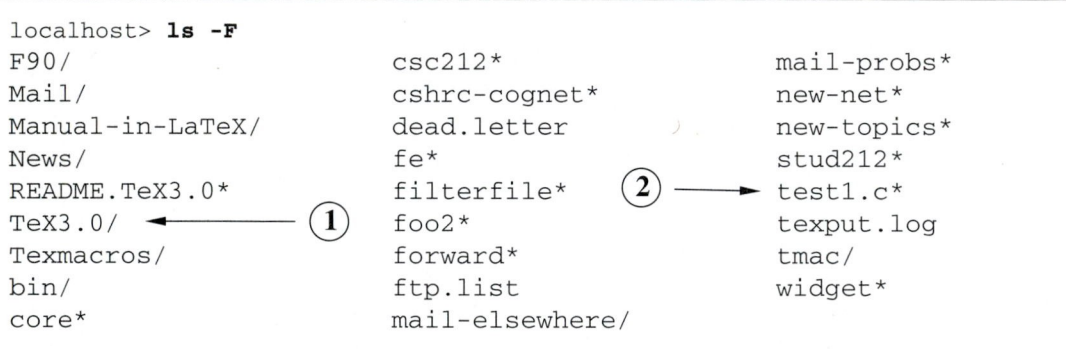

```
localhost> ls -F
F90/                    csc212*              mail-probs*
Mail/                   cshrc-cognet*        new-net*
Manual-in-LaTeX/        dead.letter          new-topics*
News/                   fe*                  stud212*
README.TeX3.0*          filterfile*          test1.c*
TeX3.0/                 foo2*                texput.log
Texmacros/              forward*             tmac/
bin/                    ftp.list             widget*
core*                   mail-elsewhere/
```

In this example, you can see that the item "TeX3.0" (at **1**) is really a directory, and that "test1.c" (at **2**) is an executable file. There are many options to the `ls` command, and you should read the man page (`man ls`) to find out more about them. Two options that are particularly useful are the '-a' (all) option and the '-l' (long) option. The '-a' option lists the contents, as above, as well as the dot files that usually aren't listed.

```
localhost> ls -aF
./                      .rnlast              filterfile*
../                     .rnsoft              foo2*
.cshrc                  F90/                 forward*
.forward                Mail/                ftp.list
.login                  Manual-in-LaTeX/     mail-elsewhere/
.login-original*        News/                mail-probs*
.mailrc                 README.TeX3.0*       new-net*
.mh_profile             TeX3.0/              new-topics*
.newsrc                 Texmacros/           stud212*
.old-cshrc*             bin/                 test1.c*
.oldnewsrc              core*                texput.log
.plan                   csc212*              tmac/
.profile*               cshrc-cognet*        widget*
.project                dead.letter
.rhosts                 fe*
```

In this example, two things are apparent. First, in the command, you can see that options can be put together (concatenated), side by side. You should put them directly together or you will have to use additional hyphens. The hyphen informs the command that whatever follows the hyphen is not the expected directory argument. Thus, you can produce any combination of effects that you want. Second, you see that there are really many more files than were displayed with the original ls command. The dot files are those files that start with a dot (or period), and are often, but not always, used for initializing and customizing the shell and other applications.

In addition, at the top of the listing there are two entries for directories which you have not seen before: a single **dot** (.) and a **double dot** (..). In the UNIX file system, the directory labeled dot is the current directory. Wherever you are located, dot will represent that directory, regardless of its name. The double-dot directory is the **parent directory**, and provides the necessary route 'up' through the file system without using *full paths* (path names starting from the root directory). You can use the capital ('A') option with the ls command to list dot files and directories *other than* the current and parent directories. You can use dot or double-dot as arguments in any command where a directory is required. ls is one such command. If you type 'ls .', then it is the same as typing ls without any argument, because the dot directory *is* the current directory. Although the use of dot in this context may appear worthless, you will see a meaning for it with other commands, particularly when moving or copying files and directories. Using the double dot as an argument to ls is immediately obvious, because you can then see the contents of the directory above the current directory.

```
localhost> ls ..
aastromo     compment     jbrandst     mmurphy      sbhimjee
abag         cpauling     jedwards     montever     scpeo
aberger      davidm       jeng         moortgat     sfch
abierman     dellis       jgemello     mpearson     sgill
aelimam      dgermann     jglenn       mreisch      shehadeh
ahhsp        dhoffman     jhodges      ncalgrnt     shelter
ajung        dleveen      jhuang       nfisher      shu
alanjung     dphsf        jjohnson     ngrafilo     smcdcs
...
```

The listing you see above is identical to the listing for the command **ls /usr/f1**, because "f1" is the parent directory for "jhodges" (i.e., is the directory in which "jhodges" resides). You can see, then, that listing directories using the double-dot can be much more efficient than using the full path, especially if you cannot remember the full path.

One last example using `ls`. You have seen how to list the contents of the current directory and its parent, to list the entire contents, and to list the contents by type. You have **not** seen how to list the contents of directories by **file attributes** (i.e., **ownership**, **size**, **creation or revision date**, etc.), all of which can be very important depending on what you are trying to do. For this you can use the '`-l`' (long) option to the `ls` command. Because the long listing displays many characteristics of each item, only one item is displayed per line, and the characteristics are displayed across the screen, in fields. The field description is shown below, followed by part of a long listing for the directory "`jhodges`."

[PERMISSIONS][LINKS][OWNER][SIZE(BYTES)][REVISION-DATE][NAME]

---

where "`PERMISSIONS`" refers to the first ten columns. The first column identifies the file description character. A 'd' means that the item is a directory, an 'l' means that it is a link, and a hyphen means that the item is a file. The "`REVISION-DATE`" columns (three) indicate when the file was last revised, and include the date and the time.

```
localhost> ls -l
total 354
drwx------   3 jhodges       512 Jan 29 20:26 F90
drwx------   9 jhodges       512 Jun 12 21:38 Mail
drwxr-xr-x   2 jhodges       512 Jun 20 10:16 Manual-in-LaTeX
drwxr-xr-x   2 jhodges       512 May 16 15:27 News
-rwx------   1 jhodges     45079 Jan 24 19:46 README.TeX3.0
drwxr-xr-x  31 jhodges      1536 Jun 17 17:28 TeX3.0
drwxr-xr-x   2 jhodges       512 Jun 21 00:47 Texmacros
drwx------   2 jhodges       512 Aug  3  1990 bin
-rwx------   1 jhodges     45056 Mar  4 14:53 core
-rwx------   1 jhodges         1 May  6 18:45 csc212
-rwx------   1 jhodges      1427 Jan 29 20:28 cshrc-cognet
```

Again, as before, the listing is alphabetical, starting with capitalized items. The actual content of the "`PERMISSIONS`" field of this listing and the notion of ownership is discussed later in this chapter, Section 3.6.2. The size of an empty directory (512, e.g. for News, at **1**) is always the same for a particular system, as this is the overhead required to set up a directory. The size of a file is listed in bytes, so the `45079` associated with the size of "`README.-TeX3.0`" (at **2**) is approximately 45K (kilo)bytes.

3.4.2 Command Wildcards

When you issue a command that might equally apply to many items at the same time, you probably will not want to issue the command for each item individually. Rather, you would like to issue the command once and have it execute similarly for all the appropriate items. There are several ways to accomplish this task, all of which use what are called **wildcards**. A wildcard matches strings in specific ways, so including a wildcard in the right position may match one or more items. Consider first the most general wildcard, the asterisk (*). The asterisk will match any number of any characters. For example, you may want to list the contents, and the subcontents of all the directories in the current directory. You could use the wildcard to do so as follows:

```
localhost> ls -l *
```

In a similar vein, you may not remember the exact name of a command argument, but are willing to see the command execute on any similar item, hoping that the one you are looking for will be one of them. For example, suppose you want to know the size of a file named "vimoves.eps" in your current directory. If you couldn't remember the name of the file but did remember that it is an EPS file (or, at least, that it has a .eps name extension), you could use the asterisk wildcard as follows:

```
localhost> ls -l *.eps
```

Note that the same command was used in both the previous examples, but the effect is quite different. Earlier it was mentioned that applying the ls command to a nondirectory would simply echo the name. However, when a wildcard or other regular expression is applied to a command, the current directory is assumed as a default. The previous command is actually interpreted as

```
localhost> ls -l ./*.eps
```

By specifying more about the characteristics of the items you are seeking, as in the second example, you have forced the command to work on a subset of the files in the directory. Two other wildcards that are generally useful are the question mark (?) and the bracket ([ ]). The question mark has a similar effect to the asterisk, except it will match any *single* character.

```
localhost> ls Ch1?
Ch10:

Ch11:

Ch12:
AWK        REGULAR SCRIPTS SED

Ch13:
ch-ext.csh                 onsince.csh              simpleif.csh
ch-ext2.csh                phones.csh               simpleswitch.csh
helloyou.csh               phonesp.csh
looptest.csh               simplegoto.csh

Ch14:
helloyou.sh      onsince.sh      simplecase.sh    untiltest.sh
looptest.sh      phones.sh       simplegoto.sh    untiltest0.sh
looptest0.sh     phonesp.sh      simpleif.sh
```

In this example, the question mark will match any *single* character, and the entries in the UNIX directory matching this template are the "Ch10," "Ch11," "Ch12," "Ch13," and "Ch14" directories, so the listing is of the contents of those directories.

The bracket is used to specify particular character *ranges*. One range would be all the lowercase letters, or a numeric ranges, such as the following:

```
localhost> ls Ch[0-2]
Ch0:
Compat212        How2UseBBS

Ch1:

Ch2:
MH-Stuff         NEWS              SAMPLES
```

which has a similar effect as the previous command, to list the "Ch0," "Ch1," and "Ch2" directories. In general, if you have specific numbers, characters, and ranges that you are sure are in the filename, then the bracket is most effective. When you have no idea what characters to use, but know how many characters there are, then the question mark is most effective. In any other case the asterisk is the way to go.

Wildcards can be used on any UNIX command, and can save a large amount of time and effort. One last directory listing option is useful when you want to look deeply into the file system for something. In that case you want a

recursive descent into the tree and a listing of what is found as you go. Recursion is a very powerful tool. In the case of `ls`, a recursive listing means that the named directory will be listed and, for every directory which is organized by the named directory, the command will be issued again. The effect of the recursive command call is to visit every directory under the one named in the command. Recursive options exist for many commands, because they work so well on tree-like structures such as directories. In the case of the `ls` command, the '`-R`' option is used to perform this task. Consider the subtree for "`UNIX/Ch6`" below:

```
localhost> ls -R Ch6
EXERCISES       MAN             PRINT-TOOLS     VGRIND
LATEX           NROFF-TROFF     UNIX-MAN1-EX

Ch6/EXERCISES:
Exercise-6.1-input      Exercise-6.1-output

Ch6/LATEX:
BIB             PAPER           TEXFORMATS      bibtex          tex
COMFILES        REAL-PAPER      TEXINPUTS       dvi2ps
FOO             RESUME          TEXMACROS       latex

Ch6/LATEX/BIB:
bibtemplates.bib        unixmanual.bib
```

`UNIX/Ch6` is called a **shallow** subtree, because it organizes other directories, but a small number of embedded levels are organized under "`UNIX/Ch6`." A **flat** subtree has no embedded directories, and a **deep** subtree has many embedded levels. `UNIX/Ch6` happens to be three levels deep (only one instance at the deepest level has been shown in the display).

You have seen how to list the contents of a directory in many ways; however, you have seen the command work only on the current directory. This need not be the case. The `ls` command, and any other UNIX command, can be issued on any path in the file system.[1] For example, suppose that you are currently located in your home directory, and you want to list the contents of the directory "`/usr/man/man1`." You could type the following:

```
localhost> ls /usr/man/man1
```

---

1. The results may not make sense if the permissions have a directory "closed," but there is nothing illegal about the usage.

3.4.3 Changing the Current Directory

You now have the ability to determine where you are in the file system and to determine the contents and attributes of the current directory. If you want to list or use the contents of another directory, however, you either need to re-member the path to that directory, or you must be able to *go* there (i.e., change the working directory to that directory). The command to change the current directory is *cd*, for change directory. The simplest usage of cd is without an argument. Unlike `ls`, when cd is issued without a directory path, the users' home directory is taken as the default directory. Two other simple examples of cd are to move down one directory into your own file system and to move up one directory into the global file system. Remember that the listing of `jhodges` had a directory called "TeX3.0." You could list the contents of that directory, directly, by typing:

```
localhost> ls TeX3.0
```

However, if you actually wanted to do something with more than one file in that directory, then you would end up typing the same paths over and over again. It would be much easier to simply move to that directory as follows:

```
localhost> cd TeX3.0
```

Suppose that you have been working in TeX3.0 for a while and want to go back and work in your home directory: that is, you want to change the directory back to that directory. Any of the following commands will do exactly the same thing from TeX3.0:

```
localhost> cd
localhost> cd ~
localhost> cd ..
localhost> cd $HOME
```

The difference between these four commands is that, although they all have the same effect when you are located in the TeX3.0 directory, the third one (cd ..) will not have the same effect as the others if you are located in a directory above your home directory or below the first level in your own file system. This is because the ".." directory is the parent of the *current* directory. The only time ".." can point to your home directory is when you are in a first-level subdirectory "below" your home directory. It should be noted that you cannot use 'cd ..' if you are in the root directory, because root has no parent directory, but you can use it anywhere else. As a matter of fact, sometimes it is the easiest way to move up through the file system. Consider the following example.

```
localhost> cd ../..
```

Remember that we are in your home directory when we started, and that the root directory is three levels up from your home directory in our examples. Then the command just issued is changing to the parent directory of your home directory, and then to its parent. If you are located deep in the file system looking around for things and do not recall (or care) where you are but, rather, what you are doing, then this is an excellent way to navigate. If the slash in the command above is bothering you, remember that the " . . " will be translated into a full path of a directory, and that all directories must be separated by slashes.

Concatenating Unix Commands

Almost every time you change your current directory you will want to list the contents of that directory to see what is there, or make sure that your current directory is, indeed, the one that you intended to change to. The reason for the first is that you presumably have some work to do in the new location, and probably want to make sure that the files you want to work on are there. The reason for the second is that, before you make any file modification, you want to guarantee that you are working on the right directory. At first, it is probably of value to type the individual commands and see what they do. But this rapidly becomes tedious, and there are ways to reduce this tedium. One way to perform the same set of tasks, in the same order, but to input them all at once is to use **command sequencing**. When you are typing UNIX commands in a command shell, you may string many commands together by separating them by semicolons (;). When you do this, each command will be executed sequentially and its results (if any) will be displayed on the terminal screen (or wherever appropriate). The general form is shown below:

```
command1; command2; command3;...
```

where it doesn't matter how many commands are sequenced. The semicolon is a command terminating character, so this is simply a faster way to type out a number of commands that you wish to execute sequentially. Suppose that you want to change your current working directory and list the contents of the new directory. You could use command sequencing (also called command concatenation) as follows:

```
localhost> cd TeX3.0;ls
```

Note that no spaces were placed between the semicolons and the commands. This was done for illustrative purposes, UNIX ignores spaces so the command below performs the same tasks:

```
localhost> cd TeX3.0  ;    ls
```

3.4.4   Directory Creation

Being able to move around and list directories is fine and good; however, in your own directory, you may want to organize your files in some meaningful way. To do so, you must be able to *create* new directories. A good method for organizing your directory is to break it up into subdirectories according to function or type. For example, consider the listing for the directory jhodges below:

```
localhost> ls -F
F90/                    csc212*                 mail-probs*
Mail/                   cshrc-cognet*           new-net*
Manual-in-LaTeX/        dead.letter             new-topics*
News/                   fe*                     stud212*
README.TeX3.0*          filterfile*             test1.c*
TeX3.0/                 foo2*                   texput.log
Texmacros/              forward*                tmac/
bin/                    ftp.list                widget*
core*                   mail-elsewhere/
```

The user jhodges has created directories for "Mail," "Manual-in-La-TeX," "TeX3.0," "bin," and so on. The first directory (Mail) was actually created by the system, and is where the MH mailer stores the mail for jhodges. The Manual-in-LaTeX directory contains this manual, formatted in latex format. The "TeX3.0" directory contains the sources and binaries for the 3.0 version of tex, the text formatting language used to write many versions of this manual. The "bin" directory contains binary files and other executables created by jhodges. Jhodges could just as easily have created directories for "Documents" or "Code," or whatever. In general, the more highly organized a user's directory, the more subdirectories you will see when you list their home directory, and the fewer executable files you will see there.

The command to create a directory (subdirectory is the same thing) is *mkdir*. For example, to create a new subdirectory Docs beneath the current directory jhodges, the command would be

```
localhost> mkdir Docs
```

Now if we list the contents of jhodges (with ls), then Docs will appear. At this point Docs is an empty directory. If we want to put something there, at least with the present level of expertise, we would be in trouble, because you have not been introduced to the editors, copying, or moving. If you want, you could create a directory under `Docs`, and under that, etc.

3.4.5 Renaming Directories

You do not have to stick to the same directory names that you start with. At any time you may change the name of a directory with the command *mv*. This command will be used to do naming and relocation of directories, and files, so it is important to understand its usage. To rename a directory, say `Docs` to "`Documents`," you would type the following:

```
localhost> mv Docs Documents
```

As you can see, the `mv` command requires two arguments. If you provide only one argument, UNIX will complain and do nothing. When you again list the contents of the directory after issuing the command above, `Docs` is no longer there and `Documents` is.

3.4.6 Relocating Directories and Their Contents

The `mv` command is also used to relocate an entire directory. Read the man page for `mv` (i.e., `man mv`) for more information; however, an example is provided here. Suppose that you have two directories, "`bin`" and "`Code/C-Code`," in your home directory. Suppose that all the binaries in `bin` are C binaries and you decide to move them under the `Code/C-Code` directory. If you want to keep the "`bin`" name intact, then you would issue the `mv` command as follows.

```
localhost> mv bin Code/C-Code
```

Because the last argument is an existing directory, `bin` directory is moved under `C-Code`. If you want to relocate and change the name of `bin` to be `C-bin`, then, instead, you could type the following:

```
localhost> mv bin Code/C-Code/C-bin
```

Because the last argument in the path is a new name, UNIX will rename *and* relocate the `bin` directory.

3.4.7 Directory Removal

You will sometimes move the contents of a directory without doing anything to the directory itself, and then remove the directory. You can remove a directory with the `rmdir` command. Suppose that you have a bunch of files off your home directory called "`bin/C-bin`" and decide that they should all be in the `bin` directory. Then you can issue the following commands:

```
localhost> cd ~/bin
localhost> mv C-bin/* .
localhost> rmdir C-bin
```

The first command moves you to the directory where you want to move the contents of C-bin. The second command moves all of the contents of C-bin to the current directory. Note the use of the wildcard (*) to denote any item in the C-bin directory.[1] The third command removes the directory. Two errors can be made when trying to remove directories: (1) the directory may not be empty, and (2) the entity may not be a directory. Consider the first case of trying to delete the nonempty directory "foo":

```
localhost> rmdir Misc/foo
rmdir: remove Misc/foo: Directory not empty
```

In this example, the directory "foo" has at least one file remaining in it when the command to remove it is issued. The following action is taken:

```
localhost> rm Misc/foo/fooblah
rm: remove Misc/foo/fooblah? y
```

here rm has been aliased to 'rm -i,' meaning **interrogate** the user before performing the action, and the user provides an affirmative response to the query. rm, mv, and cp (file copy), can each be used with a '-i' option that interrogates the user (i.e., asks for verification) before executing the command. This can be useful when deleting or replacing files because it gives you a second chance to think over what you are going to do. Many users simply alias rm to 'rm -i' in their login shell. It should be noted that the rm command is actually dangerous if not used with the interrogative option, and at many institutions, including ours, it is aliased to the interrogative version for this reason. More on that in Chapter 5. Now consider the second case, where the command rmdir is used to remove a file instead of a directory:

```
localhost> rmdir Misc/foo/fooblah
rmdir: Misc/foo/fooblah: Not a directory
```

where the correct action to take is to use the rm command on files or to issue rmdir on a directory.

---

1. The asterisk is a name completion argument in regular expressions that matches any character string. For more information on regular expressions see Chapter 12.

3.5 Files and File Manipulation

The organization of the UNIX file system is important, as is the organization of your own file system within the global file system, and so is your ability to navigate through the file system. However, the reason that file system organization is important is that our use of the computer is based on files. In this section, we look at the manipulation of files in the same manner as with directories. That is, every user must be able to create, rename, relocate, and remove files. The commands for these tasks will be presented in reverse order to the presentation of directory manipulation, because the last example presented for removing directories can also be applied to file removal:

- File removal
- File relocation
- File renaming
- File copy
- Locating files
- Looking at file contents
- Locating commands

3.5.1   File Removal

As a user, you will constantly be adding and removing files from your directory. You will add files by editing new files, saving edited files with new names, and directing the output of programs to new files. We have not covered any of these items yet. To remove a file, however, you will use the *rm* command. rm stands for remove, and can be used to eliminate single files or entire directories. For example, suppose that, instead of moving the contents of the directory "C-bin" to the directory named "bin," above, you wanted to delete the files and the directory altogether. You could use the rm command first on the files, and then remove the directory with rmdir, as follows:

```
localhost> cd ~/bin
localhost> rm C-bin/*
localhost> rmdir C-bin
```

Again, we have used the wildcard (*) to denote all items in the "C-bin" directory. Alternatively, there is an rm option that **recursively** removes the contents of C-bin and the directory itself. Recursively means that the command will be issued, by the system, on the contents of C-bin, and, if some of the contents are directories, on them, and so forth until the command has been executed on every directory and file beneath C-bin. The option is '-r' and is issued as shown subsequently.

```
localhost> rm -r C-bin
```

The recursive option is available on a number of commands, particularly cp and mv.

3.5.2   File Renaming

File renaming is identical to directory renaming. You can rename a file with the mv command, such as "widget" in the directory jhodges to "widget1" as follows:

```
localhost> mv widget widget1
```

It should be noted that, if you now now do a directory listing, "widget" no longer exists except as "widget1."

3.5.3   File Relocation

File relocation is also identical to directory relocation. If the second argument is a directory, then the file is moved to the directory. If the second argument is a new name, then the file is renamed. If the second argument is a path ending with a new name, then the file is moved and renamed. Each of these possibilities is illustrated below:

```
localhost> mv widget bin
localhost> mv widget bin/widget1
```

In the first case, the file named widget is moved to the bin directory. In the second case, the file named widget is moved to the bin directory and renamed to widget1. It should be noted, in the cases of file renaming and file relocation that if the second file already exists, its contents will be overwritten with the new file. Like the rm command, mv has an interrogative option (i.e., mv -i) which will first ask the user if he wants to overwrite the existing file. Finally, the mv command can have more than two arguments. If the last argument in a list of arguments is a directory, then all of the items but the last are relocated to the directory named by the last. The arguments can be a mixture of files and directories. This mechanism cannot be used to rename many files and directories, however.

3.5.4   File Copy

File copying is performed with the *cp* command, which takes two arguments: a file to be copied and a new name. For example, if you wanted to copy the file `widget` and then edit one of the copies, you could type the following:

```
localhost> cp widget widget-new
```

Now you would have two files with the same contents, only with different names, and you could edit the one named "`widget-new`" without worrying about loss of the original file's contents. File copy also performs the task of moving the copy if the second argument is a path and a name. For example, let's say that you want to copy `widget` and edit the copy in the directory "`new-files`." Given that the directory `new-files` exists, you could type the following:

```
localhost> cp widget new-files/widget-new
                    ↑              ↑
              directory       new name
```

In this case, `widget` continues to exist in the current directory, and a new copy of `widget`, called `widget-new`, has been created under the `new-files` directory. If `widget-new` already existed, it would have been overwritten. By using the '`-i`' option, with `cp`, you can have the system interrogate you if you are about to copy over another file. It should be noted that, when you are experimenting with files, it is generally useful to make a copy of the original before you begin, rename it something obvious like "`file.orig`," and then continue. The copy command can also be used to copy directories and to copy them recursively using the '`-r`' option.

3.5.5   Locating Files in the File System

It is not at all uncommon for you to forget where you put a file, or to forget the name of a file but be able to remember something in the file. You still need to be able to locate the file before you can execute any commands that use it. There are two commands that you will find invaluable in performing these tasks: *find* and the `grep` family: *grep/fgrep/egrep*. Given that you can locate a file, there are often cases when you will want to compare files for their differences. In such cases, you will want to use the command *diff*.

Locating a File by Name or Characteristics

Altogether too often you forget where you last saw a file. Because it is not appropriate to copy every file into your home directory, and because your own file system could be extensive, you need a command that will search any portion of the file system and return files that match your search criterion. The UNIX command *find* is the file-search utility. The syntax for the find command is shown next.

```
find [pathname-list] [expressions]
```

---

where the "pathname-list" can be one or more paths from which to start the search, and expressions represent the command options. For example, suppose that you have a file in your home directory called "widget." You could first try to see if find can locate widget when you are located in your home directory. You would type the following:

```
localhost> find . -name widget -print
```

In this example, the dot (.) represents the starting point for the search, which is the current directory. The '-name' option is used to say "look for a file with the following *name*." You could use regular expressions in this term, but wildcards (and any special characters) would have to be **escaped**. This means that a backslash (\) would have to prefix the wildcard (e.g., -name *widget would search for any file which ended in widget). Special symbols must be escaped in find because they have special meaning within the command and that meaning has to be ignored to use the symbol as a wildcard. The '-print' option specifies that any successes to the find search should be displayed with their path from the starting location. The output of this command looks as follows:

```
./widget
localhost>
```

Note that the path is ". /," meaning that widget was found in the current directory. Now try to move to another location and try the same command. Change your directory to the root directory and execute the find command again:

```
localhost> find . -name \*widget -print
...
find: cannot open < ./usr/cp1/aday >
find: cannot open < ./usr/cp1/tests2 >
find: cannot open < ./usr/cp1/vba1077 >
./usr/f1/jhodges/widget                                    (1)
find: cannot open < ./usr/f1/moortgat/bin >
find: cannot open < ./usr/f1/swilson/Mail >
find: cannot open < ./usr/f2/ghammer >
...
```

The file we are looking for is noted with (**1**). Note that unreadable directories are flagged by find. Be prepared to wait a while if you try a find from the root directory. Also, you will see "cannot open" messages for any unreadable (i.e., you do not have read permissions) directory. Note that the full path of the file is given, because the starting location was the root directory. You can also issue the same command without having to change directories, because find, like all UNIX commands, will allow an absolute path.

```
localhost> find / -name \*widget -print
```

One final, somewhat more elaborate example, is to use find to search for files that meet different criteria. To do so, you must be able to select an item that meets consecutive criterion (logical AND), and you must be able to select an item that meets one or more in a grouping of criterion (logical OR). In find, unless otherwise stated, all criteria you provide for item selection are considered as conjunctive. This means that the item must satisfy all the criterion (AND). To select one of many, you have to use some roundabout methods, as shown below. Also, I have been using the -print option, but, in this next example, I will delete any files that are located in the "/tmp" directory and are owned by the user jhodges. To do so, I must be able to execute a command on the selected set of items:

```
localhost> find /tmp \( -user jhodges -atime !2 -o -mtime 2 \) -exec rm {} \;
```

In this example, the find command is issued on the "/tmp" directory, so the user has perhaps been putting some work in the publically available temporary directory that he wants to delete. When you want to select items that match the logical value (true or false) of an expression, then you should enclose that expression in parentheses, but you must escape the parentheses as I have shown above. I have used the "-atime" option with a value of "!2" to indicate that any files which have not been accessed in 2 days. I have also used the "-mtime" option to select items that have been modified in the last "2" days. Any files that satisfy (i.e., match) one of these two criterion (using the "-o" option, for OR), AND are owned by jhodges, satisfy the overall expression. I have then used the "-exec" option to delete the files with the "rm" command. The "{}" expand to the current directory so that the items are found, and the -exec option must be terminated with an escaped semicolon (\;).

There are many additional options for `find`, as detailed below:

Table 3.3: `find` **Options reference**

`-name NAME`	⇔	True if NAME matches the current filename
`-perm XYZ`	⇔	True if the file permission flags match the octal number XYZ precisely
`-user FOO`	⇔	True if the file belongs to FOO
`-group GRP`	⇔	True if the file belongs to the group GRP
`-atime AT`	⇔	True if the file has been accessed in AT days
`-mtime MT`	⇔	True if the file has been modified in MT days
`-type TYP`	⇔	True if the item is the same type as TYP; a file, **f**, is the default, a directory is **d**, and a link is **l**
`-print`	⇔	Always true; display the current pathname
`-ls`	⇔	Always true; display the current pathname and associated statistics
`-exec`	⇔	Execute the following command and string; must be terminated with an escaped semicolon (;) — for example, `find . -name foo -exec rm {} \;` removes all files below . named `foo`
`-o`	⇔	Used to construct expressions using disjunction

Locating Files by Content

The use of `find` requires that at least part of the original file's name be remembered. When you cannot remember any part of the name of a file, it is not prudent to try repeatedly with various different names simply because the `find` command is dreadfully inefficient. Instead, you can use a **string search** command, `egrep`, `grep`, or `fgrep` to find the contents of a file. All three utilities let the user find strings within files without knowing the name of the file, and without editing the file. The difference between the `grep` family of commands is how much versatility the command allows in defining the pattern to be matched. `egrep` allows the use of full regular expressions, so we will wait on discussing it until Chapter 12. `grep` allows limited regular expressions, and `fgrep` requires fixed strings. `fgrep` is the fastest, and `egrep` is potentially quite slow. The syntax for the use of these commands (shown with `fgrep`) is the same. They all require a pattern to search for and at least one location to look for the pattern (i.e., two arguments):

`fgrep [options] expression [files]`

where the "`options`" are tabulated below, the "`expression`" is a regular expression including the string desired (or a string with `fgrep`), and "`files`" is a list of files you wish to search. For example, consider the fragment of "`widget`" below:

```
localhost> fgrep always widget
The questions *always* expect the shortest answer. If there is a
```

`fgrep` returns the string if the file name is given. This is a trivial case. Most often you use `fgrep` on all the files in a directory, and sometimes even multiple directories. In these cases, both the path and filename, followed by the content of the line in which the string occurs, are listed. For example, suppose you are looking for a function definition for "`md:create`" in a program directory. You could list the the file path and line in which the string appears as follows:

```
localhost> pwd
/usr/f1/jhodges/code/cl/SIMULATOR
localhost> fgrep md:create */*.cl
...
rep/demon-processes.t:; (set *ep* (md:create '*ep*))
rep/p1new.t:; (set *ep* (md:create '*ep*))
rep/p2new.t:; (set *ep* (md:create '*ep*))
rep/processes1.t:; (set *ep* (md:create '*ep*))
rep/processes2.t:; (set *ep* (md:create '*ep*))
utils/fixmd.t:(define (md:create . name)
find: cannot open < ./usr/f2/ghammer >
...
```

In this case, `fgrep` is being applied to two directory levels (`*/*`), using the asterisk wildcard,[1] so it will search for the string "`md:create`" in all the files ending with "`.cl`" in all the directories below "`SIMULATOR`." Each result is written on a separate line, with the path to the file first and the context (i.e., the line in the file) in which the string is found on the right

---

1. Note that the use of the asterisk as a wildcard in UNIX is different from its use in regular expressions. The wildcard can be used in `fgrep` even though other regular expression operators cannot.

Table 3.4: `grep`/`fgrep`/`egrep` Options reference

`-x`	⟺	Display only lines exactly matched (`fgrep` only)
`-c`	⟺	Display only a count of matching lines
`-v`	⟺	Display all lines that **don't** match
`-i`	⟺	Ignore uppercase and lowercase distinction during comparisons
`-l`	⟺	List only names of files with matching lines
`-n`	⟺	Precede each line by its relative line number in the file

Some of the character options for using `grep`/`egrep` are shown below:

Table 3.5: `grep`/`egrep` Regular expression operators

`^`	⟺	Matches the beginning of a line
`$`	⟺	Matches the end of a line
`.`	⟺	Matches any character
`*`	⟺	Matches zero or more regular expression instances
`+`	⟺	Matches one or more regular expression instances

Comparing Files by Content

Whenever a data or source file is used regularly, it is often the case that modifications to the file will be made, and the user will want to check on which version of the file is which. One way to keep track of versions is through the file's modification date (see long directory listing), but this mechanism will not tell the user *what* has changed, only that it *has*. The `diff` command is used to compare files by content, and is a useful means to locate and keep track of changes. The command syntax is as follows:

`diff [options] file1 file2`

where "`file2`" can be a directory, or both "`file1`" and "`file2`" can be directories. In the case where `file1` and `file2` are both regular files, they are compared line by line, and the lines where they differ are displayed. In the case where `file2` is a directory, `file1` is compared with a like-named file in the directory named by `file2`. In the case where both `file1` and `file2` are directory names, then `diff` will first sort the directories alphabetically and then do a content comparison on each file.

`diff` displays are fairly simple to read. A block of lines will be taken and that block of line numbers will be displayed. Then the lines in `file1` will be displayed, preceded by a left angle bracket (<). Then a dashed line will be displayed, followed by the corresponding lines in `file2`, preceded by a right angle bracket (>). Below is an example on two short sample files (which are comprised of this paragraph except for one change) in "UNIX/Ch3/diffex:"

```
localhost> diff filediff1 filediff2
2c2,3  ◄─────────────────────────────────────────── line numbers
< that block of line numbers will be displayed. Then the lines in file1 will
---  ◄─────────────────────────────────────────── separator
>
> that block of LINE numbers will be displayed. Then the lines in file1 will
```

In the line number reference of the display response, the line number range in each file is separated by a "c." In the example, the first "2" refers to the line in `filediff1`, while the "2,3" refers to the lines in `filediff2`. A few of the options to the `diff` command are tabulated below. More can be found in a suitable reference or the man pages.:

Table 3.6: `diff` Options reference

-b	⟺	Ignores trailing blanks and strings of blanks
-i	⟺	Ignores the case of letters ('A' will be equivalent to 'a')
-w	⟺	Ignores whitespace such as blanks and tabs . 'if (a == b)' will be equivalent to 'if(a==b)'

3.5.6 Displaying File Contents

Taking a look at the contents of a file is often enough to tell whether it is the file you are looking for. You can use `grep` or `fgrep` if you remember the contents of a file. However, if you do not remember the name or the contents, then you need some general (i.e., brute force) mechanism for listing the contents of files. Both `more` and `cat` can be used to display file contents.

Listing a File to Standard Output by Page

more is a command that takes a file (or list of files) as its argument(s) and lists the contents of the file at the standard output, and is called a **pager** because it displays one screenful at a time. For more to function properly, the terminal characteristics (as described in Chapter 5, page 143) must be set correctly. more displays a page on the screen, and then asks the user if more display is desired. You can continue to page through the file by hitting the space key <SP>, or you can exit by typing a 'q.' When a file list is given, more will display one file at a time.

```
localhost> more ftp.list
```

more supports some string search capabilities. If you are looking for a string with the word "examples" in it, then you could do a search using slash (/) followed by a regular expression for the desired string:

```
/examples
```

and more would search for the next occurrence of examples in the file and place that line near the top of the current screen. You can also use more with a process pipe (see Chapter 5, page 159) when a directory listing or other UNIX command output is too long to show on one page:

```
localhost> grep md:create */*.cl | more
```

I have not shown the output for these commands simply because this type of output has been shown already. Some useful options for using **more** are shown in Table 3.7.

Table 3.7: more Options reference

-n	⟺	Specifies how many lines to display per page
-d	⟺	The user will be prompted with the message "Press space to continue, 'q' to quit" at the end of each screenful; illegal user input is responded to with "Press 'h' for instructions"
+N	⟺	Starts the display at line number N
+/RE	⟺	Starts the display two lines above the line containing the regular expression RE
iN	⟺	Continue but redefine the page size to be N lines
is	⟺	Skip forward i lines and continue
if	⟺	Skip forward i pages and continue
ib	⟺	Skip backward i pages and continue

Listing a File to Standard Output

When a file is short or you do not really care to look closely at the contents of a file, then you might simply **dump** the contents of the file to the screen using *cat*. cat can be used the same way as more:

```
localhost> cat .login
```

This command will *scroll* through the entire contents of ".login" and return the user to the command line. cat can be used very effectively on short files, because it quickly shows an entire file, but should be used with caution on larger files unless it is used with a command like head or tail.

Two additional programs, *head* and *tail*, can be used to display portions of a file or command response. For example, consider the following command:

```
localhost> tail ftp.list
```

which would display the last 10 lines of the file "ftp.list." tail can be started at any location in the file, and it can be started with respect to the beginning of the file or the end of the file.

```
localhost> tail +20 ftp.list
```

will start displaying lines 20 lines from the beginning of the file. Had the command been issued with a -20, the display would have begun from the end of the file. Other options are available, see (man tail). The head command performs a similar function on the first 10 lines of a file or, if the "count" option is specified, the first "count" lines.

```
localhost> head -20 ftp.list
```

3.5.7   Locating Commands and Documentation

Sometimes it is difficult to find where a command or executable file resides. If you cannot find a command, then you cannot execute it, because it must be in your current directory, in your execution path, or linked to your directory for you to execute it. There are two commands that are used to locate commands or information relating to commands whose name you know: which and whereis.

Locating a Program File

The *which* command is used (in the C shell) to find program files within your execution path, and can be useful in determining how many executable files of a particular name exist and what their ordering is. which traces aliases, if they exist, to the command that is executed with the alias is invoked. The syntax for the command is

```
which filename
```

and an example is shown below

```
localhost> which tex
/usr/f1/jhodges/TeX3.0/usr/local/bin/tex
```

In this response, the path of the first executable found which matches the argument is displayed. which can be used, along with the path variable, to identify which executable is being invoked when you get bizarre program or command behavior.

Locating a Program Source or Man Page

The *whereis* command is used to find source, binary, and manual files in the same way that `which` is used, but is not limited to the user's execution path and can be used in either command shell. The command syntax is shown below, although usually the command is issued with the file name alone:

```
whereis [-sbm] filename
```

where the first field "`[sbm]`" is used to search for sources, binaries, or manuals alone. There are other option fields, that can be looked up in the man page (`man whereis`). Consider the use of `whereis` on the previous example:

```
localhost> whereis tex
tex: /usr/bin/tex /usr/lib/tex
```

Notice that the locations of both the executable and its source files is given by `whereis`, and that the previous directory, in the user's execution path, was *not* searched. `whereis` only looks in standard directories for items.

3.6 Filesystem Security

The last section of this chapter is concerned with the security of your directory or file system. When the '`ls -l`' command was demonstrated, the first few columns contained several items whose descriptions were left unexplained. These items addressed the **permissions** and **ownership** of a directory or the items in the directory. As a user, you own your own directory. This means that you control who can search your directory, who owns the files or subdirectories in your directory, and who can read, write, or execute files within your directory. It is important that every user be aware of the commands that control access to their directory, and what **access control** means. In this section, you will learn how to maintain and modify your file system. In particular, the following topics will be addressed:

- Account access
- Access permissions
- Ownership
- Directory and file creation masks

3.6.1 Account Access

The introductory chapter of this manual introduced you to the primary access control mechanism you have available. If someone is trying to obtain full rights to your files, then they must obtain your password. If you regularly change your password with `passwd`, then the chance of **account break-ins** is dramatically reduced. It is important that you not choose passwords that are *really* easy to remember, because they are the easiest codes to break. Passwords that are the same as your name, passwords with a small number of characters, and passwords with commonly used terms, products, and famous people or places are generally considered easy to break. You can selectively allow owner access to your account without revealing your password. You do this by adding machine/name pairs to a file called ".`rhosts`." This will be discussed more in Chapter 7, page 249, but the .`rhosts` file is considered a security risk because it potentially allows someone who has compromised another user's account full access to yours.

3.6.2 Access Permissions

The type of access that a user has to a file or directory is determined by the **access permissions** associated with a file. To see what permissions a file has, you can type the '`ls -l`' for a file or directory, as follows:

```
localhost> ls -l
total 356
...
-rwx------   1 jhodges        656 Mar  4 15:05 test1.c
-rw-r--r--   1 jhodges        482 Jun 17 18:25 texput.log
drwxr-xr-x   2 jhodges       1024 Jun 20 10:19 tmac          ①
-rwx------   1 jhodges       2693 Jul 14 15:10 widget
-rwx------   1 jhodges      57979 Jun  8 16:59 widget1
...
```

permissions   *owner*

The resulting long file and directory listing follows the following format:

[PERMISSIONS][LINKS][OWNER][SIZE(BYTES)][REVISION-DATE][NAME]

The permissions of the partial listing are shown in the first ten columns. The first column identifies the type of permission of an item: A hyphen identifies the item as a file, a "`d`" identifies the item as a directory, and an "`l`" identifies the item as a link. The next nine columns are divided into three sets of three columns each. Each set stands for one of three user types: **owner**, **group**, and **other**. Permissions are always written in order of owner, group, and other.

The fourth field in the listing identifies the owner of a file or directory, and only that user (or a system administrator) can modify the permissions on the item.

Three types of permissions are available: **read**, **write**, and **execute**. Like the user types, permission types are always written in the same read, write, execute order. Read permission comes first and is indicated with an "`r`." An `r` in the first column of a set means that this user type (i.e., owner, group, or other) has permission to read the file or directory. Write permission comes next and is indicated with a "`w`." A `w` in the second column of a set means that this user type has permission to write to, modify, or remove the file or directory. Finally, execute permission is indicated with an "`x`." An `x` in the third column of a set means that this user type has permission to execute the file or directory. Write permission on a directory means that the user type can create and delete directories and items in a designated directory. Execute permissions for a directory means that a user type can list the contents of or change to the location of the directory. According to this notation, the item labeled "`tmac`," above (at **1**), is a directory, the owner has read, write, and execute permission, and everyone else has read and execute permission. When a field in any set is empty (i.e., filled with a hyphen), access permissions of that type is denied for that entity. In the example above, the owner has full permissions on the files "`test1.c`," "`widget`," and "`widget1`," but has closed out all access to other users, because no entries exist in any columns after those for the owner.

Changing Access Permissions

There are two ways to modify the permissions on a file or directory. As owner of a file, you can change **access permissions**. The command to do so is *chmod*, which means "change the mode of a file." `chmod` can be issued with mnemonic (symbolic) or binary arguments.

Symbolic File Mode Change

With the mnemonic arguments, a "u" is used to designate the owner, a "g" for the group, an "o" for other users, and an "a" is used to indicate all users. A "+" is used to add a permission and a "-" is used to remove permission. For example:

```
localhost> chmod g-rwx,o-rwx tmac
```

will remove all permissions to the directory "tmac" for all "group" and "other" users.

Binary File Mode Change

Alternatively, a binary shorthand can also be used with chmod. To see how this works, we will need a brief digression to talk about binary numbers.

Binary (base 2) is an alternative way, to the decimal (base 10) way, of representing numbers. In decimal, we count using the digits 0,1,2, . . . ,9. In binary, we count using only the digits 0 and 1, called **bits** for "binary digits." Decimal numbers are very popular among humans because we have 10 fingers. Binary is used in computers because 0 and 1 can indicate that electric current is flowing or is not flowing, or the direction of a magnetic field. To write the natural numbers in decimal, we begin with 0 and cycle through the digits. When we reach 9, we represent 10 by restarting the first (rightmost) column at 0 and place a 1 in the second column (to the left). When we reach 99, we represent 100 by restarting the first two columns and put a 1 in the third column (to the left), and so on.

In binary, to represent the natural numbers, we begin with 0, then cycle through the bits. When we reach 1, we represent 2 by restarting the first column at 0 and place a 1 in the second column (i.e., 2 = 10). When we reach 7, we represent 8 by restarting the first two columns and put a 1 in the third column (i.e., 8 = 100), and so on. The same can be done with the octal (base 8) and hexadecimal (base 16) numbering systems. In the octal system, we begin with 0 and cycle through the digits until we reach 7. Using these schemes, we have the following representation of decimal, binary and octal numbers (Table 3.8).

Table 3.8:   Decimal, binary, and octal equivalents

Decimal	Binary	Octal
0	0	0
1	1	1
2	10	2
3	11	3
4	100	4
5	101 ①	5
6	110	6
7	111	7
8	1000	10
9	1001	11
10	1010	12
11	1011	13
12	1100	14
13	1101	15
14	1110	16
15	1111	17
16	10000	20

used for permissions {

As mentioned earlier, the permissions are grouped into three sets of 3. Each permission within a set may be thought of as a 0 (permission denied) or a 1 (permission granted). For example, "r-x" would be 101 in binary and equivalent to 5 in decimal and octal (noted at **1**). This octal/binary code can be used with chmod to set permissions. For example:

```
localhost> chmod 750 filename
```

would set the permissions to: rwxr-x--- which breaks down to the binary and octal representations as follows:

```
owner: 111 ⟺ 7   group: 101 ⟺ 5   other: 000 ⟺ 0
```

The first set (owner) is given the permission to read, write, and execute. The second set (group) is given permission to read and execute, and everyone else (other) has no permissions at all. Fig. 3.2 graphically depicts the relationships between type, level, and numerical representations for 744 file permissions, which give the owner full rights, and anyone else read rights.

Figure 3.2: Octal and binary codes for file permissions

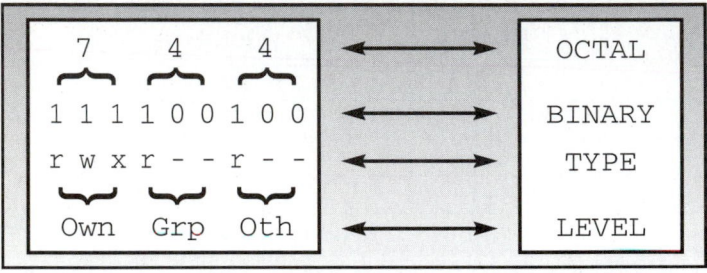

Below is a session where the permissions on the file "blah" are modified for "group" and "other" through their possible values. Note the sequencing of UNIX commands using semicolon. Also note the use of wildcards in re-executing previous commands with minor modifications. The listing is performed using the 'l' and 'F' options so that the reader will see how permissions change and how the display changes. When permissions are changed so that the owner has execute rights, an asterisk is placed on the listing of the file whether or not it is an executable file.

```
localhost> ls -lF blah
-rw-r--r-- 1 jhodges 44 Jul 18 13:46 blah
localhost> chmod 700 blah; ls -lF blah
-rwx------ 1 jhodges 44 Jul 18 13:46 blah*
localhost> chmod 711 blah; ls -lF blah
-rwx--x--x 1 jhodges 44 Jul 18 13:46 blah*
localhost> chmod 722 blah; ls -lF blah
-rwx-w--w- 1 jhodges 44 Jul 18 13:46 blah*
localhost> chmod 733 blah; ls -lF blah
-rwx-wx-wx 1 jhodges 44 Jul 18 13:46 blah*
localhost> chmod 744 blah; ls -lF blah
-rwxr--r-- 1 jhodges 44 Jul 18 13:46 blah*
localhost> chmod 755 blah; ls -lF blah
-rwxr-xr-x 1 jhodges 44 Jul 18 13:46 blah*
localhost> chmod 766 blah; ls -lF blah
-rwxrw-rw- 1 jhodges 44 Jul 18 13:46 blah*
localhost> chmod 777 blah; ls -lF blah
-rwxrwxrwx 1 jhodges 44 Jul 18 13:46 blah*
```

3.6.3 File and Directory Ownership

The column following the permissions column in a 'ls -l' listing tells how many links the item has but will not be discussed in this manual. The third column in the response identifies who the item's owner is. In the example provided, all items in the directory are owned by "jhodges." If enabled, an owner of a directory or file can change the owner of the item if they so desire using the *chown* command.[1] For example, if we want the user "geisman" to be able to cd to the "jhodges" directory and modify the file "widget," without giving everyone access to the file, then we can type the following:

```
localhost> chown geisman widget
```

where geisman is the user ID and widget is the item that will be modified. At this point, geisman owns the file and jhodges does not.

3.6.4 File and Directory Creation Masks

When a new user account is generated, the permissions of directories and files created by the user have a default setting. The setting is called a **creation mask**, because it defines the permissions that users will *not* be given rather than the other way around (as with chmod, which works after a file exists). As owner of your directory, you can set the default mask at any time using the command *umask*. The modification of this default, in the login scripts, is part of Chapter 5. umask uses the same permissions encoding scheme as chmod, except that it *clears* permissions from the full permissions set instead of adding them from the null permissions set. That is, the umask setting is the octal complement of the chmod file permissions created. For example, the default umask value is 022, which masks out no permissions (i.e., retains all permissions) for the owner, and masks out write permissions for "group" and "other" users (i.e., they have read and execute permissions). This mask corresponds to a 755 default permission on user-created files and directories. The complement of 7 is 0, and the complement of 5 is 2 (based on an octal number system).

3.7 Exercises and Sample Quiz Questions

3.7.1 Exercises

Exercise 1   Find the pathname of your home directory.

Exercise 2   Find the pathname of the TeX macros (inputs) directory.

Exercise 3   Use ls to list the contents of the directory "/usr/local/lib." Try various ls options (a, la, t, F, R, etc.) and note their effect. Determine how to use ls to list all files and subdirectories of all subdirectories.

Exercise 4   Create a subdirectory of your home directory. Call it "bin," for "binaries." Change your current directory to be bin.

---

1. Public execution permission for chown is increasingly being disabled for security reasons.

Exercise 5   Make a copy of "`~/.cshrc`" in your home directory. Call it "`csh.-compare`." Be **very** careful not to overwrite the existing "`.cshrc`" file as you are doing this. Ask for help if necessary, but do **not** let the person assisting you do the typing. This is a normal and necessary task every user must perform, and you should learn it once and for all. Once the file is in your directory, list its permissions. Who owns the new file, and what permissions do they have?

Exercise 6   Change permissions on "`csh.compare`" to `-rwx------`.

3.7.2   Sample Quiz Problems

Problem 1   What is the UNIX command to locate and print the names of all files at or below your home directory which contain "`foobar`" in their names?

Problem 2   What UNIX command(s) would you use to recursively copy the directory "`~/Docs/Letters/TeX`" to "`~/Docs/Letters/TeX-Old`"?

Problem 3   What UNIX command is used to list the entire contents of a directory and their attributes (file, directory, etc.)?

Problem 4   What is the difference between `which` and `whereis`. Give one example of when each would be used.

Problem 5   What UNIX command is used to copy a directory called "`dir`" and its contents?

Problem 6   Suppose your userid is `vcsc1999` and that your current working directory is "`~/subdir1.`" List three ways to change your current directory to your home directory with as few keystrokes as possible. Number your answers from fewest keys to most keys.

Problem 7   Show the UNIX command to change the permissions on all files in the current directory ending with "`.tex`" to *read*, *write*, and *execute* for **owner**, and *read* and *execute* for **group**, and **other**.

Problem 8   Suppose your userid is VCSC1999. What is the simplest/shortest UNIX command to remove all files ending with "`.dvi`" from the directory "`/usr/s1/vcsc1999/sub1/sub2`" without changing from your current directory, regardless of where that is?

Problem 9   Name four directories off slash (/) and what they are used for.

Chapter 4
File Creation and Editing

4.1 Introduction and Scope

By now you should be familiar with the UNIX file system: its organization, how to move around your directory and other directories, and how to manipulate files and directories. It is now important that you be able to move around within a file and manipulate its contents. By creating and editing files, you can produce programs, program data, and papers. In this chapter, we present two editors: (1) the stock UNIX editor, `vi`, and (2) a versatile and popular alternative on UNIX platforms, `emacs`. Both editors are **full-screen** editors; however, `emacs` is more extensive and takes longer to learn and master than `vi`. When you have completed this chapter, you should be comfortable using either editor on a day-to-day basis. This amounts to being able to enter the editor, use commands to move around the file, add or modify text, move text around, read another file into the current file, use commands to perform global changes as opposed to local changes, save the file, and exit the editor. Some sample files for editing can be found in the `"UNIX/Ch4"` directory, but you will find that editing your own files will be a much more valuable experiment than using someone else's files.

Ch4

4.2 File Editing

An **editable file** is a file written in *ASCII*[1] format. To modify an editable file, the user must be able to do four things:

- Access the file
- Move around in the file
- Alter the file
- Save the file

Every text editor will provide the user with different commands to perform these functions. A **line editor** is an editor which may work on many lines of a file (i.e., a block) at the same time, but only displays one line at a time. Line editors were the first editors developed. **Full-screen editors** use an entire screen to display a file, and allow the user to move around on the screen as a two-dimensional field. All modern editors are full-screen editors. The only line editor utility presented in this manual is `sed`, which stands for **stream editor**, but it will not be introduced until Chapter 12.

4.3 The `vi` Full-Screen Editor

Of the editors available, the `vi` (visual) editor is one of the most useful, accepted, and easy-to-use full-screen editors. Many UNIX applications, particularly `mail` and `rn`, assume `vi` as the default editor unless otherwise directed, so it is useful, even important, to have a basic working knowledge of `vi`. We will now use `vi` to create a file, edit the file to get acquainted with cursor controls and moving text around, and then save the file. A few of the essential commands are tabulated below, but see the man page (`man vi`), or [Joy 1980] for further details.

4.3.1 File Access: Creation or Editing

Before you move around or alter a file, you must first *gain access* to the contents of the file. When a file does not yet exist, access is called **file creation**. When the file exists, access is called **file opening**. Every editor provides access to files. In `vi`, the user accesses a file by **opening** it with the *vi* command, as shown below:

`vi [filename1 filename2 ...]`

Opening a file means that `vi` will display the file "`filename1`" and place the cursor at the top of the file and at the front of the first line in the file. Note (by the square brackets, which denote optional arguments) that `vi` has no required

---

1. ASCII is an acronym for American Standard Code for Information Interchange.

arguments; however, it is usually invoked on one or more files (e.g., `file-name1` and `filename2`). The filename can be designated with any path in the file system for which the user has write permission, as long as the last item in the path is not the name of a directory. If the file exists, then `vi` accesses it and opens the file. If the file does not exist, then `vi` reserves space for a new file with this name and opens it.[1] For example, let's open the file called `"foo"` in your home directory. Assuming that this file does not yet exist in your home directory, this will be an example of file creation:

```
localhost> vi ~/foo
```

In this example, a path has been used to show that you need not be located in the file's directory to edit it. The tilde (~) has been used to demonstrate the possibility that you could actually be located in any directory and still open a file which resides in your own directory. Opening the new file `"foo"` will look as follows:

cursor

"foo" [New file] ①

file name

`vi` will create a window for `foo`. The window will be empty except for tildes in column 1 running down the left side of the screen. The **cursor**, which locates your position in the file, will be placed in the upper lefthand corner of the edit window. `vi` is now in command mode, waiting for the user to do something with `foo`. If you were to close `foo` now, without inserting any text into it, then `foo` would not exist in your directory. Although `vi` reserves space for `foo`, it will not create a file unless it has something in it.

`vi` has two modes: **insert mode** and **command mode**, which can be toggled back and forth while editing. Insert mode is essentially a typewriter mode,

---

1. There are options to file opening, covered in the man page.

and is used to type new text into the file. Command mode is used to alter existing text. When a file is opened, the user is placed in command mode regardless of whether the file is new or already exists. During the editing of a file, a user will regularly toggle back and forth between command and insert mode.

4.3.2   Text Creation: `vi` Insert Mode

When you type a letter you are in insert mode. Everything you type goes directly onto the page. There are six places in the file to enter insert mode (see Fig. 4.1):

- At the current position
- After the current position
- At the beginning or end of the current line
- At the beginning of a new line before or after the current one

These should be self-explanatory. In insert mode, the keyboard keys have their typewriter equivalents, as detailed in Table 4.1:

Table 4.1:   `vi` Typewriter equivalents

space	⇔	Make a space between characters
backspace	⇔	Delete a character
character	⇔	Type a character
<CR>	⇔	New line, same as normal carriage return

This may seem trivial; however, in command (edit) mode, every key will have a *different* meaning. With this caveat, let's go and edit a file, by inserting some text into it, and then go back to command mode. When the file `foo` is opened, the user is in command mode and the cursor is located at the first character of the first line in the file (Fig. 4.1).

Figure 4.1: Text insertion commands in `vi`

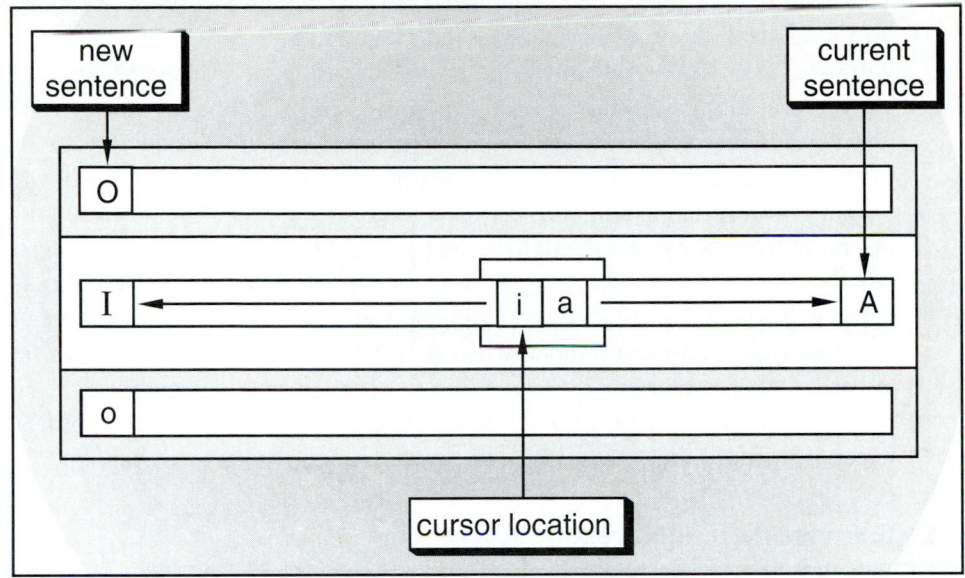

To begin typing, you want to put the editor in insert mode at the present location. To do so, type '`i`.' In command mode, nothing you type will be echoed anywhere, so you will not see the '`i`' you type. Nevertheless, you are now in insert mode, and can type for as long as you want. For example, put yourself into insert mode and type the following line exactly as it appears below:

```
She put her coat on and left the horse in a hurry.
```

This will appear on the screen as follows:

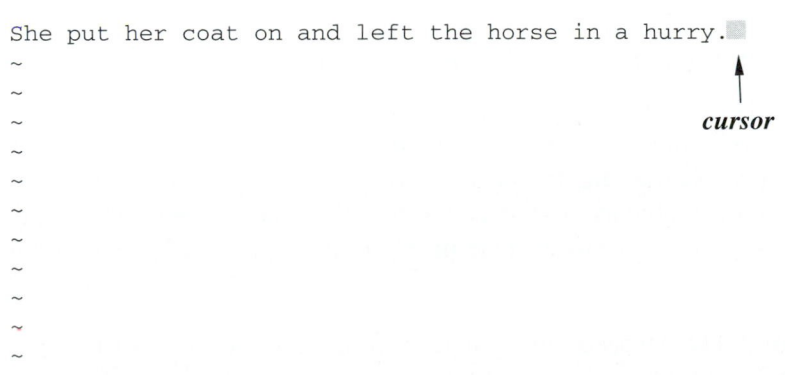

The cursor will now be to the right of the period, and you are still in insert mode.

Note that, although one can understand the sentence with "horse" in it, this is most likely an error, and that the author intended to type "house." If you make a mistake or want to stop typing in insert mode, then you must get back into command mode.[1] This is accomplished by typing an <ESC>.[2] This will toggle you to cursor movement/text manipulation mode and you can now use vi commands to get to the next position and modify or add text. The other primary insert mode commands are listed below. You may find these and other insert commands by looking in the man pages (man vi). All insert modes are entered the same way, by typing the single character you see below and in Fig. 4.1 (and Table 4.2), and then typing the text you want to enter. Sometimes users think they are in insert mode when they are not, and the terminal will beep at you to tell you that you are doing things which do not make sense. The simple solution is to type the insert command you had intended, and type some text to see if the problem goes away. This is often exactly what will happen.

Table 4.2: vi Text insertion and creation reference

a	⇔	Insert characters starting to the right of where the cursor is located
A	⇔	Insert characters at the end of the current line
i	⇔	Insert characters starting at the cursor location
I	⇔	Insert characters at the beginning of the current line
o	⇔	Insert characters on a new line below the current one
O	⇔	Insert characters on a new line above the current one

4.3.3   Text Alteration: vi Command Mode

As previously mentioned, editing a file consists of toggling back and forth between insert mode and command (edit) mode. If you are inserting text and want to edit the text, then to toggle to command mode you must press the <ESC> key. Most of the problems a user encounters with vi are related to the toggling between insert and edit modes. One problem, trying to insert when in com-

---

1. Of course, this assumes that you have typed a carriage return, because you could have backspaced in insert mode within the same line.
2. On different keyboards the escape key will be a different key. For example, on a Macintosh keyboard the tilde key is the escape key.

mand mode, was mentioned earlier. Another problem is the opposite: trying to edit when in insert mode. Because these errors are made even by advanced vi users, the novice vi user should be particularly careful or face certain confusion. All you need do to find out what mode you are in is to press the escape key. If you are in insert mode, then this action will switch you to command mode. If you are already in command mode, then either a bell will sound or nothing will happen.

Editing text amounts to searching for text matching some criterion and replacing it with something else. Depending on how severe the modification, two types of commands can be issued: (1) direct text modification and (2) global modifications. **Direct text modification** requires you to have the cursor located where you will make the change, which requires some facility with cursor positioning commands. **Global modifications** do not require knowledge of cursor positioning; however, they effectively block the screen nature of the editor, because they perform their task without the affected lines being necessarily visible to the user.

4.3.4 Moving around the File: Cursor Control

When you finished inserting the sentence:

```
She put her coat on and left the horse in a hurry.
```

into the file foo, there was an error that needed to be corrected. The first thing to do was to toggle back into command mode, which you either did, or will now do, by pressing the <ESC> key. The next thing to do, because this is a simple edit, is to **move** the cursor to the character "r" in the word horse. To do so, you need to know some cursor movement commands. The simplest way to move the cursor forward is simply to space over to the character you want. In command mode, the space bar does not insert new spaces but simply moves the cursor to the right one character at a time. The backspace key does nothing in command mode. Forward and backward movement can also be accomplished with single key commands. The 'l' key is used to move the cursor right one character, and the 'h' is used to move the cursor left one character. vi has many commands for controlling where the cursor is located in the file. It is difficult to remember all of these commands because they are character based. Fig. 4.1 and Table 4.3[1] are provided as reference tools because learning how to control the cursor in vi will speed up your editing.

---

1. Many keyboards support character and other movement with the arrow keys and function keys. Because this is not standardized on all keyboards, I am limiting the discussion to those character sequences which should work with vi on any keyboard.

Figure 4.2: Cursor movement in vi

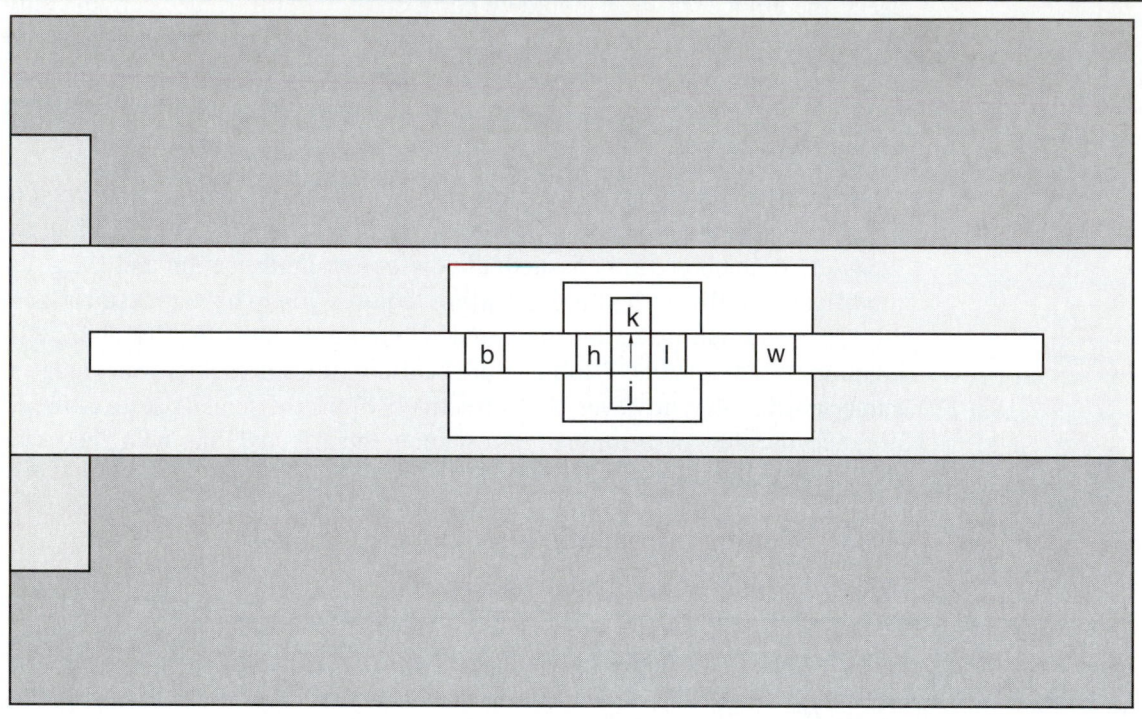

You do not have to move in one character increments throughout the file. That would make file editing an extremely tedious task. You can move forward or backward by words, sentences, paragraphs or even screens. You may want to move to the beginning of a line or sentence, or to the end of a line or sentence. Similarly, you may want to move to the beginning of the file or the end of the file. vi has commands for each of these different modes. Because the file foo only has a single line, you cannot easily test and experiment with many of these commands on this particular file. When a file becomes long the screen will change when you use certain commands, making it difficult to see what has happened. Before we go on, use some of the commands Table 4.3 to move the cursor around, but return it to the "r" in horse when you are done experimenting.

Table 4.3: `vi` **Cursor movement command reference**

j	⇔	Move cursor to the next line, in the same column as the cursor
k	⇔	Move the cursor to the previous line, in the same column as the cursor
h	⇔	Move the cursor backward one character
l	⇔	Move the cursor forward one character
w	⇔	Move the cursor forward one word
b	⇔	Move the cursor backward one word
0	⇔	Move the cursor to the beginning of the line
$	⇔	Move the cursor to the end of the line
(	⇔	Move the cursor to the beginning of the current sentence
)	⇔	Move the cursor to the end of the current sentence
{	⇔	Move the cursor to the beginning of the current paragraph
}	⇔	Move the curson to the end of the current paragraph
-	⇔	Move the cursor to the beginning of the previous line
+	⇔	Move the cursor to the beginning of the next line
<Cntl-u>	⇔	Move the cursor up one screen
<Cntl-d>	⇔	Move the cursor down one screen
nG, :n	⇔	Move the cursor to line number "n"; G without n is end of file
<Cntl-l>	⇔	Refresh the screen
<space>	⇔	Move the cursor ahead one character
<CR>	⇔	Move the cursor to the beginning of the next line

The **scope** of letter-based command keys can be extended with a preceding numeric value. For example, if you type "5j," then the cursor will move down 5 lines, and if you type "10b," then the cursor will move backward 10 words.

4.3.5 Text Editing: Altering Text

You now have a file in front of you called `foo`. `foo` has a single line in it with the following contents:

`She put her coat on and left the horse in a hurry.`

In addition, your cursor is positioned over the "r" in `horse`. There are many ways you could have gotten to the "r" in `horse`. You could have moved backward from the end of the line to the correct letter using the 'h' key, you could have used 'b' four times (bbbb) to move backward by four words and then the 'l' to space forward to the "r," and so on. Now you want to change the "r" to a "u" so that `horse` becomes `house`. The simplest editing command is the **replace** command, 'r.' This command will replace the character immediately beneath the cursor with the one you type next. In this example, you can type 'r u' to replace the "r" with a "u." Now the edit is complete. You have successfully created a new file, you have inserted text into it, and you have edited an error. You are in command mode, but you do not have a permanent version of this file because you have not saved it. The next section addresses the saving of `foo`. However, before we do that, Table 4.4 illustrates a number of other text altering commands you should experiment with and become familiar.

Table 4.4: `vi` Text alteration command reference

Nx	⟺	Delete N characters to the right, beginning with the current character; when the end of the line is reached, deletion becomes backspace
rCh	⟺	Replace the current character with Ch
J	⟺	Join next and present lines
dNd, Ndd	⟺	Delete N lines starting on the current line; if no N is provided the default is one line
D, d$	⟺	Delete to end of line
dNw, dNb	⟺	Delete N words forward or backward
dNG	⟺	Delete from line N through the current line; if no N is provided the default is the end of the file
yNy, Nyy	⟺	Copy/Yank N lines starting on the current line; if no N is provided the default is one line
yNw, yNb	⟺	Copy/Yank N words forward or backward

Table 4.4: `vi` Text alteration command reference (cont)

`P`	⟺	Paste deleted or copied text above the current line
`p`	⟺	Paste deleted or copied text below the current line
`u`	⟺	Undo the last command; this command toggles
`.`	⟺	Repeat the last command

This table is not complete but should provide you with enough tools to edit effectively. For example, the table provides methods for deleting words by combining the 'd,' "numeric," and 'w' characters. You could also delete characters by replacing the 'w' with a 'j,' 'k,' etc. Don't feel that you are limited until you try.

4.3.6   String Search and Global Edits

Suppose that, instead of spacing to the character "r" in the word horse in foo, you wanted to go directly to the word horse. In long files, a **string search**, where the string is a series of characters you are seeking, becomes extremely useful. To do this you would first type <ESC> to get into command mode, and then type '/horse'. The slash puts you into a **search mode**, and the string "horse" is the pattern that you want to match against. vi will then search for the *next* occurrence of horse in foo, based on where the cursor is currently located. Typing an 'n' will then search forward to the next occurrence. You can start a backward search by typing '?horse' instead. The 'n' still finds the next occurrence, but next now means backward. In this file there is only one instance of horse in foo, so the next occurrence will be the same occurrence.

In vi, searches, both forward and backward, are **circular**. This means that, if you are searching for the next occurrence of a string, and you come to the end of the file, the search will continue at the top of the file. Circular means that the search eventually comes back to the originating point.

You can also do a global **search and replace** with the 's' command. The 's' is invoked by: (1) identifying a starting point and range of affected lines, (2) providing a search pattern within that range, and (3) providing a string to replace strings which match the pattern. The use of a range with search and replace can be used to change all occurrences of horse to house in file "foo" as follows.

```
:1,$ s/horse/house
```

Note the colon (:) in the first column. Commands other than search (/) which are issued at the file level, are invoked with a colon (:). In this capacity, vi works like a line editor, because the : commands work on one line, or blocks of lines, at a time. In this example, the colon informs vi that a global command will be used. When the colon is followed by a range, the type of command chosen is specialized to work on that **range of lines** in the file. The "1,$" means that the range will start at line 1 in the file and will include all lines to the end of the file ($), inclusive. Now that the range is specified, the 's' identifies the command (i.e., search and replace) to invoke, horse identifies the pattern to search for, and house identifies the string which replaces it. The effect of this command is to search and replace (horse ⇒ house) between line 1 and the end of the file ($). Of course, in the file foo, there is only one occurrence of horse, so this command has a minor effect.

The command above works fine as long as there is only one occurrence of horse per line. By adding a 'g' (for global) at the end of the search, *every* occurrence of horse on any particular line will be matched and replaced:

```
:1,$ s/horse/house/g
```

where the 'g' is a modifier which follows the search 's' command. This raises a point. You have now seen several different ways to modify text, using local cursor movement to a location and alter, global search for a location and alter, and global search and replace. Each is most efficient in particular circumstances but not so efficient in others. Note that, when performing searches, any expression which would work in fgrep, grep, or egrep patterns will also work in vi patterns.

Table 4.5: vi Global command reference

/string	⇔	Search forward for string
?string	⇔	Search backward for string
n	⇔	Search for next occurrence of string; either direction
:N	⇔	Go to line number N
:s/S1/S2	⇔	Search and replace; S1 is the old string, S2 the new one

When replacing a string, be sure that the "old" string (S1 above) matches the part you want replaced and nothing else. For example, suppose a line of text reads

```
I saw the brown caw.
```

The last word should be "cow," not "caw." Suppose you try the command

```
:s/aw/ow
```

Then the result will be

```
I sow the brown caw.
```

The correct replacement would be

```
:s/caw/cow
```

or

```
:s/aw./ow.
```

4.3.7 File Manipulation and Saving

After a long digression through search and replace you are finally ready to save "foo." There are several methods for saving a file, depending on what you want to do next and what you want to do with the file. In addition, you may simply wish to quit vi without changing anything in the permanent version of foo. In this case, since foo is a new file, quitting would result in no permanent copy of foo. The easiest way to save a file (and quit vi) is to type, in command mode, two capital Zs (**ZZ**). This saves a copy of the file and exits vi. You can perform the same task by using the global command, :, as follows:

```
:wq
```

where the 'w' is a write option, and the 'q' is a quit option. On occasion, the system may become confused about whether you have write permissions on a file you own and are trying to save. In such cases, you may see a note saying that you do not have permission to write to the file, and the command mode will return. You can try to use an **override** in this kind of situation, as shown below

```
:wq!
```

If you decide to write the edited version of the file to another name, then you could type the following:

`:w filename`

---

where "`filename`" is the name of the file you want to put the current edits into. The original file name and contents remain unaltered. This particular example does not quit the editor. If you want to write the file to a new name *and* quit `vi`, then you can combine the two methods:

`:wq filename`

---

and, of course, you can also combine this with an override if necessary. One final technique that will be of value is **file merge**. If you are editing a file and decide that you want to *incorporate* the entire contents of another file, then you can merge the two files at the current location (insert the second file) with the colon command ':`r`.' The merge command is invoked as follows:

`:r filename`

---

where "`filename`" is the file you wish inserted at the present cursor location. Remember, `filename` must either be located in the present directory or you must include its path in the name. Additional commands for manipulating files are shown in Table 4.6

Table 4.6: `vi` File manipulation command reference

`ZZ`	⇔	Save the current file and exit from `vi`
`:q`	⇔	Exit from `vi` without saving the current file
`:q!`	⇔	Force an exit from `vi` without saving the current file
`:w`	⇔	Write to the file without exiting `vi`
`:w NEW`	⇔	Write to the file NEW without exiting `vi`
`:w!`	⇔	Force a write to the current file without exiting `vi`
`:wq!`	⇔	Force a write to the current file and then exit
`:r FILE`	⇔	Read FILE into the current file at the cursor location

4.3.8 `vi` Global Options

There are several options to the overall `vi` editor which the user can set before or during execution. Each of the commands is invoked with a colon command, specifically with ':`set`.' Some of these options are described in Table 4.7 for you to experiment with.

Table 4.7: `vi` Global command reference

`:set all`	⇔	Lists all option values in effect
`:set list`	⇔	Displays with special characters tab and line feed
`:set nolist`	⇔	Turns off special character display
`:set ai`	⇔	Set the automatic indent mode so that every new line starts where the beginning of the previous line did; `<Cntl-d>` backspaces over the indent
`:set noai`	⇔	Turn off automatic indentation
`:set ic`	⇔	Set the ignore case mode; when searches are performed, this will treat uppercase and lowercase characters equally
`:set noic`	⇔	Turn off case insensitivity
`:set nu`	⇔	Show line numbers in the left margin (indented)
`:set nonu`	⇔	Turn off line numbering

Each time a session of `vi` is begun, you will have to reset the options you desire, and of course, you can set them while editing. You can create a system dot file, called ".`exrc`," and add these options if you use some of them regularly, and they will automatically be applied to `vi` sessions.

4.4 The `emacs` Editor

The GNU EMACS editor provides the same capabilities as does the `vi` editor, but it also provides additional capabilities which make it a desirable editor on many platforms. In this section, the same task of opening a file, inserting some text, modifying the text, and saving the file will be performed with `emacs`. It should be noted that learning `emacs` is a more time-consuming process than learning `vi`, but that the time spent may well be worth it, depending on the environment a user has access to. `emacs` tends to be the editor of choice for users who have terminal access. For users with workstation access, the screen editors are usually `emacs` derivatives anyway. GNU EMACS sets up its own environment and window management system. As a result, a user can open many files at once and toggle between them, or "cut and paste" between them more easily than possible in `vi` where text must be explicitly marked, yanked, and put. GNU EMACS also has its own interactive help facility, but the facility assumes that you know how to manipulate `emacs` windows and buffers. The command to enter the help facility is <Cntl-h>. *Help Apropos* (<Cntl-h> a) helps you find a command given its functionality. By typing *Help name* (<Cntl-h> name), where name is a command name, information will be provided on that command. *Help Character* (<Cntl-h> c) describes a given character's effect, and *Help Function* (<Cntl-h> f) describes a given LISP function specified by name. By typing *Help Tutorial* (<Cntl-h> t) an interactive tutorial is launched that teaches beginners the fundamentals of `emacs` in a few minutes. `emacs`'s Undo can undo several steps of modification to your buffers, so it is easy to recover from editing mistakes. `emacs` also has commands that simply do not exist in `vi` and other editors. GNU EMACS's many special packages handle mail (Mail), outline editing (Outline), compiling (Compile), running subshells within `emacs` windows (Shell), running a LISP read-eval-print loop (Lisp-Interaction-Mode), and even an automated psychotherapist (Doctor). In fact, `emacs` is so complete that many users start up `emacs` when they log on and keep it running for their entire login session [Stallman 1970].

4.4.1 Getting Started with `emacs`

As with `vi`, or any other UNIX utility, the user must be able to invoke `emacs`, recognize its prompts, know how to insert and manipulate text, and know how to exit `emacs`. Before invoking the `emacs` editor, it is important to make sure that the terminal that you will be using is set up properly, because `emacs` makes use of control characters which might have dramatically different functionality with different terminal types. Have someone familiar with the laboratory environment in which you work assist you with setting up the terminal characteristics to support `emacs`. To invoke the `emacs` editor, you can use the command *emacs*, with or without an argument, as shown below.

```
localhost> emacs
```

When used without an argument, you will see the following message:

```
GNU Emacs 18.55.121 of Mon Oct 22 1990 on instamatic (berkeley-unix)
Copyright (C) 1988 Free Software Foundation, Inc.
Type C-h for help; C-x u to undo changes.  ('C-' means use CTRL key.)
GNU Emacs comes with ABSOLUTELY NO WARRANTY; type C-h C-w for full details.
You may give out copies of Emacs; type C-h C-c to see the conditions.
Type C-h C-d for information on getting the latest version.
Type C-h t for a tutorial on using Emacs.
```

```
-----Emacs: *scratch*            (LispInteraction)----All----------------
```

4.4.2   The `emacs` Window

This display will fill the entire screen, and the line at the bottom will be in reverse video (i.e., highlighted, as shown). The only difference between this display and the one where you enter a filename argument with the `emacs` command is that the initial information will not be displayed in the latter case. The blank space at the bottom is where you will type commands, and the space above is where you will insert and edit text. The space at the bottom is called a **command buffer**. The term "`*scratch*`" is the name of the edit buffer. If I had opened a file, as I will below, this would be the name of the file. The next item, "`LispInteraction`," is called the **interaction mode**, and this is the default mode when `emacs` is invoked without a filename argument. `emacs` can work in many modes, but cannot be used with more than mode at once. One reason for having different modes is they may reuse command key sequences, so the modes need to be kept distinct. For example, when writing program source code, the syntax for making comments is language dependent, and `emacs` keeps track of the differences with a mode for different languages. The next item on this line, "`All`," describes how much of the file is currently above the bottom of the screen. In this case, the file is empty and it fits entirely on one screen (hence the `ALL`). If a large file had been opened, then this term would display "`TOP`." Were we positioned part way through the file, this term would display "`N%`," where the "`N`" would refer to the amount of the file already seen, as with `more`. Finally, if the cursor was positioned at the end of the file, so that the last line was visible on the screen, this term would be "`BOT`."

4.4.3 Exiting `emacs`

To make sure that you can exit `emacs`, before we continue you should exit and re-enter `emacs`. The exit sequence is executed with two commands, `<Cntl-x>` `<Cntl-c>`, typed one after the other. You should notice that `emacs` will not immediately echo the commands entered. There is a reason for this. If you are learning `emacs`, then, if you wait a moment, the command will be echoed and you will be prompted for any missing information. If, conversely, you know what you are doing, then waiting for the command to be echoed will slow your editing down, so `emacs` doesn't echo if the commands are being typed rapidly.

4.4.4 `emacs` Special Keys

`emacs` has an extensive command set. To keep its command set clear with respect to other commands in UNIX, `emacs` uses **<Cntl-character>** sequences and **<Meta-character>** sequences in many commands. Before `emacs` can be effectively used, the user must be acquainted with these keys on their particular keyboard. The "Cntl" (i.e., control) key is the same as you have been using to end a mail message (e.g., `<Cntl-d>`) so you should not have a problem finding it. The "Meta" key is either labeled on the keyboard, or you can generally use the `<ESC>` key. While the "Cntl" key is used simultaneously with another key, the "Meta" key is pressed, and released, before the second key is pressed.

4.4.5 File Access: Creating and Editing

`emacs` and `vi` can both be invoked as shown above, with or without a file name argument. When invoked without a file argument, the file must be opened from within `emacs`. Multiple files can be opened at once while still in the editor. When `emacs` is invoked this way, it opens an empty memory space called a **buffer**, called the **Lisp Interaction** buffer, which happens to be a default. You can type in this buffer as though it were any edit file, and save it to a filename, or ignore it altogether, as you please.

To open a file of your choosing, you must first **find** it. This is accomplished with the command `<Cntl-x><Cntl-f>name`, where "name" is a file name under your home directory. You can redirect where `emacs` looks for files by typing "`<ESC>!`" and then a UNIX command to locate the file you want to open. Once found, type `<Cntl-x><Cntl-f>name` to open the file. When you select a `name`, `emacs` creates a buffer for the file and displays the buffer in the window area. Because `emacs` has only one edit mode, there is no need to toggle between command mode and insert mode, as in `vi`. In `emacs`, commands are issued to the mini-buffer (command line), and these operate on the current file buffer. If more than one file is open, then to work on it one need only find it again. This will bring that file's local buffer to the top of the buffer stack. This way, many files can be open and in various stages of editing at one time. Assuming that you have invoked emacs, we will now replicate the example from vi. Begin by finding the file named foo. Do this by typing the following:

`<Cntl-x> <Cntl-f> foo`

If you type slowly, you will see the control sequences in the mini buffer. Otherwise, emacs will simply open the file. Note that emacs will assume that the file is in your home directory, but you can backspace over this if that is not the case. emacs will open the file, replete with errors. You should now have in front of you a screen that appears as shown below:

```
She put on her coat and left the horse in a hurry.




--**-Emacs: foo              (Fundamental)----All----------------------
```

---

where I have made the blank space smaller for display purposes. The line beginning with "-**-Emacs: foo" should be reverse video on your screen as it does above. This line is important. The name of the file should appear, and the two asterisks indicate that the file has been modified. Since I just put the error back into the line from our previous correction, this makes sense. Like vi, the cursor will be located on the first character of the first line. Before continuing with the edit, you should issue two commands that will be useful. The first will be a listing of the current directory using the shell (<ESC>!) command. This will split the display into two buffers and list the directory. Consider the example on the followng page, which is a listing of my manual chapter directory.

```
<ESC>! ls
She put on her coat and left the horse in a hurry.
```

```
--**-Emacs: foo                    (Fundamental)----All-------------------
Unix-AppA-Answers.tex
Unix-Man3.tex
Unix-Mod0-Intro.tex
Unix-Mod0-Preface.tex
Unix-Mod1-Start.tex
Unix-Mod10-C3.tex
Unix-Mod11-Scripts1.tex
Unix-Mod11-Scripts1A.tex
Unix-Mod12-Scripts2.tex
Unix-Mod13-Scripts3.tex
Unix-Mod2-Mail.tex
--**-Emacs: *Shell Command Output*      (Fundamental)----TOP-------------
```

Now, you can eliminate this second (lower) buffer by typng `<Cntl-x>` 1 (a one, not the letter "el"), which leaves you with your initial file, `foo`.

```
She put on her coat and left the horse in a hurry.
```

```
--**-Emacs: foo                    (Fundamental)----All--------------------
<Cntl-x> 1
```

4.4.6   Moving Around the File: Cursor Control

You could also have eliminated the upper buffer by typing `<Cntl-x>` 0. As with `vi`, the simplest form of cursor movement is one character at a time. In `emacs`, the character movements are all done with either the "Cntl" key or the "Meta" key. The character movements are all performed with `<Cntl-character>`. For example, to move the cursor to the word "`horse`" in the file `foo` you want to move the curser **forward**. In `emacs`, this is done with `<Cntl-f>`. Try it for a few characters. To go backward, you type `<Cntl-b>`. You can move forward and backward by words using the same characters with the meta key (e.g., `<Meta-f>`). Lines and sentences work the same way as for characters and words. You can move to the beginning/end of a line with control characters (e.g., `<Cntl-a>`) and to the beginning/end of the previous/next sentence with the same characters and the meta key (e.g., `<Meta-a>`). Unfortunately, the analogy breaks down at the screen and document level. Suppose that, instead of moving many single characters to the word `horse`, you know that it is 8 words over and want to go there directly. You can perform multiple operations in `emacs` by typing `<Cntl-u>`, the number of times to repeat a command, such as "8," followed by the command, such as `<Meta-f>`. Try this now:

```
She put on her coat and left the horse in a hurry.
```

```
--**-Emacs: foo              (Fundamental)----All--------------------
<Cntl-u> 8 <ESC> f
```

The cursor should now be in the space in front of `horse`. You should take some time to wander around the screen using the `emacs` movement commands illustrated in Fig. 4.1 and in the associated Table 4.8. When done experimenting, bring the cursor back to the space in front of `horse`.

Figure 4.3: **Cursor movement in** emacs

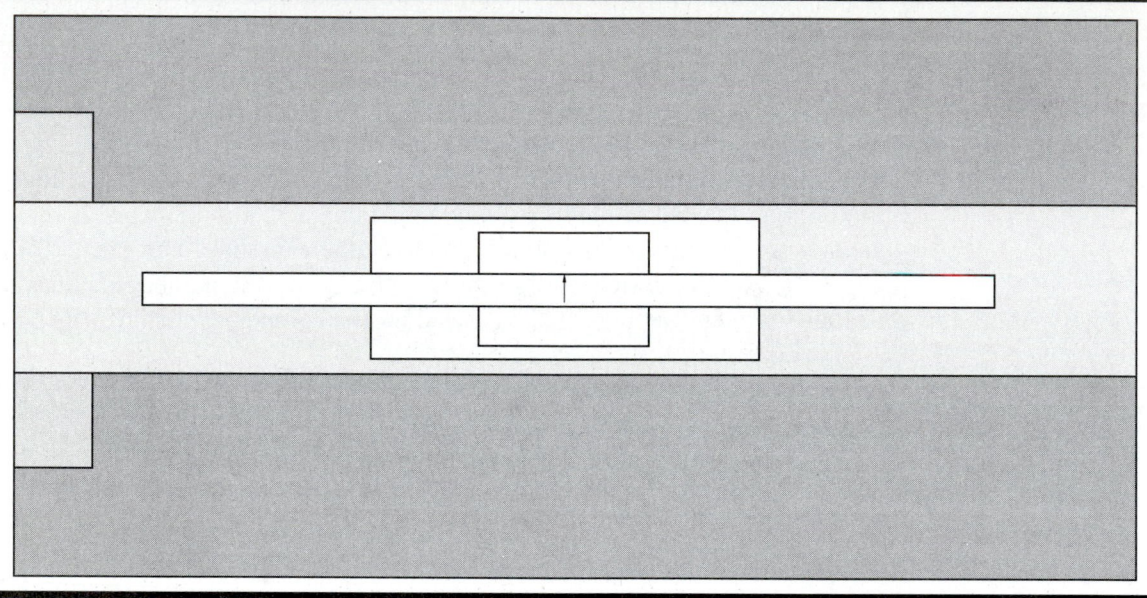

Table 4.8: emacs Cursor movement command reference (cont)

`<Meta-<>`	⇔	Move cursor to the beginning of the file
`<Meta-x> goto line`	⇔	Move cursor to a specific line # in file
`<Cntl-u>`	⇔	Repeat following command, e.g., `<Cntl-u>` 8 `<Cntl-n>` moves down 8 lines
`<Cntl-l>`	⇔	Refresh the screen with cursor location in the center
`<Cntl-g>`	⇔	Quit command but stay in emacs

4.5 Text Alteration: emacs Command Mode

We left the file `foo` with the cursor at the beginning of the word `horse`, which we want to modify to be the word "house." To do so, simply move the cursor past the "r" by typing `<Cntl-f>` four times. Now use the backspace key to delete the "r," and type a "u." Alternatively, you could use the **word delete** command in emacs, `<Meta-d>`, to delete the entire word and type the correct one. Now the file is fixed again.

4.5.1 Delete, Kill, and Paste

In emacs, there is a difference between delete and kill. **Delete** is a destructive command, which means that it cannot be undone. **Kill** is used on large pieces of text, with the assumption that the user may want to undo their action. When you perform a kill in emacs, that kill, and all previous kills, are saved, and you can retrieve the text killed after many kills if you need to. Suppose you want to move a line of text from where it is to somewhere else. The emacs command to kill the line is `<Cntl-k>`, so if you type this string, the line is killed and saved in the kill buffer. If you now move to a new location and want to retrieve, or paste, the line, you type `<Cntl-y>`. If you type `<Cntl-k>` many times, or if you use the `<Cntl-u>` N `<Cntl-k>` form, and then move to the new location and type `<Cntl-y>`, all of the lines that were removed will be pasted. Now, let's say that you killed some text up near the top of a file, and again in the middle, and again near the bottom, and now you want to retrieve the second piece of text you deleted. You now have three items in the kill buffer. If you type `<Cntl-y>` at the current location, then the last kill will be pasted. If you now type `<Cntl-y>`, the most recent kill (before the one just pasted) will replace the one you just pasted. This would be the one you were seeking. If you continued to type `<Cntl-y>` you would keep replacing from earlier kills, and, eventually, you would return to the last kill. That is, the kills are stored in a circular buffer.

4.5.2 Mark, Copy, and Paste

When you are editing a file, you will often want to copy text rather than delete or kill it. In emacs, copying text can be accomplished by putting a **mark** in the text and telling emacs to save the text as though killed but not to kill it. You can mark the text anywhere you want, using <Cntl-@>, move to a new location, and select all the intervening text using <Meta-w> (i.e., <ESC>w). You can also mark a paragraph by typing <Meta-h>. When you move to the desired location, whether in the current buffer or another buffer, and type <Cntl-y>, the marked text is pasted at the new location. Some additional emacs text editing commands are listed in Table 4.9. You should experiment with them on a file and find out which ones work best for you. The ones most useful will likely be the simple character, word, and line kills, the paste command, the undo command, the multiple command, and the mark-copy commands.

Table 4.9: emacs **File-content modification command reference**

delete	⇔	Backspace
<Cntl-d>	⇔	Character delete, like 'x' in vi
<Meta-delete>	⇔	Kill previous word
<Meta-d>	⇔	Kill next word
<Cntl-k>	⇔	Kill to end of line
<Meta-k>	⇔	Kill to end of sentence
<Meta-h>	⇔	Mark paragraph
<Cntl-@>	⇔	Mark a point
<Meta-w>	⇔	Save a marked region as though killed but do not kill
<Cntl-y>	⇔	Paste, but concatenate commands in buffer
<Meta-y>	⇔	Same as <Cntl-y> but goes back previous deletes
<Meta-Y>	⇔	Replace from <Meta-y>
<Cntl-x> u	⇔	UNDO command: can also go many commands back

4.5.3 File and Buffer Manipulation, Saving, and Killing

emacs treats files and buffers the same. As long as emacs is open, a version of every nonkilled buffer exists on a list of buffers. These buffers can be displayed in the primary buffer by **selecting a buffer** to display, using the command <Cntl-x> b. For example, suppose you want a list of all the open buffers, then you type <Cntl-x> <Cntl-b>. Now, if you want foo to become the selected buffer, you type as shown on the next page.

```
MR Buffer          Size  Mode           File
-- ------          ----  ----           ----
.   foo             50  'Fundamental    ~hodges/Documents/Classes/UNIX/Ma$
    *scratch*        0   Lisp Interaction
    *Directory*    206   Fundamental
*   *Buffer List*  270   Buffer Menu

--%%-Emacs: *Buffer List*          (Buffer Menu)----All--------------------
MR Buffer          Size  Mode           File
-- ------          ----  ----           ----
.   foo             50   Fundamental    ~hodges/Documents/Classes/UNIX/Ma$
    *scratch*        0   Lisp Interaction
    *Directory*    206   Fundamental
*   *Buffer List*  270   Buffer Menu

--%%-Emacs: *Buffer List*          (Buffer Menu)----All--------------------
<Cntl-x> b foo
```

and foo will be selected in the primary buffer window. In this way, you can select buffers without refinding the buffer, a task that may become tiring. Since editing on foo is now complete, you need to be able to save the changes and exit emacs. Saving a file is performed with the <Cntl-x> <Cntl-s> command. Assuming that you are still editing foo, save it now. If you had a number of files open at once, you could also do an incremental save, every once in a while, using the <Cntl-x> s command, which is called the "save-some-buffers" command. These same commands have analogs for killing files and buffers. The command <Cntl-x> k is used to kill the selected buffer, and <Meta-x> kill-some-buffers is used to selectively kill all open buffers. A number of additional file manipulation commands are provided below in Table 4.10.

Table 4.10: `emacs` **File manipulation command reference**

`<Cntl-x> <Cntl-f>`	⟺	Load/find a file. `emacs` prompts for a file name
`<Cntl-x> <Cntl-s>`	⟺	Save the current buffer
`<Cntl-x> s`	⟺	Save the current buffers; interrogative
`<Cntl-x> k`	⟺	Kill selected buffer
`<Meta-x> kill-some-buffers`	⟺	Kill the current buffers; interrogative
`<Cntl-x> <Cntl-b>`	⟺	Show local buffers
`<Cntl-x> b BUF`	⟺	Select buffer `BUF`
`<Cntl-x> 1`	⟺	Eliminate extra windows

4.5.4   String Search and Global Options in emacs

emacs provides a number of commands which operate on the entire document, called **global options**. The emacs string search command, `<Cntl-s>` char, works by matching characters one at a time, so if you type out a word, **slowly**, after typing `<Cntl-s>`, you will see the cursor jump around on the page, trying to match what you are typing with what is displayed on the page. When you finish typing, the cursor will be located at the first occurence of the word, if one exists in the file. After you have finished typing the string, you can locate additional occurrences of the string by typing additional `<Cntl-s>`es. If you type a backspace key, emacs will jump to previous matches of the pattern. The search ends when you type an `<ESC>` key. Some other global options are provided in Table 4.11.

Table 4.11: `emacs` Global options command reference

`<Meta-x> auto-fill`	⇔	Sets mode to word wrap mode
`<Meta-q>`	⇔	Autofills paragraph from within the paragraph
`<Cntl-s>`	⇔	Forward search; delete key moves backward; `<ESC>` terminates
`<Cntl-r>`	⇔	Backward search; delete key moves backward. `<ESC>` terminates
`<Cntl-g>`	⇔	Unhang a command; if emacs is taking too long, or if you mistype on the command line
`<Cntl-1>`	⇔	Refreshes the screen
`<Cntl-h>`	⇔	HELP; emacs prompts for a command name

4.5.5 Leaving `emacs`

When you are done editing, you can exit emacs by typing `<Cntl-x>` `<Cntl-c>`. However, if you think that you may do some editing later, you can suspend the session like any UNIX process and then come back later. This way, if you have several open buffers, there is no need to save them or kill them only to return after performing other tasks.

Table 4.12: `emacs` Session command reference

`emacs FILE`	⇔	Invoke emacs, with or without filename `FILE`
`<Cntl-z>`	⇔	Suspend emacs
`fg or %emacs`	⇔	Resume emacs
`<Cntl-x> <Cntl-c>`	⇔	Exit/Quit emacs

4.5.6 `emacs` Tutorial

In addition to the sample file edit, you should also run the emacs tutorial, which will introduce you to other features of the editor. As previously mentioned, the tutorial can be invoked by typing `<Cntl-h>` `t`. In addition to the tutorial, some useful "help" commands are listed in Table 4.13, particularly the 'a,' 'f,' 'k,' and 'w' options.

Table 4.13: `emacs` **Help options command reference**

`<Cntl-h> a`	⟺	Apropos to find command names; type a string with any term you would like information on; identical to UNIX `apropos` and `man -k`
`<Cntl-h> b`	⟺	Describe bindings; display a table of all key values
`<Cntl-h> c`	⟺	Describe a key briefly
`<Cntl-h> f`	⟺	Describe-name; type a command name and `emacs` prints full documentation for the function name
`<Cntl-h> k`	⟺	Describe-key; type a command key sequence and `emacs` will print a full description of the function associated with the key sequence
`<Cntl-h> l`	⟺	View-lossage; shows the last one hundred characters you typed
`<Cntl-h> w`	⟺	Type a command name and `emacs` prints which keystrokes invoke that command; first find the command name with apropos
`BUGS`	⟺	Generally system specific, with notes from system programmers
`<Cntl-h> t`	⟺	Run the `emacs` tutorial

4.5.7 `emacs` Integrated Packages

As mentioned earlier, `emacs` need not be exited to perform other routine tasks associated with your login session. For example, you can run UNIX shell commands from the command buffer with the "`<ESC>!`" command. You can also run a number of utilities within `emacs`, including a UNIX shell, using the `<Meta-x>` command. `<Meta-x>` is used to extend the functionality of `emacs` beyond the standard character set. For example, to open a shell in an `emacs` buffer, type `<Meta-x> shell` in the command buffer now. This will begin a shell and you can perform whatever UNIX task you want in this buffer. Table 4.14 shows a list of utilities you can invoke with `<Meta-x>`. This is not a complete list, and you should read the online `emacs` documentation at your site to find out what packages are supported.

Table 4.14: `emacs` **Utilities command reference**

`<Meta-x> shell`	⟺	Run a C shell
`<Meta-x> telnet`	⟺	`telnet` to a remote host
`<Meta-x> run-lisp`	⟺	Run a LISP interpreter
`<Meta-x> run-scheme`	⟺	Run a SCHEME interpreter
`<Meta-x> run-prolog`	⟺	Run a PROLOG interpreter
`<Meta-x> doctor`	⟺	Run the psychotherapist game
`<Meta-x> lpr-buffer`	⟺	Print a buffer using `lpr`
`<Meta-x> spell-buffer`	⟺	Run the spell cheker on a buffer
`<Meta-x> calendar`	⟺	Display a 3-month calendar in buffer
`<Meta-x> mail`	⟺	Run the mailer
`<Meta-x> rn`	⟺	Run the news reader

4.5.8 `emacs` Mode Options

As mentioned in the introduction to this section, `emacs` can run in many interaction modes, some of which can be run simultaneously. For each interaction mode, `emacs` has specific **key bindings** for that mode. A key binding simply means that the key is automatically assigned a particular value. `emacs` can only be in one mode at a time because of the possibility of key binding mismatches. A mode is entered by typing `<Meta-x> mode-name` (e.g., `c-mode`), where the different modes are tabulated below.

EMACS MODE OPTIONS
- c-mode
- emacs-lisp-mode
- fortran-mode
- latex-mode
- text-mode
- lisp-interaction-mode
- modula-2-mode
- nroff-mode
- plain-tex-mode

- prolog-mode
- scheme-mode
- scribe-mode
- tex-mode
- text-mode
- vi-mode

4.6 Exercises and Sample Quiz Questions

4.6.1 Exercises

Exercise 1   Open in a file with the `vi` editor. Enter insert mode and type 30 lines of arbitrary text. Escape to command mode and practice with the cursor control commands

Exercise 2   Type 10 more lines in your file. Make lots of errors. Use the delete and insert commands to fix the errors.

Exercise 3   Enter the line below in your file and use search and replace to fix it:

I can not have an ice cream cane todiy.

In the file you created, copy 5 lines and paste them somewhere else.

Exercise 4   Using the `emacs` editor, open the files `"foo"` and the file you created in the previous exercises. Copy the line `"I can not have an ice cream can todiy."` into the `"foo"` buffer. Now, cut the same line back into its original file.

Exercise 5   Using the `emacs` editor, open a command shell and perform the following commands: ls and pwd.

Exercise 6   Using the `emacs` editor, open the file created in exercises 1 to 3 and go to line number 10 with a single command.

4.6.2 Sample Quiz Questions

Problem 1   List four requirements/abilities associated with effective file editing.

Problem 2   What `vi` command is used to relocate the pointer to line 57 in the current file? What `emacs` command performs the same task?

Problem 3   What `vi` commands are used to save a file and exit the editor? What `emacs` commands perform the same task?

Problem 4   What two `vi` commands are used to save the current edit file and return to the command shell?

Problem 5   What is the `emacs` command to load a file?

Problem 6   What command is used to begin a search for the string `"beezlebub"` using `vi`?

Problem 7   What `emacs` command is used to save the current set of files?

Problem 8   List two **kinds** (not names) of text editors and their differences.

Problem 9   What `vi` command is used to perform a global search (entire file) and replace of the string "coconut" to "pineapple"?

Problem 10   What is the command (either editor) used to get to the end of the current line? The beginning of the file?

Problem 11   Consider the text fragments below. What `vi` command is used to produce the second fragment from the first assuming that the line numbers are known (as shown)?

```
-------------- Fragment #1 ----------------
23 The lazy brown dog
24 jumped
25 over the
26 fuzzy black
27 cat

-------------- Fragment #2 ----------------
23 The lazy brown dog
24 jumped
25 ZZZ over the
26 ZZZ fuzzy black
27 cat
```

4.7 Recommended Reading

Text Editors

Joy, W. [1980]. *An Introduction to Display Editing with Vi*, Computer Science Division, Department of Electrical Engineering, University of California, Berkeley, September.

Stallman, R. *The GNU Emacs Manual*, Free Software Foundation, Cambridge, MA.

Chapter 5
The UNIX Command Shell
and Process Control

5.1 Introduction and Scope

When you log on to a UNIX environment, you are placed in what is called a **command shell** or **command interpreter**. It is in this command shell that you issue UNIX commands. Your input device, the keyboard in general, is called the **standard input** device, and the screen you are viewing is called the **standard output** device. When you issue a command, the operating system creates what is called a **process** to execute that command. Each process is considered independently by the operating system, so it is possible to have more than one process executing at the same time. An operating system supporting this process behavior is called a **multi-tasking** system. Additionally, you may have more than one shell in use at any given time. Since the machine does not know who is logged into any given shell, many users could be running processes at once. This is called a **multi-user** system. Both of these concepts are associated with the shell environment. In this chapter, the use and manipulation of the command shell will be introduced. Then the notion of process control will be introduced so that you can use UNIX's multi-tasking capabilities to your best advantage. Specifically, the following topics will be addressed in this chapter:

- The login shell scripts
- Process control
- Process manipulation

When you have completed this chapter, you should understand your login

133

scripts, and you should feel comfortable making simple modifications to your login environment. You should also understand what initialization (dot) files are and why they are important, and be comfortable customizing them for different UNIX utilities. You should experiment with and be comfortable with the notions of multi-user, multi-tasking systems, and you should be able to demonstrate this knowledge with real examples. Finally, you should be able to determine the status of processes and control their execution.

5.2 The Login Shell Scripts

Whenever a UNIX utility is initiated, any **initialization file** associated with the utility is executed in the command shell before the user is given control. You have been introduced to a few initialization files already (e.g., the ".mailrc" file for UNIX mail, the ".mh_profile" for MH, and the ".newsrc" file for rn). These files all begin with a period and reside in your home directory; however, not all so-called *dot files* are initialization files. For example, the ".plan" and ".project" files are not initialization files, nor would be most files you name starting with a period. Assuming that your login shell is a C shell,[1] when you log on to the system, two things happen before you are able to execute commands: (1) your ".cshrc" is executed, and (2) your ".login" is executed. The .cshrc and .login are executable files called **shell scripts**. A shell script is a series of UNIX commands that are executed according to a language for manipulating UNIX commands. Each shell has its own such language The .cshrc is executed every time a C shell is created, so when your login shell is the C shell, the .cshrc is executed first, and every time you create a new shell. After the .cshrc is executed, the .login script is executed. The .login script is only executed once per login session, and sets up the login environment. Each of these shell scripts (.cshrc and .login) traditionally performs different tasks, although they can perform many of the same tasks:

- .cshrc
  - Set the terminal characteristics
  - Set the new-shell prompt
  - Set shell variable values
  - Set various command aliases
  - Execute commands

---

1. If your login shell is the Bourne shell, then the ".profile" script is executed instead of the ".login" script.

- .login
  - Set the home directory path
  - Set the mail path
  - Set the default execution path
  - Set the initial-shell prompt
  - Set various environment variables

For example, although not listed above, both scripts can set the user's default execution path. Notice that they perform some unique tasks. In the following sections two sample files, one `.cshrc` file and one `.login` file, will be looked at in some detail. These are moderate versions of either file, and are the ones used to prepare the examples for this manual.

5.2.1 The .cshrc Script

The `.cshrc` file stands for "C shell run control script." A C shell is a command shell, or environment, which is based on C type processing command control language. We will refer to it as the **C shell** script to distinguish it from other command shell types a user might use (e.g., a Bourne shell or a Korn shell). The C shell script initializes each C shell created. Generally, the C shell script is used to set terminal characteristics, local aliases, set the prompt, and run processes associated with each new shell you might want to create. Consider the sample `.cshrc` script below.

```
localhost> cat .cshrc
# this script gets executed by every shell you start                    ①
#
if ($TERM == unknown || $TERM == network) then                          ②
  set crt = 25                                                          ③
  echo "+--------------+"                                               ④
  echo "| Terminals:   |"
  echo "|              |"
  echo "|   1 (adm3a)  |"
  echo "|   2 (vt100)  |"
  echo "|   3 (vt102)  |"
  echo "|              |"
  echo "+--------------+"
  echo ""
  echo -n " Terminal Choice: "
  set choice = $<                                                       ⑤
  if ($choice == 1) then                                                ⑥
    set term = adm3a                                                    ⑦
  else if ($choice == 2) then
    set term = vt100
  else if ($choice == 3) then
    set term = vt102
  else
    echo -n " Type a termcap choice: "
    set tcentry = $<
    set term = $tcentry
  endif                                                                 ⑧
endif
if ($?prompt) then                                                      ⑨
        set prompt = "csh> "
        set notify                                                      ⑩
        set filec                                                       ⑪
        set history = 400                                               ⑫
        alias pd pushd                                                  ⑬
        alias pop popd                                                  ⑭
        alias vt52 "set term = vt52"                                    ⑮
        alias ti745 "set term = ti745 ; stty -tabs"
        alias ti785 "set term = ti745 ; stty -tabs"
        alias vt100 "set term = vt100"
endif
# safeguard against accidental removals of files with cp and mv commands
alias cp    cp -i                                                       ⑯
alias mv    mv -i
alias rm    rm -i
```

The .cshrc can look pretty unwieldy the first time you see it. However, let's break this one down piece by piece. If nothing else, you should be able to understand and appreciate what is being done, if not to tailor it to your own particular needs. What is important is that you know what tasks the `.cshrc` performs and why. The item marked (**1**) in this sample file is simply a comment line. In a shell environment, a pound sign (#) followed by anything but an exclamation point denotes a comment and the remainder of the line will not be interpreted by the shell.

The first thing this `.cshrc` file does is to determine the type of terminal the user is logging in on. Once that is determined, terminal characteristics for the session can be set. Without properly setting the keyboard characteristics, many standard UNIX utilities (e.g., `vi`) will not function properly, because the keyboard and the system will not be matched. The purpose, then, of the first `.cshrc` segment, is to identify to the system your keyboard type and then assign characteristics by setting the shell variable **term**.

The line marked with item (**2**) is what is called in programming languages a **conditional**, or **logical test**. A conditional takes the form

```
if (something is true) then
   (do something)
else
   (do something else)
endif
```

The conditional, and in particular the `if-endif`, is a basic C shell programming construct which directs control of execution. Notice that the first 29 (and then, again, the next 12 lines after that) are bounded by the words **if** and **endif**, and that they are even nested (embedded) within this construct. In this case, the string (`$TERM == unknown || $TERM == network`) is the condition/test. This test is actually comprised of two subconditions, the expression on the left of the vertical bars and the one on the right. When a condition tests true, it returns a nonzero value. The double vertical bar means *or*, so if *either* the first *or* second subcondition is true, then the entire condition is true.

In this case, the question being asked by the conditional is "is the TERM environment variable value set to either `unknown` or `network`?" If so, then the body of code following the line at (**2**) is executed. If, for example, you logged in from a terminal on campus, none of this code would be executed, because your keyboard would most likely not be associated with either of these two values. If the system initially sees your keyboard as being `unknown`, or `network`, then this `.cshrc` makes the assumption that you are logging in from a computer keyboard which is attached to the host through a modem.

In such instances, you may often have to assist in properly setting up your terminal characteristics. One of the first things to do is to set the size of the terminal display so that scrolling of files is not confusing. The expression at item (**3**) assigns a variable named **crt** a value of 25, which means that the screen will be assumed to be 25 lines (or rows) deep. The code which follows (at item **4**) is a series of echo commands to display some keyboard options to the user. Lines associated with items (**5**) – (**7**) follow a request to the user for a terminal choice, and they represent an embedded conditional. Item (**5**) assigns whatever the user types to the value of a local variable called **choice**. Item (**6**) tests to see if that value, which is accessed with a preceding dollar sign (i.e., **$choice**) is equal to "1." If so, then the line following it is executed, which assigns the value of the shell variable named **term** to be "adm3a," which corresponds to the user's first choice in the table. If the test is not true, then a second conditional is tried, and so on, until the expression (at item **8**), where the inner conditionals are terminated with the "endif" statement, followed by the termination of the outer statement.

This section of the .cshrc is not expected, at this point, to be easy to follow, since it introduces shell programming constructs that will not be discussed in detail until Chapter 13. If you are having problems with this section, simply understand that it is helping the user to interactively select a proper keyboard for the login session if it wasn't already recognized by the login host.

The first conditional illustrated identifies the terminal and assigns a variable called **term** the appropriate value. The second conditional (beginning at item **9**) checks to see if the current shell is the login shell or a new shell created by the user *during* the login session. If the latter is so, then the prompt is changed so that the user can recognize the difference between the login shell and this new one. This test is accomplished by knowing if the **prompt** shell variable has a value. The test ($?prompt) will return true when **prompt** has a value. This means that the rest of the commands will be executed if a prompt is already defined, which happens if this is a new (non-login) shell. The login prompt for these examples is set by the .login script, so these commands only get executed for new C shells created within the original login shell.

Shell Variables

Many C shell variable values are user-settable. Often users will want to set these variables themselves. For example, consider the variables at items (**10**) to (**12**) in the segment below:

```
set notify                                                    10
set filec                                                     11
set history = 400                                             12
```

In the C shell, variable values are assigned with *set*, as with the Bourne shell, but the syntax is slightly different. In each of the examples provided in this sample .cshrc, the variable is either a toggle, which is turned on or off, as in **notify** and **filec**, or can have a value assigned to them, as in **history**. The form for setting a toggled variable is the same for both the C shell and Bourne shell. The value assignment in the **history** variable has a space between the variable name, equals sign, and value, unlike the Bourne shell, which has no spaces.

Changes in System Process Status

The assignment expression (item **10**) sets a toggle variable called **notify**, which informs the user when changes in background processes occur. For example, if you are running a large text formatting job in the background, and it completes, or runs into a problem, a message is posted in the calling shell.

File Completion

Typing out all of the characters for a path, directory or file name can be tiring and unnecessary. **filec** (filename completion) is a shell variable which, when set, allows the user to type the first few characters of a name, and type an escape character, <ESC>, and the system will complete the name up to the point where it ceases to be unique. For example, if I want to change directories from my home directory to the directory "`~/Code/Lisp`," then I could type the following:

```
localhost> cd Co<ESC>de/Li<ESC>sp
```

Where you see a <ESC>, above, I typed the <ESC> key, and the system filled in the remaining characters ("`de`" the first time, and "`sp`" the second). In this C shell script, **filec** is set automatically when the user logs on.

History

The `history` command produces a listing of all the commands you have issued in the current shell. If the **history** variable is set to 20, then you will only be able to list the last 20 commands issued. The **history** variable in the sample `.cshrc` is set to 400, a fairly large number. This virtually guarantees that the user will have access to her entire command history, since it takes a long time to execute 400 commands. Most user's login sessions never reach 100 commands. Note that if you create a new shell within a shell, it will have its own command history.

At any time that you are interested in finding out what the values of shell variables are, you can issue the command `set` and a list of the bound variables and their values will be displayed.

User Aliases

Everyone has their own way of remembering command names. Often we have our own "pet" command calls with specific arguments. Instead of issuing the same command over and over, it would be nice to create a special name for a command and issue that name instead. To do so, you must tell the shell that, in the future, you will be replacing one command name with another. This is called an **alias** and is produced using the *alias* command. An alias can be typed at the shell prompt at any time.

```
    alias pd pushd                                              ⑬
    alias pop popd                                              ⑭
    alias vt52 "set term = vt52"                                ⑮
# safeguard against accidental removals of files with cp and mv commands
alias cp    cp -i                                               ⑯
alias mv    mv -i
alias rm    rm -i
```

The user may also assign a command sequence to a local variable name when they start up a new shell. The new variable is called an alias because when you type it at the command line, the system immediately translates it into the command sequence defined in the .cshrc. Items (**13**) to (**15**) illustrate a variety of alias forms and will be explained individually.

Directory Stacks

Some users work with many directories at once, editing files or compiling programs, and need ready access to their contents. If you use the same directories over and over again, then you might alias their names to something quickly typed. If, on the other hand, you use different directories all the time, then you might want to have some mechanism whereby you can quickly get to the directory without retyping the entire path. *pushd* and *popd* allow the user to place directories onto a what is called a **stack**,[1] and to manipulate directories on the stack as though they were elements in a list. When you want to move to a new directory, you type the following:

pushd new-directory

and "new-directory" gets pushed onto the stack and is cd'ed to. You can add other directories onto the stack, and cycle through them as you need them. You can refer to a directory on the stack by numeric order (+0, +1, . . .) in which it was placed on the stack, by preceding the desired directory number with a "+" sign, in which case it (the substack starting with the desired directory) is placed at the top of the stack and the current directory is changed to the desired directory. You can get a listing of the directories on the stack by issuing the command *dirs*. You can toggle between the top two directories on the

1. A stack is a data structure where items are placed in it in such a way that the first item put in is the last one taken out (or the last one in is the first one out). The operation pushd places an item onto the stack, and the operation popd takes the top item off the stack.

stack with the `pushd` command alone. When you are done working in a directory, then you can type

---

popd

---

and the top directory is taken off the directory stack, and you are `cd`'ed to the next directory on the stack. You can also take a selected directory off the stack by referencing its name or position as with `pushd`.

In this sample `.cshrc`, the commands `pushd` and `popd` have been aliased to **pd**, and **pop**, respectively. In this first example of aliases, the new command name, e.g., **pd**, is simply associated with the command `pushd` so that when **pd** is typed, `pushd` is executed.

Terminal Types

The alias at item (**15**) is a short-cut for assigning terminal characteristics. This way, if the user logs on to the system from a number of different types of terminals, even if the system doesn't immediately recognize the terminal type, the user can set it by typing the name of the terminal. The added change in this alias is setting the variable name to a string. For example, at item (**15**), the variable **vt52** is aliased to the sequence "`set term = vt52.`" In the succeeding aliases, the same operation is performed, except that command sequencing (with the semicolon) is also used.

Command Aliases

In item (**16**) of the sample `.cshrc` file, the standard file manipulation commands `cp`, `mv`, and `rm` have been aliased to their **interrogative** equivalents. This means that the system will ask for verification each time any of these commands is issued. Thus, when 'rm' is issued, the system will interpret the command with 'rm -i.' Since an alias can be typed at the command line, the interrogative versions can be changed back and forth depending on what you are doing. For example, lets take a look at what aliases are currently defined. You can do this by typing the command `alias` at the command line.

```
localhost> alias
cp (cp -i)
mv (mv -i)
pd pushd
pop popd
repl repl -filter filterfile
rm (rm -i)
ti745 set term = ti745 ; stty -tabs
ti785 set term = ti745 ; stty -tabs
vt100 set term = vt100
vt52 set term = vt52
```

Now, suppose you want to remove all the files in a directory, and there are 20 of them. If you are certain that you know what they are, perhaps you want to change the alias on rm for a while. This is shown below.

```
localhost> alias rm rm
localhost> rm fooblah
localhost> alias rm rm -i
localhost> rm fooblah2
remove fooblah? y
localhost>
```

The initial command in this example redefines the alias of rm to itself. Interestingly, on the next line the user only deletes a single file, and, on the following line redefines the alias once again. When the request to remove the file "fooblah2" is entered, the system responds with the interrogative once again. When the interrogative option is set for cp or mv, the user is asked if a file is to be replaced when a file is copied or renamed to an existing filename.

5.2.2 The .login Script and Environment Variables

The .login script initializes your login session and is only run once regardless of how many shells you open. Generally, the login script is used to identify you to the system, to set your home directory, and to set your mail path. These are all needed by various utilities. In addition, the .login is often used to set an initial execution path, terminal characteristics, and prompt. Consider the sample login script below.

```
localhost> cat .login
#
# This file gets executed once at login or window startup.
#
stty dec new cr0
tset -I -Q                                                              ①
umask 022                                                               ②
setenv MAIL /usr/spool/mail/$USER                                       ③
set mail=$MAIL
set path=($HOME $HOME/bin /usr/ucb /bin /usr/bin /usr/bin/mh            ④
         /usr/local /usr/local/bin /usr/new /usr/hosts .)
set prompt="`host`> "                                                   ⑤
setenv PAGER more                                                       ⑥
setenv TEXINPUTS ".:$HOME/Texmacros:$HOME/Texinputs"                    ⑦
setenv TEXFORMATS ".:$HOME/Texformats"
biff y                                                                  ⑧
date                                                                    ⑨
```

Each line of the script either performs some kind of function, or is related to a function. The script shown is very simple, because, unlike the ".cshrc" example just presented, every line performs a unique task. Over the course of the next few pages, each item in this script will be described, so that you understand what kinds of tasks are performed by this script. In later chapters you learn how to write your own scripts.

Terminal Characteristics

The first two things this .login script does is to set the terminal characteristics for the terminal the user has logged in from. The stty command sets up some options for the local output terminal (i.e., standard output), while the tset command uses the **term** variable determined in the .cshrc script to set up the keyboard characteristics. The stty command options listed in this example (at item **1**) are specific to the DEC ULTRIX operating system. For example, the "dec" option specifically sets up defaults for characters such as the erase and kill characters. The "new" and "cr0" options are associated with setting the terminal driver and carriage return delay. Options such as these are provided by the system administrator in the default .login script and may never be of any concern to the user. See the man pages for more discussion if interest warrants further investigation. The tset command must be used to make sure that the keyboard works properly. Without properly setting the keyboard characteristics, erase, kill, and backspace keys cannot be used, and most likely many standard UNIX utilities (e.g., vi) that associate these keys with specific functionality will produce unpredictable results.

```
stty dec new cr0
tset -I -Q
```

The other item at (**1**), *tset*, sets the terminal characteristics for this login session, so it tries to find out what the anticipated terminal type is. Then tset sets the appropriate erase and kill characters for the terminal. All terminal types are unique, but their keyboard layouts can be translated so that the computer knows what to do with each key. The terminal characteristics are stored in a file called **termcap** in the "/etc" directory ("/etc/termcap").

When you get a new account, most likely the "vanilla-flavored" login scripts do not have functionality for dealing with unexpected terminal types as does the sample .cshrc script presented above. Depending on what type of terminal you log on from, there is the possibility that the system will not correctly recognize your keyboard entries. In such a case, you need to find out what type of terminal the system *thinks* you are logged on from and change it. You can use the echo command to ask the system for the current terminal type:

```
localhost> echo $term
vt100
```

In this case, "vt100" is a response to the type of terminal in which some of the exercises in this manual are executed. If logged on from a terminal, you can look into your communications package to see what terminal type the package is using/emulating (i.e., simulating), and what options it allows. Then you simply have to make sure that the host you are logged on to recognizes one of those terminal types and either sets the terminal type directly or modify your login environment (i.e., your .login file) permanently to set the characteristics of the terminal you use. For the time being, you can manually reset terminal characteristics with the set command:

```
localhost> set term = adm3a
```

In this case, the terminal type for the login session has been set to "adm3a." If you do not know what terminal type to change, e.g., you are logged in from a modem, then you might try looking at a file called "/etc/termcap," which lists all the terminal types the host you are logged onto recognizes. You can then try them and test a few commands to see what happens.

Below is a test to find alternate entries for the VT100 terminal.

```
localhost> grep vt100 /etc/termcap
dr|vt100p|vt100p-nam|dec vt100p:\                              ①
        :rf=/usr/lib/tabset/vt100:\
        :tc=vt100p:
d0|vt100|vt100-am|dec vt100:\                                  ②
        :rf=/usr/lib/tabset/vt100:\
    :rf=/usr/lib/tabset/vt100:ku=\EOA:kd=\EOB:kr=\EOC:kl=\EOD:kb=^H:\
```

where `grep` is being used to locate lines in the file which have the string "vt100" in them. The response printed above is a partial listing of what was returned from that command. You will have to read about these in the man pages if you are interested, but the intent is to show you a way to find alternative terminal entry types if there is a problem with logging on. Notes (**1**) and (**2**) in the listing above (e.g., `dr|vt100p|` at **1**) identify two entries for VT100 terminal types. The entries on these lines refer to aliases for similar terminal types. The options for reading and understanding this file can be found in the man pages (e.g., `man 4 termcap`). All **vt100** terminal types recognized by your host will be listed in `/etc/termcap`, and you can try any one of them in search of the one which works on you particular keyboard. In general, you will want to modify your login scripts so that you can select from a range of terminal types.

Sometimes the terminal characteristics just don't get set properly. In this kind of situation, you can use the `stty` command to manually set your erase, kill and interrupt key equivalents (among others). The syntax for using this command with these parameters is illustrated below, but using it can lead to confusion so you should be careful when using this command.

```
localhost> stty erase ^h kill ^u intr ^c
```

where "`erase`" means the same as backspacing, "`kill`" means the same as deleting the entire line of input, and "`intr`" means interrupt, or the same thing as stopping a process. The character that you enter after each key (i.e., `erase`, `kill`, and `intr`) will be the character used for the associated function. In this example, the `erase` key has been set to "^h," which represents <Cntl-h>, the `kill` key has been set to "^u," which represents <Cntl-u>, and the `intr` key has been set to "^c," which represents <Cntl-c>.

New File and Directory Mask

The next item in the sample `.login` (**2**) is the new file and directory creation mask. The user mask (`umask`) is set, by default, to "022" (see Chapter 3, page

99); however, it can be modified in the `.login` or `.cshrc`.

`umask 022`

Recall (Chapter 3) that `"022"` represents the permissions that when new files and directories are created. This mask means that the `"owner"` has full permissions (nothing is masked), and that `"group"` and `"other"` users have `010` access blocked. According to the binary `"rwx"` scheme, `010` means these users do not have `"write""` permission, but that they can `"read"` and `"execute"` this user's new files and directories.

Mail Path Variable

To receive your electronic mail, there must be a host on the network, called a **mail server**, which resolves mail addresses and routes mail to the proper users. The next line in the `.login` file (item **3**) sets up the path to the file where your mail is delivered.

```
setenv MAIL /usr/spool/mail/$USER
set mail = $MAIL
```
③

Each userid is identified with mail coming through the mail server and is sent to a file called `"/usr/spool/mail/userid,"` depending on the userid, identified with the **USER** shell variable. `$USER` and `$MAIL` are references to the **USER** and **MAIL environment variables**, and **mail** is called a shell variable. The value of an environment variable is defined for an entire login session (all shells), whereas a shell variable is valid only for the context of the shell in which it was established. Since you might have many shells open at any time, each could have its own shell variables, some of which might have the same name but different values. The dollar sign (`$`) in front of a variable name (e.g., `$MAIL` for **MAIL**) is the way the variable is referenced in the UNIX shell environment. Notice that the syntax for defining a shell variable (e.g., `set mail=$MAIL`) is different than that of an environment variable (e.g., `setenv MAIL /usr/spool/mail/$USER`). This will also change with different kinds of shells.

User's Default Execution Path

Your **default path variable** is a list of directories. When a user types a command, unless that program is resident in the directory in which the user finds himself/herself, there will be an error. To get around this, each user has a list of directories which UNIX will, by default, check whenever a command is issued. If the command resides in any of these directories, then the command is executed as though it were in the current directory. Without knowing about it, you have been using your default path since you first typed `passwd` in Chapter 1, since the `passwd` program clearly does not reside in your home directory. As it turns out, `passwd` resides in "`/usr/bin`," one of the directories in your default path. Virtually every UNIX command exists off a directory in the default path; however, there are commands that you have access to in this sample `.login` which are not in the "standard" default path. For example, consider the **path** variable (item **4**) in our sample `.login`:

```
set path=($HOME                                      ④
         $HOME/bin
         /usr/ucb
         /bin
         /usr/bin
         /usr/bin/mh
         /usr/local
         /usr/local/bin
         /usr/new
         /usr/hosts
         .)
```

In this path, there is one directory that is not in the standard default path. The directory "`/usr/bin/mh`" has been added by the user so that MH commands will be properly found. Actually, if you look at your own `.login` file, it will be formatted as in the original listing. These lines have been listed vertically to show more clearly the directories and their ordering. The path is designated by a list bound by left and right parentheses. Each item in the path is separated by at least one space, since UNIX does not read extra spaces. Additionally, each item is listed as a regular directory path.

Commands will be sought in the order the directories are listed in the path. For example, if you know that MH commands (a mailer, see Chapter 2) reside in the directory "`/usr/bin/mh`," and you issue an MH command, such as `comp`, then UNIX will first look in "`$HOME`" for `comp` (HOME is an environment variable like `MAIL`), then in "`$HOME/bin`," then in "`/usr/ucb`," then in "`/bin`," "`/usr/bin`," and, finally, in "`/usr/bin/mh`." When the command is found, it is executed.

If there are different copies of a command in different directories, and the one you seek is listed second in your path variable, then it will never execute unless you provide its full path at the command line. This is important, because you may want to override your path variable, and you may make a mistake. Note that the last item in the sample `.login` path is a dot. As you know from Chapter 3, the dot represents your current directory. If you are a programmer, then you might want to place the dot much higher in the path, because you might be rewriting system functions. If, on the other hand, you are just learning UNIX, then you might want to make sure that your programs are the last ones tried. Suffice it to say, you are free to add directories to your path as you wish.

Shell Prompt

The next thing being done (at item **5**) in the sample `.login` is to set the shell prompt to something more meaningful than the default.

```
set prompt="`host`>"
```

Ch5

The double quotes after the equal sign mean that the resulting environment variable will be a string. The single backquotes surrounding the word "`host`" mean that this item will be evaluated by the shell. In this case, then, `host` must be a command or executable program. This particular program is a shell script which can be found in the "`UNIX/Ch5`" directory, and it will be explained in Chapter 12. The result of this command's execution is concatenated with an angle bracket. The result is to produce a string which looks just like the C shell prompt in this manual.

As a user, you can define your prompt any way you want. Beware, however, that the size of the window may place effective limitations on the size of your prompt. Suppose, for example, that you wanted to have your current location in the file system be part of your prompt. You could do this by inserting the command **pwd** after the command *hostname*, as follows:

```
set prompt="`hostname`:`pwd`[\!] "
```

The result of this exercise can complicate your shell as much as any good it can bring. Why? Look at the effect of this prompt below:

```
localhost.inst.edu:/usr/f1/jhodges/TeX3.0/usr/local/lib/tex/inputs[23]
```

which doesn't leave a lot of room for work! If you are deep inside the file system, as in this example, there will not be any space to type commands after your prompt prints. Users beware!

File Display Variable

By default, many UNIX utilities redirect file display through the `more` paging utility. However, the user can define the utility with which they want to use to page files by modifying the environment variable **PAGER**.

Item (**7**) in the sample `.login` sets the **PAGER** environment variable used to display files. In this `.login` the **PAGER** environment variable is set to `more`.

```
setenv PAGER more
```
(6)

LaTeX Path Variables

The next two items (**8**) in this sample .login file define execution paths for a specific application, latex, which was used to format this book for publication (and is described in detail in Chapter 6). To work properly, latex must be able to locate certain files. It has a set of default files, but you can also tell it to look elsewhere for files with these variables.

```
setenv TEXINPUTS ".:$HOME/Texmacros:$HOME/Texinputs"
setenv TEXFORMATS ".:$HOME/Texformats"
```

Note that the paths in an environment variable take a different form than your path (shell) variable. The entire list is enclosed in double quotes, and directories are separated by colons (:).

Message Notification and Date

The last two items in this sample .login file (items **9** and **10**) are processes that the user has decided to execute whenever they log on. Each executes once. The first is *biff*, which, when set to "y," notifies the user whenever new mail has arrived. The second, *date*, displays the current time and date.

```
biff y
date
```

5.2.3 Changing and Customizing the Login Scripts

The entire notion of the .cshrc and .login scripts is to set variables and execute commands that the user would probably always execute, to make life easier. If you want to design your own shell environment, these script files are *not* the place to begin experimenting, simply because changes made to these files will affect your login environment. Because any command you can execute in a shell script can also be executed at the command line, you are encouraged to test every command you might place in your login scripts *before* changing your login scripts. When you do make changes to these files, use the following guidelines and you will be much happier if you get unexpected results:

- *Always* test the command at the command line first.
- *Always* save the original file before making any changes.
- Modify small pieces of one of these files at a time.

When you rename a file that you are going to edit, it is normal practice to call it something similar. For example, if you want to modify your .login file, first copy the original to something like .login-orig or .login.-orig before making the changes.

5.2.4 Changing the Default Shell Type

Some users do not like to execute commands in the C shell, but, rather, in the Bourne shell or the Korn shell. There are actually many different shell environments, some of which are supported at different sites. To change your default shell from the C shell to something else, issue the command *chsh*, as follows:

```
localhost> chsh
Changing login shell for jhodges
Shell [/bin/csh]: <CR>
Login shell unchanged.
localhost>
```

In this example, the user typed a carriage return instead of modifying the shell type. The bracketed item (/bin/csh) was the existing, and default value, so typing the carriage return resulted in no change. If you ever change your login shell to the Bourne shell (/bin/sh), make sure to edit your ".profile" file, which is the Bourne shell equivalent of the C shell .login file.

5.3 Shell Control

Executing commands is synonymous with running processes. When you issue a command, UNIX creates a process to execute the command. Each process is managed independently. Each process can potentially take input and produce output. For example, the ls command can be issued alone or with arguments. The arguments are the input data, and what the system produces as a result, the directory listing, is the output. By default, the **standard input** is the keyboard, and the **standard output** is the screen. These can be modified by users to suit their needs. The use of the command shell can be facilitated by understanding how processes interact and how the user, and the system, keep track of processes. A minimum knowledge of processes is important in keeping track of your own tasks and those of other users on the system.

- Shell evaluation
- Process status
- Process removal
- Process sequencing
- I/O redirection
- Process I/O piping
- Backgrounding a process
- Multi-processing
- Command modification

5.3.1 Evaluating Commands in the Shell

You can use the *source* command to tell the shell to read and interpret commands from a particular file, even though you have already started a shell environment. Often this is done when you edit or modify a dot file such as the .login and want to execute the commands in the new file as a test. The command is easy to use, as shown below.

```
localhost> source ~/.login
Mon Jan 18 16:48:17 PST 1993
localhost>
```

5.3.2 Status of Processes

The UNIX operating system manages the execution of processes. Whether a process is created to execute an ls command issued by a user, or whether a process is created to perform nightly backups of all user files makes no difference to the operating system. As a result, at any given time there will be many processes on the system, each at potentially different stages of completion. To determine the status of any given process, the *ps* command is used. ps stands for 'process status,' and, like most UNIX commands, has a number of options (man ps). In its simplest form, the ps command will provide a minimal listing of a user's current processes, as shown below.

```
localhost> ps
  PID TT STAT   TIME COMMAND
10001 qc S      0:00 -csh (csh)
10061 qc R      0:00 ps
```

The format of the system response is shown below. The "PID" field is the process ID number and is used so that you can stop or remove (i.e., kill) the process if necessary. The "STAT" field is the status of the process. According to the tables below, the first process above (PID 10001), is sleeping (waiting for input), and the second process (PID 10061) is running. The "TIME" field is the total amount of time the process has been running, and the "COMMAND" field is the command that created the process.

Table 5.1: ps Display field descriptions

USER	⟺	The process owner
PID	⟺	Process identification number
%CPU	⟺	CPU utilization of the process
%MEM	⟺	Percentage of real memory used by this process
SZ	⟺	Size in virtual memory, measured in 1024-byte blocks
RSS	⟺	Size in real memory, measured in 1024-byte blocks
TT	⟺	Control terminal of the process
STAT	⟺	Status: a sequence of up to four characters, for example, RWNA
TIME	⟺	How long the process has been running; both user and system time
COMMAND	⟺	The command that created the process
NICE	⟺	Process scheduling increment, 1–20

Other fields can be found in the man page for ps. The "STAT" field consists of a sequence of three or more letters. I will describe the three most commonly used ones. The first letter describes the process's ability to execute and can be one of the following letters: 'R,' 'T,' 'P,' 'D,' 'S,' 'H,' 'U,' or 'I,' as described in Table 5.2.

Table 5.2:   ps Status execute field value descriptions

R	⟺	Running process
T	⟺	Stopped process
P	⟺	Process in page wait
D	⟺	Process in disk (or other short-term) waits
S	⟺	Sleeping process
H	⟺	Halted process
U	⟺	Uninterrupted process
I	⟺	Idle processes (sleeping longer than about 20 seconds)

The *second* letter of the three to four character status sequence indicates what a process's status in memory is, and can be one of the following letters: 'W,' 'Z,' 'bl,' or '>,' as shown in Table 5.3:

Table 5.3: ps Status swap field value descriptions

W	⇔	Process is swapped out
Z	⇔	Process that is killed but not yet removed
bl	⇔	Process that is in core
>	⇔	Process that has exceeded its soft limit

The *third* letter of the three to four character status sequence indicates whether a process is running with altered CPU scheduling priority, using *nice* (man nice). Nice is used when, for example, you have a particularly large job to run, and you lower its priority so that other users are not hampered by your work. In addition, it is traditional to nice your jobs when running them remotely on someone else's console. As an aside, the use of **nice** follows:

```
nice [ -number ] command [ arguments ]
```

and is usually applied as follows:

```
localhost> nice +10 more Exercise-6.1-output
```

I have omitted the output because it is simply a display of a document. The third letter in a process's "STAT" field can be one of the following letters: 'N,' '<,' or 'bl.'

Table 5.4: ps Status priority field value descriptions

N	⇔	The process priority is reduced; values can range from 0 to 20, with 20 having the lowest priority
<	⇔	The process priority has artificially been raised
bl	⇔	Process is running without special treatment

Given these metrics for interpreting process status, you will notice that most ps listings will use a single or double letter rather than more. Moreover, generally a user only wants to know if the process is running or not, and if not, why not. In each of the processes in the example, below, only the first character is used, and only the R-Running, S-SizeInMemory, and I-Idle are represented.

Table 5.5: ps Options command reference

#	⇔	Represents any given process number and must be the last option given; you cannot use this option with the -a and -tx options
-a	⇔	Displays information for processes executed from all user's terminals
-g	⇔	Displays all processes within the process group
-l	⇔	Displays information in long format
-u	⇔	Displays user-oriented output, which includes fields USER, %CPU, and %MEM
-v	⇔	Displays process system time and user time in addition to cumulative time
-w	⇔	Produces 132-column rather than 80-column output
-x	⇔	Displays information for all processes

Using this table as a guide, the following example can be interpreted. The 'u' option is given to get user information, the 'x' is used to get all the information for a process, and the 'a' option is used to get all the processes. Note that the options are concatenated together.

```
localhost> ps uxa                                                    ①
USER        PID %CPU %MEM   SZ  RSS TT STAT   TIME COMMAND
jhodges   10067 83.0  0.9  530  369 qc R      0:00 ps uxa
vcsc2107  10060 13.5  0.2  282   71 p8 S      0:00 vi lexer.c
homels32  10054  3.9  0.3  245  119 pe S      0:00 bbs unix
vcsc2096  10038  3.5  0.9  627  383 pc S      0:00 emacs list.c
vcsc2095   9561  0.8  0.2  282   64 pb S      0:01 vi create.c
vpcsc4    10004  0.6  0.2  283   75 qb S      0:00 vi cost.mod
pbourne    9160  0.6  0.3  268  137 q7 I      0:03 bbs            ②
root         255  0.4  0.0    6    4 ?  S      0:48 /etc/update
root          78  0.3  0.1   93   46 ?  S      0:05 /etc/portmap
jcheung     8629  0.3  0.3  268  127 q8 S      0:01 /usr/local/bin/bbs
root        8562  0.3  0.1  106   34 q7 S      0:02 telnetd
vcsc2185    9195  0.2  0.2  290   80 q9 S      0:02 vi dirutil.c
vcsc2199    9858  0.2  0.2  282   58 p3 I      0:00 vi sos.c
root        8571  0.2  0.1   96   40 q8 S      0:01 rlogind
vcsc2109   10040  0.2  0.1   62   24 pa I      0:00 page
pbourne    10045  0.2  0.1   62   22 q7 I      0:00 more -d
oracle      3473  0.1  0.8 1792  322 ?  S      0:09 ora_dbwr_gold
jhodges    10001  0.1  0.2  236   68 qc S      0:00 -csh (csh)     ③
vcsc2106    9401  0.1  0.2  249   63 q5 I      0:00 -csh (csh)
shahryar    7153  0.1  0.6  345  262 p0 S      0:08 i2
jchan      10014  0.1  0.3  256  118 q4 S      0:00 ftp sfsuvm
homels32    8428  0.1  0.2  250   95 pe S      0:01 -csh (csh)
root        9222  0.0  0.1  106   34 pd S      0:03 telnetd
fbuenafe    8625  0.0  0.2  172   70 p6 I      0:01 learn
azhao       9867  0.0  0.1   30   29 p9 I      0:00 sh
root         258  0.0  0.0   39   12 ?  I      0:02 /etc/cron
daemon       129  0.0  0.2  123   83 ?  I      0:04 /etc/syslog
chance      9814  0.0  0.2  228   64 qa I      0:00 -csh (csh)
root         111  0.0  0.2  125   83 ?  S      0:00 /usr/etc/statd
goldstei    7187  0.0  0.3  189  127 q2 I      0:12 kermit         ④
root          83  0.0  0.3  145  105 ?  S      0:00 /etc/mountd
```

Several valuable pieces of information can be gleened from the listing above. First, note that the ps process that generated the listing is shown at the top (item **1**). Also notice that a user may have many processes scattered throughout the table. Notice the variety of tasks the users are working on, and how many processes are sleeping, how many are idle (e.g., item **2**), and how many are running. Often you will want to know which process is most recent, so that you can kill the newest or oldest process. Notice (at item **3**), that the user jhodges has a shell process running, and that its PID is 10001. Also note that the ps command just executed has a PID of 10067. Because the ps command must have been issued after the shell was created, this is an informal proof that PIDs increase.

None of this may make sense at first, but all of it is useful in different contexts. One thing you can tell right away is whether someone is on the system, and you may be able to tell how long they might be on the system based on what they are doing. For example, someone who is using `kermit` to transfer a file (**4**) is likely to be doing so for some time, but cannot be reached while they are using `kermit`.

5.3.3 Removing Processes

If a process **hangs**,[1] then it has stopped running and something may be wrong. If the user can create another shell in which they can do a `ps`, or if the process was run in the background so that they can run a `ps` command in the foreground (see Section 5.3.8, page 161), then its status can be known. In many circumstances, the only thing that can be done is to remove, or *kill* the process. This is accomplished using the `kill` command. The example below

```
localhost> kill 10001
```

will terminate the process numbered `10001`. You need to know the process number of the job that you wish to kill, which is one of the reasons why the `ps` command is valuable. Two versions of `kill` are used regularly. The first kills *nicely*, meaning it removes the process without doing damage to related processes. The second method is called the "**blast**" method, because it removes the process without any consideration for the side effects that removal may produce. The syntax for each is shown below.

```
localhost> kill pid
```

```
or
```

```
localhost> kill -9 pid
```

You should always try to use `kill` alone, first, as sometimes the blasting method has poor (or devastating) side effects. For example, many processes are running subprocesses, and it may be one of the parent processes that appears to be hung. If a blast is issued on this process, then it will probably kill all the child processes as well. This may not be something the user wants and should be carefully considered. Sometimes a machine will appear to be hung when a renegade process is really using up many of its resources, or has created a block to further processing. Instead of rebooting the machine, if someone can still login remotely, the offending process might be removed. This could potentially save the work of many users and should always be considered a first

---

1. Another common term for stopped processes is wedged.

line of defense in multi-user systems. Refer to Chapter 7 for the network solutions to this kind of problem.

5.3.4 Process Sequencing

In Chapter 3, the notion of command sequencing was introduced. In UNIX, commands may be sequenced by separating them with semicolons. A common sequenced command is to cd to a directory and then ls its contents. One way is to issue the commands separately, as below.

```
localhost> cd tmac
localhost> ls
```

However, the same effect can be realized with a single line, as follows:

```
localhost> cd tmac; ls
```

Another example is moving up directories using the dot-dot command with pwd:

```
localhost> cd ../..;pwd
```

This example moves up two directories and then displays the name of the directory.

5.3.5 Redirecting Process Input or Output

There are two ways to modify the I/O behavior of processes, by (1) redirection and (2) piping. **Redirection** means that a process takes its input from some place other than the standard input (i.e., the keyboard), or sends its output to some place other than the standard output (i.e., the screen). The >, < and >> signs are used to perform the redirection. Options are shown in Table 5.6:

Table 5.6: Process redirection options

process < file1	⇔	Input from file1
process > file2	⇔	Output to file2
process < file1 > file2	⇔	Input from file1 and output to file2
process >> file2	⇔	Output is appended to file2

To illustrate I/O redirection, the cat command concatenates two files. Normally the output from cat is displayed on the screen (standard output). By using the > symbol with a filename, cat can send its output to a file.

```
localhost> ls -F
...
TeX3.0/                 forward*                texput.log
Texmacros/              ftp.list                tmac/
bin/                    mail-elsewhere/         widget*
blah                    mail-probs*             widget1*
localhost> cat blah > fooblah; ls -F
...
TeX3.0/                 fooblah   ◄──── ①       test1.c*
Texmacros/              forward*                texput.log
bin/                    ftp.list                tmac/
blah*                   mail-elsewhere/         widget*
```

The first listing shows that "fooblah" does not exist. After the redirection to "fooblah," another listing is done, and now fooblah exists (item **1**). If fooblah had existed already, then it would be overwritten with the contents of blah. All other lines in fooblah would be lost. An example of limited practical value which you can easily do yourself involves the echo command, which prints its arguments on the screen. Try typing the command echo with the arguments shown below.

```
localhost> echo my home directory is $home
my home directory is /usr/f1/jhodges
```

This should display the sentence directly. Now do the same thing, but redirect the output to a file called "HOME."

```
localhost> echo my home directory is $home > HOME
localhost> more HOME
my home directory is /usr/f1/jhodges
```

If you now do an ls on your directory, the file "HOME" will exist (assuming it wasn't already there), and, if you cat or more the file, as I have done above, you will see that it has the sentence in it.

The symbol >> can be used to **append** the output of a command to the end of an existing file. That is, the file will be appended with the output of the command. This is very useful when creating a small file without using an editor. Suppose, for example, we wanted to create a file with two lines

```
my home directory is $home
my user execution path is $path
```

where the two shell variables **home** and **path** are expanded out to their true values in the file. This can be accomplished by typing the following:

```
localhost> echo my home directory is $home > HOME
localhost> echo my execution path is $path >> HOME
```

and, as before, HOME can be listed to show that the append worked:

```
localhost> more HOME
my home directory is /usr/f1/jhodges
my execution path is /usr/f1/jhodges/bin /usr/ucb /bin
/usr/bin /usr/bin/mh /usr/local /usr/local/bin /usr/new
/usr/hosts .
```

Process Redirection and Email

Redirection can also be used with the standard UNIX mailer (/usr/ucb/ mail). Suppose you have written a file "myfile" with your favorite editor and you want to sent the file to a friend, "myfriend," on localhost. Instead of entering the mail environment, you can direct the input to the mail message from the file. Consider the sample scenario below:

```
localhost> mail myfriend < myfile
```

will send the user myfriend a copy of the file myfile. There is a limitation to this approach of course. The entire process is a single command. You cannot edit it further after you have begun. If you want to use this approach, then make sure that you have everything you want to say in the file.

Redirecting Input and Output at the Same Time

Input and output redirection can be done in the same command. For example, you may wish to find all references to a type of string in a directory and later go into the associated files and do something to them. Suppose you want to look for the string "SDRAW" in all files in your "Lisp" directory that end in ".lisp," and that you want to place the list of names into a file "items." This can be done with redirection as follows.

```
localhost> fgrep SDRAW < Lisp/*.cl > items
localhost> more items
;;; -*- Mode: Lisp; Package: SDRAW -*-
;;; SDRAW - draws cons cell structures.
;;; (SDRAW obj) - draws obj on the terminal
;;; (SDRAW-LOOP) - puts the use in a read-eval-draw loop
(in-package "SDRAW")
;;; and lines (vertical). They apply to all versions of SDRAW,
;;; SDRAW and subordinate definitions
;;; SDRAW-LOOP and subordinate definitions.
```

Remember that `fgrep` takes a string and a path and returns each item that matches string along with its pathname. In this example, the matched lines and their pathnames will end up in the file "`items`." Notice that each line in the `items` file has the string "`SDRAW`" in it somewhere.

5.3.6   Piping Process Input or Output to Another Process

Whereas redirection performs process $\Rightarrow$ file tasks, sometimes you will want to perform process $\Rightarrow$ process tasks. When you want to send the output from one process directly to the input of another process, you use a **pipe** (|). Process piping eliminates the intermediate process of sending the output of the first process to the standard output and then using that as the standard input to the second process. The symbol for a pipe is a vertical bar (|). A simple example is to take a long directory listing and send it to **more**.

```
localhost> ls -l | more
```

The '`ls -l`' command can produce a long directory listing because each item is displayed on a line by itself. With many directories, this list may be too long for a single screen display. By piping the output of the '`ls -l`' command directly into `more`, you never see the initial listing at all, since the intermediate step is eliminated. There is no limit to the number of pipes you can use in a command, as long as the pipes make sense. For example, years ago (before I began using LaTeX) I used the Troff text formatter. In Troff, there was a `tbl` utility for making tables, a `pic` utility for making figures, an `eqn` utility for making equations, and a `refer` utility for making bibliographies. It was not at all abnormal to take a file and pipe it through all of these utilities, and then on to a printer.

```
localhost> troff parse | tbl | pic | eqn | refer | lpr
```

Although this is obviously an absurd example, it illustrates just how effective process piping can be.

5.3.7 Splitting Output to Different Locations

There are circumstances where a user may want to combine the effects of process-to-file and process-to-process behavior. For example, suppose you want to send the output of a command to a file *and* to the standard output at once. That way you can see what is going on, and later have it to work with. There is a UNIX command called *tee* which performs a branching of output. One copy goes directly to the standard output, whereas the other goes to a specified file. One example is shown below.

```
localhost> fgrep SDRAW < Lisp/*.cl | tee foo
;;; -*- Mode: Lisp; Package: SDRAW -*-
;;; SDRAW - draws cons cell structures.
;;; (SDRAW obj) - draws obj on the terminal
;;; (SDRAW-LOOP) - puts the use in a read-eval-draw loop
(in-package "SDRAW")
;;; and lines (vertical). They apply to all versions of SDRAW,
;;; SDRAW and subordinate definitions
;;; SDRAW-LOOP and subordinate definitions.
localhost> more foo
;;; -*- Mode: Lisp; Package: SDRAW -*-
;;; SDRAW - draws cons cell structures.
;;; (SDRAW obj) - draws obj on the terminal
;;; (SDRAW-LOOP) - puts the use in a read-eval-draw loop
(in-package "SDRAW")
;;; and lines (vertical). They apply to all versions of SDRAW,
;;; SDRAW and subordinate definitions
;;; SDRAW-LOOP and subordinate definitions.
localhost> ls
CCode       Lisp        foo         pcl-tar-orig.Z
Items       descartes   pcl
```

where our previous example sent the result of the `fgrep` to the file "`items`," the use of `tee` will also send the results to the screen. The use of `tee` is particularly useful during debugging.

5.3.8 Process Backgrounding and Multi-Tasking

Wouldn't it be nice if you could perform many tasks at once, even though you may only have one command shell? The utilities that you have been looking at (command sequencing, redirection, and piping) allow a user to perform many tasks with a single line of commands; however, they are all related through output. If a user wants to run many "unrelated" tasks, then something else must be done.

When you issue commands at the shell prompt, they are run in the visible shell or what is called the **foreground**. Each process must take its turn, because you can only type one thing at the shell prompt at a time. Because the UNIX operating system treats each process uniquely, there is no reason why a process (let's call it a **job**) cannot be **stacked** (i.e., put in a queue) and executed by the machine when it has the resources to do so without tying up the user's ability to continue working. When a job is stacked, it is placed in what is called the **background**. This "backgrounding" of a process simply means that the system will keep track of the job's progress and notify the user of status changes if desired. When a job is placed in the background, a new subshell is created for the process and control is returned to the user so they can perform other tasks in the foreground or parent shell.

When you want to put a process in the background, you type an ampersand (&) after the command and its arguments, as follows:

```
localhost> latex Unix-Man &
[1]938  ◄──────────────────────────────────── [job number]  process ID
```

The system then returns, as shown above, a **job number** and a **process ID number**. To poll the system on the progress of jobs currently running, you can use the *jobs* command:

```
localhost> jobs
[1]938
```

In this case, there is only one job running in the background and its process ID was "938." The system will tabulate the process and provide the user with information on its status. To retrieve the process, one would type

```
localhost> fg 1
```

where '*fg*' stands for "foreground," and "1" is the job number. Let's say that you are running a job in the foreground but it turns out to be taking too much time and you have other things to do. In this case, you want to stop running a process in the foreground and put it in the background. This is accomplished by typing the following:

```
localhost> <Cntl-z>
localhost> bg
```

An actual example is shown below, where I began to run a latex job, stopped it, and then placed it into the background.

```
localhost> latex Unix-Man
This is TeX, C Version 3.0 <Cntl-z>
Stopped
localhost> bg
[1] /usr/f1/jhodges/latex Unix-Man &
```

where <Cntl-z> (^Z) temporarily stops the job, and '*bg*' puts it into the background. These commands have the same effect as would '&' upon issuing the original command. You can see, when the command is pushed into the background, that this is what is happening. When you background a process, you are creating a **subshell** in which to execute the process. This is also called **forking a shell**, because, in the process hierarchy, the calling shell is a **parent process**, and the subshell is a **child process**. The number assigned to the subshell is what is returned when you background the process, and you can refer to it with this number, preceded by a percent sign (%). For example, if you decided that you wanted to kill this process, you would either have to do a process listing, find out its PID, and then issue a kill on the PID, or you could type the following:

```
localhost> kill %1
[1] Terminated latex Unix-Man
```

5.4 Command Manipulation

Every user will issue many commands in a given login session. Many of the commands issued will be repeated with minor modification, while others may be completely identical, differing only by what the current directory is. There should be no reason to retype (sometimes long) commands when the system keeps a running list of the commands you have executed. By manipulating commands already issued, the user can be more efficient.

- Command history
- Command repetition
- Command modification

5.4.1 Command History

In order to make use of previously issued commands, the user must have access to the list of commands issued. This is achieved with the history command. history displays a list of the commands issued in the order they were issued at the command line. The shell variable **history** determines how far back the history is retained and can be modified by the user. For example, the following is a history of a user's session:

```
localhost> history
    1   scan
    2   cat .login
    3   cat .cshrc
    4   ps
    5   ps uxa
    6   who
    7   rwho -a
    8   rwho
    9   ruptime
   10   ls
   11   more README.TeX3.0
   12   finger jhodges
   13   cat .plan
   14   cat ,project
   15   cat .project
   16   chfn
   17   last jhodges
   18   whoami
   19   who am i
   20   pwd
   21   ls
   22   mv blah fooblah
   23   ls
   24   mv mkdir Misc
   25   mkdir Misc
   26   mv fooblah Misc
    .
    .
    .
   39   ls Misc
   40   rm -rf Misc
   41   history
```

which shows many of the commands that you have seen in this chapter (even the mistakes, if you can find them :-). As a user, you can always issue the history command to see what commands you have executed, and then reissue them or modify them to suit your current activity. If your prompt has the current command number in it, then you may remember, or even see on the screen, the command number. In such cases, the user need not issue the history command unless the desired command is off the screen already.

5.4.2 Command Repetition

The most often-used command modification is to repeat a command. The exclamation point (!) is used to repeat a command. The exclamation point is often termed "**bang**," so the command given below might be called "bang 27."

What follows the exclamation point tells the operating system which command to work with (called an **event selector**). Table 5.7 shows how event selection works:

Table 5.7: Command history event selection

!N	⟺	Repeat the Nth command; if the number is preceded by a hyphen, then the command N back from the current position is executed
!!	⟺	Repeat the last command
!string	⟺	Repeat the most recent command instance starting with string

For example, the following command will repeat command number 39, which was **ls Misc**.

```
localhost> ls Misc
Misc: No such file or directory
```

However, since that did not work so well (the directory had been deleted in command "40"), another example was tried. This time, command 23 was reissued.

```
localhost> !23
ls                                                              ①
F90                   cshrc-cognet          new-topics
Mail                  dead.letter           news-groups
Manual-in-LaTeX       fe                    steph
News                  filterfile            stud212
README.TeX3.0         foo2                  test1.c
TeX3.0                forward               texput.log
Texmacros             ftp.list              tmac
bin                   mail-elsewhere        widget
blah                  mail-probs            widget1
core                  new-net
```

Notice that the command, as reinterpreted by the operating system, is echoed (item **1**) before running. The next step is to repeat a command, but to add onto it with something else. For instance, below is the same command reissued with another directory after it. Although this example would not suggest it, this method is often easier than typing the entire command.

```
localhost> !23 TeX3.0
ls TeX3.0
BibTeX.inputs          README.METAFONT          fontutil
COPYING.POLICY         README.RT                make.history
CWEB                   README.SCORE             makefile
ChangeLog.WEB-to-C     README.WEB-to-C          makefile.bak
DVIware                README.WRITE-WHITE       mf
Install_INPUTS         README.distrib_info      mfware
Install_INPUTS.bak     README.version           plain.log
LaTeX                  Spiderweb                site.h
LaTeXfonts             TeXcontrib               site.h.bak
MACHINES               TeXdoc                   stamp-web2c
MACHINES.tex82         TeXemacs                 tex
MFcontrib              TeXfonts                 texput.log
MFdoc                  TeXgraphics              texware
MFtexfiles             TeXmacros                usr
Man-pages              aix                      utilityfonts
PROBLEMS               ams                      web
PROJECTS               bibtex                   web2c
README                 cmfonts
README.APOLLO          defaults.h
```

Notice that this time the effect of the reinterpretation is to execute the **ls TeX3.0** directory command, which is what is listed on the line after the command.

5.4.3   Last Command Modification

Sometimes you will want to do the same operation over and over again, but change one thing, like the name of a file. This example was provided in the file system security section of Section 3.6.2, page 94, and is repeated below. The use of the up carat (^) is used to set off the string to be replaced from the string which will replace it. The template is shown below.

^pattern1^pattern2

Examples are shown below, where the access permissions for a file are changed to illustrate how they look in a long listing.

```
localhost> ls -1F blah
-rw-r--r-- 1 jhodges 44 Jul 18 13:46 blah
localhost> chmod 700 blah; ls -1F blah
-rwx------ 1 jhodges 44 Jul 18 13:46 blah*
localhost> ^700^711          ◄──────────────────────────────── ①
chmod 711 blah; ls -1F blah
-rwx--x--x 1 jhodges 44 Jul 18 13:46 blah*
localhost> ^711^722
chmod 722 blah; ls -1F blah
-rwx-w--w- 1 jhodges 44 Jul 18 13:46 blah*
```

The string change starts at the command labeled (**1**), where the 700 (original permission code) is replaced with 711 (new permission code) prior to re-issuing the command. On the following line, the reinterpreted command is echoed, and then the result of the command is displayed. The same command is performed on the new "most recent" command. You can see that you could keep modifying the most recent command.

5.4.4 Command Substitution

More often than not you will find it easier to reissue a specific command with minor modifications than to retype it. In such circumstances, you need a combination of the repeat command and the string modification command, in which you tell the operating system what part of the string to replace. This is accomplished with ':s,' or search and replace command. Below is an example where both are used together. Note the use of two exclamation points (!!), which means re-execute the last command. In this case, the repeated command is !23 TeX3.0.

```
localhost> !!:s/TeX3.0/tmac
ls tmac
tmac.Franz       tmac.Xrefs     tmac.an6n     tmac.imagen     tmac.skeep
tmac.X           tmac.Xtra      tmac.an6t     tmac.os         tmac.srefs
tmac.XP          tmac.Xtras     tmac.ayday    tmac.r          tmac.syb
tmac.Xalg        tmac.a         tmac.bib      tmac.s          tmac.vcat
tmac.Xref.acm    tmac.an        tmac.cp       tmac.scover     tmac.vgrind
tmac.Xref.ieee   tmac.an.new    tmac.e        tmac.sdisp
```

This example is a bit overdone since the same result could be accomplished with '^TeX3.0^tmac'; however, the ":s" will work on any command and the '^' will only work on the most recently issued command. In the last example, the selection of what to modify was based on a pattern match. The selection of command argument to modify can also be made with reference to the order of arguments.

Table 5.8: Command modification word selection

0	⇔	Command name itself (e.g., `!!:0`)
1 or ^	⇔	First argument (e.g., `!!:^`)
$	⇔	Last argument (e.g., `!!:$`)
N	⇔	Nth argument (e.g., `!!:4`)
N1-N2	⇔	Range of arguments argument (e.g., `!!:2-4`)

The ':s' modifier after the event designator is also but one option for working with commands in the history. Below is a short reference of alternative modifiers.

Table 5.9: Command modification reference

:s/pat1/pat2	⇔	Replace regular expression `pat1` with regular expression `pat2`; slashes can be replaced by any symbol
:h	⇔	Remove a trailing pathname component
:t	⇔	Remove all but a trailing pathname component
:r	⇔	Remove a trailing ".xxx" component, such as ".eps" from "rp0.eps," leaving the head "rp0" (i.e., `!!:r`)
:e	⇔	Remove all but the trailing component
:g	⇔	Perform change globally
:p	⇔	For debug; print the modification but do not execute it

5.5 Linking Files and Directories

You have learned about shells and processes, how to recognize them, how to customize them, how to keep track of them, and how to control them. For each of these, however, the assumption has been made that you either have access to a command or that you would obtain access by placing the proper directory in your default execution path. Sometimes this can get unwieldy, though, and you do *not* want to keep putting directories into your path. Why? Consider the following example. If someone develops a program that you want to use, then they can make it read/executable by you. Then, depending on how deeply the program was nested in their directory, you would be adding a long item to your path. If they suddenly decided to move the program, your path would no longer be valid. In general, you do not want to place items in your execution path which are not in your own directories, or in directories higher in the UNIX file system. What you do for the other cases is make a symbolic link.

A **symbolic link** is a **pointer** to a location in the file system. A link is like an alias, but it is a permanent part of your directory rather than something which is started when you log on. It looks like a file, or a directory, and shows up on a directory listing. The command for creating a symbolic link is *ln*, and the format for creating a symbolic or soft link follows:

```
ln -s original-path your-path
```

where the 's' option means *symbolic*, "original-path" is the true path of the file or directory, and "your-path" is the location and name, within your directory file system, of the file or directory. For example, suppose you want to link to a program in the UNIX directory called "latex," and that you want to retain the name in your directory. You could do that as follows:

```
localhost> ln -s UNIX/CH6/LATEX-STUFF/latex latex
```

In general, you will want to retain the same names (i.e., latex in this case). It does not matter whether the original is a file or a directory. For example, consider my directory, which has a number of links in it. I will show a partial long listing so that you can see a few such links and what they look like.

```
localhost> ls -l
total 35
-rw-r-r- 1 jhodges 106 Jan 27 21:24 #blah#
-rw-r-r- 1 jhodges 0 Jan 28 22:58 #diss.doc#
-rw-r-r- 1 jhodges 52 Jan 28 22:58 #foo#
.
.
.
lrwxr-xr-x 1 jhodges 27 Nov 7 15:23 dvi2ps -> TeX3.0/usr/local/bin/dvi2ps
lrwxr-xr-x 1 jhodges 42 Sep 30 17:09 latex -> ~jhodges/TeX3.0/usr/local/bin/latex
                                              ↑                ↑              ↑
.                                           local            real           real
.                                           name             path           name
.
localhost>
```

In this example, you can see that the first field of the permissions descriptor shows the link with an 'l' flag. When the listing shows the full path for the link, it displays both the local name and the real path and name.

5.6 Exercises and Sample Quiz Questions

5.6.1 Exercises

Exercise 1   Write a command that will display the message, `"These are all the files in the directory ..."` along with the list of all the filenames.

Exercise 2   Create two test files with a few lines each. Use cat to concatenate the two files. Redo this but have the output sent to a third file. Do it again, but this time append a third file to the concatenation of the two files.

Exercise 3   Run a test on one of your UNIX commands in the background.

5.6.2 Sample Quiz Questions

Problem 1   Suppose you want to make some modifications/customizations to your ".login" or ".cshrc" login script. Outline how you would go about this and what considerations you should address along the way.

Problem 2   Explain how the semicolon is used in process control.

Problem 3   Consider the ps listing below and answer the following questions:

- Which is the most recently used command shell?
- Explain the status fields of process 59
- Can you tell, from this table, which shell process spawned process 2608?

USER	PID	%CPU	%MEM	VSIZE	RSIZE	TT	STAT	TIME	COMMAND
hodges	2630	1.5	1.4	1.34M	400K	q1	S	0:00	-bin/csh (csh)
root	2543	0.5	1.1	1.27M	312K	p0	S	0:11	layers
root	1	0.0	0.8	1.31M	224K	?	S	0:00	/usr/etc/init -xx
root	54	0.0	0.9	1.24M	256K	?	S	0:00	/usr/etc/syslogd
root	59	0.0	1.4	6.37M	392K	?	S N	0:22	/usr/etc/nmserver
root	66	0.0	1.0	1.25M	288K	?	S	0:00	/usr/etc/nibindd
root	63	0.0	0.9	1.23M	248K	?	S	0:05	/usr/etc/portmap
root	0	0.0	8.8	14.3M	2.45M	?	R N	78hr	(kernel idle)
hodges	2539	0.0	1.4	1.34M	392K	p0	S	0:00	-csh (csh)
hodges	2544	0.0	1.4	1.34M	408K	q0	S	0:01	-bin/csh (csh)
hodges	2608	0.0	1.7	5.56M	480K	q0	S	0:05	vi Unix-AppA-SF.tex
root	93	0.0	1.2	1.34M	344K	?	S	0:00	/usr/lib/sendmail -bd -q1h

Problem 4   When is I/O redirection most useful? When is piping most useful? Provide an example which exemplifies each answer (can be written).

Problem 5   What is process backgrounding? Provide an example of stopping a process, backgrounding it, checking its status, and bringing back into the foreground.

Problem 6   Explain the use of the history command in performing command repetition and modification. Provide an example of each.

Problem 7   When you log on to a UNIX platform, explain what happens, what order they happen in, and why.

Problem 8   Explain what an environment variable is, and what the USER, HOME, and MAIL variables are. What shell are these variables most likely to be set in?

Problem 9   What is a "command alias," as used at the command prompt or in the ".cshrc?" Give two examples of legal alias commands and explain what they do.

Problem 10   Suppose you are logging on from a modem at home. When you try to use the vi editor, the backspace and escape characters do not work and you have a hard time getting out of the editor. What is the problem most likely to be? List, in order of priority, the steps you would take to correct this problem.

Problem 11   Your last command was: `% chmod 755 fileA`. Show how you would make your next command change permissions to owner read, write, and execute, only, on a file named "fileB" using command modification.

Problem 12   The sample process status listing given below lists all current processes running on a platform by the userid hodges. Assuming for a moment that your userid is hodges, provide (1) a list the process ids for all sleeping processes, (2) give the UNIX command to blast one of the process jobids.

```
USER       PID   %CPU %MEM VSIZE RSIZE TT STAT   TIME COMMAND
hodges     202   47.7 37.4 30.4M 12.0M ?  R     30:59 - console (WindowServer)
hodges     216   44.1  5.4 4.15M 1.72M ?  R N   22:04 /LocalApps/BackSpace.app/Ba
hodges     215    2.9 15.7 8.61M 5.03M ?  S      2:46 /LocalApps/FrameMaker.app/F
hodges     210    0.0  6.9 5.56M 2.20M ?  S      0:04 /usr/lib/NextStep/Workspace
hodges     208    0.0  1.3 2.07M  432K ?  SW     0:00 (appkitServer)
hodges     206    0.0  1.6 1.72M  528K ?  S      0:00 /usr/etc/pbs -a
hodges     214    0.0  4.2 4.92M 1.36M ?  SW     0:00 /NextApps/Edit.app/Edit -NX
hodges     211    0.0  4.1 5.27M 1.31M ?  SW     0:00 /NextApps/Preferences.app/P
hodges     212    0.0  4.8 3.88M 1.52M ?  SW     0:01 /Users/hodges/Apps/Date -NX
hodges     217    0.0  1.1 1.62M  368K p1 S      0:00 -csh (csh)
```

5.7 Recommended Reading

Shells

Joy, W. [1980]. *An Introduction to the C Shell*, Computer Science Division, Department of Electrical Engineering, University of California, Berkeley, November.

Chapter 6
File Formatting and Printing

6.1 Introduction and Scope

One of the primary services a computer provides is the ability to print documents. In this chapter, three techniques are presented for formatting and printing documents. For each, an overview and command syntax will be presented, along with examples for its use. The examples will be illustrated on files which you should be able to replicate directly. You will be expected to understand the differences between wordprocessing and text formatting, and to be able to format and print simple documents. A simple document will be a code listing, the documentation for a program in manual format, and a simple paper suitable for turning in as a term project. Samples will be provided and discussed. Additional examples are provided in Appendix L. We will leave up to you the decision of which, if any, to use on a long-term basis. Specifically, the following document preparation techniques will be presented:

- `vgrind`
- `nroff` and `troff`
- `latex`

Within the context of printing documents with a particular package, or in a particular fashion, is the basic process of printing a document at all. This chapter is divided into sections that address the process of printing, and specialize in later sections to printing with a particular method, to achieve a particular end.

173

6.2 Printing Etiquette

Printing is very important to students in computer science, because programs cannot always be read and edited (online) effectively. At some point you just have to see code in print. In the past decade, the preparation of documents: for assignments, reports, papers, and publications has also risen steadily. The need for printing diversity, and applications which support all phases of code and document preparation, has become commonplace. Historically, high-speed line printers have been available to print out galleys of programs in draft mode, while dot matrix and laser printers have become available for higher=quality work. Although the trend has been toward higher quality printers, the cost of printing remains relatively high, so it is important to keep in mind a few commonsense guidelines when you decide to print a document.

- Being able to print code and documents is a privilege, not a right. Never abuse printing privileges with excessive or inconsiderate use.
- If you need to print source code, then use a line printer whenever possible.
- If you need to print code on standard-sized paper, say for a report, then use `vgrind` (or its equivalent), in landscape format.
- Never print man pages. System manuals are provided by the people who administer a system and generally exist on line. In general, if documentation exists on line, don't print it.
- Printing large documents is *extremely* cycle intensive. When you print out something like a thesis, you are keeping other people from finishing homework, theses, or publications. Remember that, if everyone thinks only of themselves, then the network comes to a screeching halt.
- In general, it is considered in poor taste, and, at many institutions, not allowed, to print online manuals. Before considering printing a manual, consult your local administrator and find out what the rules are.
- When printing a large job is justified, print it in chunks rather than all at once so that other users with smaller jobs can get their work done.
- Print large jobs when CPU loads are low.
- Text formatting is cycle intensive. Try to run print jobs on lower priority (i.e., `nice` them) whenever possible.
- Pictures, such as PostScript, Ecapsulated PostScript (**EPS**), Tagged Interchange Format (**TIFF**), and Bitmapped screen dumps take up a lot of space. It takes a laser printer a long time to format pages with graphics. Try to break up print jobs so that pages with graphics are printed separately.
- Whenever possible, use a speller and a previewer (when applicable) *before* you print a document. This will save a lot of trees, and it will decrease your edit time.
- When your document has many figures that must be placed, often it is more efficient to test print the figures separately to make sure they look right. Then, in the document, reserve space for figures, tables, and captions, and format the document without them until all figures and tables are correctly

placed. Then insert them into the document for printing. The method for doing this with `latex` will be explained.

The more you work with text formatters and printing on a network, the more these rules will affect you. More often than not, you will be the brunt of someone else's negligence, so the more people who actively adhere to these guidelines, the better off the network community will be.

6.3 **Printing Tools**

Ch6

print-tools

Before a document is printed, every user should know of the document preparation utilities available to assist in preparing the document and using the printing resources wisely. In this section several tools for checking and validating a document before printing will be introduced, along with the print commands themselves. The files and test output for these examples can be found in the "`print-tools`" directory. The following tools can be used to edit an ASCII document before it is formatted or printed, in order to help edit the file and eliminate or reduce excessive printing. For example, when you prepare a document, you always want to check the spelling in it before printing. UNIX has a utility called *spell* that can be invoked on a file that returns a list of misspelled words. Consider the small document presented below, called "`real-paper`."

```
localhost> cat real-paper
Graduating in Four Years: A Forgotten Trust
Bachelor O. Science
Abstract
A decade ago, the promise of a college education in four years was a
real expectation for students in american universities. With the advent
of ...
Introduction
This year will mark a decade in the information age. And with this age
has come a terrifying realization that students cannot hope to
assimilate the information required of them in an undergraduate program,
and somehow put themselves through school, in a four-year term...
The Demise of Student Support for Higher Education
The major threat to higher education in the past half decade has been
the lack of educational support by the taxpaying public. The effective
result is that students are, to an increasing extent, being forced to
pay for their own educations. Tie this into increased costs and time
to graduation and the result is an ever decreasing number of graduating
students.
The Increase in Required Information
```

`real-paper` represents a simple ASCII file, what might be the beginning of a fictitious term paper. We will use this text to illustrate the use of various utilities in the following sections. For example, to run `spell` on `real-paper` you type the following:

```
localhost> spell real-paper > rspell
localhost> more rspell
american
```

This command applies the `spell` utility to the file `real-paper` and redirects the output to the file "`rpspell`." Had the redirection been omitted, the results of spell would have been displayed onscreen. If the list of misspelled words had been long, this might not have been desirable. Note that there is only one mispelled word, "`american`," which should be "American." In general, the list of mispelled words is given alphabetically, and the correct spellings are not provided. Use `look` for finding possible spelling for words flagged using `spell`. Five additional UNIX utilities which can be used to prepare your document: `wc`, `spell`, `style`, `diction`, and `explain` are shown, with their arguments, in Table 6.1.

Table 6.1: ASCII file checking utilities

spell FILE	⇔	Runs a spell checker on the document FILE
wc FILE	⇔	Counts words, lines, and characters in FILE
look WORD	⇔	Looks up spelling on WORD as you spell them
style FILE	⇔	Analyzes the readability of your FILE
diction FILE	⇔	Looks through the file for outdated and awkward phrases
explain PHRASE	⇔	Gives thesaurus entries for an awkward PHRASE

6.3.1 Finding Word Spellings

The `look` utility is a companion to `spell`. `look` takes a particular word as its argument, as you would spell it, and finds words that are spelled similarly, with the assumption that you can recognize which one is correct. For example, when I ran spell on the file `real-paper`, the word `american` was called out as misspelled. Running look on this word produced the following response.

```
localhost> look american
American
Americana
Americanism
```

6.3.2 Counting Word, Lines, and Characters

The *wc* program is probably used most often of the document preprint programs. wc counts characters, words, and lines in a file. When you are preparing a paper for a class, or for publication, and have a word minimum or maximum, wc will come in handy. wc can be invoked as follows:

```
localhost> wc real-paper
28 156 969 real-paper
```

The first column of this output is the number of lines in the file. The second is the the number of words, and the third is the number of characters. Thus, real-paper is a whopping 28 lines long.

6.3.3 Checking Document Readability

Although not used as often as spell or wc, the other four utilities are available for those who wish to try them out. The *style* function is used to compare the **readability** of your text. The man page can give more detail, but the essence of the command is to show the approximate reading level of the sentences of the paper, as defined mostly by length and phrase complexity. The figure on the following page is an example of style invoked on real-paper. The display shows five different components: (1) readability grades, (2) sentence info., (3) sentence types, (4) word usage, and (5) sentence beginnings.

In general, as a writer, you are trying to maintain the content of your paper while lowering the readability ratings (highlighted) of this output. The common belief is that the easier it is to read a document, regardless of the content, the more people who will understand, and, hence, appreciate what you are trying to say. Notice that there are four different rating scales provided (Kincaid, auto, Coleman-Liau, and Flesch), and that the score under each scale is different. In general, scores under 10 are considered good.

```
localhost> style real-paper
  real-paper
readability grades:
        (Kincaid) 15.3  (auto) 15.3  (Coleman-Liau) 12.8  (Flesch) 15.8 (31.5)
sentence info:
        no. sent 6 no. wds 155
        av sent leng 25.8 av word leng 5.05
        no. questions 0 no. imperatives 0
        no. nonfunc wds 87  56.1%   av leng 6.78
        short sent (<21) 67% (4) long sent (>36)  17% (1)
        longest sent 64 wds at sent 3; shortest sent 5 wds at sent 6
sentence types:
        simple  67% (4) complex  17% (1)
        compound   0% (0) compound-complex  17% (1)
word usage:
        verb types as % of total verbs
        tobe  46% (6) aux  31% (4) inf  23% (3)
        passives as % of non-inf verbs  10% (1)
        types as % of total
        prep 14.8% (23) conj 2.6% (4) adv 1.3% (2)
        noun 29.0% (45) adj 20.6% (32) pron 1.9% (3)
        nominalizations   4 % (6)
sentence beginnings:
        subject opener: noun (2) pron (0) pos (0) adj (0) art (2) tot   67%
        prep  17% (1) adv   0% (0)
        verb   0% (0)  sub_conj   0% (0) conj  17% (1)
        expletives   0% (0)
```

Sentence info. and sentence types are both based on sentence length, while word usage and sentence beginnings are based on the types of words found in each sentence. It even looks for expletives.

6.3.4   Checking Phrase Style

The *diction* program is used to find phrases which are considered awkward or outdated. When executed on your file, **diction** produces a listing of sentences with awkward phrases, set off by asterisks and brackets * [. . .] *. An example that applies **diction** to real-paper is shown below.

```
localhost> diction real-paper
  real-paper
Tie this into increased costs and time to graduation and the
result is an ever decreasing *[ number of ]* graduating students.

  number of sentences 12 number of phrases found 1
```

This output means that the phrase "number of" is improperly used in the context of this sentence. This phrase can then be used as input to explain.

6.3.5 Correcting Phrase Style

The *explain* program takes phrases indicated as awkward by diction and returns thesaurus entries for the phrase which the author can replace the odd phrase with. The phrase "number of" from real-paper is applied to the explain program below:

```
localhost> explain
phrase?
number of
use "many" for a "a large number of"
use "several, many, some" for "a number of"
use "usually" for "except in a small number of cases"
use "some" for "in a number of cases"
use "enough" for "sufficient number of"
use "often" for "in a considerable number of cases"
phrase? <Cntl-c> ◄─────────────────────────────── ①
```

It is clear that explain leaves something to be desired, because a better replacement would begin at "is" and would be "fewer graduating students." Nevertheless, the program offers another viewpoint, and that is sometimes valuable. The program will continue to prompt for phrases until you kill the process, as shown at item (**1**).

6.4 Printing a Document

Regardless of what means one chooses to print (e.g., laser or line printer), one must know how to invoke the printer, how to check the print queue, and how to remove a print job from the queue. When a document is prepared to a point where editing a hard copy would be useful, the command used to print the document is *lpr*. lpr (man lpr) stands for "off line print" and has options for telling which pages to print, how many copies to print, what printer to select for printing, and so forth, as described in the manual page. The general format is shown below.

```
lpr [ options ] [file ... ]
```

where some of the "`options`" from the man page are listed below, and where "`file`" is the file to print.

Table 6.2: `lpr` **Command option reference**

-h	⇔	Do not print the banner page
-in	⇔	Indent printed output by n spaces
-Jjob	⇔	Print the argument "`job`" as the job name on the banner page
-m	⇔	Send a mail note to you when the job has been completed
-Pprinter	⇔	Send the output to the spool queue for the printer specified by `printer`
-Ttitle	⇔	Print the argument `title` at the head of each page
-#N	⇔	Print N copies of the specified files

6.4.1 Line Printers

There are generally two types of printers available on a system: draft mode line printers and laser printers. The **default printer** is usually a line printer, so any output sent to the printer will be printed on the line printer. The procedure for printing a file on the line printer is shown below. Use the following UNIX command format:

```
lpr -J BIN## filename
```

where '`-J`' is an `lpr` option used to print a banner on the first page of the printer output. A **print banner** is simply a large font used for easy identification and can be anything that can assist in identifying your print job. "`BIN##`" is an example of a banner that is used as a sorting mechanism at this institution. For example, if I type the command

```
localhost> lpr -J BIN20 myfile.c
```

to print a file named "`myfile.c`" to a line printer and, using the sample mechanism, above, pick up my output in the designated location, sorted into "`BIN20`." The bin number allows the person who sorts the print jobs to split them into smaller, more identifiable bundles. Often print jobs which are print-ed to a shared printer are sorted by the file name being printed, or by the name of the user. You should write down the locations of local printers and the mechanisms used for sorting jobs here, and on the inside flap of this book.

```
Printer Location          _____
Line Printer Name         _____
Laser Printer Name        _____
Banner Requirements/Options _____
```

6.4.2 Laser Printers

There may also be laser printers available for your use. Please reread the print-ing etiquette rules above prior to using a laser printer, because they are expen-sive and someone has to pay for them. Use the following UNIX command for-mat as a template for printing on a laser printer:

```
lpr -J BIN## -Pprintername filename
```

where the '-P' option is being invoked to redirect the output to the printer named "laser." The naming convention for printers will change from loca-tion to location, but there will always be a difference in the names of line and laser printers unless there are no line printers. The command can be used in conjunction with a text formatter and various preprocessors/postprocessors (or filters), as illustrated below.

```
localhost> nroff real-paper.troff | tbl | lpr -Plaser
```

In this example, the nroff text formatter is used on the file "real-pa-per.troff" and the output is sent into the tbl utility to format tables in the document, and then to the printer.

When your work is PostScript, or includes PostScript or Encapsulated PostScript files, then you *must* send your print file to a laser printer which sup-ports PostScript printing. In the preceding example, this is why the '-P' option was used.

6.4.3 Checking Status of Print Jobs

When you print a job, you generally like to know when it is done printing, or where it is in the stack of jobs (i.e., the queue) waiting to print. You can check the status of your job easily enough with the line **printer queue**, *lpq* com-mand. An example is shown below.

```
localhost> lpq -Plaser
laser is ready and printing via lat
Rank    Owner       Job  Files                  Total Size
active jhodges       34  um3.ps                 2246554 bytes
```

The first display column, "Rank," will list the order of jobs in the queue, with the job which is printing on top. The job which is printing is labeled "active." The "Owner" column is the userid that sent the job, the "Job" column is an identifier, the "Files" column identifies the file that is printing, and the "Total Size" indicates how much space is required to print the job. Notice that um3.ps, which is the PostScript of the current version of this book, is rather large (2.25 Meg). Normally it would be considered in poor taste to print this all at once, so I will use the print job removal command in an example below to kill it.

6.4.4   Removing Print Jobs from the Print Queue

Occasionally when printing a job, you may have cause to remove the job from the print queue. One such case would be if you were demonstrating how to use the printer and the printer status commands, as I am now. More realistically, if you realize that you have made a mistake, or if you change your mind, you might want to cancel the job. One way to gauge a mistake is by the size of the file. If you have a general idea of how large the file should be, then if it is much smaller or larger than that size, it might be worthwhile looking at the file. The command to remove a file from the queue is *lprm*. When using the lprm command, you must identify which job to remove, and which printer to remove it from. If you do not, then all your jobs will be removed. An example that removes the job I sent to the printer, shown above, is shown below.

```
localhost> lprm 34 -Plaser
dfA034sfsuvax1.sfsu.edu dequeued
cfA034sfsuvax1.sfsu.edu dequeued
localhost> lpq -Plaser
no entries
```

6.5 Laser Printing in Draft Mode

After a line printer, the next least expensive way to print a document is laser draft mode. Laser draft mode is generally used when code is being turned in with a report and must be on standard paper and look good. The utility *vgrind* is used to send files to the laser printer. For example, to vgrind a file "file1" and save the output to a new file, "file1outvg," you can type as follows:

```
vgrind file1 -t > file1outvg
```

This now creates a PostScript file that can be sent directly to a laser printer, such as shown in the command below.

```
localhost> lpr -Plaser -J BIN20 file1outvg
```

along with whatever options that are requested. For the case above, the file file1outvg will be printed on a laser printer. Some of the vgrind options are listed below.

Table 6.3: vgrind **Command option reference**

-h HEAD	⇔	Causes the output to have HEAD printed on every page
-l LANG	⇔	Specifies the language, LANG, to use in choosing printing style (C, PASCAL, LISP, CSH, SH)
-sN	⇔	Printing point size given a N
-t	⇔	Sends output to the standard output rather than to lpr
-W	⇔	Forces output to a wide printer
-x	⇔	Outputs index file in pretty format

Ch6

vgrind

Consider a program file named "shortlispfile.cl," which can be found in the "vgrind" directory. In the example below, the file is printed using vgrind. Because it is a lisp file, the '-l' option '-lisp' has been used to format it. Were the file a C program, this same option would have been '-lc.' The '-t' option sends the output to the standard output, which has, in this example, then been redirected to a file ending with ".ps." This has been done to show you that the file is a PostScript file. The command below also prints an optional header, "MISSIONARIES" at the top of every page.

```
localhost> vgrind -lisp -t -h "MISSIONARIES" shortlispfile.cl > vgrind2.ps
localhost>
```

The file generated in this process, vgrind2.ps, is shown in Fig. 6.1.

Figure 6.1: A PostScript file generated for laser draft with vgrind

shortlispfile.cl   MISSIONARIES   **shortlispfile.cl**

```
; Cannibals and Missionaries
;
; There are three functions:
;
;          way to invoke          its function
;          ————————————          ————————————
;          (dfs–mandc)            depth–first solution
;          (bfs–mandc)            breadth–first solution
;          (best–mandc)           best–first solution using a simple cost function
;          (this is missing the branch and bound search since I cannot think
;           of a good heuristic)
;
; A state is represented by four numbers.  The first number is the number
; of cannibals on the left bank, the second number is the number of
; missionaries on the left bank, the third is the number of cannibals on the
; right bank, and the fourth is the number of missionaries on the right bank.
; For example, (0 3 3 0) means 3 missionaries on the left and 3 cannibals on
; the right.   The start state therefore is (0 0 3 3) and the goal state is
; (3 3 0 0).
; Moves are represented by a pair of numbers.   The first number is subtracted
; from the number of cannibals on the left bank and added to the number on
; the right bank.   The second number is subtracted from the number of
; missionaries on the left bank and added to the number on the right bank.

; All moves to the left.
(setq *neg–moves* '((0 –1) (–1 0) (–1 –1) (–2 0) (0 –2)))

; All moves to the right.
(setq *pos–moves* '((0 1) (1 0) (1 1) (2 0) (0 2)))

; Print out the moves of the missionaries and cannibals problem in a nice way.

(defun nice–print–mandc (history)
    (if (null history) nil
        (progn
;           (pprint (car history))
            (fresh–line)
            (print–statop (car history))
            (fresh–line)
            (nice–print–mandc (cdr history)))))

; Print the state–operator in a pretty way.
(defun print–statop (statop)
        (print–bunch 'C (caar statop) 3)
        (print–bunch 'M (cadar statop) 3)
        (write–string "   ")
        (if (cdr statop) (print–oper (cadr statop))
            (write–string "            "))
        (write–string "   ")
        (print–bunch 'C (caddr (car statop)) 3)
        (print–bunch 'M (cadddr (car statop)) 3))
```

6.6 Text Formatters versus Word Processors

A **text formatter** or **markup language** is used to organize the material contained in a text file into an attractive format similar to what a word processor does on a personal computer. Text formatters are generally used when draft mode produces insufficient quality. For example, a letter, a set of lecture slides, a paper, a thesis, a report, an article, and a book are increasingly complex documents which can be prepared with text formatters. Until every UNIX platform has the ability to display documents in "What You See is What You Get" (WYSIWYG) format, document formatters will continue to be valuable tools. Some people continue to use text formatters even though they have access to excellent word processing and page layout applications. Two of the primary reasons for this are: (a) the actual document is an ASCII file, so it is smaller and can be easily sent anywhere (and then recompiled) via email, and (b) the formatting is semantically clear, meaning that the author selects a style and leaves it up to the implementation to decide how to interpret that style. One of the most popular text formatters today is the Hyper Text Markup Language (HTML), which is used to format documents for the World Wide Web (W3). The primary reason that HTML is used on the Web is that many different types of computers are used to interpret a document. HTML specifies the names of commands used to format a document, and suggests how the commands will display text, etc., but it is left to the local browser to determine exactly how the text will appear on a particular screen.

A text formatting language is a set of commands writers use in their documents to produce the desired appearance when the document is later displayed online or printed. All word processing programs use a text formatting language, but generally hide the commands from the user (with menus, mouse clicks and the like) to improve user friendliness. In this respect, an understanding of text formatting is extremely useful to anyone who is writing documents on a computer.

A text formatter is a type of compiler. It has expressions which operate on text, and those expressions are placed in the document according to the language definition. Each formatter has its own language, but an **interchange format** is slowly emerging for transferring documents from one hardware platform, and formatter, to another. An interchange format enables the translation of a document written with one formatter into an application independent ASCII file. Another text formatting language can then be applied to the interchange file, and, whatever commands are supported by the new application will be translated properly. Those capabilities that are not supported are converted to text.

6.6.1   Text Source File

A user begins using a text formatter by creating the text which will be formatted using an editor such as vi. This text file is called the **text source file**. When the text is written, formatting commands may be inserted into the document which will tell the formatter how to format the file. When the document is prepared, the text formatting application is invoked to **compile** the document. The result is a new file with the interpreted document translated into a form a printer can understand. Sometimes this stage can be printed directly, while other times another program, a translator/converter, will be needed to produce a printable file.

6.6.2   Features of Text Formatters

Text formatters are generally *very* versatile, usually sacrificing user friendliness for the sake of feature versatility and user control. Some of the features needed to produce high quality documents are listed below. Although most users do not have an immediate need for some of these features, they should be kept in mind when you choose a text formatter or word processor, and they should be compared to the overall cost of the formatter in terms of required memory, performance, ease of use, etc.

- Page layout (margins, tabs)
- Document organization (outlining)
- Document control (type, page numbering)
- Paragraph control (line spacing, indentation, styles)
- Font control (type, size, spacing)
- Table control (generation, placement, labels)
- Graphics control (generation, placement, labels)
- Equation control (generation, placement, labels)
- Cross referencing (sections, cites, figures, tables)
- Lists and indexes (table of contents, list of figures and tables, index)
- Bibliographic support
- Document sharing (incorporating and exporting text and graphics in different formats)
- Header and footer control
- User customization

This is not an exhaustive list, but should provide a basis for the capabilities that are required in constructing a document. Many of these features are not needed by everyone, or by every application; however, they are fundamental to text production. In the following sections, we will address the formatting of text files with two popular formatting languages. The nroff/troff package will be presented because it is a standard UNIX utility that is used to prepare manual pages. We will also present the L^AT_EX package (pronounced LAH-TECH), because it easier to use, in some respects, and is specifically directed at high quality document preparation [Lamport 1986]. For those who are interested, HTML is similar to L^A_T_EX, and learning to use L^A_T_EX will simplify the process of learning HTML. For both `nroff/troff` and `latex`, a text file will be formatted without any commands, and then we will slowly add commands so that new users can develop an understanding of how to use the utilities to their best advantage.

6.7 `nroff` and `troff`

Ch6

nroff-troff

`nroff` is a text formatting language that formats text in files for typewriter-like output devices such as display terminals. The UNIX manual pages are formatted using `nroff`. `nroff` is designed to produce documents with relative ease, and uses macro[1] packages to increase its versatility. `nroff` has been around for a long time, and, to some degree, has outlived its usefulness. Nevertheless, `nroff` is a part of a standard UNIX distribution and should be learned by all UNIX users. After `nroff` is understood, other text formatting and printing applications can more easily be appreciated. Examples in this section can be found in the "`nroff-troff`" directory.

6.7.1 Simple Application of `nroff` on a File

One strength of `nroff` is that it can be applied to an unformatted file at the command line. Thus, `nroff` can be applied to "real-paper" as follows:

```
localhost> nroff real-paper
```

`nroff` produces a result similar to `cat` in that it scrolls off the page. This problem can be resolved by piping the `nroff` output through the `more` utility. The `nroffed` file is minimally justified in 80 columns, the standard terminal window size. This can be useful when writing documents which will be sent through `mail` or posted to newsgroups. When the `nroff` is issued, the file does not change, since the text formatter merely reads the file and reformats it. `nroff` sends this new form to the standard output, to a file, to another process, or to a printer, depending on what the user wants to do.

6.7.2 Simple `nroff` Commands

In general, `nroff` is used to modify the appearance of files in more dramatic ways than just forcing them to a particular page size. In order to accomplish this, `nroff` has command options which can be embedded into the text file by

---

1. A macro is a series of formatting commands associated with a particular function and invoked with a specific name.

the user. For example, if you wanted to produce a file with the lines double spaced, the embedded `nroff` command to do this is '`.ls 2`' (for double line spacing) alone at the beginning of a line. Lets put a few simple `nroff` commands into `real-paper` and see how they affect the display appearance of the document. The file below can be found in the "`real-paper`" directory.

```
localhost> cat real-paper.nroff
.ce 1                                                              ①
Graduating in Four Years: A Forgotten Trust
.ce 1
Bachelor O. Science
.ce 1                                                              ②
.sp 1                                                              ③
Abstract
.ti +.75in
.ll -.75in
A decade ago, the promise of a college education in four years was a
real expectation for students in american universities. With the advent
of ...
.ti -.75in                                                         ④
.ll +.75in                                                         ⑤
Introduction
.sp 2
.ls 2                                                              ⑥
This year will mark a decade in the information age. And with this age
has come a terrifying realization that students cannot hope to
assimilate the information required of them in an undergraduate program,
and somehow put themselves through school, in a four-year term...
.ls 1
.sp 5
The Demise of Student Support for Higher Education
The major threat to higher education in the past half decade has been
the lack of educational support by the taxpaying public. The effective
result is that students are, to an increasing extent, being forced to
pay for their own education. Tie this into increased costs and time
to graduation and the result is an ever decreasing number of graduating
students.
The Increase in Required Information
```

Notice that every command starts with a dot/period "`.`" at the beginning of a new line, and that the command is not followed by any text. I have flagged six `nroff` commands that are worth noting in this sample. First, at item (**1**), the command "`.ce 1`" tells `nroff` to center the next line, so as to look like a title. The next item (**2**) sets a temporary indent of whatever the indent currently is plus .75 inches. In order for this to work on both margins, the line length has been reduced by the same amount with the "`.ll -.75in`" command (item **3**). This will create an abstract for the paper. After the abstract, the indent and line length are returned to their starting values. Item (**4**) "`.sp 2`" simply tells `nroff` to space two lines in the output, and item (**5**) changes the line spacing so that this paragraph is double spaced, as previously mentioned. The line spacing is returned to single spacing with ".`ls 1`" at item (**6**). The execution and output for this file is shown below.

```
localhost> nroff real-paper.nroff
             Graduating in Four Years: A Forgotten Trust
                        Bachelor O. Science


                            Abstract
          A decade ago, the promise of a  college  education
          in  four years was a real expectation for students
          in american universities. With the advent of ...

Introduction

This year will mark a decade in the  information  age.  And  with

this  age  has come a terrifying realization that students cannot

hope to assimilate the information required of them in an  under-

graduate program, and somehow put themselves through school, in a

four-year term...



The Demise of Student Support for Higher Education
The major threat to higher education in the past half decade  has
been the lack of educational support by the taxpaying public. The
effective result is that students are, to an  increasing  extent,
being  forced  to  pay for their own education. Tie this into in-
creased costs and time to graduation and the result  is  an  ever
decreasing number of graduating students.

The Increase in Required Information
```

6.7.3 `nroff`, `troff`, and Macro Packages

`nroff` is used for displaying on typewriter-like devices, such as terminals. When you want to prepare a document that will be displayed in WYSIWYG format, or be printed on a high quality printer, then *troff* can be used. The differences between `nroff` and `troff` are related to the quality of the output device. On a workstation or laser printer, where the size, type, and resolution of characters can be controlled, `troff` will produce superior quality over `nroff`. For the most part, `troff` and `nroff` have compatible command sets, the output just looks different. For example, in `nroff` emphasized text comes out as an underline, because on a typewriter device italics are not available. Using `troff` emphasized text is italicized. When you execute `nroff` on a file, you are using what is called **plain nroff**. The major drawback of `nroff/troff` is an awkward command set that is difficult to remember. Several macro packages have been developed that make it easier to format documents, where a **macro** is a mechanism whereby the commands needed to perform a particular function are clustered together and invoked with a single command. The user can use the macro packages or even develop their own macros. When `nroff` is invoked with the '-m' option, a macro package is loaded that can be applied to the text file. Whatever appears directly after the 'm' must be a file located in the path "`/usr/local/tmac`," and the file must be named "`tmac.CH`," where "`CH`" stands for the file identifier. For example, the following command:

```
localhost> nroff -me real-paper.nroff
```

should execute `nroff` on the file `real-paper` using the "`/usr/lib/tmac/tmac.e`" macro package available to `nroff`. You can find out more about how to get macro packages to work by reading the man page for `nroff` (`man nroff`). Four macro packages which are generally supported are the **me** (`man 7 me`), **ms** (`man 7 ms`), **mm** (`man 7 mm`), and **man** (`man 7 man`) packages. Examples in this section will describe how to load and use the **me** macros. Following the examples in this section, some plain `nroff` commands and some `me` commands will be tabulated for reference.

6.7.4   Loading a Macro Package or Input File

In order to load your own macro package, or input file, place a line similar to the one below at the top of your document source file:

```
.so ~/tmac/memacros
```

Ch6

**nroff-troff/
memacros**

The "`.so`" nroff command means switch the input **source** to the file following the `.so` command. In this example, the path and filename following the "`so`" command point to a macro package where user-defined macros reside. In this example, some macros from the user's personal "`tmac/memacros`" file have been loaded. A copy of this file can be found in the "`memacros`" directory. Inside the `memacros` file, there are several user-defined (some commented) macros which can be used to format complex documents. The `.so` command can also be used to input files which have their own separate `nroff/troff` commands.

6.7.5   Creating a Simple Document File

Each `nroff` document is created with an editor such as `vi`. The macro package load line, if such a package is used, is at the top of the page, and the remainder of the document consists of text and `nroff` (or macro) commands. As previously mentioned, an `nroff` command starts with a period in column 1 of any particular line, and is immediately followed by the command name. The same is true of me macro commands. Most macros have different commands to begin and end the context of the macro. For example, to begin a list item with me, the macro '. (l' is used, and to end the list, the macro '.) l' is used. Macros that are part of **me** are generally lowercase. Macros that are user defined are generally uppercase. Try running `troff` on the sample file `"real-paper.me"` shown below.

```
localhost> cat real-paper.me
.so UNIX/Ch6/nroff-troff/memacros/memacros              ①
.ls 1
.in +.5in
.ll 5.7i
.fi
.ce 1
Graduating in Four Years: A Forgotten Trust
.ce 1
Bachelor O. Science
.sp 1
.ce 1
Abstract
.(q                                                     ②
A decade ago, the promise of a college education in four years was a
real expectation for students in american universities. With the advent
of ...
.)q                                                     ③
.sh 1 "Introduction"                                    ④
This year will mark a decade in the information age. And with this age
has come a terrifying realization that students cannot hope to
assimilate the information required of them in an undergraduate program,
and somehow put themselves through school, in a four-year term...
.sh 1 "The Demise of Student Support for Higher Education"
The major threat to higher education in the past half decade has been
the lack of educational support by the taxpaying public. The effective
result is that students are, to an increasing extent, being forced to
pay for their own education. Tie this into increased costs and time
to graduation and the result is an ever decreasing number of graduating
students.
.sh 1 "The Increase in Required Information"
```

This example is fairly typical of a simple **me** paper. In this example, the primary commands are those for headings and references. Item (**1**) begins what is called the **preamble**. A preamble is a set of locally defined macros and commands which will be effective for the entire document, but are not specifically related to the text. At item (**1**), a macro file is being loaded using the ".so" command. The abstract is created by centering the abstract line and then using what is called a quote **paragraph environment**, which is begun with a '.(q' command (item **2**) and ended with a '.)q' command (item **3**). Item (**4**) is a **heading**. The heading level (here 1) indicates to the formatter how to number the sections. The text of the heading is wrapped in double quotes. This heading is thus a first-level heading, or section. The output of running this example with nroff is shown below:

```
localhost> nroff real-paper.me
        Graduating in Four Years: A Forgotten Trust


        Bachelor O. Science



                Abstract


        A decade ago, the promise of a college  edu-
        cation  in four years was a real expectation
        for students in american universities.  With
        the advent of...


1.   Introduction

This year will mark a decade in the information age.  And
with this age has come a terrifying realization that stu-
dents cannot hope to assimilate the information  required
of  them  in  an  undergraduate  program, and somehow put
themselves through school, in a four-year term...


2.   The Demise of Student Support for Higher Education

The major threat to higher education  in  the  past  half
decade  has  been  the lack of educational support by the
taxpaying public. The effective result is  that  students
are,  to  an  increasing  extent, being forced to pay for
their own education. Tie this into  increased  costs  and
time  to  graduation and the result is an ever decreasing
number of graduating students.


3.   The Increase in Required Information
```

6.7.6 `nroff` and `troff` Formatting Tools

The `nroff` text formatter has four utilities for generating specialized text types that can be used as pre or post processors with `nroff` itself. A preprocessor is a utility whose output you can send to `nroff` before printing, and a postprocessor is a utility through which you pipe the output from `nroff` before sending the final output to a printer. Although we will not illustrate the use of these utilities, the interested user can find more information in the man pages and references at the end of this chapter.

Table 6.4: `nroff` Formatting utilities

pic	⇔	Generates line graphics
eqn	⇔	Generates equations
tbl	⇔	Generates tables
refer	⇔	Generates bibliographic references

6.7.7 Plain `nroff/troff` Command Reference

In the following sections, several plain `nroff/troff` commands will be introduced. Use the examples as guidelines for understanding the usage of these commands.

PAGE CONTROL

One of the first things a writer wants to do when formatting a document is to set the pagination. In the me package, a couple of commands are used to define the page: '`.pl`' and '`.bp`.'

Table 6.5: `nroff` Page control option reference

.pl ± **Ni**	⇔	Page length, where `Ni` is the number of inches (default is 11)
.bp	⇔	Start a new page
.pn ± **N**	⇔	The next page will be numbered `N`

LINE CONTROL

Table 6.6: `nroff` Line control option reference

`.ll Ni`	⟺	Line length, where `Ni` is the number of inches (default is 6.5)
`.na`	⟺	No adjust on justification; leaves ragged right page
`.nf`	⟺	No fill; same as verbatim (left justify; for code display)
`.fi`	⟺	Fill; same as full justification left and right
`.ce N`	⟺	Center the next `N` lines
`.ul N`	⟺	Underline the next `N` lines
`.cu`	⟺	Continuous underline
`.sp N`	⟺	Space vertically `N` lines
`.ls N`	⟺	line spacing (e.g., single spaced: `N = 1`)
`.nm N M S I`	⟺	Turn on output line numbering
	`N`	Line number starts with, or incremented to, `N` (e.g., `N=3` starts line numbering at `3`)
	`M`	Line numbers for lines of multiples of `M` (e.g., `M=2` numbers every other line)
	`S`	Line numbers and lines are separated by `S` spaces
	`I`	Line numbers are indented by `I` spaces

MARGINS AND TABS

Table 6.7: `nroff` Margin and tab control option reference

`.in ± Ni`	⟺	Indentation, when `Ni` specifies the number of inches offset.
`.ti ± Ni`	⟺	Temporary indentation. + before paragraph and - after paragraph
`.ta Nt`	⟺	Tab; `N` identifies location and `t` the type as declared by the characters below:
	`R`	Right justified tab
	`C`	Center adjusted tab
	`L`	Left adjusted tab

FONT TYPE AND SIZE

Table 6.8: `nroff` Font type/size control option reference

.ps ± N	⇔	Set point size, can also use `ps ± N` inline	
.ft F	⇔	Font changed to F, where F is the font name (default roman)	
		R	- Times roman
		I	*- Times italic*
		B	**- Times bold**
		S	- Symbol
.fp N F	⇔	Font position, where font is loaded (1-4) where the correspondence between character font type and font position is tabulated below	
		F1	- roman
		F2	*- italic*
		F3	**- bold**
		F4	`- courier`

Point size and font commands can be issued inline with the use of the command. For example, the following command changes the font types using both the character and font position methods:

```
\fB See \fR Spot \fI run \fR
```

will produce

See Spot *run*

The same effect can be produced with the font position

```
\f3 See \f1 Spot \f2 run \f1
```

HYPHENATION

To prevent a word from being hyphenated, type % at the beginning of the word with no space.

Table 6.9: `nroff` **Hyphenation control option reference**

`.nh`	⇔	No hyphenation
`.hy N`	⇔	Automatic hypenation on; the number N indicates how many characters to keep together before splitting

MISCELLANEOUS

Table 6.10: `nroff` **Miscelaneous options reference**

`.tl 'left'center'right'`	⇔	Three-part title; text between quotes will be left justified, center justified, and right justified with the current margins of a line
`.de xx`	⇔	Define a macro xx
`..`	⇔	End a macro definition
`.ds xx string`	⇔	Define a string xx containing string

6.7.8 Command Reference for the me Macro Package

SECTIONING

Table 6.11: me Heading control option reference

`.sh LEVEL "LABEL"`	⇔	Create a section heading, with LABEL as its title, and LEVEL as its depth; level values are associated with the following section types ($0 \leq \text{LEVEL} \leq 6$):
		0 - Title (no number, left justified)
		1 - Section (1.)
		2 - Subsection (1.1)
		3 - Subsubsection (1.1.1)
`.$c "LABEL"`	⇔	Start a new chapter, with LABEL as the chapter title
`.he 'x'y'z'`	⇔	Make a page header with x being left justified, y being center justified, and z being right justified
`.fo 'x'y'z'`	⇔	Make a page footer with x being left justified, y being center justified, and z being right justified

COLUMN AND LINE CONTROL

Table 6.12: me Column control option reference

`.1c`	⇔	Single-column text
`.2c`	⇔	Two-column text
`.bc`	⇔	Begin a new column here
`.pp`	⇔	Begin a new paragraph here
`.xp N`	⇔	Print index N here

PARAGRAPHS

Table 6.13: me **Paragraph style option reference**

`.(c CP .)c`	⇔	Begin a centered paragraph environment for paragraphs CP; end a centered paragraph environment
`.)f FN .)f`	⇔	Begin a footnote definition for footnote FN; end a footnote definition
`.(l LI .)l`	⇔	Begin a list environment for list item LI; end the list environment
`.(q QP .)q`	⇔	Begin a quote environment for quote paragraph QP; end the quote environment
`.(x IX .)`	⇔	Begin an index definition for index item IX; end the index item definition
`.bu`	⇔	Begin a bulleted paragraph
`.ip x y`	⇔	Begin a hanging indent (aka description) paragraph, where x is the hanging item and y is the indentation space for the rest of the paragraph
`.np`	⇔	Begin a numbered paragraph
`.(x IX .)`	⇔	Begin an index definition for index item IX; end the index item definition

6.8 Online Documentation using `nroff`

One way to document a program or utility that you have developed is to write comments in the code or a supporting paper which accompanies the code. Another method is to write online documentation, which can be read by a user with or without access to hardcopy. The UNIX online manual pages are written using `nroff` and a macro package specifically oriented toward creating and displaying documentation on terminals. This package can be used to document any programs which you develop and intend to use, and its use will be introduced and illustrated here. Specifically, we will address the creation and viewing of an online document, and followup with a listing of the *man* macro commands available for producing online documentation. The process of developing an online document is iterative, and should be maintained as you develop the application. There are three steps in producing an online document.

- Create the online document
- Test the online document
- Make the online document available to those who will use it

6.8.1   Creating Online Documentation Files

An example of an online document, one which prints the title and sections for an imaginary (dummy) program FOOBAR is created in `vi` and saved into the file "`sample-man.nroff`," and can be found in the "`man`" directory. The file is shown below:

```
localhost> cat sample-man.nroff
.TH FOOBAR 1L "vax version 1" "CSC212 Demo Man"          (1)
.SH NAME                                                 (2)

FOOBAR - A sample program documentation file

.SH SYNOPSIS                                             (3)

foobar file [ list1 ] ... [ listn ]

.SH DESCRIPTION

Foobar doesn't do anything. This is simply a syntax example.

.SH AUTHOR

Jake Foobar

.SH EXAMPLES

Try:

.EX                                                      (4)

% foobar sampman
.EE
.SH SEE ALSO
.SH FILES
.SH KNOWN BUGS
There are no known bugs, yet, but there isn't any code either.
```

The noted items are described below. The headings are taken from the standard cluster of man page headings that was mentioned in Chapter 3 and page 65. The .TH (item **1**) creates the title bar of the online document. The first and second items are the program name and section, respectively. They should not be quoted. The third item is a reference to the architecture the program is running on. The fourth item is a comment written in the footer. The third and fourth items must be quoted. Notice that this is an adaptation from the `nroff` three-part title.

Item (**2**) uses the .SH command to produce a subject header. Item (**3**) is just text associated with the heading for item (**2**). Without other commands text is justified as normally the case in `nroff`. Item (**4**) identifies a macro for formatting an example. The .EX begins the example, and the .EE ends the example. The macro formats an example by setting a temporary indent for the paragraph.

Additional commands for designing more elaborate documents are tabulated below.

6.8.2   Viewing the Online Documentation File

You can view the document you create by calling nroff with the appropriate arguments. The commands provided below are the ones used when man pages are displayed:

```
tbl file | nroff -man - | col | more
```

The `tbl` utility was mentioned in a previous section. It is an `nroff` pre/postprocessor which formats tables. The *col* utility works with `tbl` for displaying multiple column text. If you want to produce a simple document, such as that above, then these commands can be left out. The part which you must use is the **-man** macro call and the subsequent (recommended) pipe through `more`. The hyphen in the sixth position in this command is often used with utilities which expect a filename as an argument, and represents the standard input even though the utility is getting its input piped in. Below is an example of this command applied to the sample document file "`sample-man.-nroff`."

```
localhost> nroff -man sample-man.nroff | more
FOOBAR(1L)              UNIX Programmer's Manual                FOOBAR(1L)



NAME
     FOOBAR - A sample program documentation file



SYNOPSIS
     foobar file [ list1 ] ... [ listn ]



DESCRIPTION
     Foobar doesn't do anything. A complete fake.



AUTHOR
     Jerk Foobar
```

continued

```
EXAMPLES
     Try:

     % foobar sampman


SEE ALSO
FILES
KNOWN BUGS
     There are no known bugs, yet, but there isn't any code
     either.
```

The output for man formats is the standard 80 columns by 66 lines. Page numbers appear at the bottom of each output page with odd page numbers appearing on the right side and even page numbers appearing on the left side. I have collapsed some of the lines from this output to save space, but you should get the idea.

6.8.3   Making the Online Document Available

When you finish writing the program and the online document is also correct, then you need to place the document into the directory where the application will reside and make sure that the command to read the document is available also. These considerations will be continued when the C programming language is introduced, because program writing and documentation are very closely related.

6.8.4   `nroff` Man Macro Package Command Reference

Some of the commands for creating online documentation are included in the following table. Refer to (man 7 man) for additional commands. The entries below pertain only to `nroff`.

Table 6.14: `nroff` **Man macro options reference**

`.B [TEXT...]`	⇔	Sets text TEXT in boldface; if no text is specified, the next text line is set in boldface
`.CT CHAR`	⇔	Prints the keyboard control character indicator <Cntl-CHAR>; for example, `.CT A` prints <Cntl-A>
`.CW`	⇔	Sets text in constant width font until another font change is found
`.EE`	⇔	Ends an example and restores basic text defaults and indents
`.EX [i]`	⇔	Starts an example. Text between `.EX` and `.EE` is printed in a constant width font with 'no fill' mode (no text wrapping and blank lines allowed) in effect
`.HB [words...]`	⇔	Sets the text in underline mode
`.I1 word`	⇔	Sets a temporary indent to the length of the specified word
`.I2 word`	⇔	Reverses one line and then sets a temporary indent to the length of the specified word
`.PN x[y]`	⇔	Sets x in a constant width typeface and then reverts to the previous typeface, y
`.PP`	⇔	Starts a block paragraph; sets the prevailing indent to `.5i`
`.R`	⇔	Sets the text in a roman typeface until another font change is encountered. Also ends `nroff` underline mode if it was in effect
`.RN`	⇔	Prints the return character indicator, <RET> or <CR>
`.RS [i]`	⇔	Shifts the left margin to the right (relatively) the amount of i indents. The `.RS` macro can be nested up to nine levels deep
`.SH TEXT`	⇔	Creates a section header with TEXT
`.SS TEXT`	⇔	Creates a subsection header with TEXT
`.TH ncafx`	⇔	Begins a new reference page and sets the page title; **n** refers to the file name; **c** to the section; **a** to an optional machine architecture, such as "VAX", **f** to a footer component; and **x** to an extra optional commentary such as "unsupported"
`.TP [i]`	⇔	Sets the prevailing indent to i, then begins the indented paragraph with a hanging tag given by the next text line; if the tag does not fit, the macro places the next text on a separate line

6.9 L^A T_E X

L^A T_E X and T_E X are text formatting languages similar to `nroff/troff`. `latex` and `tex` are the associated compilers which are widely used for producing articles, books, and letters which can be sent directly to a phototypesetter such as a Linotype®. Their popularity is based partly on their semantic clarity, partly on a more mnemonic set of commands, partly on the development of bitmap previewers, and partly on the fact that the source file remains in ASCII. `latex` and `tex` can be used on a wide variety of hardware platforms: Sun, HP, DEC, NeXT, Apple, and IBM, to name a few. The commands are fairly easy to follow, although the learning curve is gradual for complex documents. In general, and especially compared to the competition, `latex` (`tex`) is quite reasonable. Presented here are a few examples for using `latex`. There are six important things to consider when using `latex`: (1) the environment, (2) the source file, (3) command files, (4) running `latex`, (5) printing the file, and (6) supplementary utilities. Sample examples will be provided, annotated, and explained. The files used in these examples can be found in the "`latex`" directory. More examples appear in Appendix L along with some comparisons to HTML.

Ch6

latex

6.9.1   L^A T_E X **Source for a Simple Paper File**

As in `nroff` and `troff`, the basis for `latex` is a **source file** containing text and `latex` commands. Unlike `nroff`, however, `tex` and `latex` do not have a terminal equivalent, so all examples must first be converted to Post-Script and then placed into this document. Also, because `latex` is not designed to send its output to a terminal, it cannot be run on raw text files as can `nroff`. The simplest form of `latex` source must still have a few `latex` commands embedded in it.[1] Consider a simple modification to `real-paper`, called "`real-paper0.tex`," and located in the "`real-paper`" directory, which can be compiled with `latex`. All that you do is wrap the text inside the following lines:

Ch6

**latex/
real-paper**

```
\documentstyle{article}                                    ①
\begin{document} ◄─────────────────────────────────────── ②
%   .
%   . BODY OF REAL-PAPER                                    ③
%   .
\end{document} ◄───────────────────────────────────────── ④
```

The `latex` document is comprised of three sections. The first section is called the **preamble**. In the preamble, the type of document is established. For

---

1. Unless a command file is used.

example, the first line of the file, at item (**1**), defines the **documentstyle**. This is a required line in the file, because the document must be formatted to some particular style. In this example, `real-paper` is being formatted according to an "article" style, which is the format for a journal article. Other items which can be found in a preamble are user-defined macros, page numbering commands, title information, and so on.

The second part of the document is the **document body** itself (item **3**), and must be identified by a beginning (item **2**) and an end (item **4**). The text of the document, and its formatting, are written where item (**3**) is. The percent-sign (%) is the `tex` and `latex` comment character. All three segments are required statements in a `latex` source file. Given these minimum requirements, `real-paper` can be formatted. Granted it will not look too pretty, because nothing else has been added, but will be equivalent to running `nroff` on the plain version of `real-paper`.

The last section of a `latex` document is the closing segment, or **postamble**, which is located between the document ending item (**3**) and the end statement (**4**). In the example above there isn't anything of note in the closing segment, but this is where the bibliography style would be identified.

6.9.2   Executing `latex` on the Simple Paper Source File

Once the source file has been created, it is a simple matter to use `latex`. Apply the function *latex* to the source file as follows:

`latex sourcefilename`

Below is the trace of `latex`'ing "`real-paper0.tex`":

```
localhost> latex real-paper0.tex
This is TeX, C Version 3.0                                                    ①
(real-paper0.tex                                                              ②
LaTeX Version 2.09 <7 Dec 1989>
(/usr/f1/jhodges/TeX3.0/usr/local/lib/tex/inputs/article.sty                  ③
Document Style 'article' <16 Mar 88>.
(/usr/f1/jhodges/TeX3.0/usr/local/lib/tex/inputs/art10.sty)) (real-paper0.aux)
[1] (real-paper0.aux) )                                                       ④
Output written on real-paper0.dvi (1 page, 1628 bytes).                       ⑤
Transcript written on real-paper0.log.
sfsuvax1[272] dvi2ps real-paper0 > rp0.ps                                     ⑥
[/usr/f1/jhodges/TeX3.0/usr/local/lib/tex/tex.ps] [1]
```

The execution trace shown above should be explained. First, item (**1**) shows the tex version number, which may be significant if you ever have problems with it. Second, item (**2**) shows what file `latex` is compiling. Item (**3**) shows where `latex` has found the requested documentstyle. In this case, all files relating to tex reside in the "`/usr/local/lib/tex/inputs`" directory off the directory where tex is installed. At item (**4**), note the [**1**]. This signifies that page 1 has successfully been compiled. You can always tell how far the compilation has gotten because the page numbers are listed in this way. As the compilation proceeds, tex also displays line numbers in the text file if something interesting is detected. When an error is detected, the line number and context will be displayed. In this example, there was only one page of text, so the compilation was successful. The final output is noted at item (**5**) and is written to "`real-paper0.dvi`." **dvi** stands for **device independent** file. This file can be translated to forms suitable for display and printing, such as PostScript.

Item (**6**) is a new command, one of many possible "next steps." In this case, I decided to run a conversion from `real-paper0.dvi` to a PostScript file, which I have included below. This was done with the function *dvi2ps*.[1] Note that I have directed the output to the file "`rp0.ps`." This file can be printed with lpr or, in this case, input into this book with the special command.[2] As with the compilation phase, when `dvi2ps` begins working on the "dvi" file, it lists the page numbers as it completes its translation. The final product is shown in Fig. 6.2.

---

1. Some versions use a function called `dvips`.
2. One way to incorporate a postscript figure into a `latex` document is shown in Appendix B.

Figure 6.2: Result of minimal changes to `real-paper` for latex compilation

Graduating in Four Years: A Forgotten Trust

Bachelor O. Science

Abstract

A decade ago, the promise of a college education in four years was a real expectation for students in american universities. With the advent of ...

Introduction

This year will mark a decade in the information age. And with this age has come a terrifying realization that students cannot hope to assimilate the information required of them in an undergraduate program, and somehow put themselves through school, in a four-year term...

The Demise of Student Support for Higher Education The major threat to higher education in the past half decade has been the lack of educational support by the taxpaying public. The effective result is that students are, to an increasing extent, being forced to pay for their own education. Tie this into increased costs and time to graduation and the result is an ever decreasing number of graduating students.

The Increase in Required Information

1

6.9.3   Debugging a `latex` Compilation

If the `latex` compilation runs into problems, then they will be flagged as the compilation continues. If the compilation runs into a problem it cannot resolve, then it stops and waits for your instructions. When the compilation stops, you will see a question mark (?). If you type an 'h' after this, tex will try to assist you in debugging the compilation. Some of its comments are pretty useful and others aren't. You can always type a carriage return and try to resume the compilation. You can also type an 'x' to quit, or an 'e' to edit, at which point your default editor will be invoked and place at the line where the error occurred. When you exit the editor, you will be able to recompile the file.

6.9.4 The Command File

Wrapping a couple of commands around the text in a file is fairly harmless, but it detracts from the intent of the writer; to prepare the document. When you add many such commands to the file, then it becomes more and more difficult to discern the administrative commands (i.e., the preamble and postamble) in the first and last segments from the paper itself. As a result, sometimes it is easier to consider placing these commands, the **preamble** in particular, into a separate file, called a **command file**. Then, the general commands are always executed the same way, and they do not get in the way of formatting the document. Although unnecessary, a command file enables the user to keep a document and commands somewhat separate, and to define useful macros for massaging the document appropriately. A simple command file, "rp0com.tex," one that can be used to format "real-paper0.tex," is shown below. This file can be found in "comfiles" directory. In addition, two sample command files ("com.tex" and "sfsu.tex") are provided and explained in Appendix L.

Ch6

latex/ comfiles

```
localhost> cat rp0com.tex
\documentstyle{article}
\begin{document}                                                    ①
\include{real-paper0}                                               ②
\end{document}                                                      ③
\end
```

Note that this file looks very much like the template provided above. The difference is that, instead of placing the text associated with real-paper0 in between the lines labeled item (**1**) and item (**3**), the paper is being read into this document with the "\include" command (item **2**). The **include** command searches the current directory for a file named "real-paper0.tex." If it does not find one, then it will prompt the user for another name. latex will require that the file name end in ".tex." but you do not have to type the suffix. The file real-paper0.tex can now be comprised of text and "inline" latex commands only.

6.9.5 Preparing the L^AT_EX Document File

So far, you have seen how to execute latex on a minimally altered file. The reason for that was to prove to you that you can do it. Preparing a document with a formatting language can be as frustrating as writing a computer program, maybe more so. You want the result to look a certain way, and you sense that it can be done, but you keep getting compile errors. In a program, at least it works or it doesn't, but in a document errors aren't always obvious, nor easy to locate and eradicate. As an introduction to text formatting with `latex`, we will take a look at preparing `real-paper0.tex`. This time, the required formatting commands will be embedded, and we will look at each one and explain what it does. We will then execute `latex` on the file, and print out the result as before. After that, you can simply take a copy of the source file and replace it with your own text, and it should prepare a nice looking class paper for you. There are two *types* of commands that you should be familiar with in `latex`: (1) preamble commands, which you have seen a few of already; and (2) text (inline) commands. `latex` commands are different from `nroff` commands in that they look like words. For example, the command for making a title is called "title," and the command to make a section-level heading is called "section."

Preamble Commands

Although `latex` is designed to produce a document whose page layout is predefined, the preamble consists of all the commands that either initialize `latex` and select the paper layout, or tell `latex` how to override or add to the paper format as a whole. These are **page layout** commands. For example, consider the first line of the file `rp0com.tex` above.

```
\documentstyle{article}
```

The essence of a `latex` document is the **documentstyle**. The document-style file, in this case `"article"` stands for `"article.sty,"` which is a template or **style file** for the document. The style file tells `latex` how to format the document. For example, `article.sty` tells `latex` that the document will use a technical article format. The style file for articles then sets the page size, margins, font type and sizes, headings, text spacing, etc. for a paper that might go into a journal. The article style file can also be used for term papers, since it is already a formal presentation. A style file is designed using the macros defined in **tex** and `latex`. The idea is to hide from the user the task of building a page and a paragraph and leave the author the task of preparing the content of the paper. If you change the style file of the document, but keep everything else the same, then the document will look very different. This is one of the strengths of `latex`. A `latex` document style is only a template, and can be modified by adding other styles on top of it. That is, documentstyle files are hierarchically organized and support property inheritance. The general syntax for documentstyle use in a `latex` file follows:

```
\documentstyle[ option1, option2,... ]{style}
```

where "`style`" can be any of the following (partial list):

- book.sty
- article.sty
- report.sty
- msthesis.sty
- diss.sty
- letter.sty

Notice that the files have the suffix "`.sty`." As with other `latex` files, the suffix is not required but assumed. Options can be used to modify a style, For example, the default type size for the "`article`" style is `10pt`. But the user can elect to have the document printed in 11pt or 12pt by providing an optional argument:

```
\documentstyle[12pt]{article}
```

A few of the options available are tabulated below:

- 10pt
- 11pt
- apalike
- twocolumn

Ch6

**latex/
texmacros**

When the author decides to modify the style of their document, they only need change the documentstyle and future versions of the file will be changed. This capability makes `latex` an extremely powerful tool. Of course, a documentstyle can be edited to suit one's particular needs, but then you must understand **tex** much better. All the standard documentstyle files are located in the "`/usr/local/lib/tex/inputs`" directory. In addition, if you are interested, there are some home-brewed document styles in the "`texmacros`" directory.

Text Commands

There are two types of text commands in `latex`: (1) **line commands** and (2) embedded or **inline commands**. `latex` commands are different than `nroff` commands in that they look like words. A `latex` **line command** starts with a backslash (`\`) at the beginning of a new line. A `latex` inline command is set off with curly braces (`{}`) within the text. An example of each is provided below.

```
\small
this text would appear smaller than normal
\normalsize
this text would appear normal again
```

However, the same thing could be done, inline, as follows:

```
{\small this text would appear smaller than normal} \\
{\normalsize} this text would appear normal again}
```

Line commands are used to change paragraph styles and more global changes, while inline commands are most often used for emphasis, cites, and other references. The double backslash (\ \ ) forces a carriage return.

6.9.6   The Source File for a Simple Paper

Now we will look again at `real-paper.tex`, a version which has `latex` commands for formatting it in article style. I have not used a command file so that the reader can appreciate the difference.

```
localhost> cat real-paper.tex
\documentstyle{article}

\begin{document}

\title{Graduating in Four Years: A Forgotten Trust}        (1)
\author{Bachelor O. Science}                               (2)
\date{}                                                    (3)
\maketitle                                                 (4)
\vspace{0.5in}                                             (5)

\begin{abstract}                                           (6)
A decade ago, the promise of a college education in four years was a
real expectation for students in american universities. With the advent
of ...
\end{abstract}

\section{Introduction}                                     (7)

This year will mark a decade in the information age. And with this age
has come a terrifying realization that students cannot hope to
assimilate the information required of them in an undergraduate program,
and somehow put themselves through school, in a four-year term...
```

continued

```
\section{The Demise of Student Support for Higher Education}

The major threat to higher education in the past half decade has been
the lack of educational support by the taxpaying public. The effective
result is that students are, to an increasing extent, being forced to
pay for their own education. Tie this into increased costs and time
to graduation and the result is an ever decreasing number of graduating
students.

\section{The Increase in Required Information}
\end{document}
\end
```

This example is fairly typical of `latex` papers not using a command file. I will show a sample command file for the paper after I discuss this version. The line labeled (item **1**) indicates the paper title. Titles cannot be broken into lines arbitrarily, so you cannot use two backslashes, as mentioned above, to start a new line. The paper's author is formatted with the `\author` command at item (**2**). With this command, you *can* use backslashes to break up the author field in `\author`. This will allow you to put your address, school, or course in the same format and location. Item (**3**) illustrates the use of `\date` to label the date of the publication. This can be made blank as shown. The `\maketitle` command (**4**) generates the title. Note that maketitle must be after the beginning of the document. The line in which item (**5**) occurs illustrates the creation of vertical space using the `\vspace` command. Vertical and horizontal space require an argument. The argument must have units, and the units can be inches, centimeters, millimeters, picas, and points. An abstract can be created with the paragraph command `\begin{abstract}...\end{abstract}`, as noted at item (**6**). All paragraph styles start with *begin* and end with *end*. The abstract paragraph creates a title and an indented paragraph in smaller type. The line in which item (**7**) occurs creates a first-level heading. There are six heading depths in `latex`, but only part, chapter, section, and subsection are numbered. In `latex`, all numbered sequences are generated during the compilation, so the author need not worry about section numbering. If sections are moved, `latex` reorders the numbering the next time the document is compiled. The final note (item **8**) illustrates how the document is ended, which ends the document paragraph style, and the paper.

As an aside, the file `real-paper.tex` need not have a preamble if the author had decided to use a command file. A command file for this paper would have been simple to produce, as I have done in the next example.

```
\documentstyle{article}
\begin{document}
\title{Graduating in Four Years: A Forgotten Trust}
\author{Bachelor O. Science}
\date{}
\maketitle
\vspace{0.5in}
\begin{abstract}
A decade ago, the promise of a college education in four years was a
real expectation for students in american universities. With the advent
of ...
\end{abstract}
\include{real-paper}
\end{document}
```

6.9.7 Running L^AT_EX on the Simple Paper

The file was compiled with `latex` as shown below and printed as illustrated in Fig. 6.3

```
localhost> latex real-paper
This is TeX, C Version 3.0
(real-paper.tex
LaTeX Version 2.09 <7 Dec 1989>
(/usr/f1/jhodges/TeX3.0/usr/local/lib/tex/inputs/article.sty
Document Style 'article' <16 Mar 88>.
(/usr/f1/jhodges/TeX3.0/usr/local/lib/tex/inputs/art10.sty)) (real-paper.aux)
[1] (real-paper.aux) )
Output written on real-paper.dvi (1 page, 1720 bytes).
Transcript written on real-paper.log.
localhost> dvi2ps real-paper > rp.ps
[/usr/f1/jhodges/TeX3.0/usr/local/lib/tex/tex.ps] [1]
localhost>
```

Figure 6.3: PostScript output from latex applied to `real-paper.tex`

Graduating in Four Years: A Forgotten Trust

Bachelor O. Science

Abstract

A decade ago, the promise of a college education in four years was a real expectation for students in american universities. With the advent of ...

1 Introduction

This year will mark a decade in the information age. And with this age has come a terrifying realization that students cannot hope to assimilate the information required of them in an undergraduate program, and somehow put themselves through school, in a four-year term...

2 The Demise of Student Support for Higher Education

The major threat to higher education in the past half decade has been the lack of educational support by the taxpaying public. The effective result is that students are, to an increasing extent, being forced to pay for their own education. Tie this into increased costs and time to graduation and the result is an ever decreasing number of graduating students.

3 The Increase in Required Information

1

6.9.8 Preparing Complex Documents

To use `latex` on a complex document, several passes must be executed. If the document has a bibliography, then the bibliography can be included directly, at the end of the document, or be included separately, in which case it will be placed on a separate page. The format for creating bibliographic entries, index entries, and cross references are discussed in Appendix L. All included files start on a separate page. Either way, you must run bibtex on the file after you run `latex` on the file. Likewise, if you have an index in the document, and have prepared the index entries, then you must run makeindex on the file after you have run `latex` on the file. The order between `bibtex` and `makein-dex` is unimportant. Next, if you have any cross references in the file, then you have to run `latex` on the file again just to generate and resolve the references. They are gathered together after the first pass and then placed on the second one. Finally, if you are planning to put a table of contents, list of figures, or list of tables into the document, you have to run `latex` again, because these functions lag the processing by one cycle. Of course, a single pass can accomplish any of these tasks, but generally two `latex` compilations are required in addition to any postprocessor runs, such as `bibtex` or `makeindex`. At each stage, `latex` produces a file called `"file.dvi"` which can be sent to an output device. So you need not run all these passes when you are still trying to compile the document. Nevertheless, only after you have done all these passes will the document print correctly. It should be noted that if you do not modify the index entries or the bibliographic entries, then you do not have to keep running `makeindex` and `bibtex`. The overall template is shown below:

- Run `latex` on the document file
  ("file.tex" ⇒ "file.aux," "file.toc," "file.lof," "file.lot," "file.dvi")
- Run `makeindex` on the document file
  ("file.aux," "file.idx" ⇒ "file.ind")
- Run `bibtex` on the document file
  ("file.aux," "file.bib" ⇒ "file.bbl")
- Run `latex` on the document to import ".ind" and ".bbl" files
  ("file.aux," "file.ind," "file.bbl" ⇒ "file.aux," "file.toc," "file.lof," "file.lot," "file.dvi")
- Run `latex` on the document to resolve references
  ("file.aux," "file.ind," "file.bbl" ⇒ "file.aux," "file.toc," "file.lof," "file.lot," "file.dvi")
- Run `dvi2ps` on the document
  ("file.dvi" ⇒ "file.ps")

`latex` is the executable which compiles the document file in a manner similar to `nroff`. `latex` produces a number of files which are editable but not, in general, of much use to the `latex` neophyte. One of these files is called `"file.aux,"` which is required by the bibliographic reference utility `bibtex`. An embedded preamble command, *makeidx*, produces a file called `"file.idx."` This file can be used with the program `makeindex` to produce an index. The resulting file is called `"file.ind."` The reason that so many passes are required is to build the "file.bbl" file (the reference file), and to resolve cross references within the document. When this process is done, the user can execute the utility `dvi2ps` on the `"file.dvi"` file created. `dvi2ps` takes the *device independent* file created by `latex` and translates it to Post-Script suitable for printing with lpr or previewed on a workstation which supports a PostScript previewer.

```
dvi2ps file > file.ps
```

which will write the output to the file "`file.ps`." Note that `dvi2ps` does not need you to type the ".dvi" suffix on the file. `latex` does not need the ".tex" postamble, and `bibtex` does not need the ".aux" postamble. All of these are the default expectations for their respective utilities. When the document is properly formatted, it can easily be printed on a laser printer with the following command:

```
dvi2ps file | lpr -Pprinter-name
```

or you can use the "`file.ps`" created from a `dvi2ps` run directly, as follows:

```
lpr -Pprinter-name file.ps
```

6.9.9 L^A_T_EX Command Reference

In each item in the following tables, an N refers to a unit of measurement and the associated value. If unspecified, the unit is assumed to be pixels in 72 dots per inch (dpi). Inches can also be specified as "in." Every command is assumed to follow the format above. That is, each item starts with a backslash (\) in column 1 of a line, or it is enclosed in curly braces ({}) and the backslash. An "item" assumes curly braces around it. When "begin" and "end" are used, they must be used only at the beginning of lines since they reflect an entire paragraph style. Paragraph styles can be nested but must be balanced appropriately.

DOCUMENT CONTROL

Table 6.15: `latex` **Document control options reference**

`\documentstyle[options]{style}`	⇔	Basic document page layout, font selection, etc.
`\pageheight{N-units}`	⇔	Length of page
`\pagewidth{N-units}`	⇔	Width of page
`\leftmargin{N-units}`	⇔	Size of left margin
`\rightmargin{N-units}`	⇔	Size of right margin
`\title{TITLE}`	⇔	Document title
`\author{TEXT}`	⇔	Names, addresses, etc. of authors
`\thanks{TEXT}`	⇔	Acknowledgments
`\begin{abstract}...\end{abstract}`		Abstract environment
`\tableofcontents`	⇔	No argument
`\listoffigures`	⇔	No argument
`\listoftables`	⇔	No argument
`\date{item}`	⇔	Current date
`\begin{document}...\end{document}`		Document environment
`\maketitle`	⇔	Put the title here, after `\begin{document}`
`\include{DOC}`	⇔	Insert DOC to compile here; DOC name ends with ".tex"
`\appendix{TEXT}`	⇔	Chapter level header with TEXT text
`\printindex`	⇔	Print the index now
`\bibliography{FILE}`	⇔	Name of file of bibliographic entries; FILE name ends with ".bib"
`\bibliographystyle{STYLE}`	⇔	Type of bibliography formatting desired; STYLE type ends with ".sty"

PAGE CONTROL

Table 6.16: `latex` **Page control options reference**

`\newpage`	⇔	Break page here and start a new page

FONT TYPE

Table 6.17: `latex` **Font type options reference**

`{\bf item}`	⇔	**bold font**
`{\em item}`	⇔	*emphasis, italic*
`{\sf item}`	⇔	san serif
`{\sl item}`	⇔	*slant type*
`{\tt item}`	⇔	`typewriter (constant width) font`

FONT SIZE

Table 6.18: `latex` **Font size options reference**

`\tiny`	⇔	tiny text
`\footnotesize`	⇔	footnote-sized text
`\normalsize`	⇔	normal-sized text (for style option)
`\large`	⇔	large text
`\Large`	⇔	Large text
`\huge`	⇔	huge text
`\Huge`	⇔	Huge text

HEADINGS

The following list illustrates the font type and size, and numbering schemes, for the "book.sty" documentstlye. Different documentstyles, such as article.sty, will differ in how headings are formatted.

Table 6.19: `latex` Section header options reference

`\part{Part}`	⇔	**Part I**
`\chapter{Chapter}`	⇔	**3 Chapter**
`\section{Section}`	⇔	**1.1 Section**
`\subsection{Subsection}`	⇔	**1.1.1 Subsection**
`\subsubsection{Subsubsection}`	⇔	**Subsubsection**
`\paragraph{Paragraph}`	⇔	**Paragraph**
`\subparagraph{Subparagraph}`	⇔	Subparagraph

PARAGRAPH STYLES

Table 6.20: `latex` **Paragraph style options reference**

`\begin{enumerate} ...items...\end{enumerate}`	⇔	1. Numbered list of items
`\begin{itemize}..items...\end{itemize}`	⇔	• Bulleted list of items
`\begin{description}...items...\end{description}`	⇔	**Item** text in the paragraph is indented under item
`\begin{abstract}...text...\end{abstract}`	⇔	**abstract** Indented and justified text with "abstract" centered above
`\begin{quote}...text...\end{quote}`	⇔	Indented and justified text
`\begin{verse}...text...\end{verse}`	⇔	Indented and not justified text
`\begin{verbatim}...text...\end{verbatim}`	⇔	`Format exactly as typed in constant width font`

For each item in a paragraph style, the item is designated as shown below for the *itemize* paragraph style:

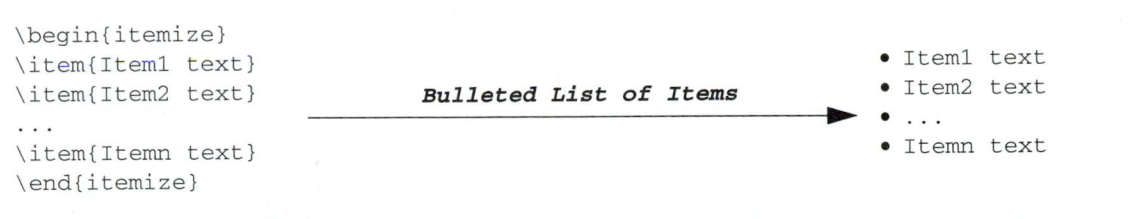

```
\begin{itemize}
\item{Item1 text}
\item{Item2 text}
...
\item{Itemn text}
\end{itemize}
```
Bulleted List of Items →
```
• Item1 text
• Item2 text
• ...
• Itemn text
```

The *itemize* and *enumerate* paragraph styles have optional arguments which enable the writer to modify how items will appear. The optional arguments are used in the same manner as for the required argument to the *description* format.

```
\begin{description}
\item[Item1]{Text for item1. We will
show how the description format dis-
plays with these items.}
\item[Item2]{Text for item1. This
one we will make extend to a new line
also.}
\end{decription}
```

⟶

Item1 Text for item1. We will show
how the description format
displays with these items.

Item2 Text for item2. This one we
will make extend to a new
line also.

where the description in square brackets, for the *description* format, is bold. For the *itemize* and *enumerate* paragraph styles, the optional bullet type, or numbering mechanism, are placed in the square brackets. See [Lamport 1986] for details.

FIGURES and TABLES

Table 6.21: `latex` **Figure control options reference**

`\begin{figure}[htbc]..stuff..\end{figure}`	⟺	Figure environment
`\begin{table}[htbc]..stuff..\end{table}`	⟺	Table environment
h ⟺		Place the figure or table here
t ⟺		Place the figure or table at the top of a page
b ⟺		Place the figure or table at the bottom of a page
c ⟺		Place the figure or table at the center of a page
`\caption{text}`	⟺	Creates a caption for figure or table
`\vspace{size-units}`	⟺	Creates vertical space (e.g., for figure or table) between paragraphs

The figure and table environments do not reserve space for the figure. The user should make sure that vertical space is made (this only applies to included artwork). The figure or table can be located ([loc] above) according to a hierarchical scheme. The options are "h – here," "t – top of page," "b – bottom of page," and "p – own page."

REFERENCES

Table 6.22: `latex` **Reference control options reference**

`\footnote{item}`	⇔	Inserts a footnote with `item` as text
`\cite{bibitem}`	⇔	Inserts a bibliographic cite for reference associated with `bibitem` key
`\ref{label}`	⇔	Inserts section number in which `label` occurs
`\pageref{label}`	⇔	Inserts a page number where `label` occurs

Referenced items, such as the ones above, are included as inline commands. In the case of a footnote, the footnote will be placed at the bottom of the page, separated from the page with a horizontal bar. The "`cite`" reference item is a key from the bibliographic item in the ".bib" file mentioned in Table 6.15. The "`label`" item can be placed anywhere, and will print according to the section where it is placed. Accordingly, the "`ref`" and "`pageref`" labels reference the labeled item. Sample template and real bibliographies are included in Appendix L.

Suffice it to say that this small set of commands hardly begins to scratch the surface with L^{A}T$_E$X. A writer can set up equations using a wide variety of symbols, build tables and graphics inline, design document and page styles, and on and on. If you want to get serious with L^{A}T$_E$X, see the reference [Lamport 1986].

6.10 Exercises and Sample Quiz Questions

6.10.1 Exercises

Exercise 1   Below is the text of a document and, on the following page, is the same text but formatted using nroff. Copy the text exactly as it appears into a file and then add nroff commands to produce the desired result. Your task is to determine which plain nroff commands should be placed in the file to obtain the desired output.

Source File

```
'Title - CSC 212'Chapter 6'nroff'
Use nroff commands to create the desired effect in the file. Don't type them
in yourself. This top paragraph for example, should be double spaced. Determine
the appropriate nroff command to accomplish double spacing. (Hint: ls)
Now
Center
These 3 lines
Now skip 5 lines.
Turn fill off.
In these lines
with fill off
type three words
per line. In
the next few
lines turn fill
on but still
type only three
words per line.
But use the
fill command to
fill the lines.
Leave fill on.
These next lines should be justified. Type several lines
with the right hand side "jagged", and see if the justification
will line them up properly. Write at least three or four lines
to test this out.
Turn justification off.
Start a new page here.
End of file.
```

Output displayed

```
Title - CSC 212              Chapter 6                           nroff
Use nroff commands to create the  desired  effect  in  the  file.
Don't  type  them  in  yourself.  This top paragraph for example,
should be double spaced. Determine the appropriate nroff  command
to accomplish double spacing. (Hint: ls)
                              Now
                            Center
                        These 3 lines
Now skip 5 lines.
Turn fill off.
In these lines
with fill off
type three words
per line. In
the next few lines turn fill on but still type only  three  words
per  line.  But  use  the fill command to fill the lines.  Leave
fill on.  These next lines  should  be  justified.  Type  several
lines  with the right hand side "jagged", and see if the justifi-
cation will line them up properly. Write at least three  or  four
lines to test this out.  Turn justification off.  Start a new
page here.
End of file.
```

Exercise 2   Using the source text for problem 1, perform the same formatting with
L^{A}T$_E$X.

6.10.2 Sample Quiz Questions

Problem 1   What UNIX utility can you use to count the number of lines in a file?

Problem 2   Explain why PostScript figures are a potential problem for printing
documents on a shared printer, and how to reduce the affect of this
problem on the community.

Problem 3   You have been using the online manuals since Chapter 3, if not earlier.
Suppose that you are developing a program for a programming class
and want to document the code (the program) both within the code and
have an online reference page similar to the online manual page.

- Present three (3) headings you think should be in your reference
  page that are consistent with the online manual pages.
- Describe two commands used to format your reference page
  and headings using nroff.
- Describe the method whereby your reference page is displayed
  on the monitor.

Problem 4   Consider the text below. Which nroff/troff paragraph command is used to format this text exactly as it appears? Which L^AT_EX paragraph command is used to produce the same result?

> The wired white poodle jumped over the pink rose bush and into the mud. What an ugly sight it was, seeing the poodle looking more like the mud than the mud itself.

Problem 5   Consider the text below. Which `nroff/troff` paragraph command is used to format this text exactly as it appears? Which `latex` paragraph command is used to produce the same result?

The lazy brown dog jumped over the pink rose bush ...

The lazy brown dog jumped *over* the pink rose bush.

Problem 6   How is an itemized list created using `nroff`, in `latex`? Create an itemized list in the sample file provided for Chapter 6 in which you take each of the following phrases as an item:

1. less student support
2. increased tuitions and fees
3. lower motivation

Problem 7   What does the following command do?

```
sfsuvax1> vgrind -h "myfile" code.c
```

Problem 8   What is the standard sequence used to compile and print a document that has embedded bibliographic references with `latex`?

Problem 9   Provide the `nroff` and `latex` commands to (1) create a title for and (2) introduction-level heading with the following text: "Mating Habits of Computer Generated Amoebas."

Problem 10   Consider the text below. Which `nroff/troff` paragraph command is used to format this text exactly as it appears? Which `latex` paragraph command is used to produce the same result?

```
The lazy brown dog jumped
over the
pink rose bush and into
the
mud.
```

6.11 Recommended Reading

nroff/troff

Kernighan, B.W. [1976]. "A TROFF Tutorial," Bell Laboratories, internal
    memorandum.

Ossanna, J.F. "Nroff/Troff User's Manual," Bell Laboratories, internal
    memorandum.

latex/tex

Leslie Lamport [1986]. *LaTeX: A Document Preparation System: User's
    Guide and Reference Manual*, Addison-Wesley, Reading, MA.

Donald E. Knuth [1986]. *The TeXbook*, Addison-Wesley, Reading, MA.

makeindex

Chen, Pehong and Harrison, Michael [1987]. "Automating Index Preparation,"
    Computer Science Division, University of California, Berkeley,
    technical note 87/347, March.

Chapter 7
Network Processing

7.1 Introduction and Scope

The last six chapters have introduced you to the UNIX operating system. You have learned how the file system is organized and how to create and manipulate files and directories. You have learned how to control the processing of jobs and how to utilize the system to your advantage. Nevertheless, what you have done to date involves you and a single machine, and other users through `mail`, `talk`, or `rn`. The machine your account is on is likely one piece of a larger puzzle, a puzzle that you have access to and which your actions can affect. As a result, it is exciting to learn what you can do outside of the machine where your account resides, and it is also important that you develop a "network attitude" about this "shared resource." In this chapter, the notion of a network and resource sharing will be introduced. The methods whereby you can use other computers and obtain access to information from them will be addressed. Along with these will be the supporting utilities for testing the network and who is using it, for determining your effect on the network, and for managing your environment so that you maintain and protect your personal file system and that of the global processing environment. The following topics will be presented in this chapter:

- Network etiquette
- Single-user status
- Network-user status
- Network status
- Remote processing
- File system management

227

When you have completed this chapter, you should understand how (1) your host fits into the network as a whole, (2) to determine the number of users on the system, (3) to determine the system load, and (4) to check and understand the processes running on your host or other hosts. You should also understand and be able to log onto other hosts in various ways, depending on what task you are trying to accomplish. You should understand the differences between those methods. Finally, you should understand how to maintain your personal file system, and be able to do so with the various methods available.

7.2 Shared Resources and Network Etiquette

There is so much information in our world that no one person can keep track of its increase, let alone what already exists. Our computing environments are rapidly moving toward a day when information is *transparently* available from any source to any application, meaning that we will not need to know where the information is actually located or even where it is being processed. This is called **shared information**. Moreover, the computers themselves are increasingly being shared: their disk space, their CPU cycles, and their peripheral devices. This is called **resource sharing**. For example, there is no need to have a large number of printers on a network that get used part of the time, when you can have a few printers strategically placed which are used by many people. There is also no need to have one machine used very lightly and have another machine loaded to the limit when their resources could be averaged to benefit both. One of the advantages of the UNIX operating system is its support for diverse users and devices; it is the operating system for shared resources. Here are some things to keep in mind, a **network etiquette** if you will, when using a shared resource environment.

- Do not waste resources. The network exists to help us learn, communicate, and share what we have learned. Useless comments and information clutter the network and are sure to attract flames to your institution.
- Do not copy man pages and manuals to your own directory. The network exists so that resources can be shared. Make a link to the files you need, use the man pages, but do not waste disk space by making duplicates of everything you need.
- Archive files and directories that are not actively being used. This saves space, and reduces disk space shortages on shared file systems.
- Remove support files regularly, such as binary (.o) files, ".dvi," ".aux," ".log," etc. files. Compress the source and remove the rest.
- Do not run remote processes during peak periods unless you `nice` them. The console user should always have privileges.
- Do not try to log on to a system illegally. If you do not have an account, then you have no business there.
- Never write or send an electronic virus; the machine it infects may well be

your own, and the files it corrupts may belong to someone you care about.

- Keep your finger file up to date so that network users can locate you if necessary.

- Do not abuse dial-in privileges. Systems are generally not designed to handle large numbers of users or traffic through modems. Dialin access is really a courtesy, since most institutions simply do not have the physical resources to support all users on local terminals. Also, one might need to read or respond to mail remotely. Try to perform your tasks which can be performed remotely on the remote machine, and transfer the results to the local host. Do your best to use local facilities and leave the dial-in lines to those without the choice of direct access.

7.3 Single-User Status

Using a network can be tricky. Unless you can tell, at any given time, who is running what processes on which machine, then you will be at the mercy of other users. Knowing this information will enable you to run your processes on machines which are less heavily loaded, and to avoid system *hogs* (users who use lots of processing cycles and memory). There are two ways to determine the status of the file system: (1) find who the users are and what they are doing, and (2) find out what machines are available and what their processing loads are. In the next two sections, you will learn techniques for obtaining this information for yourself and for anyone else on the network

7.3.1   Your Status

Sometimes it is important to know what your login name is. It will become more important in later sections, but you can tell with the command `whoami`:

```
localhost> whoami
jhodges
```

Alternatively, the `who` command has an option, `who am i` (with two arguments), which will tell the current user/host combination, the login port, the date and time of login, and port (e.g., tty) of login.

```
localhost> who am i
sfsuvax1!jhodges ttyqc Jul 18 13:35 (modem13.sfsu.edu)
```

7.3.2   Anyone's Status

The *finger* utility was introduced in Chapter 3. `finger` is useful on a network to find out who is on the system, and can be used when trying to find out who is logged on to a host whether you know a user's account name or not. `finger` can also be used as a general rolodex for users, because it displays general information about a user that the user has decided to make available to the general public. The standard syntax for finger is shown below:

```
finger [name]@host
```

where "name" is optional, and can be any single string of characters, representing a person's userid, their first name, their last name, etc. If name is omitted from the command, finger will list all users logged onto "host." Likewise, host can be a local host, a full internet symbolic name, or an IP address. On a local host you can issue the finger command without a host and the local host is assumed. Likewise, you can issue the finger command without a name and a list of all users on that system will be displayed. For example, let's say you want to see if anyone is logged on to the host humpback:

```
localhost> finger @humpback
[humpback]
Login       Name              TTY Idle    When             Office
hodges    Jack Hodges          co 101d Fri 15:05
hodges    Jack Hodges          p1      Fri 15:05
```

finger used without a "name" argument will poll the host selected (in this case, humpback) for all users and return a list of userids (plus information) currently active on the host. In this example, the full symbolic address for humpback was not necessary, because the system had an alias for humpback in its "/etc/hosts" table or equivalent. The information that is displayed along with the userid resides in a **finger file**.

The contents of the finger file are displayed differently when the finger command is issued for a specific user. For example, you can also finger a user knowing only part of their name. For example, suppose you know that a user's name *in real life* is Jim. Then you can type

```
localhost> finger jim@sfsuvax1
```

which will produce a display of finger files for all the users with the string "Jim" in their finger file (i.e., in their userid or their **name alias**) on the system. In this particular case, seven user's finger files were displayed (but not shown here). You could then try to identify which "Jim" is the person you are seeking information for. It should be noted that finger does not guarantee that a user is on the network; however, you will be able to tell when they were last logged on and whether they are currently logged on because finger will display the user's **login status**. A significant aspect of finger is that a user may have a different finger file on different hosts. When you "finger a user," every host on which the user has active processes on localhost will display *its* finger file for the user. Consider the `finger` command issued for the user "jhodges" below. On the `sfsuvax1` the finger file looks as follows:

```
localhost> finger jhodges
Login name: jhodges                In real life: Jack Hodges      ← name
Office: TH 970, 338-2335           Home phone: NA                   alias
Directory: /usr/f1/jhodges         Shell: /bin/csh
On since Jul 18 13:35:36 on ttyqc from modem13.sfsu.edu   ← login status
Project: Lets find out what makes this thing tick.
Plan:
Assistant Professor (Artificial Intelligence)
Computer Science Department
Office Hours:    T 1-4
```

whereas the same user has a different account (i.e. `hodges`) and finger file on the host `futon`:

```
localhost> finger hodges@futon
[futon.sfsu.edu]
Login name: hodges                 In real life: John Hodges      ← name
Directory: /Users/hodges           Shell: /bin/csh                  alias
On since Aug 20 15:30:33 on ttyp3 from huckleberry.sfsu
Project: Pull the wool over your own eyes!    ←          .project
Plan:
I plan to use this machine as little as possible, so don't  ←   .plan
plan on finding out when I log in by using this finger
file.
```

In these examples, I could have used the `finger` command with "Jack" or "John" or "Hodges" just as easily as the userid on that host. In both cases, `finger` displays the login name (i.e., the userid), what is called a **name alias** (what follows "In real life:"), the user's office location, their home phone, the path to the user's home directory, the path of their login shell, a line describing their last login session, and the contents of two files, ".plan," and ".project." All of the information displayed in the finger command response can be modified/customized by the user with the commands `chsh` (Section 5.2.4, page 150) and `chfn`.

Changing Your `finger` File

Users can modify the contents of their finger file using the *chfn* command, as shown below.

```
localhost> chfn
Changing finger information for jhodges
Name [Jack Hodges]:<CR>
Office number [Thornton Hall 970]:<CR>
Office Phone [338-2335]:<CR>
Home Phone [NA]:<CR>
```

where the bracketed ([]) items are the defaults from the existing finger file contents, and the <CR>s on the right indicate the responses given by the user. In this case, no modifications were made to the finger file. The item that follows "Name" fills the name alias field for the finger file. The name alias, like the other fields in the finger file, need not have your *real* name in it, and many users insert aliases. Remember, though, that often this alias is used by mail handlers to indicate who email is from, and it may not be very valuable to a mail recipient to receive mail from some bizarre name alias.

The `.plan` File

There are two user created and configured files, `.plan` and `.project` which, in addition to `chfn` and `chsh`, determine how the `finger` display will appear. Both files are used to display a message to those who would `finger` you, and can contain whatever text you want to place in them, although a certain amount of discretion would be wise. The `.plan` file can have multiple lines, as shown for one of my old "`.plan`" files below:

```
localhost> cat .plan
Assistant Professor (Artificial Intelligence)
Computer Science Department
Office Hours:   T 1-4
```

This example is basically a form of signature, where I was providing information that is not normally found in the finger file. Users often make their `.plan` file quite elaborate, and sometimes even have a program executed when someone fingers them. It should be mentioned that when someone fingers you, they often just want to find your login ID or to find out when you last logged on. Deluging them with lots of information could be considered a form of poor taste, so you should be careful in selecting the content of these files.

The .project File

The .project file is a shorter, one-line, file, as illustrated below:

```
localhost> cat .project
Lets find out what makes this thing tick.
```

New accounts are generally given a stock .plan and .project which are resident somewhere in the file system other than the user's account, so if you want to modify the information in your .plan and/or .project, you will likely have to create these files with a suitable text editor. They should be placed in your home directory.

7.3.3 Your Login History

One of the best ways to determine a user's usage is with *last*. last lists the user's login history from some date (usually since the last time the wtmp file was deleted) to the present. Each entry in the history looks as follows:

userid terminal host login-date time-on-off (login-time)

last is often used to determine whether a user is currently active. If the user is currently logged on, then the top-most "time-on-off" and "(login-time)" entries of the last response history cannot be filled in, and will say "still logged in." For example, consider the login history below:

```
localhost> last jhodges | more
jhodges    ttyqc    modem13.sfsu.edu Thu Jul 18 13:35    still logged in    ①
jhodges    ttyp2    huckleberry.sfsu Wed Jul 17 17:53 - 17:54  (00:01)
jhodges    ttyp7    modem13.sfsu.edu Tue Jul 16 09:06 - 09:06  (00:00)
jhodges    ttyp0    Matterhorn.COGNE Mon Jul  1 23:44 - 23:45  (00:00)    ②
jhodges    ftp      toaster.sfsu.edu Fri Jun 21 00:30 - 00:33  (00:02)
jhodges    ftp      sfsuvax1.sfsu.ed Sun Jun 16 15:47 - 15:47  (00:00)
jhodges    ttyp3    huckleberry.sfsu Sun Jun 16 13:12 - 16:57  (03:45)    ③
jhodges    ttyp2    oad-8cs1d.sfsu.e Sat Jun  8 11:37 - 11:50  (00:13)
jhodges    ttyp7    sutro.sfsu.edu   Thu May 30 17:03 - 17:09  (00:06)
jhodges    ttypa    couch.sfsu.edu   Sat May 11 14:47 - 14:48  (00:00)    ④
jhodges    ttyq5    telnet.sfsu.edu  Mon Mar 11 10:22 - 10:36  (00:13)
jhodges    ftp      huckleberry.sfsu Sun Feb 24 14:08 - 14:08  (00:00)
jhodges    ftp      Maui.CS.UCLA.EDU Thu Feb 14 13:45 - 13:45  (00:00)    ⑤
jhodges    ftp      Maui.CS.UCLA.EDU Thu Feb 14 13:43 - 13:43  (00:00)
jhodges    ftp      huckleberry.sfsu Tue Jan 29 20:20 - 20:28  (00:08)
...
wtmp begins Wed Dec 31 16:00
```

The login history above is a truncated version of the real listing, with a few items selected. The history shown above indicates a number of things about a user. If you look closely at a `last` response, you can tell what a user's schedule is, where they do their work, where they hide, and other good things. Consider the output above. When the history was taken the user was still logged in from `modem13.sfsu.edu` (item **1**). The other entries show the amount of "login-time" in parentheses (hours:minutes). For example, on Sunday, June 16 "`jhodges`" logged on at `huckleberry` at `13:12` (i.e., 1:12 in the afternoon) for (`03:45`), or 3 hours and 45 minutes (item **3**). Also note that "`jhodges`" logs in from many different hosts (e.g., `huckleberry`, `Matterhorn` [item **2**], `Maui` [item **5**], `toaster`, `sutro`, `couch` [item **4**]), from different networks (e.g., `sfsu`, UCLA), and by different modes (e.g., direct and modem). Finally, note that "`jhodges`" logs in at any time of the day between 9 a.m. and midnight, usually for a short amount of time, but sometimes for extended periods. One note of caution. The `last` command is going to display all login sessions from the last time the system file "`wtmp`" was removed. In many cases, this could result in a very long listing. Hence the use of `more` above. You could also use the `head` command, but there are options to the last command so that this isn't necessary. For example, if you use the '`-N`' option, where '`N`' is a number, then only `N` lines of the total number of lines will be displayed in the response:

```
localhost> last -2 jhodges
jhodges    ttyqc    modem13.sfsu.edu Thu Jul 18 13:35    still logged in
jhodges    ttyp2    huckleberry.sfsu Wed Jul 17 17:53 - 17:54  (00:01)
```

7.4 Network-User Status

There are two reasons to look for activity on the network. The more obvious case is one in which you are looking to see if specific users are logged in, so that you can get in touch with them. The other case is one in which you are trying to find out what the big jobs are, who is running them, and when they run their jobs so that you can do your work some other time (or on some other host). Either way, it is important to be able to look at the activity on the network and understand what it means. "Activity," in this context, means (1) the users who are logged in and (2) what they are doing. There are two ways to determine activity across the network. The first is to poll the machine on the network to see who is active. The second is to poll the machines on the network for how active *they* are. These methods can be accomplished with the `who`, `users`, and `w` commands.

7.4.1 Who Is Out There

If you already know who a user is on the network, having determined their userid with `finger`, then a simple listing of who is on the system tells you if they are there or not. You can then decide whether you want to be on the system or not. Two commands are used to poll the network for users. The *who* command polls the local host for active users. A sample **who** is shown below for the host `localhost`:

```
localhost> who
shahryar ttyp0   Jul 18 09:01   (rincon.sfsu.edu)
vcsc2087 ttyp1   Jul 18 13:13   (hh-302dync.sfsu.)
vcsc2162 ttyp2   Jul 18 13:12   (bus212d10.sfsu.e)
arichard ttyp4   Jul 18 11:10   (gisps2-1.sfsu.ed)
rlee     ttyp5   Jul 18 12:02   (ac-pc2.sfsu.edu)
fbuenafe ttyp6   Jul 18 12:49   (oad-8cs1d.sfsu.e)
davidm   ttyp7   Jul 18 10:42   (lib-e145cs1a.sfs)
vcsc2107 ttyp8   Jul 18 13:12   (lib-maccs2a.sfsu)
azhao    ttyp9   Jul 18 13:01   (ac-allen.sfsu.ed)
vcsc2095 ttypb   Jul 18 12:22   (bus212d21.sfsu.e)
vcsc2123 ttypd   Jul 18 13:27   (telnet.sfsu.edu)
homels13 ttype   Jul 18 13:38   (futon.sfsu.edu)
vcsc2177 ttypf   Jul 18 13:18   (oad-8cs1d.sfsu.e)
vcsc2085 ttyq1   Jul 18 11:20   (lib-maccs2a.sfsu)
goldstei ttyq2   Jul 18 11:22   (mdmsrv4.sdsu.edu)
vcsc2014 ttyq3   Jul 18 12:04   (oad-8cs1d.sfsu.e)
jchan    ttyq4   Jul 18 10:46   (ac-jchan.sfsu.ed)
vcsc2106 ttyq5   Jul 18 13:28   (138.202.2.1)
pbourne  ttyq7   Jul 18 13:20   (modem11.sfsu.edu)
jcheung  ttyq8   Jul 18 13:21   (russian.sfsu.edu)
vcsc2185 ttyq9   Jul 18 13:26   (bus212d19.sfsu.e)
chance   ttyqa   Jul 18 13:32   (net-chance.sfsu.)
vpcsc4   ttyqb   Jul 18 13:34   (telnet.sfsu.edu)
jhodges  ttyqc   Jul 18 13:35   (modem13.sfsu.edu)
vcsc2105 ttyqd   Jul 18 13:37   (modem11.sfsu.edu)
```

This was only a partial list! The who command is output with a simple format:

[USERID] [TTY] [LOGIN-DATE] [LOGIN-TIME] [LOGIN-SITE]

Note that the user IDs appear to be listed in random order, since the list is ordered by which device they logged in from (i.e., TTY, the second field). A who listing can be useful in determining how much load is likely to occur on a host. In contrast, when the who command is issued on a workstation, the number of users may be dramatically different.

```
huckleberry[1] who
hodges ttyp0 Aug 13 14:31 (modem14.sfsu.edu)
```

The **remote** who command, rwho, performs the same function as who except that rwho traverses the local network that the host is attached to. Issuing this command on our example LOCALHOST proves fruitless because it has no local network to which it is connected:

```
localhost> rwho
localhost>
```

Conversely, issuing the same command from a workstation which is networked to many other (and sometimes heterogeneous) hosts, can be entirely different:

```
huckleberry[2] rwho
eisman    toaster:ttyp1 Aug 13 13:43 :08
jessica   futon:ttyp3   Aug 13 14:23 :01
sheehan   walnut:ttyp0  Aug 13 14:02
```

In this example, notice that the syntax of the table is slightly different:

[USERID] [HOST:TTY] [LOGIN-DATE] [LOGIN-TIME] [IDLE-TIME]

so this command, when effective, additionally provides information about how long the user has been idle (i.e., how long it has been since the user issued a command). Specifically, the user "jessica," in the table above, has been idle for about one minute, so we know that she is currently very active. When the '-a' (all) option to rwho is issued, *all* local networks are polled and the resulting users are shown, again for a workstation hooked up to a local network, as follows:

```
huckleberry[3] rwho -a
eisman    toaster:ttyp1 Aug 13 13:43    :08
jessica   futon:console Aug 13 14:22 99:59
jessica   futon:ttyp3   Aug 13 14:23    :01
sheehan   walnut:ttyp0  Aug 13 14:02
sherif    futon:ttyp0   Aug 13 09:33  4:35
```

Notice that the display for rwho is different from that of who, but similar to and longer than that for last. rwho lists the userids, the host they logged on to, the data and time they logged on, and the amount of idle time they have had since their last command. This is similar to the `last` command entry.

7.4.2 Identifying User Names on the Network

The second command to find out what users are on the network is *users*, which, like `whoami` for a single user, lists the userids of users currently logged on to the system. An example for `localhost` is shown below:

```
localhost> users
epearson jason jhodges jkelley ramberg schwartz vcsc2195 vpcsc21
```

However, when the similar *remote* version of the `users` command (called *rusers*) is issued, we see that the command is not supported:

```
localhost> rusers
Command not found.
```

Issuing the `users` command on a workstation provides the following result:

```
huckleberry[4] users
hodges
```

and the remote command `rusers` is now supported:

```
huckleberry[5] rusers
stars.sfsu.e cook carpente
gibbs.sfsu.e gronerts
esmeralda.sf aragons
futon.sfsu.e jessica sherif jessica
walnut       sheehan
homer.sfsu.e jason
lisa.sfsu.ed goel
lentil.sfsu. levine
bart.sfsu.ed bregler
kumquat.sfsu kroll
marge.sfsu.e goel
quark.sfsu.e ramberg
huckleberry  hodges
```

host   userids

In this example, the first item in any row is the name of a host on the network, while the remaining items in a given row are names of users logged on to the host. For example, jessica, sherif, and jessica are logged on to `futon.-sfsu.edu`. This means that jessica has two active command shells. Also note that user goel is logged on to both `lisa.sfsu.edu` and to `marge.sfs-u.edu`.

7.4.3   Host Information and User Information

Finally, the *w* command is an integration of `who` and `uptime`. As mentioned, the w command integrates `uptime` and `who`. The command displays who is logged in *and* what they are doing. Below is an example:

```
localhost> w
  4:14pm   up   9:15,   8 users,   load average: 1.04, 1.01, 0.76      line 1 like
User       tty from            login@  idle   JCPU    PCPU   what          uptime
pbourne    p0 modem11.sfsu.e   4:13pm                        mail
vpcsc11    p1 dh9.uccs.edu     3:59pm            2       2   rn
jhodges    p2 huckleberry.sf   4:06pm                        w
shahryar   p3 rincon.sfsu.ed   2:10pm           18      18   i2          other lines
robinson   p5 modem11.sfsu.e  12:12pm    12     17           -csh        similar
jchan      p6 ac-jchan.sfsu.   2:08pm  2:05                  -csh        to who
vpcsc21    p7 lib-maccs2a.sf   3:18pm            4       4   vi dis.out
wkwong     p8 oad-8cs1d.sfsu   4:07pm     1      2           -csh
```

As you can see, the first line is identical to `uptime`, while the remaining lines represent users on the system. Notice that the last field shows *what* the user is doing. Very nice! The columns are explained as follows:

Table 7.1: w Display field descriptions

Field 1	⇔	The user's login name (userid)
Field 2	⇔	The name of the tty[a] the user is logged in on
Field 3	⇔	The host from which the user is logged on
Field 4	⇔	The time of day the user logged on
Field 5	⇔	The number of minutes since the user last issued a command
Field 6	⇔	The CPU time used by all processes and their children on that terminal
Field 7	⇔	The CPU time used by the currently active process
Field 8	⇔	The name and arguments of the current process

a. A tty is a special device file associated with a terminal line.

You can force w to display only information for a particular user by issuing the command with the userid (e.g., **w userid**). Because the w command provides such a variety of information, it is often the only command used to check users and system status.

7.5 Network Status

The commands who and users are excellent ways to find out who is logged on to a particular system and what tasks they are working on. Sometimes, however, all you really care to know is whether a particular host is accessible on the network, or what the processing load on a particular host is. In such cases, the commands *ping*, uptime and ruptime can be used.

7.5.1 Statistics for a Specific Host

Sometimes you will have a difficult time connecting to a host, or you will find that the performance of the network isn't what it might be on other occasions. In such cases, you will probably want to find out if the problem is with you or with the machine you are trying to work with. This can be easily accomplished with the ping command, as shown below:

```
localhost> /etc/ping huckleberry.sfsu.edu
PING huckleberry.sfsu.edu: 56 data bytes
64 bytes from 198.137.218.1: icmp_seq=0. time=5. ms
64 bytes from 198.137.218.1: icmp_seq=1. time=1. ms
64 bytes from 198.137.218.1: icmp_seq=2. time=1. ms
64 bytes from 198.137.218.1: icmp_seq=3. time=1. ms
64 bytes from 198.137.218.1: icmp_seq=4. time=1. ms
^C
----huckleberry PING Statistics----
5 packets transmitted, 5 packets received, 0% packet loss
round-trip (ms)  min/avg/max = 1/1/5
localhost>
```

When the ping command is issued with the name of a network host, the local host sends a data packet to the remote host (it could be the local host, it doesn't make a difference to the command), which is then sent back. A packet is sent every second, and the statistics for each packet are displayed on the screeen. This process is continued until the number of counts that was requested by the user is reached, or until the process is terminated. The general format for the ping command is shown below:

```
ping [ -r ] [ -v ] host [ packetsize ] [ count ]
```

In this template, the '-r' and '-v' options (i.e., routing and verbose options) will not be discussed here, and the interested reader should see a reference or the man page for more details (man ping). The host is the required argument to the command, and both the packetsize and the count (the number of transmissions to make) can be provided to the command. For example, the previous example could be modified as follows without changing the response:

```
localhost> /etc/ping huckleberry.sfsu.edu 64 5
```

The results of a ping command can be very useful to even the novice network user, because it provides network load information. While packets are being sent, each packet has a status line that looks as follows:

```
64 bytes from 198.137.218.1: icmp_seq=0. time=5. ms
```

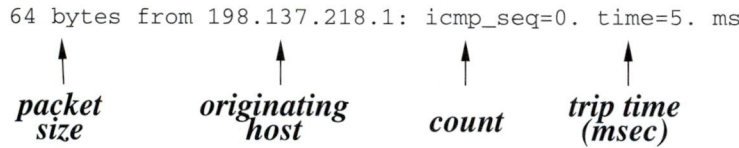

packet size   *originating host*   *count*   *trip time (msec)*

The last item, the trip time, is a reasonable indicator of the status of the connection between the two machines (your local host and the one you are `pinging`). The final display from the command shows a cumulative summary of all the packets sent, where the number of packets sent and received are noted, and, importantly, the percentage of packets lost in the process.

```
----huckleberry PING Statistics----
5 packets transmitted, 5 packets received, 0% packet loss
round-trip (ms)  min/avg/max = 1/1/5
```

This is also a good indicator of the network connection. When the remote host is down, this number will typically be 100%. The last value gives an effective measure of the network load, since, over the time it takes to run the number of packets sent, the average load can change measurably.

7.5.2   Host Processing Load

When a host is up and running, it is often useful to look at what its actual performance is, in terms of how many effective users are running jobs, over a period of time. This can be accomplished with the *uptime* command. The example below shows the format which uptime displays:

```
localhost> uptime
4:26pm up 9:42, 8 users, load average: 0.84, 0.74, 0.62
```

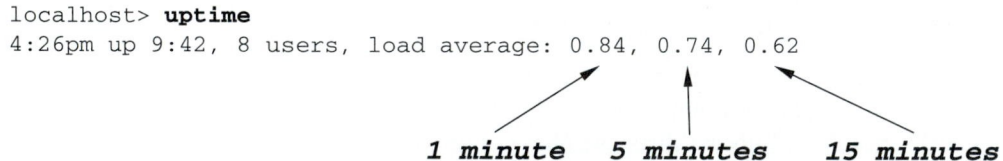

1 minute   5 minutes   15 minutes

There are ten fields in the display. The first field is the current time. The second field tells if the host is "up" (i.e., running). The third field tells how long the host has been up (in this case 9 and 42 minutes). The fourth field tells how many users are active, and the fifth field is a text field (i.e., "users") for the fourth field. The sixth and seventh fields are text fields (i.e., "load" and "average") for the last three fields. Fields eight ⇒ ten show the **load averages** over the last 1, 5, and 15 minutes, where load is measured in the number of users. The following example shows that LOCALHOST cannot display load information for other machines using *ruptime*, because it isn't on a local network, as was seen with the commands rwho and rusers:

```
localhost> ruptime
no hosts!?!
```

The same command, when issued from a workstation on a local network produces a different result and form:

```
huckleberry[6] ruptime
couch        up   6+20:39,      0 users,   load 0.00, 0.00, 0.00
cs           up   6+00:25,      0 users,   load 1.00, 1.00, 1.01
futon        up   5+22:34,      1 user,    load 0.00, 0.00, 0.00
huckleberry  up   3+16:03,      1 user,    load 0.00, 0.00, 0.00
springfield  up 112+13:01,      0 users,   load 0.00, 0.00, 0.00
toaster      up  99+00:32,      1 user,    load 0.00, 0.00, 0.00
walnut       up  24+14:07,      1 user,    load 0.00, 0.00, 0.00
```

There are nine fields in this table. The first field is the name of a host, such as huckleberry. The second field tells whether the host is currently "up." The third field tells how long the host has been up. The "N+" syntax means that the host has been up for "N" days "plus" whatever time follows in hours:minutes format. The fourth field tells how many users are logged on to the host. The fifth field is just the text field (i.e., "user") for the fourth field. The sixth field is the text field (i.e., "load") for the seventh ⇒ ninth fields, which tell what the average load (in users) has been over the last 1, 5, and 15 minutes.

7.6 Remote Processing

The notion of multi-user computing environment is associated with the ability to run many shells at once. The system does not know who the owner of each shell process is, so any particular user can be running processes on any particular machine, and any particular user can be running multiple processes on any machine he/she can log on to. In this section, the different methods whereby a user can run multiple shells or shell commands on remote machines will be introduced. A **remote machine** is any machine other than the one the user is currently logged onto. The notion of running a shell on a machine which is located somewhere other than where the user is located is called **remote processing**.

Remote processing is the essence of a shared resource network, since a user can run processes on machines which are less heavily loaded as well as on the one where they are sitting. In this section, you will learn how to perform three tasks:

- send and receive files with other (remote) hosts
- remote login to or from another host on a network
- create and execute shell commands on remote hosts

7.6.1   Experimenting with Remote Processing

Because you most likely do not have accounts on other machines, and since this chapter is specifically *about* performing work on other machines, do not despair. UNIX does not care, when you issue a command, if you are sitting at the machine you issue the command from. Thus, if you want to test any of the commands you will learn about in this chapter (except anonymous ftp), you can issue the command with the host argument being the machine on which your account resides. For example, if you have an account on the host `foobar.cs.oz.edu`, and you want to experiment with `rcp`, then (as long as you have created a "`.rhosts`" file in your directory) you can issue the following command:

```
localhost> rcp foobar.cs.oz.edu:blah foobar.cs.oz.edu:blech
```

and you should see a duplicate of the file "`blah`" appear as "`blech`" in your home directory. All of the commands in this section can be experimented with this way (i.e., using your own host as a target). Have fun!

7.6.2   File Transfer Protocol

The **File Transfer Protocol**, or *ftp*, is commonly used to transmit files from one machine to another without the use of magnetic tape media. `ftp` is especially useful for single-file (vs. directories) transfers, so it is good to use with the **Tape ARchival** (*tar*) and `compress` utilities. Some of the command syntax for `ftp` is given below, and more details can be found in the man page (`man ftp`).

```
ftp [ -v ] [ -i ] [ host ]
```

The '`-v`' option stands for **verbose mode**, in which case `ftp` will display everything it does. The '`-i`' option turns off interrogation when multiple file transfers are being made (e.g., with `mput` or `mget`). Normally when performing these tasks `ftp` will ask for authorization on each file. If you specify the client host (machine) that `ftp` is to communicate with on the command line, `ftp` immediately attempts to establish a connection to an **ftp server** on that host. Otherwise, it will enter its command interpreter and await instructions from you. When `ftp` is awaiting commands, it prompts you with 'ftp>.' The typical invocation may look as follows:

```
localhost> ftp huckleberry.sfsu.edu
Connected to huckleberry.sfsu.edu
220 huckleberry FTP server (Version 5.18 (NeXT 1.0) Wed Aug 23, 1989) ready.
Name (huckleberry.sfsu.edu:): hodges <CR>                                    ①
331 Password required for hodges.
Password: [MY-PASSWORD]<CR>                                                  ②
230 User hodges logged in.
ftp> ls
200 PORT command successful
150 Opening ASCII mode data connection for file list.

... DIRECTORY LISTING ...

ftp> quit                                                                    ③
221 Goodbye.
```

The user typically is provided with a default login in square brackets, which can be overridden as shown in the example (at item **1**). Then a password request is made and the user completes the login on the remote host (item **2**). After issuing whatever commands the user wants to execute, such as 'ls' in this example, the quit (or bye) ftp command is issued to log off the remote host (item **3**). Some of the more commonly used commands are described in Table 7.2.

Table 7.2: `ftp` Command reference

open HOST	⇔	Establish a connection to the specified host ftp server, HOST
pwd	⇔	Display the name of the current working directory on the remote machine
cd DIR	⇔	Change the working directory to DIR on the remote machine
lcd DIR	⇔	Change the working directory to DIR on the local machine
ls DIR	⇔	Display a directory listing of DIR on the remote machine
!ls DIR	⇔	Display a directory listing of DIR on the local machine
mkdir DIR	⇔	Make a directory DIR on the remote machine
rmdir DIR	⇔	Delete a directory on the remote machine
delete FILE	⇔	Delete the file on the remote machine
get FILE	⇔	Retrieve the file named FILE and store it on the local machine

Table 7.2: `ftp` Command reference (cont)

`mget FILES`	⇔	Retrieve the specified `FILES` from the remote machine; `FILES` can be specified with wildcards
`put FILE`	⇔	Store a local file named `FILE` on the remote machine
`mput FILES`	⇔	Transfer multiple local files (`FILES`) from the current local directory to the current working directory on the remote machine; `FILES` can be specified with wildcards
`send FILE`	⇔	Perform the same functions as put
`status`	⇔	Show the current status of `ftp`
`!`	⇔	Invoke a shell on the local machine
`?command`	⇔	Obtain help for the command
`binary`	⇔	Set the file transfer mode to support binary image transfer
`bye, quit`	⇔	Terminate the `ftp` session with the remote server and exit `ftp`
`close`	⇔	Terminate the `ftp` session with the remote server and return to the `ftp` command interpreter

One of the truly amazing capabilities offered by networked computers is our access to other machines and applications across a network. One such example I will present is **anonymous ftp** which is used to send files to and retrieve files from remote hosts where you do not have an account, usually called **public archives**.

Copying Archived Remote Files

Occasionally you might hear of software databases (perhaps in a newsgroup, in email, or from friends) and want to gain access to the software located there. In other situations you might find yourself looking for useful information on machines at other institutions and other locations. Many machines have an *anonymous* `ftp` capability that enables users without accounts to log in and acquire software. Machines with this capability are generally called *archives*. I have included the protocol for using this utility in the next example.

```
localhost> ftp huckleberry.sfsu.edu
Connected to huckleberry.sfsu.edu.
220 huckleberry FTP server (Version 5.18 (NeXT 1.0) Wed Aug 23, 1989) ready.
Name (huckleberry.sfsu.edu:jhodges): anonymous          ◄─────────── ①
331 Guest login ok, send ident as password.
Password: [jhodges@sfsuvax1.sfsu.edu]   ◄─────────── ②
230 Guest login ok, access restrictions apply.
ftp> ls   ◄─────────── ③
200 PORT command successful.
150 Opening ASCII mode data connection for file list.
bin
etc
pub
.forward
.hidden
.places
226 Transfer complete.
37 bytes received in 0.01 seconds (3.6 Kbytes/s)
ftp> quit
221 Goodbye.
```

In the example above, the ftp prompt is "ftp>," and my responses are shown after these, in bold. What I did was to issue the ftp command with a local machine, huckleberry, as an argument. I already knew this host had a version of "TeX3.0" on it. The procedure is to use the "anonymous" as your user ID (at item **1**) and, when asked for your password, to type in your mail address (i.e., userid and host address). In this case, I typed "jhodges@sf-suvax1.sfsu.edu" (item **2**). It was not echoed because this login is part of the standard login script and expects a password. Once I was accepted, I then listed the available directories (item **3**). Really quite straightforward. In general, anonymous users are given severely restricted access to the machine, usually to specific directories where public software is kept. In the preceding example, the directory I have been given access to is the "pub" directory.

To use anonymous ftp to look around on the network, you must know *where* to look. One way to find out where archives of a particular sort are is through newsgroups, at least this is the way it was done until very recently. If you were interested in a particular topic, and subscribe to the appropriate newsgroup(s), then sooner or later you would see mention of locations where the archives for that topic reside. You could then ftp to the archive and look around. Of course, this method still works, and you can also ask friends who might remember where an archive resides.

Recently an online database has been developed to keep track of ftp sites around the globe, along with servers to query the database from anywhere on the network. The utility is called *archie* and was originally written by Alan

246 Chapter 7 Network Processing

Emtage and Peter Deutsch at McGill university. `archie` has become an invaluable aid to help users around the globe locate and acquire software. It also helps to reduce replication in archives since there is now a consistently updated database of `ftp` sites. `archie` is used at the command line like any UNIX utility. First you have to find out if `archie` is supported on your host. To do so, use the `which` command with "archie" as its argument:

```
localhost> which archie
/usr/local/bin/archie
```

This will work if `archie` is located in any directory in your search path. If not, it may still reside on the system, in which case you might try invoking the man page (`man archie`). If all else fails, you could request assistance from the system administrator.[1] Below is a list of options for using `archie`, followed by a simple session using it.

Table 7.3: `archie` Command reference

-c	⇔	A case sensitive substring search
-e	⇔	An exact string match
-r	⇔	A regular expression search
-s	⇔	A case insensitive substring search
-l	⇔	List one match per line
-t	⇔	Sort inverted by date
-m #	⇔	Specifies the maximum number, #, of hits to return
-h HOST	⇔	Specifies the server HOST
-N#	⇔	Specifies query niceness level (0-35765)

Using these options, you can now access `archie` and locate an archive site. For example, I have decided to look for no more than five (5) sites which support latex. I use the '-m' option to select the number of sites to display, and "LaTeX" is the string I want to search for. Since I did not use an option, the

---

1. Many systems have a "help" newsgroup that is monitored by the system administrator and other interested users. You can send mail to this address if it exists, or you could send mail to "root."

search is based on an exact match. Below is the output from the command.

```
localhost> archie -m 5 LaTeX
Host cnam.cnam.fr
     Location: /pub/TeX/TeX3/TeX3.0
        DIRECTORY drwxrwxr-x        512  May  4 1991   LaTeX
Host emx.cc.utexas.edu
     Location: /pub/mnt/source/tex/tex-3.14/TeX3.14
        DIRECTORY drwxr-xr-x        512  Jan 15 00:00   LaTeX
Host ics.uci.edu
     Location: /mac
        DIRECTORY drwxrwxr-x        512  Aug 17 04:15   LaTeX
Host liasun3.epfl.ch
     Location: /pub/tex/tex3.14-imake202
        DIRECTORY drwxr-xr-x        512  Aug 16 20:15   LaTeX
Host walton.maths.tcd.ie
     Location: /src/TeX/TeX3.14
        DIRECTORY drwxr-xr-x        512  May  8 1991   LaTeX
```

There are three lines in each response, as illustrated by the shaded portion of the response. The first line identifies the host symbolic address on the network, such as `ics.uci.edu`. The second line identifies the directory in which the search item resides, such as "`/mac`." The third line describes the directory in which the search item resides, which should have the search item in its name. This will essentially be the output from '`ls -l`' on the directory.

Bear in mind that `ftp` uses the network and that you should use some discretion about when to transfer files from one site to another. Generally speaking, the later the better. Most users agree that anonymous ftp should be used only during nonprime hours (i.e., 1900 - 0600 hours local time for the remote site, although it might be considerate to select non prime-time hours on both ends of the network, when possible).

7.6.3   Remote Copy

Remote copy is probably more useful than `ftp` in some circumstances, because you needn't actually log on to the remote host to copy a file; however, you must have an account on the target machine. In order to use remote copy, you must have, or create, a file in your home directory named "`.rhosts`." This file must reside on the machine which you wish to log onto, so you must have an account on that machine. The `.rhosts` file consists of a list of entries, each of which has a machine address and a list of userids. Any user/machine combination that exists in your `.rhosts` file can `rlogin` to your account without a password and can use `rcp` to copy files and directories from your account or to your account. As you have probably heard, `.rhosts` files are dangerous for system security, because they allow anyone with access to one of your accounts the potential to log on to other machines easily. However, there are advantages, and *rcp* is one of them.

A .rhosts file must reside in your home directory, and has a line for each user and platform that you want to have access to your account. I have a dummy file below:

```
hobbes.cogent.ucla.edu freebie
fuzz.cogent.ucla.edu zorch
laina.cs.ucla.edu corrigan
huckleberry.sfsu.edu smith
sfsuvax1.sfsu.edu cohen
```

    ↑   ↑

host address   userid list

Note that user "zorch" at UCLA has been given access to the account in which the sample .rhosts file resides when she logs on from the host fuzz but not from other hosts. You may want other users to be able to test software or edit files that belong to you, without the hassle of copying files through other means. One very important thing about a .rhosts file is that it must never be made readable by others, since they might then obtain access to someone who has privileges to your account. They might also be able to break the password of someone who has access to your account even if they cannot break yours. Using remote copy is quite simple, as evidenced by the following session:

```
localhost> rcp -r maui.cs.ucla.edu:/usr/lib/tex/macros sfsuvax1:Texmacros
```

This example illustrates the coping of the entire "macros" directory subtree (i.e., recursively) from the host maui.cs.ucla.edu over to the "Texmacros" directory on the host sfsuvax1. The colon (:) is used after each host as shown in the template below. You need not be logged on to either machine to perform this task, as long as your userid exists on both systems in a .rhosts file:

```
rcp flags host1:path1 host2:path2
```

When you really get rolling with UNIX you will probably use rlogin and rcp all the time. It just turns out that, when you have lots of work to do, you end up using all kinds of machines to do it, and rlogin enables you to execute shell commands on any machine as though you are sitting at the machine directly. telnet is similar to rlogin, but I will present a session anyway.

7.6.4 Remote Login

rlogin stands for "Remote LOGIN." When you issue the command, the system looks into a file called "/etc/hosts" (or equivalent) for the host (machine) that you name. If you have a .rhosts file and entry on that machine, then you are logged in as though you had logged into that machine directly. If you do not have a .rhosts file and entry on that machine, then you are asked for your password on that machine, and, if you provide it correctly, you are logged on. I will first show you how to use it, and then I will describe some of the commands:

```
localhost> rlogin sfsuvax1.sfsu.edu -l jhodges
last login: Thu April 18 17:36:16 from huckleberry.sfsu
ULTRIX V4.1 (Rev.52) System #2: Thu Jan 17 11:53:02 PST 1991
You have mail.
sfsuvax1>
```

This command could have been issued without the '-l jhodges' and it would have worked, but it would have asked for a password. For the purposes of this example I created a .rhosts file. With that file I was able to log in without using a password. Notice that, as soon as I execute the command, my .login and .cshrc on the host sfsuvax1 execute and the new shell is run with the standard output on my local terminal. Once you are logged on to the remote host, you can perform any task that you can perform from that account when logged in directly. Remember that the shell scripts which are run, and hence your path variable, etc., will be those on the target machine.

7.6.5 telnet

telnet is very similar to both rlogin and ftp. The functionality is the same as rlogin, and the syntax is very similar to ftp. The primary difference between telnet and rlogin is that no .rhosts file is used/required for telnet. On the other hand, you cannot use rcp (or rsh) either. When you use telnet, the entire login script will be executed, so you will be prompted for both your ID and password. Consider the sample session and commands shown on the next page.

```
localhost> telnet sfsuvax1
Trying 130.212.10.102...
Connected to sfsuvax1.sfsu.edu.
Escape character is '^]'.
Ultrix-32 V3.1B (Rev. 10) (sfsuvax1.sfsu.edu)
login: jhodges <CR>
Password: <MY PASSWORD> <CR>
Last login: Thu Apr 18 17:37:14 from huckleberry.sfsu
ULTRIX V4.1 (Rev. 52) System #2:
Thu Jan 17 11:53:02 PST 1991
You have mail.
sfsuvax1[1]
```

Should you *not* succeed in logging on to the machine of choice, `telnet` will communicate with you with a 'telnet>' prompt similar to that of `ftp`. In such a case the following commands will be useful:

Table 7.4: `telnet` **Command reference**

open HOST	⟺	Open a connection to the named host, HOST
close	⟺	Close a `telnet` session and return to telnet command mode
quit	⟺	Close any open `telnet` session and exit `telnet`
status	⟺	Show the current status of `telnet`

7.6.6 Remote Shell Commands

The *rsh* command, or "**remote sh**ell," is the same as `rlogin`, except that you use `rsh` to execute *single* commands rather than to open a shell. Instead of logging you on to the host and providing you with a command shell, `rsh` gains access to the machine, executes your command, displays whatever output is associated with the command on your local terminal, and quits.

```
localhost> rsh sfsuvax1 -l jhodges ls
F90/
Mail/
README.TeX3.0*
TeX3.0/
TeX3.0.tar*
bin/
core*
.
.
.
localhost>
```

Notice that I have provided the remote host name, the account which I have access to, and the command to execute. To use `rlogin` and `rsh`, you will need to have a `.rhosts` file on the remote machine with an entry for you, because there is no request for a password from the shell using this utility. Also note that, after the command has executed, control is returned to the shell on `localhost`.

7.7 File System Management

All network users have the responsibility to maintain their accounts in such a way as to optimize resources for all users. This means that you should be able to clean up after yourself and back up your files regularly. To do so, you must be able to generate statistics on your local host (where your directory is located), as well as network-wide. In general, you should strive to eliminate files in your directory that are unneeded, such as binaries not being used regularly or, if the binaries are being used regularly, the source files. You generally do not need both at the same time. As an example, latex files ending with ".aux," ".log," ".bbl," and ".dvi" can be removed since they are produced as a result of tex compilation. These and other commonsense guidelines have been discussed already. In this section, you will be introduced to utilities for obtaining information about your disk space allocation, your usage of disk space, the system overall usage of disk space, and two utilities for managing your personal file system.

- Account allocation
- Disk free space
- Disk usage
- File and directory archival
- File compression

7.7.1 Account Allocation

Each account can potentially be allocated a specific disk space limit. Not all system administrators invoke disk space limits, and, when they are used, the amount of disk space allocated to accounts varies with institution, with department, and with users. There are two important things to remember about account allocations (or **quotas**): (1) that you can determine what your quota is and current usage with the `quota` command, and (2) you can possibly get your allocation increased if you can justify it.

The `quota` command is invoked under different circumstances. You may want to see how close you are to your limit before trying to transfer a large file on to your account. You might also want to check your quote before executing a job which might exceed your quota, because you may lose some of your work. The easiest way to find out is to issue the command.

`quota [user]`

---

where user represents a userid and is an optional argument. When the command is issued without a user argument, the default is your own userid, as illustrated below:

```
localhost> quota

Disc quotas for jhodges (uid 326):
   Filsys current   quota  limit  #warns    files  quota  limit  #warns    ①
   /usr/f1   94474  95000  100000            4438      0      0             ②
   /usr/cp2     19  95000  100000              10      0      0
```

`quota` will return a table showing what your allocation is and how it is being used on the various file systems your account current has disk space usage. Generally an account has a quota and a limit which is generally set to 5-10% beyond your quota. If you exceed your quota, then you will be notified at the terminal and you will not be allowed to perform tasks that would increase your disk space usage.

Table 7.5: `quota` Field description

Filesys	⇔	The file system for which allocation is being reported
current	⇔	The current disk space usage on this file system (in 1024 byte blocks)
quota	⇔	The user's quota on this file system
limit	⇔	The maximum disk space limit for user on this file system
#warns	⇔	The number of warnings that have been posted to the user
files	⇔	The number of files using the current disk space

7.7.2 Display Free Disk Space

Users can determine the current status of mounted drives on the local host with the `df` command. A **mounted device** is a peripheral device, such as a disk drive or a tape drive, which the computer knows how to address by associating with it a device file and a local directory. Those interested in computer architecture are encouraged to take a course specializing in the topic.

`df` displays a line for each mounted file system, telling how much space it has and how much space is available, as shown in Table 7.6.

Table 7.6: `df` Field description

Filesystem node	⇔	Location and name of associated device file
Total kbytes	⇔	Total (unformatted) space for the device
Kbytes used	⇔	How much of the space has been used
kbytes free	⇔	How much space is available
% used	⇔	How much space has been used as a percentage of the total space
Mounted on	⇔	File system directory associated with the device

A sample usage of the *df* command is shown below:

```
localhost> df
Filesystem    Total      kbytes    kbytes    %
node          kbytes     used      free      used    Mounted on
/dev/ra0a      15551      7514      6482     54%     /                      ①
/dev/ra0d     201919    127494     54234     70%     /usr
/dev/ra0e     201919     15061    166667      8%     /var
/dev/ra0h     257407    168621     63046     73%     /usr/users
/dev/ra1a       7423         3      6678      0%     /usr/ra1a
/dev/ra1d     201919     21216    160512     12%     /usr/s1
/dev/ra1e     201919     14029    167699      8%     /usr/s2
/dev/ra1h     265575    184084     54934     77%     /usr/cp1
/dev/ra1f     404127    299980     63735     82%     /usr/f1               ②
/dev/ra2a       7423        10      6671      0%     /usr/ra2a
/dev/ra2d     201919       597    181131      0%     /tmp                  ③
/dev/ra2e     201919    101245     80483     56%     /usr/f2
/dev/ra2h     265575    189453     49565     79%     /dba
```

The first entry in the table always represents the device file and file system for the host from which you are issuing the command. Thus, the host is associated with the device "`/dev/ra0a`." All devices which are attached to (mounted on) the host are associated with such an entry. Notice, on the far right, the column titled "`Mounted on`." This entry means that the device which is associated with device file `/dev/ra0a` is mounted on the local directory "`/`" (item **1**). Thus the drive associated with the device file `/dev/`

ra0a is the **root disk**, or **root volume**. The second entry in the table indicates how much space the device *can* hold, i.e., its capacity. The value is measured in kilobytes (i.e., thousands of bytes) and usually refers to an unformatted capacity rather than an actual (i.e., usable) capacity. In this case, the slash disk (/dev/ra0a) has 15,551 kilobytes, or 15 megabytes of total storage space, of which 6,482 bytes are free (i.e., 46%).

By issuing a pwd command, you can determine on which device your home directory resides. Then you can look in the df table to see how much space is available on the device that includes that directory. The third column tells how much space, in kilobytes, is currently being used on the device. For example, the "/dev/ralf" device (item **2**), on which my directory resides (/usr/f1), has a total capacity of 404,127 kilobytes (i.e., 404 Megabytes), and 299,980 kilobytes (300 Meg) are being used. The fourth column tells how many kilobytes are still available, and the fifth column gives that value as a percentage of the total disk space on the device. Notice that these numbers do not add up. When a device is formatted, some of its space (e.g., say 10%) is generally reserved, and this accounts for the discrepancy. When the utilization reaches 100%, no users will be able to execute any commands requiring the usage of additional space until some files are deleted. The last entry identifies which directory subtree is associated with the device on the system. This is commonly referred to as the **mounting point** for the device. All directories below the one mentioned in this entry physically reside on the device associated with the device file in the first entry. This is how you will find "your" device with the pwd command.

Finally, note (item **3**) that there is a physically separate device on this file system associated with the "/tmp" directory. This space is writable by all users, but is for temporary, rather than permanent, storage.

7.7.3   Disk Usage

du is similar to df insomuch as it tells how much storage is being used. du stands for "display amount of **D**isk **U**sage" and will display the disk space taken up by a local directory. For example, if you want to know how much space your home directory uses, type the following:

```
localhost> du ~
```

An example is shown on the following page for the directory of the user "jhodges".

```
localhost> du
2           /usr/f1/jhodges/bin
171         /usr/f1/jhodges/tmac
9           /usr/f1/jhodges/mail-elsewhere
120         /usr/f1/jhodges/TeX3.0/docs/manual
        .
        .
        .
3           /usr/f1/jhodges/TeX3.0/usr/spool
15040       /usr/f1/jhodges/TeX3.0/usr
15167       /usr/f1/jhodges/TeX3.0                          ①
2           /usr/f1/jhodges/News
27551       /usr/f1/jhodges/AKCL
728         /usr/f1/jhodges/Mail
1067        /usr/f1/jhodges/lib
33          /usr/f1/jhodges/F90
362         /usr/f1/jhodges/Texmacros
2649        /usr/f1/jhodges/Manual-in-LaTeX
31654       /usr/f1/jhodges/Archive-TEX
11965       /usr/f1/jhodges/Code
3           /usr/f1/jhodges/MX-TESTS
34          /usr/f1/jhodges/LATEX-TESTS
91746       /usr/f1/jhodges
```

In this example, I have spared you the entire list. du will display an entry for each subdirectory below the directory where the command was issued. The display will use full paths. Thus, the "TeX3.0" directory is listed as "/usr/f1/jhodges/TeX3.0" (at item **1**). The du command displays directories from the inside out, or deepest to shallowest. Thus, the last term in the display of any particular directory will show the space used by that directory subtree. For example, the last line of the TeX3.0 directory (item **1**) has as its first argument the value "15167," which stands for 15,167 disk blocks,[1] or 15+ megabytes. Each of the following entries shows the value for the home directory (the others were omitted for the sake of brevity). The last entry is the space used by the directory originally called with the command (tilde expands to "/usr/f1/jhodges"), which is a soaring 91+ megabytes. This is an excellent example of a **disk hog**. Not a nice term, and maybe not so deserved, since this I am responsible for the port of a number of utilities to the host SFSUVAX1. You can use the du command to keep tabs on your own directories and maintain them as necessary by deleting files or decreasing their size with the tar and compress utilities presented in the next section.

---

1. This means that the block size on this device is 1024 bytes, or 1 kilobyte.

7.7.4 File and Directory Archival

I have noted that `ftp` is useful for sending a file or files. However, often you will be interested in sending large files or directories over to a remote machine. As `ftp` can take a while to send large files, and cannot send directories at all, except file-by-file, one must use other methods with `ftp` to achieve such ends. **Tape ARchival** (`tar`) is a method originally designed for efficient archiving of files onto magnetic medium. It is also commonly used to move directories from one machine to another. The standard form for `tar` is

```
tar key [ blocksize ] [ name ] files
```

where the keys are described below and the blocksize and name arguments are defined better in the `tar` man page. Generally, the use of `tar` will be as follows:

```
localhost> tar cvf tarfile.tar filenames
localhost> tar xvf tarfile.tar
```

The first command will take the files (or directories) and put them all onto a single file "`tarfile.tar`." The 'c' key means **create** an archive. The second line will then take them out of the tar file and place them in their same order, ownership, and protection starting in the now-present location. The 'x' key means to **extract** the contents of the archive. A sample session is shown below, followed by a description of the keys that can be used. It should be noted for emphasis that the 'v' in the above examples is a **verbose** key which echoes everything that **tar** does. The 'f' key tells `tar` that the next argument will be the name of the `tar` file to write the files to.

```
localhost> cd tmac; ls
ditroff              tmac.Xref.ieee       tmac.ayday       tmac.sdisp
pic                  tmac.Xrefs           tmac.bib         tmac.skeep
psroff               tmac.Xtra            tmac.cp          tmac.srefs
tmac.Xtras           tmac.e               tmac.syb         tmac.vcat
tmac.Franz           tmac.a               tmac.imagen      tmac.vgrind
tmac.X               tmac.an              tmac.os
tmac.XP              tmac.an.new          tmac.r
tmac.Xalg            tmac.an6n            tmac.s
tmac.Xref.acm        tmac.an6t            tmac.scover
localhost> tar cvf tmac.tar *                                           ①
a ditroff 272 blocks
a pic 272 blocks
a psroff 18 blocks
a tmac.Franz 38 blocks                                                  ②
a tmac.X 16 blocks
a tmac.XP 2 blocks
a tmac.Xalg 2 blocks
a tmac.Xref.acm 5 blocks
.
.
.
localhost>
```

Because the 'v' option was used in this command (at item **1**), each file is displayed on the monitor as it is being archived. Notice that for every file archived there is an 'a' in the first column (item **2**), followed by the name of the file. A number follows the file name, and this number represents the size of the file, in blocks. When the command has completed, every file in the "tmac" directory is now copied in the file "tmac.tar." The files are not removed, copies have been made and put into tmac.tar. Also note that I used the wildcard (*) to denote all items in the directory. Now I will create a directory on the host TOASTER, to demonstrate how to extract, or "**untar**," files using tar.

```
localhost> ftp toaster
(... other responses omitted ...)
ftp> mkdir tmac                                                    ①
257 MKD command successful.
ftp> cd tmac
250 CWD command successful.
ftp> pwd
257 "/Users/hodges/tmac" is current directory.
ftp> binary                                                        ②
200 Type set to I.
ftp> put tmac.tar                                                  ③
200 PORT command successful.
150 Opening BINARY mode data connection for tmac.tar.
226 Transfer complete.
local: tmac.tar remote: tmac.tar
237497 bytes sent in 1.6 seconds (1.4e+02 Kbytes/s)
ftp> ls
200 PORT command successful.
150 Opening ASCII mode data connection for file list.
tmac.tar
226 Transfer complete.
12 bytes received in 0 seconds (0.012 Kbytes/s)
ftp> quit
221 Goodbye.
localhost>
```

In this example, I ftp to the host, create a new directory for my files (at item **1**), and cd to that directory. Notice (item **2**) that I used the **binary** option with ftp. I find that this option provides a more reliable file transfer, even when the file isn't binary. If the file *is* binary and you send it in ASCII mode, then you end up with a **corrupted file** and you may be able to extract some, but perhaps not all, of the files in the tarfile. Once in binary mode I issue the put command (item **3**) to transfer the tarfile. Now, after ftp logs me out, I go rlogin in to toaster (procedure not shown, but notice the different C shell prompt) and I can type the following.

```
toaster[1] cd tmac; ls
tmac.tar
toaster[2] tar xvf tmac.tar
x ditroff, 139264 bytes, 272 tape blocks
x pic, 139264 bytes, 272 tape blocks
x psroff, 9184 bytes, 18 tape blocks
x tmac.Franz, 19444 bytes, 38 tape blocks
x tmac.X, 8113 bytes, 16 tape blocks
x tmac.XP, 841 bytes, 2 tape blocks
x tmac.Xalg, 639 bytes, 2 tape blocks
x tmac.Xref.acm, 2317 bytes, 5 tape blocks
.
.
.
toaster[3]
```

When I logged on to `toaster`, I created the directory where I wanted to place the files. Had I created the tar file with embedded directories, they would be created on the fly when I **untar** the file on `toaster`. Then I change directories to "`tmac`" and untarred the file. Here are some of the keys used with tar on a common basis:

Table 7.7: `tar` Options command reference

c	⇔	Create a new archive
t	⇔	List the names of all the files in the archive
x	⇔	Extract the named items from the archive; if one of the items is a directory, tar recursively extracts the directory and all files and subdirectories it contains
f FNAME	⇔	The key must be followed by a space and the name, FNAME, of the archive you want tar to read from or write to
v	⇔	This option makes tar display the name of each file it archives or extracts, preceded by a function letter that indicates what it is doing with the file

One nifty thing about `tar` is that you can copy the contents of a user directory on one file system (disk) to that of another. The syntax follows, but you can find the example in the man page for `tar`.

```
cd fromdir; tar cvf - . | (cd todir; tar xv - )
```

In this command, the first part of the command gets you to the directory you want to archive. The second part of the command issues the tar command to create and archive with the 'f' option, but the file selected is '-' which stands for the standard output. The files selected are those in the " . " directory. Now the results are piped into another command sequence that starts with locating to the new directory and ends by extracting the archive from the standard input. Note that the verbose option is being used throughout so the user can watch the progress of the transfer.

7.7.5   File Compression

Every once in a while, you look at a tarfile and it looks enormous, or you decide that you are simply using too much disk space and want to cut down to be conscientious. This is a time for file compression. *compress* compresses files to a more compact version, and replaces the file name with "**file.Z**" if the compression resulted in a smaller file. For example, we could try to compress "tmac.tar" and see what happens, but first we should take a look at its original size so that we can tell if anything good results from the application of compress:

```
localhost> ls -l tmac.*
-rw-r--r--  1 jhodges     471040Apr 18 14:19 tmac.tar
localhost> compress tmac.tar
localhost> ls -l tmac-*
-rw-r--r--  1 jhodges     237497Apr 18 14:19 tmac.tar.Z
```

The original copy of tmac.tar is 470K bytes and the compressed version is 237K bytes. You can see that using compress amounts to quite a savings in space. The next question that you might ask is "HOW DO I GET MY FILES BACK!" Simple: type *uncompress* tmac.tar at the C shell prompt as follows:

```
localhost> uncompress tmac.tar
localhost>
```

Notice that you do not need to provide the " . Z," as it is the expected suffix for uncompress. The tar and compress utilities are naturals for file archives, since it is far easier to transfer a single, smaller file over the network and then use uncompress and tar, locally, to restore the archive.

7.8 Exercises and Sample Quiz Questions

7.8.1 Exercises

Exercise 1   Using your own directory as a source and target, try the `rlogin`, `telnet`, `ftp`, `rcp`, and `rsh` commands. Find an anonymous `ftp` site and bring something *small* back to your local host.

Exercise 2   Issue the `who`, `rwho`, `uptime`, `ruptime`, and `w` commands. Note their differences.

Exercise 3   Practice file system management by tarring and compressing a file and a directory, and then reversing the process.

7.8.2 Sample Quiz Questions

Problem 1   List three different ways to find out information about a user whose real name is Dr. Jerk Foobar, assuming Dr. Foobar is logged on.

Problem 2   Explain what `tar`, `compress`, and `uncompress` are used for and why. What are the options to

- create an archive
- view the contents of an archive
- extract an archive

Problem 3   What is the minimum set of commands, and their correct order, to anonymously log onto a host named `sumex-aim.stanford.edu`, retrieve a file in binary format, and exit?

Problem 4   Approximately how much space is saved using `compress`.

Problem 5   What UNIX command do you use to list the contents of a `tar` archive named cl3.1.2.tar?

Problem 6   You are logged onto the LOCALHOST. You have an account on the host `fuzz@cs.blowtorch.edu`, and have a ".`rhosts`" file. You want to retrieve the files in "`/usr/lib/tex/inputs`" to a directory called "texinputs" at `localhost`. What command(s) do you issue from your terminal and `fuzz`?

Problem 7   Which of the following provides the most explicit information about a user and what they are doing? Which is the fastest way to find out if they are logged on? Which is the fastest to find out how long they have been idle?

- who
- rwho
- users
- rusers
- w
- finger
- last

Problem 8   What does file system management mean and how can you apply the notion of file system management in your day to day use of a shared resource environment? Which four utilities are particulary useful in this regard and why are they useful?

Problem 9   You are working with a Computer Science faculty member to port an X server to the VAX. The `tared` and `compressed` file takes up 6 Megabytes, and the `uncompressed` directory uses 16+ Megabytes. Assuming your faculty member has access to these filesystems,

- Which filesystem(s) in the two listings below would you *least* likely want to try to bring the server up on?
- Why?
- Which UNIX command produced these listings?

A:

Filesystem node	Total kbytes	kbytes used	kbytes free	% used	Mounted on
/dev/raom	15551	7514	6482	54%	/
/dev/raoa	7423	3	6678	0%	/usr/raoa

B:

Filesystem node	Total kbytes	kbytes used	kbytes free	% used	Mounted on
/dev/ratn	201919	597	181131	0%	/tmp
/dev/raon	265575	189453	49565	79%	/non1

Problem 10   You are logged onto the SFSUVAX1, doing some minor processing task, when the time between what you type and what gets echoed on the screen goes **way** up. After a few minutes, reponse time returns to normal, only to become sluggish again, and again, over the entire period you are logged on. Please identify

- What type of problem you think it is
- *How* you would identify what type of problem this is
- What one could do to avoid this from happening in the future

7.9 Recommended Reading

UNIX References

Sobell, Mark, [1989]. *A Practical Guide to the UNIX System*, 2nd Ed., Benjamin-Cummins, Redwood City, CA.

Advanced UNIX Principles

Rochkind, Marc J. [1985]. *Advanced UNIX Programming*, Prentice Hall, Englewood Cliffs, NJ.

PART II
Programming Languages and ANSI C

The intent of this part of the book is to introduce the student to the concepts associated with programming. You are not expected to become fluent in C, nor are you expected to become a good programmer by writing a few simple programs. However, you *are* expected to learn how to write a program, which includes proper code presentation, debugging, and function. You are also expected to learn the concepts in programming that are applicable to any programming language. No aspect of the C programming language is presented in very much detail. Generally, a topic is introduced that covers a broad range of programming situations. An example is discussed that illustrates how that topic fits into the programming environment and how it is used. Throughout the chapter the example will be modified to add to its functionality. Where alternative approaches are possible, the alternatives will be tabulated so that you can modify the example code to experiment with them. By the end of each chapter, you should have a few template examples that enable you to construct simple working programs that exhibit behavior commensurate with the topics leading up to and including those introduced in the chapter.

Chapter 8
Introduction to
C Programming

8.1 Introduction and Scope

Programming is an empirical skill of writing instructions to control a computer. Programming is both rewarding and fun, but you will never understand a programming language without writing and correcting (i.e., debugging) computer programs. In this chapter, the C programming language will be introduced, along with methods for writing, compiling, executing, and debugging simple programs. In subsequent chapters, more complex notions will be introduced which will enable you to write programs that can perform more elaborate tasks. The following topics will be covered in this chapter:

- Programming languages
- The C programming language
- A simple C program
- C language operators

At the conclusion of this chapter, you should be able to look at a C program and understand how and why it is laid out. You should know how the file is named, how a compiler is invoked to translate it, and what the executable file will be called. You should understand the differences between syntax and semantics of a programming language, and you should know some of the syntax and semantics of C. Finally, you should know how to write simple C programs that make use of simple expressions and variable assignments.

8.2 Programming Languages

A **programming language** is a set of rules for evaluating instructions to a computer. A **computer program** is a set of instructions (like a recipe) the computer follows to perform a specific task. An **instruction** can be as simple as a variable assignment or a call to a function. **Expressions** are combinations of operators and their operands (data). A programming language consists of operations on data, and the rules for combining and evaluating the resulting expressions. The instructions which comprise a computer program can be expressed in different languages just as the thoughts I am conveying to you can be expressed in different natural (spoken) languages. The underlying concepts are the same, but the grammar and style for expressing concepts change. The essence of programming is to understand the underlying concepts that are being expressed, and to recognize how they are captured in any particular programming language.

There are different kinds of programming languages. The computer hardware manipulates electrical signals, and the instructions which tell the computer what to do with electrical signals are called **machine language**. *Machine language* is appropriately called a **low-level** language. It is both awkward and unnecessary to communicate in low-level languages. Most programmers communicate with the computer with **high-level** languages such as PASCAL, C, LISP, FORTRAN, or COBOL.

The computer cannot execute the instructions of these programming languages directly. They must first be translated into low-level machine language. The translation process is called **compilation**. The translation is performed by another program, called a **compiler**, which reads the expressions from the high-level language, interprets them, and rewrites them in machine language. The executable expressions of a computer program are called *code*. A program in a high-level programming language has two code components: **source code** and **object code**. Both source code and object code reside in files. The source code file is the editable version of the program and is the file that is compiled. The object code file is the translation produced by the compiler, and, for smaller programs, is often the executable version of the program.

8.2.1 Programming Language Syntax and Semantics

A programming language evaluates expressions by first recognizing the symbols which comprise expressions. Once recognized, the symbols can be clustered together into meaningful units, which the computer can then execute. The symbols and their organization into expressions is called the language's **syntax** and **grammar**, whereas the interpretation and meaning of expressions is the language's **semantics**. Writing a successful computer program requires an understanding of the language's syntax and semantics.

Grammar and Syntax

The compiler must read a program according to specific and consistent rules. These rules are called *grammar* rules. If the compiler is able to read the data, it can then use these rules to construct, or **parse**, the data into recognizable expressions, interpret their meaning, and continue the translation. To parse expressions, the language expects certain symbols to have specific meanings. For example, the language must be able to determine when the end of an expression occurs. It must recognize the *end of expression* character. Likewise, each language has a specific character sequence which it recognizes as a *comment*, after which it does not try to parse meaning. The interpretation and order of symbols is a language's *syntax*. Programs which violate a language's syntax rules will not compile and will produce errors. Programs with syntax errors cannot be executed because the compiler never succeeds in creating the object code file.

Structured Languages

A **structured** language has an extensive syntax and grammar. The more structured a programming language, the more grammar rules it will have. As a result, the errors (or **bugs**) detected by the compiler during translation may be easier to find and **debug** (resolve). The opposite is true of unstructured languages; however, their advantage is a freedom from strict rules for how expressions are presented. Both structured and unstructured programming languages have their advantages, but this is an issue which is best addressed by a course in programming language design. C is considered a structured programming language, because it has a rich syntax, although it is less structured than, say, PASCAL.

8.3 The C Programming Language

C is a versatile language, and its structure enables **portability** between hardware platforms, meaning that programs written in C can be used on different computers with little or no modification. We will be using examples based on the ANSI C standard. Although ANSI C is not currently the most portable version of the language, because it is relatively new, it may become the most portable version in the future. The language will be introduced by looking at some simple examples which illustrate some of the language's syntax in proper presentation format (called **style**). Following the examples will be an introduction to C operators, program compiling, execution, and debugging.

- Writing a C program
- Basic syntax of a C program
- Compiling a C program
- Executing a C program

Before we begin, it should be reiterated that C, like UNIX, is **case sensitive**. This means that lowercase and uppercase characters are unique and are not interpreted as having the same meaning in any context. For example, an identifier such as "Total" is different from "TOTAL" or "total." When you use a variable name, you must be very careful to reuse it exactly the way it was originally used.

8.3.1   Writing C Programs

Programming style concerns how a program is presented visually, as opposed to how it executes. Style includes comments, format, and object naming conventions, none of which affects how a program executes. The purpose of style guidelines is to make programs easier to read, so that programs can be used properly, fixed, updated, and rewritten in different languages by different people at different times. Consider the following properly written program, "UNIX/Ch8/First.c," which is nothing more than comment lines and an empty program:

Ch8

Figure 8.1:   Use of input parameters in First.c

```
/*********************************************************/
/* FILE:       First.c                               */   ①
/*                                                   */
/* AUTHOR:     J.B. Hodges                           */
/* DATE:       August, 1993                          */
/* FUNCTION:   NONE                                  */
/* APPROACH:   NA                                    */
/* COMMENTS:   Demonstrates the use of banner comments */
/*             for program documentation.           */
/*********************************************************/

int                                                       ②
main(void)                                                ③
{                                                         ④

   return (0);                                            ⑤
}                                                         ⑥
```

This example program does nothing at all, but it illustrates what is minimally necessary to start programming. The numbered items in the right margin have nothing to do with the program and will be used to identify lines where comments are being made.

Banner Comments

Even an empty program should have some statement indicating what it is intended for. Although it is not a formal component of a computer program, a program's **documentation** plays a crucial role in how the program is presented. In the program in Fig. 8.1, item (**1**) is called a **banner comment**, and is comprised of a series of global comments. Every programming language has a mechanism for making a comment, which is a line of text that is not parsed or evaluated in any way by the compiler. In C, comments are delimited by **/*** at the beginning and ***/** and the end, and can span more than one line. The banner comment shown has comment opening and closing characters on each line. This is partly for readability, as the reader need not search for the end of the comment, and for security, since the programmer can delete a line without accidentally removing a comment's beginning or ending.

The banner itself contains information which documents the program's design and implementation. There are different kinds of banners: main function or program banners, function banners, header file banners, etc. Each banner documents the aspects of the program specific to its associated procedural component. A list of information which is commonly placed in a main and other function banner comments is shown below. In general, the more information that is provided in the banner, the easier it will be later to understand what a program was intended to do and how it was done.

FILE: The most obvious part of the banner should be the name of the program or file. In the example above, the program is named after the file in which the source code resides, `"First.c"`

FILE LOCATION: It is easy to lose files, and it is often a good idea to identify the location in the banner, in case someone has a hard copy but not the soft copy.

VERSION and **DATE**: When many iterations of a program exist, then version number and modification date are important data to maintain in the banner.

AUTHOR (account ID): The person who designs and writes a program should always get credit for it. The account ID is only important to locate the files later.

CLASS and **INSTRUCTOR**: This is clearly academically motivated; however, the same mechanism could just as easily work for department, etc.

CREDITS: If an algorithm or code segment is borrowed from another programmer, it is only common courtesy to give them credit for their work.

PURPOSE: What the program is supposed to do, and should be a component of every banner comment. Purpose, or function, is generally what the program takes as input and what it produces as output.

METHODOLOGY (algorithms/theories used): What the program does and how it is accomplished need not be differentiated in simple programs.

In complicated programs, the mechanisms invoked to achieve a program's function may not be at all obvious and should be documented.

FORMULAS: Where appropriate, it is much easier to follow someone's source code if the equations/logic being implemented are documented up front. It is also good to cite where the equations were found. Otherwise, even the author may forget what is being implemented and where it was found, making corrections, updates, and extensions difficult.

VARIABLES and **PARAMETERS**: A parameter is an input/output variable which is specific to a function. When the primary program banner is created, the main function's variables should be declared and described. When a function banner is created, the function's parameters should be identified as input, output, or input/output parameters in addition to their declaration and description. It is better to describe variables/parameters in a banner than inline because it reduces clutter and all the documentation is in one place.

IMPLEMENTATION NOTES: Even mentioning the methodology or algorithms used to implement a function may not be explicit enough to remember how a program was developed, so specific comments on the implementation may be appropriate.

USAGE: In function banners, a sample function call could save a lot of time later on. Programmers often forget how a function was supposed to be used, so providing an example of its use on legal data, and naming the function(s) which call it, is often later appreciated. One way to provide a usage comment is to provide the calling function (say, in square brackets) followed by a sample function call with real arguments.

A banner should be obvious and clear. A box is used in the example banners in this text to clearly distinguish documentation from source code, and the horizontal lines of asterisks provide clear boundaries between these sections, making the documentation and the associated source code easy to locate.

There are actually two types of comments, of which banner comments are used for documentation. There are also **inline** comments which you will see soon, which are embedded within the source code, often for debugging purposes. Inline comments can be problematic in C, because the language doesn't support comment nesting (i.e., comments within comments). If you have comments inside the source code, and you decide to **comment out** (i.e. block out) a section of the source code, then you have to specifically edit out the comment characters within the block. By placing as many comments into banners as possible, much of this type of problem can be avoided.

Program Blocks

Every C program is comprised of a main function component and additional function components when appropriate. The main function is a required component of every C program and coordinates the procedural elements of the program. In every other respect main is like any other function. A **function** is a structure which performs a task, whose definition is semantically comprised of three component *blocks*: (1) a header, (2) declarations, and (3) statements. The **header** block is used as an interface to other programs or functions through argument passing. The **declarations** block identifies the objects and processes which will be used. The **statement** block consists of the expressions which will be executed by the program. Although the simple program presented above will do nothing, it is a legal C program: it has a single main function which has a header, declaration, and statement block.

Item (**2**) in Fig. 8.1, "int," in this case on a line by itself, is a **declaration**. A declaration is a definition of what type of value a variable or function can take on. Every object or function in C can have a type. An object, such as a number or a character, always has a type. For example, an integer is the type int, and a real number is the type double. A function in C is a procedural construct, like a program, which can be called with arguments and can return a value. In mathematics, square root is a function which takes a number and returns its square root. A C function works the same way, and the language needs to know what kind of value will be returned. The reason is that C functions, like square root, can be embedded in expressions. In mathematics, the human interprets the result of the square root and (hopefully) knows whether its use makes sense in the expression. In C programming, the value returned by a function may not be appropriate for the expression it is embedded in, and this can be checked during compilation to help the programmer find errors. The int before "main" simply means that main is a kind of function that will return an integer value.

Item (**3**), the line that says "main(void)" is the main function's **header**. As mentioned, the header identifies how a function interacts with other functions. It is done through what is called its **parameter list**. The string "main" identifies this as the primary or organizational function of the program and is *always* required in a C program. main organizes other components in the program and interfaces to other programs. The string, "main," must appear as it is, and there can be space between it and the open parenthesis, although not shown that way in the figure. The set of parentheses next to main delimits the parameter list. There is a single item void in this particular parameter list. A void in a parameter list is simply a statement that there are no parameters for the function. It is a matter of style. Neither a void as a declaration, nor a void in the parameter list is required by the language semantics. However; both make sense because they declare to the compiler, and to anyone who reads the program source code what the programmer's original intent was, something which is often lost in the documentation.

Items (**4**) and (**6**), the open and close curly braces (`{` and `}`) comprise the statement block for the sample program. Although the only expression in this segment is a return statement, this is still a legal statement block. You will see the use of statement blocks like this when stubbing is discussed in Chapter 9.

Each function can return a single value to the function or environment from which it was called, as specified by a `return` statement. Item (**5**) is a `return` statement, and specifies what value will be returned by the function `main`. Since no function called `main`, the value is returned to the environment which called the program, namely the UNIX command shell. This particular `return` statement returns a value of 0, which is (and must be) consistent with the `int` (i.e., integer) type associated with the function's definition. The value of 0 is chosen because the information sent back to the operating system is often used as an error function, to signify whether or not the program executed successfully. Operating sytems will vary in what value (e.g., 0, 1, negative integer) is associated with "success." In general, we will adhere to using a `return` statement in all example programs, if only to remind the programmer that `main` is itself a function. I will use 0 to signify success in main return statements and, where appropriate to the interpretation of a return statement of an embedded function, I will use a 1, because C views 1 as a "true" logical value.

A sequence of statements is often grouped together functionally, called a **functional context**. A sequence of executable statements is called a **compound** statement. In C, the beginning and ending of a functional context, such as compound statement sequences, are marked with curly braces (`{` `}`). The open curly braces after the "`main`" function header denotes the beginning of the context of the function, and is balanced at the end of the context. In a functional context, the closing brace marks the end of the function.

Because this program is not intended to do anything, we will not show it being compiled or executing. In future examples, the compilation will be shown if it illustrates a facet of programming which will be valuable to the novice. In most cases sample input and output will be provided.

Simple Program Statements: Display Information

Now that you have seen a program that works, but does nothing, let's add a statement which does something and see what it takes to make it work. Suppose that you want to display a greeting to the user of this program, then you would add a `printf` C function to our sample program as shown in Fig. 8.1.

Figure 8.2: Use of input parameters in FirstOut.c

```
/*******************************************************/
/* FILE:       FirstOut.c                              */        ①
/*                                                     */
/* AUTHOR:     J.B. Hodges                             */
/* DATE:       August, 1993                            */
/* PURPOSE:    Displays a string                       */        ②
/* LIBRARIES:  Uses stdio.h function library           */
/* COMMENTS:   Demonstrates the use of the I/O function */
/*             library and the printf function on a    */
/*             simple string.                          */
/*******************************************************/

#include <stdio.h>                                                ③

int
main(void)
{
  printf("\nHello there future ANSI C wizard!\n\n");              ④

  return (0);
}
```

This program, "FirstOut.c," will print the line "Hello there future ANSI C wizard!" by itself and stop. Nevertheless, it introduces four new concepts: (1) the inclusion of standard libraries, (2) the use of standard functions, (3) the executable expression, and (4) the expression terminating character. The notes labeled item (**1**) and (**2**) in the margin of the program indicate changes to the banner which result from the change in program name and functionality.

To use the printf function, which clearly was not written in this program (or there would be a function definition for it), it must be made available to this program. printf is one of many functions which is associated with input and output (called I/O or IO) and resides in a library of functions called "stdio.h" or "standard input and output." stdio.h is called a **header file**[1] and represents a standard library that is provided with the C programming language, but, like other libraries, it is not made available to the programmer's environment unless the programmer specifically requests it. The request is done with the include statement. Item (**3**) is a type of header statement, because it defines an interface between the current program and other programs. It is called an **include** statement, and the pound sign (#) is required. The #include statement is called a **precompiler directive**, because the inclusion of

---

1. A header file is so named because it includes the function headers for each function in the library.

this library must be performed before the source code in the file is compiled. Other precompiler directives will be introduced and discussed as their functionality merits. Although not shown that way, there can be space between the pound sign and the the the string "include." When the include statement is added to the program, all of the functions in the stdio library are made available to FirstOut.c for local use. One of these functions is printf.

Item (**4**) is the application of the printf function, called a **function call**. As previously mentioned, every function is associated with a type and has a parameter list. printf is no exception: although it is used to display strings it returns nothing to the program. printf takes at least one argument but may have many arguments, depending on what the programmer is trying to dispay. The required argument is a string, called a **control** (or format) **string**. The number of additional arguments is identified by the contents of the control string. A **string** is any set of numbers, characters, spaces, and special symbols delimited by double quotes. As such, it is seen as a single object.

The printf function takes the control string argument, interprets its contents, and displays the results where and how the string dictates. Each of the items which are to be printed, if any, must be identified in the control string and told how to print.

In the sample printf function call, printf is not instructed to display any items, only the string "Hello there future UNIX wizard!" However, it *is* told *how* to print the string, with the special characters (\n) in front of the string and the two (\n)s in back of the string. These characters have special meaning in the control string: to print a line feed or carriage return. The first one simply moves the print position to the first character of the next line before printing the string, and the last two print a blank line after the string. Were we to print a variable using printf, the variable type and formatting commands for printing the variable would have to be included in the string, as well as the name of the variable as a separate argument. Before compiling and running this program, let's look at some of the other options for controlling printf.

Table 8.1: `printf` **formatting options**

`\n`	$\Rightarrow$	Print a line feed
`\t`	$\Rightarrow$	Print a tab
`%d`	$\Rightarrow$	The argument is displayed in decimal notation
`%c`	$\Rightarrow$	The argument is displayed in character format
`%s`	$\Rightarrow$	The argument is displayed in string format
`%f`	$\Rightarrow$	The argument is displayed in fixed point format: [-]mmm.nnn
`%e`	$\Rightarrow$	The argument is displayed in floating point format: [-]m.nnne [±]xx
`%g`	$\Rightarrow$	Display in %f or %e format, whichever is shorter

```
printf("There were %d rainy days in the U.S. last year\n", foo);
```

control string with one
integer print argument

integer
variable

At the end of the `printf` statement in the example (item **4**) there is a semicolon (;). The semicolon is the expression terminating character in C (and many other programming languages). Every line inside the statement block must begin or terminate a functional context or be terminated with a semicolon. Long lines can also be extended to the next line with a backslash character (\).

8.3.2 Compiling a C Program

Since the program `FirstOut.c` will actually do something, let's introduce the compiler now and slowly talk more about the compiler as more complicated examples are introduced.

The C compiler we will use is the GNU C compiler and is invoked (on this particular host) with the command *gcc*. We will use this compiler because it is compatible with ANSI C. Many other C compilers exist, and the programmer should find out about the characteristics of their compiler and related utilities. The compiler takes a file as a mandatory argument, as shown below. The general template for compiling a source file is shown below

```
gcc [options] sourcefile ...
```

where `"sourcefile"`[1] is the file name containing the program you have

---

1. Traditionally, readable program code is called source or source code.

written and wish to compile. The name of the file must end with ".c." Lets use this template to compile `FirstOut.c`.

```
localhost> gcc FirstOut.c
localhost>
```

where no options are used, and the "sourcefile" command argument used is the file "`FirstOut.c`." A few other compiler options are listed below.

Table 8.2: `gcc` **Compiler options**

-bsd	⇒	Enforce strict BSD semantics
-g	⇒	Produce additional symbol table information for the debugger
-I DIR	⇒	Specify the directory DIR to search for #include files
-o OUTF	⇒	Name the output object file OUTF
-O	⇒	Uses the object code optimizer
-p	⇒	Returns a count of how many times each routine is called
-v	⇒	Compile verbosely
-Y ENV	⇒	Compiles for environment ENV (e.g., BSD, POSIX, SYSTEM_FIVE)

If there are no compilation errors, the next response will get a shell prompt without any other notification. Unless otherwise stated, the compiled version of the code (the object code), which, in this case, is also the **executable file**, is called "`a.out`." After the program is compiled, you are ready to execute it. This is done by entering "`a.out`," along with any arguments required by the program, as follows:

```
localhost> gcc FirstOut.c
localhost> gcc ./a.out
Hello there future ANSI C wizard!
```

It is possible that you could fail to get the program to execute even though you have successfully compiled the program. This could happen if your UNIX execution path does not include '.' in it. In this case, simply type "`./a.out`" instead of "`a.out`" to tell UNIX what directory the executable is in. If you want to change the name of the executable file to something other than `a.out`, you can use the '-o' compiler option as follows:

```
localhost> gcc -o foc FirstOut.c
```

This will name the object code file for "`FirstOut.c`" to be "`foc`." Be careful to not confuse the small 'o' with the large 'O,' which is the compiler option to *optimize* the compilation. Do (man gcc) for more information on compiler options and their applicability.

8.3.3 Errors Detected During Compilation

If your program doesn't compile, then it has syntax errors in it. A syntax error is one where you have either typed something incorrectly or have added or forgotten to add something which is required by the C language syntax. Often these errors will be displayed on the screen. Errors will be identified by line number. The line number in the error may not be the line where the error occurs, since the error is flagged when the error is first identified. But it should be close. As an example, consider a slight modification to FirstOut.c which generates a syntax error, shown below. This program is called FirstOut.c but is in a file called "FirstBug.c":

Figure 8.3: An intentional syntax error injected into FirstOut.c.

```
localhost> cat FirstBug.c
/*****************************************************/
/* FILE:        FirstOut.c                      */
/*                                              */
/* AUTHOR:      J.B. Hodges                     */
/* DATE:        August, 1993                    */
/* PURPOSE:     Displays a string               */
/* LIBRARIES:   Uses stdio.h function library   */
/* COMMENTS:    Demonstrates the use of the I/O function */
/*              library and the printf function on a     */
/*              simple string.                  */
/*********************************************            ◄── ERROR

#include <stdio.h>
void
main(void)
{
  printf("\nHello there future UNIX wizard!\n\n");

  return;
}
```

where the terminating portion of the banner comment (*/) is removed. Compilation produces the following list of syntax errors.

```
localhost> gcc FirstBug.c
ld: Undefined symbols:
_main
```

where, in this case, we are lucky. In many cases, a simple 'typo' will result in many errors *downstream* of the error. This effect is called **error propagation**. There are two types of syntax errors: (1) **warnings** and (2) **fatal** errors. The difference between them is that warnings are recoverable but may point to a problem with the program logic. A fatal error will produce non-executable code. Errors have a tendency to propagate. One error early in the program may cause other errors further along. For example, if you have a missing left parenthesis, you might generate two errors - one for the missing left parenthesis and one when the compiler finds the right parenthesis. Because of error propagation, it is a good idea to correct the first error that occurs, compile the program again, and see if other errors disappear.

You can fix bugs (called **debugging**) by editing the source file. You may want to keep different versions of the source code when you start debugging, to avoid destroying a partially working program. Techniques for debugging will be addressed in Chapter 11.

8.3.4 Using `printf` to Request Input and Reading It

Many programs require the user to type data which is requested by the program. Anytime a program interacts directly with a user, regardless of the interaction mode, the program is called an **interactive program**. Programs which are called and perform their function without interaction are called **batch programs**. Inputting large amounts of data is tedious and programmers generally avoid interactive input of large amounts of data; however, for small amounts of data it is all right. We will now modify `FirstOut.c` to signal the user to type some data to be read and then displayed.

Figure 8.4: Use of input/output functions in `FirstIO.c`

```
/******************************************************/
/* FILE:      FirstIO.c                            */
/*                                                 */
/* AUTHOR:    J.B. Hodges                          */
/* DATE:      August, 1993                         */
/* PURPOSE:   Reads user's initials and number of dogs */
/*            and then prints them on one line.    */
/* LIBRARIES: Uses the stdio.h function library    */
/* COMMENTS:  Demonstrates variable declaration.   */
/*            Demonstrates use of scanf on char and */
/*            int variable types. Demonstrates use of */
/*            printf to output variable values.    */
/******************************************************/

#include <stdio.h>

int
main(void)
{
  char first, middle, last;   /* Initials of user's name */
  int  ndogs;                  /* Number of dogs          */

  printf("\nPlease type your initials, separated by no spaces: ");
  scanf("%c%c%c", &first, &middle, &last);
  printf("\nPlease type how many dogs you own: ");
  scanf("%d", &ndogs);
  printf("\nHello, %c %c %c, you own %d dogs, right?\n\n", \
          first, middle, last, ndogs);

  return (0);
}
```

① ② ③ ④ ⑤

I will mention once more that I have changed the name of the file and its function, so I have modified the banner statement accordingly. Henceforth this kind of change will be assumed to be important but will not be mentioned. This program is essentially identical to `FirstOut.c` in that no new libraries are needed and we are only using standard (sometimes called **canned functions**). However, we are now using variables, since this program will ask the user to type some data and that data has to be remembered (i.e., stored in memory) until it is used. We are also going to read that data from the keyboard, so we will use the scanf function. Finally, we will use the printf option to display variables. Item (**3**) is a variable declaration. In C, variable declarations define both the **type** of variable that it will be and its **identifier**. As previously mentioned, the type precedes the identifier, so char is the type associated with the variable identifiers `first`, `middle`, and `last`, and int is the type associated with the variable identifier ndogs. Variable names should always be chosen to be functionally appropriate. The variable names in this example are at least possible to remember, but they are slightly cryptic. When variables are cryptic it is possible to forget, later, what they were for. This makes reading code some time in the future difficult. This is when an **inline comment** may be of value, since the programmer can write what the variable means and what it does. Notice that the comments line up left and right. This simply makes the comment easier to read, but is not required syntactically. In general, this type of comment may save some space, but confuses the distinction between documentation and source code. It would be better, and cleaner, to have the variables described in the function banner. For the purposes of saving space, only, variables in our examples will be documented inline.

It should be noted that variable names have thus far been simple character combinations. It is legal to use an underscore (_) to separate characters into meaningful units, and to use numbers in variable names; however, it is not legal to begin a variable name with a number, nor is it legal to use any other special characters (e.g., $, >, <, %, &, *) in a variable name.

Also notice that there are three variables declared on the same line, separated by commas. This is all right as long as they are all the same type (i.e., char). It is also all right to type them on separate lines. You can declare different typed variables on the same line, but not separated by commas.

Item (**4**) illustrates the use of the keyboard reading function, scanf. Although printf and scanf are both I/O functions, they are different kinds of functions. printf always displays its result and doesn't return any values to the function or program which calls it. As a result, printf is called an **output** function. scanf always assigns a value to a variable in the calling function or program and is called an **input** function. scanf also returns a value, the number of items read. The arguments to printf and scanf differ as a result. Notice that the argument names in the scanf function are preceded by ampersands (&). When scanf reads the variable values typed at the keyboard it assigns those values to its local parameters. In order to have those values be associated with the parameters in scanf, and to the variables in main (which may have different identifiers), they must refer to the same location in memory. Hence the user has to provide, as the argument to scanf, the location of *where* the variables are located in memory. The ampersand is an operator (called an **address-of operator**) used to do so.

Each variable in C has associated with it an identifier (or name), a type, and a value. In terms of memory; however, each variable has an **address** and a **value**. The address is the location where the value is stored. When the identifier is used to refer to a variable, the memory address is traced to the value, which is returned. You do not need to understand any more about variable addresses and value right now. It is only important that you recognize that there are similarities and differences between printf and scanf, and that you remember to precede a variable name in scanf with an ampersand (&). Notice how the three variables are written right next to each other in the formatting string, and how the variable arguments are separated by commas in the remainder of the call. Also, note that the formatting of arguments is the same for both printf and scanf. Item (**5**) illustrates the printf function being applied to the four variables, and the application of a line continuation character to make the line more readable. The line extension character is the backslash, \. The program "FirstIO.c" is shown executing below.

```
localhost> gcc -o fioc FirstIO.c
localhost> fioc
Please type your initials, separated by no spaces: jBh
Please type how many dogs you own: 2
Hello, j B h, you own 2 dogs, right?
```

8.3.5 Inputting Strings into Programs

Although more will be said on this topic in Chapter 10, many novice programmers want to read and print strings and should be able to do so right away. Let's modify FirstIO.c to become "FirstStringIO.c," as illustrated in Fig. 8.5. In doing so, we will introduce an **array** variable type, but will not go into any detail describing it. Simply use it for now in the limited capacity available.

Figure 8.5: String variable application in `FirstStringIO.c`

```
/****************************************************/
/* FILE:        FirstStringIO.c                     */
/*                                                  */
/* AUTHOR:      J.B. Hodges                         */
/* DATE:        August, 1993                        */
/* PURPOSE:     Reads a name of < 20 characters as a */
/*              string. Reads an integer. Displays the */
/*              string and integer on one line.     */
/* LIBRARIES:   Uses stdio.h and string.h libraries */
/* COMMENTS:    Demonstrates the use of printf to   */
/*              request data, and scanf to read the data */
/*              into variables which are then printed. */
/****************************************************/

#include <stdio.h>
#include <string.h>                                    (1)

int
main(void)
{
  char name[20];                                       (2)
  int  ndogs;

  printf("\nPlease type your name: ");
  scanf("%s", name);                                   (3)
  printf("\nPlease type how many dogs you own: ");
  scanf("%d", &ndogs);
  printf("\nHello, %s, you own %d dogs, right?\n\n", name, ndogs);

  return (0);
}
```

A couple of changes have been made to the `FirstIO.c` program to make it usable for simple string I/O. First, a new function library "`string.h`" is being included into the program (item **1**). This makes available several functions that are specific to strings. Second, a variable is declared, called "`name`" that is a character (char) type. The variable is followed by a bracketed 20 (item **2**). This syntax is used to define a type of variable called an **array**, and the number 20 indicates how many items are going to be associated with the variable. In this case, we are defining 20 variables, each of which is a character, but all of which are associated with the single variable identifier, `name`. This is simply how strings must be defined in C, as character arrays.

The reader should note that the banner suggests that the name will be limited to 19 characters, and the array is defined to be 20 characters, but there is nothing in the program which checks to makes sure that only this many characters are typed by the user. This could be problematic and will be discussed in Chapter 11. Item (**3**) illustrates the difference in use in scanf between the character variable and the character array (string) variable. Unlike the character variable, whose location in memory must be identified in scanf, the character array does not need to be similarly identified, because the two are represented differently in memory. An array is always identified by its starting address in memory, so no specific mention of it is needed when reading a value into it. Notice the sample I/O for this program below.

```
localhost> gcc -o fsioc FirstStringIO.c
localhost> fsioc
Please type your name: Jack
Please type how many dogs you own: 2
Hello, Jack, you own 2 dogs, right?
```

When the %s format is used in scanf, characters will be placed into the string variable until the first space is encountered. Thus "Jack" is reasonable input for the program, as shown above, but "Jack Hodges" would not be.

8.3.6   Input from a Separate Function

One final use of the scanf function is in a separate function. In most programs, the overall function of the program is broken down ("decomposed," or "refined") into smaller (at least, more specific) subtasks, and these are further refined into yet smaller subtasks. This approach may continue until a subtask is nothing more than a single expression. At that point the program is constructed by defining the required variable types and identifiers, and setting up interfaces between each of the subtasks and the top-level function, main. This process is called **iterative refinement**. When programming subtasks are implemented using constructs which control the flow of execution, this process is also associated with what is called **modular programming**. The predominant feature of modular programming is the use control structures that have predictable control behavior. As such, the structure should have a single entry point and a single exit point. A C function is a control stucture, or module: it defines and orders a sequential block of statements. A C function has a single entry point in the function header. Although it is possible for a C function to have more than one exit point, it is wise to use only one, so a C function is also a module. The use of functions as one type of control structure in the refinement process is called **procedural abstraction**.

To introduce the notion of modular programming, using functions, we will write a small program which does exactly the same thing as the FirstIO.c program; however, the display and input segments of the code will be considered separate functional subtasks and will be performed by their own functions. One function (PrintVals) will be an output function, which will do nothing more than display the final results, and one function (`GetArgs`) will be the input function, which obtains data in the first place. The `main` function will coordinate the activities of the functions.

Figure 8.6: Modular programming for simple I/O in `FirstModIO.c`

```
/******************************************************/
/* FILE:        FirstModIO.c                      */
/*                                                */
/* AUTHOR:      J.B. Hodges                       */
/* DATE:        August, 1993                      */
/* PURPOSE:     Reads user's initials and number of dogs */
/*              and then prints them on one line. */
/* APPROACH:    Uses stdio.h function library. Input is  */
/*              separate from MAIN. Output is separate   */
/*              from MAIN.                        */
/* FUNCTIONS:   GetArgs:   reads the input data  */
/*              PrintVals: displays the output   */
/* COMMENTS:    Demonstrates modular design for I/O with */
/*              functions.                        */
/******************************************************/

#include <stdio.h>

void PrintVals(char arg1, char arg2, char arg3, int arg4);           ①
void GetArgs(char *firstp, char *middlep, char *lastp, int *ndogsp);

int
main(void)
{
  char fi, mi, la;                                                    ②
  int  nd;

  GetArgs(&fi, &mi, &la, &nd);                                        ③
  PrintVals(fi, mi, la, nd);

  return (0);
}
```

This program is a large departure from other programs which have been presented so far, but performs the same task as `FirstIO.c`. The difference is that each of the component subtasks of the original program (i.e. requesting and reading input, and printing the values) are placed into separate functions. This is an example of procedural abstraction. Although the function-based approach initially involves an increase in program complexity, the overall savings far exceeds the pain. Generally, procedural abstraction is advantageous in three ways: (1) readability, (2) testability, and (3) modularity.

The `main` function has two new declaration components, called **function**

prototypes (at item **1**), which declare the function type, parameter types and their order. This allows the placement of the function definitions anywhere in the file and allows the programmer a lot of flexibility when implementing the program. A function's prototype is simply a copy of its header, but terminated like an expression.

The variable declarations shown at item (**2**) correspond in a one-to-one fashion with the paramter declarations in the function definition and function call (item **3**).

Figure 8.6: Modular programming for simple I/O in `FirstModIO.c` (cont.)

```
/*********************************************************/
/* PrintVals:   Prints output variables                 */
/* INPUT:       first, middle, last, ndogs              */
/* OUTPUT:      None                                     */
/* RETURN:      None                                     */
/* USAGE:       [main] PrintVals(fi, mi, la, nd);       */
/*********************************************************/

void
PrintVals(char arg1, char arg2, char arg3, int arg4)              ④
{
  printf("\nHello, %c %c %c, you own %d dogs, right?\n\n", \
          arg1, arg2, arg3, arg4);

  return;
}


/*********************************************************/
/* GetArgs:   Reads input variables                     */
/* INPUT:     None                                       */
/* OUTPUT:    first, middle, last, ndogs                */
/* RETURN:    None                                       */
/* USAGE:     [main] GetArgs(&fi, &mi, &la, &nd);       */
/*********************************************************/

void
GetArgs(char *firstp, char *middlep, char *lastp, int *ndogsp)    ⑤
{
  printf("\nPlease type your initials, separated by no spaces: ");
  scanf("%c%c%c", firstp, middlep, lastp);                        ⑥
  printf("\nPlease type how many dogs you own: ");
  scanf("%d", ndogsp);

  return;
}
```

Clearly, each function shown above has fewer lines of executable code, and the code is specifically associated with the task of the particular function. The code is easier to read, because you need not search around for the code segment that performs the subtask you are looking for. When you design programs using functions, you can initially write the statement block in main that calls the functions, the header and a blank function statement block (called a **stub**) for each function, and the associated function prototypes. This enables you to compile the program, and to develop the internal workings of each function at your own pace. Debugging and testing is easier, because you can isolate the effects of the function from the rest of the program. Finally, changes to the function need not require changes to the entire program, nor do the other functions really need to know how a subtask is solved as long as the values that are communicated between functions work together effectively.

In general, you should work toward developing programs which make use of modular programming methods and procedural abstraction. The first thing that you should notice about this sample program is that each function has its own banner comment. The banners associated with a function are different than those for a program, usually shorter. Unless a function is undergoing a large amount of revision, it will generally just require a banner that tells what the function name is, what it does, what its input and output parameters are, and what it returns. Sometimes, a sample call is useful in the function banner. In our examples, the function from which this function is called is included in the sample call, in brackets. This can be good for small programs; however, if a function is later used in a library, or if the number of functions in which a function is used is large, it might be misleading to the reader. This is an issue which can really only be resolved by the programmer.

If you look closely at the three function definitions you will see that they all follow the same general form: (1) the function is declared, (2) the parameter list is defined, (3) the local variables are declared, and (4) the statements are elaborated. Because main has thus far had no parameters, the parameter lists of GetArgs and PrintVals appear much more elaborate. On the other hand, GetArgs and PrintVals are our first examples of functions which return no values. Such a function is declared as void to signify that it is the programmer's intention to return no values. The associated function return statement is simply terminated instead of providing it with a value. In item (**4**), for example, instead of having 4 variable defined within the body of main, we now have 4 variables declared in the parameter list of PrintVals. A parameter list simply declares the items which will be shared between the calling function and the function being called, and sets up an interface for doing so. The only requirement to the interface is that the parameter types and order be maintained. When the function PrintVals is called from main, the values of the variables used as arguments in the function call are copied into the PrintVals function parameters. We say that the values are *passed into* the function *from* main. PrintVals does not change the values of these variables in any way, so they are called **output parameters** and PrintVals is called an **output function**.

The parameter list for GetArgs (item **5**) is somewhat different than for PrintVals. Because GetArgs starts with no variable values and reads variable values from the keyboard, these are called **input parameters** and GetArgs is called an **input function**. In this case, the variable values are completely different than those in main, because they do not *have* values until they leave GetArgs. Moreover, since these variables will actually be the result of a scanf function, which returns the location of a variable in memory rather than the value itself, the parameters in the GetArgs header must refer to the locations of those variables in memory. Since the parameters of GetArgs must be used in expressions within GetArgs, as objects, a simple address is not adequate. Thus the parameters declared in the GetArgs header are 'objects that represent addesses,' commonly referred to as **pointers**. A pointer is declared by placing an asterisk in front of the paramter name, after the type declaration. More on this in Chapter 9. When a parameter is declared as a pointer, then the associated argument in the function call must refer to the variable with an **address-of operator**, &. [1] This is how the arguments in the call to GetArgs (at item **3**) are given.

Item (**6**) shows that the variables associated with the values read in GetArgs must be declared in main, because the values are returned by GetArgs to main before they are sent into PrintVals. This is called variable reference or **call by reference**. Anytime a function references a value, it must declare an object for the value. Notice that the variable names are not the same in main that the parameter names in GetArgs. This is quite all right, because the consistency check is based on the type declaration and order of variables in the function call with parameters in the parameter list. As long as the arguments sent to the function when it is called are consistent, it doesn't matter what they are named. The program "FirstModIO.c" is compiled and run below:

```
localhost> gcc -o fmioc FirstModIO.c
localhost> fmioc
Please type your initials, separated by no spaces: JBH
Please type how many dogs you own: 2
Hello, J B H, you own 2 dogs, right?
```

---

1. This is true for simple variables, or scalars, but not so for array variables.

8.4 C Types, Operators, and Expressions

In the C programming language, a program is comprised of processes and objects. A process is comprised of the three component blocks mentioned previously (header, declaration, and statement blocks). A process is a dynamic entity, in that it performs a task. A process performs a task by executing statements, which involve the manipulation of objects. A program, a function, and an operator are all examples of processes and each has its own identifier. An object is a data item, and also has a label or identifier. A constant and a variable are examples of programming objects.

The program examples that have been presented so far make use of standard library functions. Although the functions that are provided in C libraries are very useful, they are provided as support and cannot *solve* problems. In order to write meaningful programs, programmers must learn how to declare their own variables, write their own expressions, and develop their own functions. In order to introduce the concepts in this section, we will further modify the program `FirstIO.c` to become "FirstExpr.c" (see Fig. 8.7).

`FirstExpr.c` illustrates a few things that were mentioned before. The first is the declaration of a global (program-wide) constant (item **1**) named "PI." A constant is an object whose value does not change during the course of execution, and is declared using the `#define` syntax, which is similar to the `#include` syntax. There is no semicolon after the definition. As a constant, `PI` can be used in expressions and as a function argument, but it cannot be on the lefthand side of an assignment statement.

The second item of interest is the variable naming convention in C. You can use an underscore, as done at item (**2**), to make an identifier easier to read or more descriptive, but care should be taken not to confuse cases, not to use numbers as the first character, and not to use other special characters (such as $, &, *, \, #). For example:

```
int state_tax;
```

is a legal variable identifier, whereas:

```
int state*tax;
```

is not a legal variable identifier.

Figure 8.7: Simple variable assignment expressions in `FirstExpr.c`

```
/*++++++++++++++++++++++++++++++++++++++++++++++++++++++++*/
/* FILE:      FirstExpr.c                                 */
/*                                                        */
/* AUTHOR:    J.B. Hodges                                 */
/* DATE:      August, 1993                                */
/* FUNCTION:  Calculates the volume of a cylinder and     */
/*            displays cylinder characteristics.          */
/* LIBRARIES: Uses the stdio.h function library           */
/* COMMENTS:  Demonstrates variable declaration.          */
/*            Demonstrates constant declaration.          */
/*            Demonstrates variable assignment.           */
/*            Demonstrates field format specifier.        */
/**********************************************************/

#include <stdio.h>
#define PI 3.14159                                              ①

int
main(void)
{
    char   obj_type;                                            ②
    double radius,
           height,
           cyl_area,
           obj_volume;                                          ③

    printf("\n**** THIS PROGRAM CALCULATES THE VOLUME OF A CYLINDER" \
           "****\n\n");
    printf("\nPlease input the following information for the cylinder:" \
           "\n\n");
    printf("\tradius: ");
    scanf("%lf", &radius);
    printf("\n\theight: ");                                     ④
    scanf("%lf", &height);
    printf("\nYou have entered the following:\n\n");
    printf("CYLINDER RADIUS: %6.3f\nCYLINDER HEIGHT: %6.3f\n\n", radius, \
           height);

    cyl_area   = PI * radius * radius;                          ⑤
    obj_volume = height * cyl_area;

    printf("The volume of the cylinder is: %6.3f\n", obj_volume);  ⑥

    return (0);
}
```

Also note that we have placed four floating point identifiers (i.e., `radius`, `height`, `cyl_area`, and `obj_volume`) on separate lines in the program (item **3**), but they share the same declaration. This was done for readability. In-line comments could have been placed to the right of these declarations. Item (**4**) illustrates the use of a formatting directive, \t for printing tabs.

Item (**5**) illustrates our first use of an **assignment statement**. An assignment is used to define the value of a variable, and is always associated with the equal sign symbol (=). When you see a variable name, an equals sign, and then some expression, it means that the variable on the left of the assignment is *getting* the value on the right. It doesn't matter whether the item on the right is a number or a complex expression. Whatever the expression evaluates to will become the new value of the variable on the left. Only variables can be assigned values; however, they can be reassigned new values over and over again. It should be noted that an assignment statement is *not* the same as an equation. In mathematics, what is on the right side of an equality is identified with what is on the left hand side. In programming languages; however, what is on the left hand side is identified with what is on the right hand side. It is a one-directional relationship, right to left. You cannot have an expression on the left of the assignment symbol as you can in a mathematical equivalence.

The assignment statement at item (**5**) defines the value of the variable cy-l_area to be the result of the expression:

```
PI * radius * radius;
```

This expression uses three C objects in a mathematical expression. All three objects are user defined: one constant, PI, for the approximation to pi, and two uses of the floating point variable, radius. The asterisk (*) is a symbol for the multiplication operator, so this expression multiplies the values associated with the constant PI, radius, and radius. The result is made the new value of the variable cyl_area. On the next line (item **6**), this variable is used in an expression (again, a multiplication) to calculate the volume of the cylinder. Both mathematical expressions could easily have been collapsed into a single line. Also, had we included the standard math function library, we could have used the **pow** function instead of explicitly multiplying radius by itself.

```
obj_volume = height * PI * pow(radius, 2);
```

Table 8.3 presents the mathematical operators available in C and their evaluation precedence. You can experiment with them by modifying the expressions in FirstExpr.c.

Table 8.3: Mathematical operators in C

Precedence	Operator		Function
least	+ -	$\Rightarrow$	addition and subtraction
	*	$\Rightarrow$	multiplication
	/	$\Rightarrow$	real division if **either** operand is real, integer division if **both** operands are integers
greatest	%	$\Rightarrow$	integer remainder

Expressions are evaluated in a particular operator order, or **precedence**. With respect to mathematical operators, division operators are applied first, then multiplication, and finally addition and subtraction. In order to modify this order, the programmer must simply enclose the expressions in parentheses. The use of parentheses overrides normal precedence. In addition to the standard (canned) mathematical operators, there is a standard math library (math.h) with the following functions in it:

Table 8.4: Functions in the math.h function library

Function	Description
`ceil(x)`	Returns smallest integer less than x
`cos(x)`	Returns the cosine of x (x in radians)
`exp(x)`	Returns e to the power x, where e = 2.718 . . .
`fabs(x)`	Returns the absolute value of x, where x can be real
`floor(x)`	Returns largest integer not greater than x
`log(x)`	Returns the natural logarithm of x
`log10(x)`	Returns the base 10 logarithm of x
`pow(x, y)`	Returns x raised to the power y
`sin(x)`	Returns the sin of x (x in radians)
`sqrt(x)`	Returns the square root of x
`tan(x)`	Returns the tangent of x (x in radians)

Item (**5**) in `FirstExpr.c` illustrates a form of printf which makes use of the optional **field specifier**. The field specifier defines how a variable's value will be printed. In the example, the variable `obj_volume` is being printed as a floating point variable with the `%f` format specifier. In addition, the field specifier, "6.3" precedes the type specifier. The general format is 'X.Yf', where X refers to the total number of spaces allocated to print the value, including the decimal point, and Y refers to the precision allocated beyond the decimal point. In this example, then, six spaces are allocated for the number and decimal point, and three spaces are allocated for precision. Below is the program compilation and execution. Note the effect of the printfs on the printing of floating point variables.

```
localhost> gcc -o fexpr FirstExpr.c
localhost> fexpr
**** THIS PROGRAM CALCULATES THE VOLUME OF A CYLINDER ****
Please input the following information for the cylinder:
        radius: 3
        height: 4
You have entered the following:
CYLINDER RADIUS:   3.000
CYLINDER HEIGHT:   4.000
The volume of the cylinder is: 113.097
```

Included below is a brief table of examples which illustrate different field specifiers on different variables, and what the `printf` prints as a result, based on evaluation of the following expressions:

```
#define PI    3.14159
#define jack "academic"

int     x;
double  y;

x = 210;
y = PI + 3;
```

Table 8.5: printf field specifier for fixed and floating point doubles

1	`printf("The sum is @%f@\n", y)`	$\Rightarrow$	`The sum is @6.141590@`
2	`printf("The sum is @%5.0f@\n", y)`	$\Rightarrow$	`The sum is @    6@`
3	`printf("The sum is @%5.2f@\n", y)`	$\Rightarrow$	`The sum is @ 6.14@`
4	`printf("The sum is @%5.4f@\n", y)`	$\Rightarrow$	`The sum is @6.1416@`
5	`printf("The sum is @%5.5f@\n", y)`	$\Rightarrow$	`The sum is @6.14159@`
6	`printf("The sum is @%6.4f@\n", y)`	$\Rightarrow$	`The sum is @6.1416@`
7	`printf("The sum is @%5.2e@\n", y)`	$\Rightarrow$	`The sum is @6.14e+00@`
8	`printf("The sum is @%6.4e@\n", y)`	$\Rightarrow$	`The sum is @6.1416e+00@`
9	`printf("The sum is @%e@\n", y)`	$\Rightarrow$	`The sum is @6.141590e+00@`
10	`printf("The sum is @%g@\n", y)`	$\Rightarrow$	`The sum is @6.14159@`

The field specifier controls how the variable will be displayed. In example 3, the field specifier is "5.2f" and controls how the value of variable "y" is printed. The first number specifies how many columns the number will be displayed in, in this case 5. The second number specifies how many significant figures will be displayed after the decimal point, in this case 2. As mentioned before, the character specifies what type of format to display the number in, and defines how the numbers which precede it will be interpreted. The "f" specifies display of the number in floating point notation. When the field variable is too small for a number (as in example 1), C ignores the field variable and prints whatever number of spaces is required for the entire number. C will give as many significant figures as requested. In example 2, the number is truncated as a result. When a number is truncated, C will round it off to the next significant place, as shown in examples 2, 3, and 4. If the overall number of spaces is insufficient for the number of significant places requested, C will add (pad) the remaining spaces, as in 4 and 5. If the number of spaces requested is large, then the variable value is right justified and may result in leading blank characters, as in examples 2 and 3. Examples 7 and 8 show the same `printf` field specification as for examples 3 and 6 except that the exponential format (%e) is being used instead of the floating point format (%f). As before, C will provide enough space to print the number of significant figures requested. Example 9 is a comparison to example 1. Finally, example 10 uses the %g format, which chooses between the %f and %e formats and drops nonsignificant zeros.

The same tables can be generated for integers (i.e., %d) and strings (i.e., %s) using the same example variables (and values) above.

Table 8.6: **printf field specifier for integers and strings**

1	`printf("x is @%d@\n", x)`	$\Rightarrow$	`x is @210@`
2	`printf("x is is @%1d@\n", x)`	$\Rightarrow$	`x is @210@`
3	`printf("x is is @%4d@\n", x)`	$\Rightarrow$	`x is @ 210@`
4	`printf("Jack is @%s@\n", jack)`	$\Rightarrow$	`Jack is @academic@`
5	`printf("Jack is @%5s@\n", jack)`	$\Rightarrow$	`Jack is @academic@`
6	`printf("Jack is @%9s@\n", jack)`	$\Rightarrow$	`Jack is @ academic@`

As with real variables, integer and string variables are printed right justified. If the field specifier is smaller than the integer, or string, C will print the entire number or string. If the field specifier is larger than the number or string, then C will right justify the number or string with leading blanks.

8.5 Variable Type Conversion

In C, the variable on the lefthand side of an assignment must be compatible with the resulting type of the expression on the right. In some cases, an error will be flagged (i.e., noted) by the compiler if assignment compatibility is not maintained. However, in many cases the variable types are different but compatible, and no error will be flagged. The programmer should be aware that when unlike variable types are used together in an assignment statement, C will convert the value of the expression to the type of the variable on the left. This is called **implicit type conversion**, or type **coercion**, as illustrated below.

```
y = PI + 3;
```

In the formatting examples above, y was declared as a real variable (double), while PI was declared a real constant. In this example, 3 is an integer literal. When y is being assigned a new value, C will convert the result on the righthand side of the expression to a real value before assigning it to y. Consider a slightly more obvious example which uses characters and integers.

```
y = 'a' + 3;
```

The character 'a' is converted to its ASCII value before adding 3, and the combination is converted to float before assigning the value to y. This is an example of where implicit type conversion can trip up the unwary programmer, since the addition operation cannot be applied to characters, but the internal representation of characters, in C, is as integers.

C also allows the programmer to **force** a type conversion using what is called a **cast**. A cast is an **explicit type conversion** since the programmer must change program code to make the conversion happen. A cast is invoked by wrapping the type declaration in parentheses, as shown below.

```
(double)3  ⟹  3.0
```

8.6 Program Layout and Organization

In addition to the style presented in examples above, the following general guidelines can be followed to produce programs with maximum readability and reusability. In addition to readability, here are a few additional motivations for paying particularly close attention to programming style.

- Programs that are difficult to read get thrown away because they can't be fixed, improved, or moved to other hardware.
- The simpler the style, the easier the code will be to read.
- Consistency within the program, and with other programmers, requires less reading effort, because you know where to look for what.
- If you start writing the program with good style, you might avoid generating errors you might get if you tried to put it in later.

8.7 Style for C Program Layout

The program layout should be similar to the outline of a paper. There should be vertical separation (with blank lines) between major functional components. Here are some guidelines for *vertical* spacing.

- One blank line before every function.
- One blank line before and after every block or banner comment.
- Sometimes before and after programming constructs such as loops.
- There should usually be one statement or declaration per line.

Code is easier to read when it is indented with respect to its function. For example, when you type an "if-else" segment, which is used to make branching decisions, then the code associated with the if-else should be indented equally. Here are some guidelines on indentation:

- Compound statements should be indented two to four spaces to the right of the "containing" statement (e.g., code associated with the while example, above, was indented two to four spaces horizontally with respect to the line on which the while occurred.

- The identifier in declaration lists should be indented the same amount as surrounding statements. Variable names should line up vertically.
- In segment comments are easiest to read when they use the entire line, although many programmers indent them the same as surrounding code.
- Inline comments are easiest to read when they are justified together.

Spacing within statements is also important for readability. C does not recognize multiple spaces, so you could write the following:

```
a=b+c*e/f+g;
```

Unfortunately, this is really hard on the eyes! By simply spreading symbols, operators, etc. out, the code becomes much more readable.

```
a = ( b + c ) * e / ( f + g );
```

Of course, too much space and the program becomes incoherent.

```
a =    ( b + c )    *   e / (    f + g      );
```

Here are some guidelines for *horizontal* spacing.

- Put one space between identifiers and operators (e.g., `a = b + c`).
- Put punctuation symbols directly after identifiers (e.g., `p(a, b)`; note space *after* comma).
- Put space before and after curly braces (`{` and `}`), because they are difficult to distinguish from plain parentheses.

8.7.1   Organization of C Programs

The organization of a program is as important as any other aspect of its preparation. If you see functions that run on for many screens, then you will understand. Here are some guidelines which will be useful:

- Functions should usually be less than a page or so long.
- Pass variables needed by functions as arguments; avoid using global variables.
- Cluster similar items. Put related variables close to each other within a declaration, and put related functions near each other.[1]

One last comment. Every programmer works hard to make their programs

---

1. Functions that perform similar tasks should be organized in the same place. Also, most programs have low-level functions on which higher-level tasks are based. Functions of the same abstraction level should be located in the same place.

run well. However, no one will appreciate a program unless they can understand how it works. Make all of your programs stand out as examples of simplicity and clarity, and everyone will enjoy reading your code.

8.8 Exercises and Sample Quiz Questions

8.8.1 Exercises

Exercise 1   Change the message printed in "FirstOut.c" to "Learn C and be free." Recompile and run.

8.8.2 Sample Quiz Questions

Problem 1   What is the difference between syntax and grammar in C (any language)? Give an example of each.

Problem 2   What is the difference between a low-level programming language and a high-level programming language. What is C? What are the strengths of this type of language?

Problem 3   Explain the notion of language portability, and why ANSI C is a good dialect to learn.

Problem 4   What is all the fuss about programming style (documentation and readability) . . . what is the reasoning behind the use of consistent style conventions? Provide two examples, each, of (1) itemsthat are commonly placed into a program/function banner, and (2) readability guidelines.

Problem 5   There are different semantic blocks of information which comprise a C program. What are they, and what task does each perform?

Problem 6   What do the symbols { and } mean in a C program? When can they be used, and when should they (according to convention) be used?

Problem 7   Name a standard function and the library in which it is found. How are library functions of this kind made available for use in a C program?

Problem 8   Show a C expression in which the value of an integer variable, named "foo", is assigned a value of 65. Show a C expression in which the following line is displayed:

```
The annual rainfall in Springfield, MA is 65 inches
```

where you can assume that the value (65) is associated with the integer variable named "foo."

Problem 9   Why is it the case that it is always best to correct the first error that you find after compiling a program, rather than to fix as many as you can?

Problem 10   What is a function prototype, and why is it important to use them?

Chapter 9
Decision Making, Iteration, and Functions

9.1 Introduction and Scope

Although you have learned how to write simple programs in C, you do not have the basic tools to construct real programs. For example, you can read a number of values into the program, but you do not know how to compare them, say to see if they fall in a certain range. If you wanted to perform a task over and over again, you would have to repeat the expressions as many times as you wanted the task repeated, instead of using a iteration construct. This chapter will teach you the elements of programming in C that will provide you with these necessary capabilities, and it will also show you how to write your own functions so that your code need not always be in a single **main** function. The examples illustrated in this chapter provide a starting point for using these programming constructs, and are available to the student in the `"UNIX/Chapter9"` directory for manipulation and modification. The following topics are be presented in this chapter:

Ch9

- Decision making
- Iteration
- Functions and program structure

At the completion of this chapter, you should be able to design and implement simple functional segments which demonstrate flow control and iteration with the different constructs available in the the C programming language. You should be able to write functions, and you should be able to return values from

299

the functions you write. You should understand the difference between parameters called by value and those called by reference, and you should be able to use variable addresses to properly assign and return parameter values through function headers. These abilities should be demonstrated in simple programs, such as those presented in this chapter.

9.2 Making Decisions

In order to make a choice between alternatives, you must have alternatives to choose between, you must have some operator which is used to make comparisons, and you must have some metric for evaluating the comparison. One example of two alternatives is to execute one of two sets of expressions. The associated comparison might be based on which of two variables has the greater value. Making different kinds of comparisons thus provides a mechanism for choice.

9.2.1 Simple Comparisons

Suppose that you have two numbers and you want to know which one is numerically larger (i.e., greater). In C, you use a **relational** operator for "greater than" between the variables you want to compare. The combination is an expression which can be evaluated, and the result is 0 or 1. If the one variable's value is greater that the other, a 1 is returned by the operation, otherwise a 0 is returned. Such expressions are called **logical expressions**, because they return a truth value of the relational operator applied to the operands. It is called a truth value because it can only have a binary value (i.e., zero or nonzero), as do false and not-false. Logical operators and expressions are thus also called boolean operators and expressions. The value of all logical/boolean expressions is either zero or nonzero. Consider the logical expression in "Simple-Comparison.c," shown in Fig. 9.1. This example illustrates the use of a variable that is assigned the truth value of a simple logical expression. Variables which represent boolean variables are often called **logical flags**, because they can be used to later decide whether to perform an action.

Figure 9.1: Relational operators and comparison in `SimpleComparison.c`

```
/*****************************************************/
/* FILE:        SimpleComparison.c           */
/*                                           */
/* AUTHOR:      J.B. Hodges                  */
/* DATE:        August, 1993                 */
/* FUNCTION:    Displays the result of a simple    */
/*              comparison between two integers.   */
/* LIBRARIES:   Uses stdio.h function library */
/* COMMENTS:    Demonstrates the use of > relational op */
/*              Demonstrates the use of if-else    */
/*****************************************************/

#include <stdio.h>

int
main(void)
{
  int x, y, z;

  printf("Enter two integers separated by spaces: ");
  scanf("%d%d", &x, &y);
  z = x > y;                                          ①
  printf("The value of z is: %d\n", z);

  return (0);
}
```

In this simple example, the value of **z** will be 0 or 1. If the value of **x** is 3 and the value of **y** is 2, then the value of the logical expression is 1. If the variables or variable values are switched, then the value of the expression is 0:

```
localhost> gcc SimpleComparison.c
localhost> a.out
Enter two integers separated by spaces: 3 2
The value of z is: 1
localhost> !!
a.out
Enter two integers separated by spaces: 2 3
The value of z is: 0
```

This is a pretty trivial example; however, there are many comparsions that you can make. The > operator is called a **relational** operator, because it makes comparisons based on how variables relate to each other. Table 9.1 shows other relational operators available in C.

Table 9.1: Relational operators in C

`x < y`	$\Rightarrow$	returns 1 if x is **less than** y
`x <= y`	$\Rightarrow$	returns 1 if x is **less than or equal to** y
`x == y`	$\Rightarrow$	returns 1 if x is **equal to** y
`x != y`	$\Rightarrow$	returns 1 if x is **not equal to** y
`x > y`	$\Rightarrow$	returns 1 if x is **greater than or equal to** y
`x >= y`	$\Rightarrow$	returns 1 if x is **greater than** y

Relational operators always return a value which can be interpreted as true or false. In addition, any expression whose value is nonzero can be interpreted as a *true* logical value, while an expression whose value is zero can be interpreted as a *false* logical value.

9.2.2 Using Comparisons to Make Choices

In C, comparisons such as that shown above are usually part of a choice between options. In this example we determined whether x was greater than y. We can use the result of this comparison by asking a "what if" question. For example, **if** x is greater than y, then maybe we want to add PI to x, and **if** it isn't maybe we want to subtract PI from y, as shown in "SimpleIF.c" (Fig. 9.2). If we can express this in C, then we can ask the question "what if x has the value of 3 and y has the value of 5"?

Figure 9.2: Simple path decisions in `SimpleIF.c`

```c
/******************************************************/
/* FILE:        SimpleIF.c                           */
/*                                                   */
/* AUTHOR:      J.B. Hodges                          */
/* DATE:        August, 1993                         */
/* FUNCTION:    Displays the result of a simple      */
/*              comparison between two integers.     */
/* LIBRARIES:   Uses stdio.h function library        */
/* COMMENTS:    Demonstrates the use of > relational op */
/*              Demonstrates the use of if-else      */
/******************************************************/

#include <stdio.h>

#define PI 3.14159

int
main(void)
{
  int x, y, z;

  printf("Enter two integers separated by spaces: ");
  scanf("%d%d", &x, &y);
  z = x > y;
  printf("The value of z is: %d\n", z);
  if ( z )                                              ①
     printf("Result of choice is: %6.4f\n", x + PI);
  else
     printf("Result of choice is: %6.4f\n", y - PI);

  return (0);
}
```

It should come as no surprise that the C construct which performs this type of comparison and decision making is called if-else. The if-else (or if-then-else) is one of the most powerful control structures in any programming language. The component inside the parentheses is called a **conditional**, and is used as a **test** in the if statement. The test is used to decide between two sets of compound expressions. If the test returns a nonzero (true) value, then the first set of expressions is selected. Otherwise the second set of expressions is selected. Note the format of the if else construct (at item **1**). The if and else are reserved words, so they must be typed exactly as they appear. The condition is always wrapped in a set of parentheses, and, in this example, the parentheses are spaced from the expression for readability. All statements that are executed, either from a successful test or an unsuccessful test, must be terminated. If the statements associated with either the condtional or the alternative (i.e., else) form a compound statement, then they *must* be enclosed in curly braces. When curly braces are used, the closing curly brace for the conditional expressions should precede the else. The same effect could be produced by replacing the expression (z) at item (**1**) with the following:

```
if ( x > y ) {...
```

without changing the way the program works. The if construct can be illustrated by compiling and executing `SimpleIF.c`:

```
localhost> gcc SimpleIF.c
localhost> a.out
Enter two integers separated by spaces: 3 2
The value of z is: 1
Result of choice is: 6.1416
localhost> !!
a.out
Enter two integers separated by spaces: 2 3
The value of z is: 0
Result of choice is: -0.1416
```

An important point about the if is that the expressions which are executed if the condition is true cannot be reached otherwise. If the condition fails, then control **falls through** the if to the next executable expression. Two other forms of the if can be used in C. The first is an if without an else. If the if condition is not met, then control falls through to the end of the if. The format is the same as before, namely:

```
if ( condition ) {
   expressions
}
```

The second form allows for multiple tests, by immediately following the else with another if-else statement as follows:

```
if ( condition1 ) {
   expressions1
} else if ( condition2 ) {                                    (1)
   expressions2
} else
   expressions3
}
```

In this construct, a second if-else construct is embedded in the code at item (**1**). The effect of this set of tests is to say that *if* condition1 is not met, and *if* condition2 is met, *then* perform the second set of expressions, and so on. This construct describes an OR relation, meaning that exactly one of these sets of expressions will be performed and that they are mutually exclusive.

Any of the three forms of if can be used to **nest** tests. Nesting means that one test is made based on the success of the previous test. Thus the set that describes the range of values which meet both criterion is smaller than that which met just the first test, or the second:

```
if ( condition1 )                                         (1)
   if ( condition2 )                                      (2)
      if ( condition3 ) {                                 (3)
         expressions3
      } else {
         expressions2
      }
   else {
      expressions1
   }
else {
   expressions0
}
```

This is called an AND statement, because each successive test is further constraining the possibility of inclusion in the final set. Of course, any combination of the ifs can be done as well, and is worth experimenting with. Notice that the actions of the first two conditionals are themselves other if statements. No matter how complex these embedded if statements are, they represent single control structures, so the "outer" ifs need not (and, in general, should not) use curly braces. I have used the plural of expression (i.e., expressions3, expressions2, etc.), so the use of curly braces is mandated after the third conditional. Also note that all the statements associated with an if are indented the same.

9.2.3   Making Choices from More Than Two Alternatives

The previous decision-making constructs each select a set of expressions to evaluate based on the result of a comparison test. The basic mechanism allows a choice between two alternatives. The case where more than two alternatives exist can be handled with embedded if else constructs, but it is a bit cumbersome. C has an alternative construct, called switch that selects one set of expressions among many possible cases. The switch is a multiple-branch construct. The format is shown in "SimpleSwitch.c" below:

Figure 9.3: Multiple choice path decisions in SimpleSwitch.c

```
/*********************************************************/
/* FILE:       SimpleSwitch.c                           */
/*                                                      */
/* AUTHOR:     J.B. Hodges                              */
/* DATE:       August, 1993                             */
/* FUNCTION:   Displays information about a dog based   */
/*             on family membership.                    */
/* LIBRARIES:  Uses stdio.h function library            */
/* COMMENTS:   Demonstrates the use of                  */
/*             switch-case-break-default                */
/*********************************************************/

#include <stdio.h>

int
main(void)
{
  char dog;

  printf("Enter the type of dog that you own by character.\n");
  printf("Below is a list of options you can use.\n\n");
  printf("\tGolden Retriever        -- G\n" \
         "\tLabrador Retriever      -- L\n" \
         "\tFlatcoat Retriever      -- F\n" \
         "\tChesapeake Bay Retriever -- B\n" \
         "\tCurlycoat Retriever     -- C\n\n" \
         "Choice: ");
  scanf("%c", &dog);

  switch ( dog ) {                                        ① 
    case 'G':
    case 'g':                                             ②
      printf("\nGolden retriever: child friendly.\n");
      break;                                              ③
    case 'L':
    case 'l':
      printf("\nLabrador retriever: dives for rocks.\n");
      break;
    case 'F':
    case 'f':
      printf("\nFlatcoat retriever: black-gold.\n");
      break;
    case 'B':
    case 'b':
      printf("\nChesapeake bay retriever: bird hungry.\n");
      break;
```

Figure 9.3: Multiple choice path decisions in `SimpleSwitch.c` (cont)

```
    case 'C':
    case 'c':
      printf("\nCurlycoat retriever: never seen one.\n");
      break;
    default:
      printf("\nYou need a retriever!\n");                    (4)
    }

  return (0);
}
```

The **switch** is invoked as shown at item (**1**). The programmer supplied variable (in this case `dog`) is provided as the condition (in parentheses) and its value is interpreted at run-time. The various options are provided as per items (**2**) and (**3**), where the string `"case"` is required, as is the colon after the choice. In this program, character variables are used in the condition and case; however, integers can also be used in the condition. Both upper and lower case options were used in this program, to allow for user discretion. Notice that the empty statement body after the first case (at item **1**). When the cases are stacked in this way, the first nonempty statement block will be applied to all of the cases preceding it. Once a match is found between the value of the condition and one of the options, the corresponding expressions are evaluated until a **break** is found. In the **switch-case** construct, there is no need to define a compound statement and enclose it in curly braces; it is assumed that there will be a number of expressions to evaluate. Unfortunately, the construct doesn't automatically fall through to the end of the `switch` after executing the statements, and, without a `break` statement, will continue to execute the statements in cases which follow, until a `break` statement is found or the construct is ended. At that point the `switch` is exited. If none of the options match the condition and there is a `"default"` expression (item **4**), then the statements following the `default` are executed. Otherwise the `switch` is exited. An illustration of `SimpleSwitch.c` in operation is shown below.

```
localhost> gcc SimpleSwitch.c
localhost> a.out
Enter the type of dog that you own by character.
Below is a list of options you can use.
          Golden Retriever          -- G
          Labrador Retriever        -- L
          Flatcoat Retriever        -- F
          Chesapeake Bay Retriever -- B
          Curlycoat Retriever       -- C
Choice: G
Golden retriever: child friendly.
```

9.2.4 Increasing the Specificity of Comparisons

So far, we have talked only about simple comparisons within a condition, those which utilize a single relational operator and two variables. However, it is often the case that you will want to have a condition which makes a more complex comparison, such as to check if values are within a range. For example, you might want to find out if some person's age is between 21 and 30. If so, then you might want to perform some task on the person, and another task if not. In order to determine whether a variable's value is within a range, you have to perform two comparisons. This can be done with nested ifs of course, but that is not a single condition. Multiple comparisons in a single condition require the use of **logical connectives**.

In programming it is a frequently desirable to combine expressions with logical tests. For example, if you want to say:

```
IF x1 AND x2 AND x3 OR y1 THEN actions1
```

where "x1," "x2," "x3," and "y1" are potentially complex expressions, then you need to have some mechanism for performing the AND and OR tests. These are called *logical connectives* or *logical operators*. The logical connectives in C are demonstrated in the program "CompComp.c."

Figure 9.4: Compound logical expression comparisons in `CompComp.c`

```c
/********************************************************/
/* FILE:        CompComp.c                              */
/*                                                      */
/* AUTHOR:      J.B. Hodges                             */
/* DATE:        August, 1993                            */
/* FUNCTION:    Performs a compound comparison regarding */
/*              the use of specialized cloth for sewing. */
/* LIBRARIES:   Uses stdio.h function library           */
/* COMMENTS:    Demonstrates the use of C logical opers. */
/*              for AND (&&) and OR (||)                 */
/********************************************************/

#include <stdio.h>

int
main(void)
{
  char matl;
  int  hweave, lweave;

  printf("Enter the type of material you are using.\n");
  printf("Below is a list of options you can use.\n\n");
  printf("\tLight Packcloth  -- L\n" \
         "\tMedium Packcloth -- M\n" \
         "\tCordura          -- C\n\n" \
         "Matl: ");
  scanf("%c", &matl);

  switch ( matl ) {
    case 'L':
    case 'l': hweave = 220;
              lweave = 420;
              break;
    case 'M':
    case 'm': hweave = 420;
              lweave = 420;
              break;
    case 'C':
    case 'c': hweave = 520;
              lweave = 1000;
              break;
    default:  hweave = 1000;
              lweave = 1000;
  }
```

Figure 9.4: Compound logical expression comparisons in `CompComp.c` (cont.)

```
if ( ((matl == 'L')   ||
      (matl == 'l'))  &&
     (hweave >= 200)  &&
     (lweave >= 400) ) {
   printf("\nLight duty: stuff sacks.\n");
} else if ( ((matl == 'M')  ||
             (matl == 'm')) &&
            (hweave >= 400) &&
            (lweave >= 400) ) {
   printf("\nmedium duty: back packs.\n");
} else if ( ((matl == 'C')  ||
             (matl == 'c')) &&
            (hweave >= 500) &&
            (lweave >= 1000) ) {
   printf("\nheavy duty: mountaineering packs.\n");
} else
   printf("\nMake jackets with oxford cloth.\n");

   return (0);
}
```
①

In this example, both the **OR** (||) and the **AND** (&&) operators are used in compound tests. In the first such test (item **1**), the first test is to check the material type (a char variable). Both upper and lower cases are acceptable answers from the user and so an OR relation is used. If the material type is acceptable, then the vertical and horizontal weave is checked. These are deemed constraining tests, so an AND is used in the expression. The program is shown in execution below.

```
localhost> gcc CompComp.c
localhost> a.out
Enter the type of material you are using.
Below is a list of options you can use.
        Oxford            -- O
        Light Packcloth   -- L
        Medium Packcloth  -- M
        Cordura           -- C
Matl: C
heavy duty: mountaineering packs.
```

9.3 Iteration

Programs are most useful in allowing tasks which are performed repetitively to be codified into a single package. In a similar vein, some tasks are inherently repetitive, and programs which solve them are particularly useful. Consider a simple program which counts from one number to another number in user-provided increments. None of the programming constructs which have been presented so far can perform this task with variable limits or a variable increment. You would have to print the starting value, add the increment to it, test to see if the new value was greater than the ending value, print the new value, and so on until you had written all the statements. If you changed the ending value, then you would have to rewrite the program by adding or subtracting groups of statements. Fortunately, C has three iteration constructs which perform this task for you: (1) `while`, (2) `for`, and (3) `do-while`. Each of these is called a **looping construct** and will generally be referred to as such. We will introduce the `while` construct with the simple counting program called "`Count-ByN.c:`"

9.3.1 While Loops

A looping construct needs to know: (1) when to perform iteration, and (2) what to iterate. The `while` loop construct is the most general iteration mechanism in C, because it gives the programmer the most control over when and how iteration is performed. The `while` loop has two components: (1) a conditional, and (2) a body, but must explicitly control four related tasks: (1) initialization, (2) an entry/exit condition, called a **loop control expression**, which is based on a **loop control variable**, (3) an update mechanism, and (4) a **loop body** of associated executable statements.

Figure 9.5: Simple iteration using a while loop in `CountByN.c`

```
/***********************************************************/
/* FILE:        CountByN.c                             */
/*                                                     */
/* AUTHOR:      J.B. Hodges                            */
/* DATE:        August, 1993                           */
/* FUNCTION:    Displays a table of integers counted   */
/*              by an increment between two values.    */
/* APPROACH:    Uses stdio.h function library and while */
/* COMMENTS:    Demonstrates the use of the while loop  */
/*              Demonstrates the use of two assignment  */
/*              operators, var++ and +=.               */
/***********************************************************/

#include <stdio.h>

int
main(void)
{
    int first, last, incr, counter, current;

    printf("Input the starting/ending integers, and step: ");
    scanf("%d%d%d", &first, &last, &incr);

    current = first;                                        ①
    counter = 1;                                            ②

    while ( current < last ) {  ◄──────────────────         ③
      printf ("%5d %5d\n", counter, current);
      counter++;  ◄──────────────────────────              ④
      current += incr;                                      ⑤
    }

    return (0);
}
```

The **initialization** assigns values to the loop control variables which are used in the entry condition and the update mechanism. In `CountByN.c`, the initialization is noted at item (**1**), where `current`, which is the loop control variable, is assigned its initial value. Item (**2**) also notes an initialization of the `counter` variable, which is used in the program to keep track of how many times the loop body is executed. Part of the initialization for the while can be considered the reserved word while itself, which invokes the construct. The while reserved word must be followed by the entry condition and the body of the loop.

The loop control expression defines the loop entry condition and exit condition. The **entry condition** is a test which must be met before the loop body can be executed. The entry condition in the example (at item **3**) is a simple comparison between the value of `current` and the value of `last`. When the while entry condition is met, the while body is executed exactly once. This is called a loop **pass** or **cycle**. After the pass, the entry condition is tested again. The body of the while in `CountByN.c` should be cycled as long as the entry condition is satisfied (i.e., as long as the value of `current` is smaller than the value of `last`).

The **update mechanism** modifies the variables in the loop control expression so that it is *possible* to exit the loop. In order to determine whether the loop can ever be exited, the exit criterion should be looked at. The **exit condition** is the negation (i.e., logical complement) of the entry condition. In this example, the exit condition is satisfied when the value of `current` is greater than or equal to the value of `last`. Since `last` is static (i.e., it never changes throughout the program execution), the update mechanism must alter `current` upward toward `last`, as noted at item (**5**).

The while **body** is the compound statement which is executed when the entry condition is satisfied. In `CountByN.c`, the body consists of a printf statement, a counter update (item **4**), and an update of `current` at item (**5**). As with the decision-making constructs, the while signals a new context, and that is why the associated compound statments are indented with respect to the while statement and not with respect to the outer function (`main`).

Increment and Decrement Operators

The two update expressions in `CountByN.c` present the application of two new kinds of operators. The first is an increment operator (`++`), and the second is an assignment operator (`+=`). An **increment** operator performs the same task as adding 1 to a variable value, except that the change in variable value takes place at a different time depending on whether the `++` is placed before or after the variable identifier. A **prefix increment** is when the `++` precedes the variable, as shown below.

```
new = ++counter
```

In this case, the value of the `counter` is incremented, the expression is evaluated, and then the value of `new` is assigned. That is, *after* incrementing `counter`. If the `++` follows the variable identifier, the operation is called a **postfix increment**.

```
new = counter++
```

In postfix increment, the expression is evaluated, and the value assigned to new, based on the present value of counter, *before* incrementing counter. In both examples, after the expression is evaluated counter has been incremented and has the same value. When used alone, as in Count-ByN.c, the two operators have the same effect, but increment operators can be a source of off-by-one errors and care should be taken when using them. There are also decrement operators which function the same way as the increment operators.

Table 9.2: Increment and decrement operators in C

Expression		Initial Value	New Values
`new = current++`	$\Rightarrow$	`current = 1`	`current = 2, new = 1`
`new = ++current`	$\Rightarrow$	`current = 1`	`current = 2, new = 2`
`new = current--`	$\Rightarrow$	`current = 2`	`current = 1, new = 2`
`new = --current`	$\Rightarrow$	`current = 2`	`current = 1, new = 1`

Assignment Operators

An **assignment** operator modifies the basic assignment of variables in an arithmetic way. The assignment operator shown in CountByN.c at item (**5**) is an addition operator and works as follows. The two following expressions below are equivalent:

```
current = current + incr;
current += incr;
```

Thus, instead of simply incrementing or decrementing the variable current, this operator lets the programmer select what the increment will be. Likewise, there are assignment operators for the other arithmetic operations (Table 9.3).

Table 9.3: Assignment operators in C

Operator	Example Expression		Equivalent Expression
+=	current += expr	$\Rightarrow$	current = current + expr
-=	current -= expr	$\Rightarrow$	current = current - expr
*=	current *= expr	$\Rightarrow$	current = current * expr
/=	current /= expr	$\Rightarrow$	current = current / expr
%=	current %= expr	$\Rightarrow$	current = current % expr

The use of arithmetic assignment operators is illustrated in the execution of CountByN.c shown below:

```
localhost> gcc CountByN.c
localhost> a.out
Input the starting/ending integers, and step: 3 31 4
    1       3
    2       7
    3      11
    4      15
    5      19
    6      23
    7      27
```

where the increment is 4 and the arithmetic operator adds 4 to the current value of current during any particular iteration.

9.3.2 For Loops

The C for loop performs the same function as the while loop; however, instead of the abstract structure in the while, the initialization of the loop control variable, the entry condition, and the updating mechanism for the loop control variable are defined in the syntax of the construct, so as long as they are defined properly the loop will exit normally. The format of the for is shown below:

```
for ( loop-control-variable-initialization;
      entry-condition;
      loop-control-variable-update-expression ) {
  loop-body
}
```

As an example of its use, CountByN.c has been rewritten with a for loop below. Execution produces identical output.

Figure 9.6: Simple iteration using a for loop in CountByNFor.c

```
/**********************************************************/
/* FILE:       CountByNFor.c                           */
/*                                                      */
/* AUTHOR:     J.B. Hodges                             */
/* DATE:       August, 1993                            */
/* FUNCTION:   Displays a table of integers counted    */
/*             by an increment between two values.     */
/* LIBRARIES:  Uses stdio.h function library           */
/* COMMENTS:   Demonstrates the use of the for loop    */
/**********************************************************/

#include <stdio.h>

int
main(void)
{
    int     first, last, incr, counter, current;

    printf("Input the starting and ending integers and the step: ");
    scanf("%d%d%d", &first, &last, &incr);

    counter = 1;

    for ( current = first;                                          ①
          current < last;
②         current += incr ) {                                       ③
        printf ("%5d %5d\n", counter, current);
        counter++;
    }

    return (0);
}
```

In "CountByNFor.c" the for reserved word invokes the construct. The three components of the for control mechanism are all embedded in a set of parentheses. Only the entry condition is a logical expression, the other two can be any legal expression. The initialization expression (at item **1**) is an *assignment* of the value of first to the variable current, which is the loop control variable in this example. The entry condition is the test (item **2**) of whether current is less than the terminating value, last. The updating expression (item **3**) applies the incrementing assignment operator to current with the value of incr. Note that the variable counter is used in the body of the for, but is otherwise not used in the control of the construct. The loop control variable should not be modified in the loop body.

9.3.3 Do-While Loops

The do-while loop is identical to the while except that it is used when the loop body should be continually cycled *until* a condition is met. One of the most frequent uses of a do-while loop is for user input. For example, if the programmer wants the user to keep typing values until a non-negative value is entered, then a do-while is an appropriate construct to use. Consider the program "Get-PosValues.c" below.

Figure 9.7: Simple iteration using a do while loop in GetPosValues.c

```
/**********************************************************/
/* FILE:        GetPosValues.c                            */
/*                                                        */
/* AUTHOR:      J.B. Hodges                               */
/* DATE:        August, 1993                              */
/* FUNCTION:    Reads and displays integers until a non-  */
/*              negative value is read.                   */
/* APPROACH:    Uses stdio.h function library             */
/* COMMENTS:    Demonstrates the use of the do-while      */
/**********************************************************/

#include <stdio.h>

int
main(void)
{
  int readval;

  do {                                                      (1)
      printf("\nInput an integer: ");
      scanf("%d", &readval);
      printf("\nInteger value read is: %d\n", readval);
  } while ( readval <= 0 );                                 (2)
      printf("\n\nFinal integer value read is: %d\n\n", readval);

  return (0);
}
```

The construct is invoked with the reserved word do (at item **1**), followed by the compound statement which defines the loop body. The construct is terminated by the loop entry condition, which includes the reserved word while (item **2**). The effect of this construct is to guarantee at least one pass through the loop body, since the conditional is tested after the body is executed.

```
localhost> gcc GetPosValues.c
localhost> a.out
Input an integer: -1
Integer value read is: -1
Input an integer: -10
Integer value read is: -10
Input an integer: 0
Integer value read is: 0
Input an integer: 10
Integer value read is: 10
Final integer value read is: 10
```

9.3.4   Operations with Loops

Many tasks can be performed with loops that will not be presented here but that you should experiment with on your own. A common use is to **nest** looping constructs so that you perform the same operations on different variables. For example, if you wanted to produce an addition table, you could run one loop whose control variable is the first addend, and you could run a second loop and whose control variable is the second addend. The operation would only be performed on the **inner loop** and would perform the addition of the two addends. In a nested loop, the inner loop cycles through all of its values for each value of the outer loop, so the inner loop initialization must occur within the **outer loop**. Nesting can be done with any number of variables.

Another task that can be performed with loops is to count events while cycling. One simple example is to read in integer values until some criterion (say, a negative integer is input) is met, and to count the number of even values and the number of odd values. The programmer must create variables to keep the current tally of even and odd values, and increment them within the loop body.

9.4 Functions

As a program becomes more complex, it also becomes more difficult to read, debug, and test. The design of a program is usually accomplished using an approach called **iterative refinement**. In this approach, the original problem is broken into identifiable subtasks. Then each of those subtasks is, in turn, refined to its subtasks, and so on until each subtask is finally refined to the point where it can be written as source code directly. The problem with this approach is that none of the code gets written until the most specific code is designed and written, even though all of the higher-level organization has already been done. Another approach which uses iterative refinement is called **modular programming**. In modular programming, the overall problem solution is associated with the main function; however, each subtask can be associated with a function **called** by main. As the refinement process deepens, the programmer can define new functions to solve the related subtasks. The functions are themselves miniprograms which address a particular component of the overall problem. The construction of functions and their interaction with the program which calls them will be addressed in the sections which follow.

9.4.1 Function Format and Definition

All functions (e.g., system library functions, user-defined functions, the main function[1]) have the same general structure: a header, declarations, and a statement block, as shown in the function "MySquare:"

Figure 9.8: Function structure in MySquare

```
/*********************************************************/
/* MySquare: Calulates the square of a values           */
/*                                                       */
/* INPUT:    varval                                      */
/* OUTPUT:   None                                        */
/* LOCAL:    sqval                                       */
/* RETURN:   double                                      */
/* USAGE:    [main] MySquare(4) => 16.0                  */
/*********************************************************/

double                                    function type declaration
MySquare(double varval)                   function header
{
  double sqval;

  sqval = varval * varval;                function body

  return (sqval);                         function return
}
```

Comments in Functions

The first thing that you should notice about this sample function is that it has its own banner comment. The banners associated with a function are different from those for a program, usually shorter. Functions generally require a banner that tells what the function name is, what it does, what its input and output parameters are, and what it returns. Sometimes, a sample call is useful in the function banner, to remind the reader of how the function is invoked.

---

1. main is a function that is the starting point for all programs. It organizes the source code fragments of a program.

Function Parameters

The source code shown in Fig. 9.8 defines a function called `"MySquare"` which has one parameter `"varval,"` and one local variable, `"sqval."` A **parameter** is a variable which is declared in the function header and serves as an interface element to the calling module. Each function parameter must have a one-to-one correspondence with a function argument when the function is called. A **local variable** only has meaning in the scope of the function. That is, the value of the *local* variable is restricted to the context of the function body. If there is another variable with the same name in another function, or the function which called `MySquare`, it can have a different value assigned to it without adverse consequences. This is called **lexical scoping**, because the scope of a variable's value is restricted to the local statements.

Function Types

There are two types of functions: (1) functions intended to return a value; and (2) functions intended to communicate, and perhaps modify, variable values shared with other functions. The function `MySquare` is one of the former function types; it returns a value. Functions which return values can be used on the right-hand side of expressions, since the value they return is typed and should fit into the context of the expression. The library functions sqrt and pow return values and can be used in expressions directly. The value they return takes the place of the function call when the expression in which they reside is evaluated.

Function Type Declaration

Whether or not a function returns a value, it should be declared as though it will. A `void` function need not be declared, but good programming style suggests that it is best to declare even `void` functions. To specify the type of value returned, it is necessary to specify the function type along with the function name in the declarations. This is done just prior to the function header. The function `MySquare` is declared a `double` function, meaning that the function should return a `double` value. If a function is not declared, the compiler default is type `int`.

9.4.2 Function Application

A function is invoked (i.e., applied) with a **function call** from another function. The program shown in Fig. 9.9, `"FirstModRet.c"` demonstrates the organization and use of `MySquare`.

Figure 9.9: Function structure in `FirstModRet.c`

```
/**********************************************************/
/* FILE:        FirstModRet.c                            */
/*                                                       */
/* AUTHOR:      J.B. Hodges                              */
/* DATE:        August, 1993                             */
/* FUNCTION:    Reads a value to square, squares it, and */
/*              and then prints both on a line.          */
/* APPROACH:    Uses stdio.h function library. The       */
/*              calculation is performed in function     */
/*              MySquare.                                */
/* FUNCTIONS:   MySquare: calculates the square          */
/* COMMENTS:    Demonstrates modular design for a        */
/*              function with a return value.            */
/*              Demonstrates the use of prototypes.      */
/**********************************************************/

#include <stdio.h>

double MySquare(double varval);                              ①

int
main(void)
{
   double val, sq;                                          ②

   printf("\nInput a value to square: ");
   scanf("%f", &val);
   sq = MySquare(val);                                      ③
   printf("\nThe square of %6.4f is %6.4f\n\n", val, sq);

   return (0);
}
```

Figure 9.9: Function structure in `FirstModRet.c` (cont.)

```
/*************************************************************/
/* NAME:      MySquare: Calulates the square of a values */
/* INPUT:     double varval : the value to be squared    */
/* LOCAL:     double sqval  : the squared value          */
/* OUTPUT:    None                                       */
/* RETURN:    double sqval                               */
/* USAGE:     [main] MySquare(4) => 16.0                 */
/*************************************************************/

double                                                    ④
MySquare(double varval)
{
  double sqval;

  sqval = varval * varval;                                ⑤

  return (sqval);
}
```

Program Organization

The first thing that you need to notice in this listing is the organization. The main function is listed first, and `MySquare` is listed second. This is made possible by the function prototype noted at item (**1**). A **function prototype** is a copy of the function declaration and header (item **4**) without the associated function body. The prototype is terminated with a semicolon. The prototype must come before any function definition and there should be one prototype for every function in the file, *except* for main. The prototype allows the programmer to position functions anywhere in the file, because it already has a definition of the declaration, number, and type of parameters for the function. If the prototype is left out, the program will compile with warnings, since the functions will automatically be declared as type int, which may clash with the actual declarations when found.

Variable Type Consistency

The second item of interest is the variable declaration in main (item **2**). It is very important that the variable and function types be consistent throughout the program and its functions. The function `MySquare` is declared as a type double, so the value returned should be consistent with the double type. The parameter varval is declared as a double in `MySquare` and, after multiplication, is assigned to a double variable sqval. The value of sqval is returned to main (item **5**). The value returned by `MySquare` is assigned to the variable sq (item **2**) in the function call (item **3**), which is declared in main as double, so the type logic is consistent throughout.

Function Call

The final note of interest is the function call itself. When a function is defined, each of its parameters must be declared. They can have any names the programmer wishes because of variable scoping; however, the order and types **must** be consistent with the function call, in which function arguments will be paired by order. Because of this requirement, the variable identifiers used in the calling function need not be the same as those in the function parameter list. There are advantages and disadvantages to doing so. First, by keeping the variable identifers the same between functions, the programmer is less likely to get confused with many variable identifiers floating about. Second, the variable identifiers will probably make more sense to the programmer if kept consistent with the main, or calling, function. On the other hand, an important strength of modular programming and procedural abstraction is the separation of functions so that they are't mutually dependent. If the function parameters are associated with what the function does, and not with what it is used for by any particular function or program, then the function can be used by many programs. This extends its usefullness.

The function call for MySquare, in main (item **3**), has the single argument val. When the function is called, the value associated with val is copied into the MySquare parameter varval. As long as the types are assignment compatible there is no problem. In this case, both val and varval are declared double.

```
localhost> gcc FirstModRet.c
localhost> a.out
Input a value to square: 5.874
The square of 5.8740 is 34.5039
```

9.4.3   Functions that Pass Variable Values

As mentioned previously, there are functions which return values and there are functions which manipulate variables. There are three kinds of functions that manipulate variables: (1) output functions, (2) input functions, and (3) input/output functions.[1]

Output Functions

An **output function** is one that may have values which are passed to it from the calling function, but the function itself does not modify the values in any way which would affect the calling function. The most common form of output functions are those which print initial instructions to a user or print variable

---

1. Strictly speaking, one thinks of input, output, and input/output parameters, rather than functions; however, there are examples of functions which perform these tasks.

values, such as "PrintVals" in Fig. 9.10.

Figure 9.10: Function structure in PrintVals

```
/**********************************************************/
/* PrintVals: Prints output variables                     */
/*                                                        */
/* INPUT:     char   first, middle, last                  */
/*            int    ndogs                                 */
/* OUTPUT:    None                                         */
/* RETURN:    None                                         */
/* USAGE:     [main] PrintVals(ch1, ch2, ch3, num);       */
/**********************************************************/

void
PrintVals(char arg1, char arg2, char arg3, int arg4)           ①
{
  printf("\nHello, %c %c %c, you own %d dogs, right?\n\n", \
          arg1, arg2, arg3, arg4);

  return;
}
```

This function has four parameters: arg1, arg2, arg3, and arg4. The first three parameters are char types, and the last is an int type. This is our first function example with more than one parameter, and it has no return value. It is important to declare each parameter separately. This is noted at item (**1**). Notice that there is only one expression in the function other than the return statement, and that there are no assignments in the function. Thus, the PrintVals function only produces a **side effect** to display some values, but otherwise has no effect on the program which calls it. Besides functions that return a value, output functions are the easiest to understand, because they effectively take a copy of the value associated with a variable and perform some task on it. This is called **call by value**. Because a copy of the value associated with a variable is provided to the function, the value in the original value is not affected.

Input Functions

An **input function** is one that has parameters whose values will be used in the calling function, but are initially assigned values in the local function. If more than one variable's value is needed in the calling module, then the return statement cannot be used. In general, call by value would be inefficient in such a case, because many variables use a lot of memory. Copying of variable values would be computationally costly and would take up even more memory.

Since the programmer already knows that the variable value is going to change, the original memory address and value can be manipulated directly.

This is called **call by reference**, because the function call uses the address of the variable rather than the variable value itself. The main program can provide to the function the address of the variable whose value is to change, and the function can return a value into that address which `main` can use. The only thing passed to the function is the memory address for the variable (see Fig. 9.11):

Figure 9.11: Function parameter passing, memory addresses, and pointers

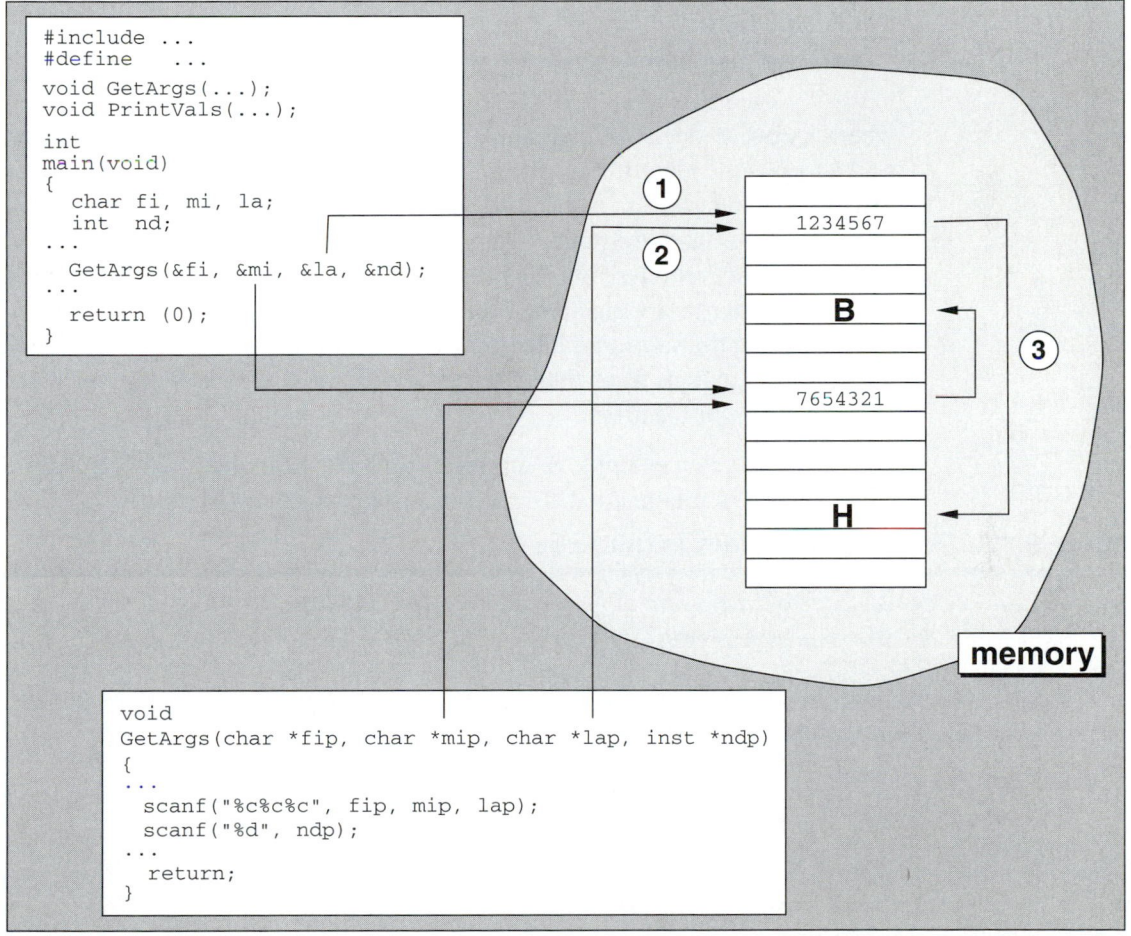

The `main` function and the function it calls can share the same address and values, but have different identifiers. In Fig. 9.11, the address-of operator (&) is used (at item **1**) to reference the addresses of the `char` variables `mi` and `la`. In the `GetArgs` function header, parameters are declared of type 'address-to-char' variables. These are called **pointers**, because they "point" to the variable. A pointer is an object that can be referenced like a variable, but represents an address. A pointer is declared as follows.

```
type  *identifierp
    └┘
```

Example		Type	Pointer Identifier
char *fip	$\Rightarrow$	char *	fip
int *ndp	$\Rightarrow$	int *	ndp

where **type** * declares a variable to be a pointer of type **type**, and **identifierp** is the identifier for the pointer. Using this notation, fip, mip, and lap are pointers to char variables, and ndp is a pointer to an int variable. The "p" in the identifier name helps to remind the programmer that this is a pointer. It is not required, but is a useful mechanism for keeping track of pointers. The pointer to a variable and the address of a variable are different ways of referencing the same variable (item **2**). The (variable) value associated with the address (at item **3**) is then the same even though it is being referenced through different identifers.

Fig. 9.12 shows an example of a typical input function that reads values from the keyboard in the function GetArgs and returns them to main.

Figure 9.12: Output parameters in GetArgs

```
/*****************************************************/
/* GetArgs:   Reads input variables                  */
/*                                                   */
/* INPUT:     None                                   */
/* OUTPUT:    char *firstp, *middlep, *lastp         */
/*            int  *ndogsp                            */
/* LOCAL:     None                                   */
/* RETURN:    None                                   */
/* USAGE:     [main] GetArgs(&fi, &mi, &li, &nd);    */
/*****************************************************/

void
GetArgs(char *firstp, char *middlep, char *lastp, int *ndogsp)       ①
{
  printf("\nPlease type your initials, separated by no spaces: ");
  scanf("%c%c%c", firstp, middlep, lastp);                           ②
  printf("\nPlease type how many dogs you own: ");
  scanf("%d", ndogsp);

  return;
}
```

The function parameters: firstp, middlep, lastp, and ndogsp (at item **1**) are the **addresses** in memory (pointers) where the variable values are stored. Notice at item (**2**) that the variables being read with scanf do not require ampersands (**address-of** operators). This is because the parameters already represent memory addresses.

The use of input and output functions, particularly PrintVals and GetArgs is illustrated in the following complete program, "FirstModI-O.c," illustrated in Fig. 9.13. This program does the same thing as the FirstIO.c program; however, the display and input segments of the code are implemented with the functions we have just presented. In this program, the two functions are repeated for coherence. Note that the main function is organized at the top of the file, because C allows the programmer to organize functions in any order. This program is similar in organization to FirstModRet.c. Item (**1**) notes the function prototypes for GetArgs and PrintVals. Also similar to the previous program is the use of local variables in main (item **2**), which hold the values that are associated with the functions.

Figure 9.13: Use of input parameters in `FirstModIO.c`

```
/***********************************************************/
/* FILE:        FirstModIO.c                               */
/*                                                         */
/* AUTHOR:      J.B. Hodges                                */
/* DATE:        August, 1993                               */
/* FUNCTION:    Reads user's initials and number of dogs   */
/*              and then prints them on one line.          */
/* APPROACH:    Uses stdio.h function library. Input is    */
/*              separate from main. Output is separate     */
/*              from main.                                 */
/* FUNCTIONS:   GetArgs:   reads the input data            */
/*              PrintVals: displays the output             */
/* COMMENTS:    Demonstrates modular design for I/O with   */
/*              functions.                                 */
/***********************************************************/

#include <stdio.h>

void PrintVals(char arg1, char arg2, char arg3, int arg4)
void GetArgs(char *firstp, char *middlep, char *lastp, int *ndogsp);    ①

int
main(void)
{
  char fi, mi, la;                                                      ②
  int  nd;

  GetArgs(&fi, &mi, &la, &nd);                                          ③
  PrintVals(fi, mi, la, nd);

  return (0);
}
```

Referring back to Fig. 9.12, the function call for `GetArgs` (item **3**) illustrates the use of call by reference, since the address-of operator refers to the address of the associated variable. So any variable which is manipulated in a function will be referenced in the function call with an address-of operator (just as for **scanf** and for the same reasons). This is why the four arguments to `GetArgs` are passed in with address-of operators. On the other hand, an output function does not need to have consistent values for variables with its calling function, so a **copy** of the variable value can be sent into the function. Although our examples have used all call by reference or call by value, this is not a requirement. What is important is that the programmer recognize which arguments are somehow coming back into the **main** or calling function and which are not.

Figure 9.13: Use of input parameters in `FirstModIO.c` (cont.)

```
/*********************************************************/
/* GetArg: Reads input variabless                       */
/*                                                       */
/* INPUT:     None                                       */
/* OUTPUT:    firstp, middlep, lastp, ndogsp             */
/* LOCAL:     None                                       */
/* RETURN:    None                                       */
/* USAGE:     [main] GetArgs(&fi, &mi, &li, &nd);        */
/*********************************************************/

void
GetArgs(char *firstp, char *middlep, char *lastp, int *ndogsp)      ①
{
  printf("\nPlease type your initials, separated by no spaces: ");
  scanf("%c%c%c", firstp, middlep, lastp);                          ②
  printf("\nPlease type how many dogs you own: ");
  scanf("%d", ndogsp);

  return;
}

/*********************************************************/
/* PrintVals: Prints output variables                   */
/*                                                       */
/* INPUT:     first, middle, last, ndogs                 */
/* OUTPUT:    None                                       */
/* RETURN:    None                                       */
/* USAGE:     [main] PrintVals(ch1, ch2, ch3, num);      */
/*********************************************************/

void
PrintVals(char arg1, char arg2, char arg3, int arg4)
{
  printf("\nHello, %c %c %c, you own %d dogs, right?\n\n", \
         arg1, arg2, arg3, arg4);

  return;
}
```

The program `FirstModIO.c` is compiled and run below.

```
localhost> gcc -o fmioc FirstModIO.c
localhost> fmioc
Please type your initials, separated by no spaces: JBH
Please type how many dogs you own: 2
Hello, J B H, you own 2 dogs, right?
```

9.4.4 Modular Programming and Procedural Abstraction

The design of programs using functions utilizes the method of iterative refinement discussed on page 319. The idea of looking at a problem statement and identifying the different tasks which need to be performed is the basis for all program development. The **modular** approach to program development uses programming constructs with predictable behavior to design the program. **Procedural abstraction** means that the conceptual subtasks which are used to solve a problem, or a subproblem, make up what is called an abstraction level for the problem. If these subtasks can be implemented with functions, then the solution to a subtask is kept distinct from the problem itself, because only the interface is shared between the original function call and the function implementation. If each conceptual level is implemented in this way, then the programmer is free to (later) change how a task is implemented, or solved, without affecting the other components of the problem. Procedural abstraction has many benefits, some of which are discussed in Chapter 11.

In order to illustrate the application of modular programming and procedural abstraction, let's construct a program to solve the simple but possibly real problem presented below:

Balls in a Box

Suppose that you have a number of balls that you want to store in boxes, and that you want to store as many balls per box as possible. Write a program which, given the diameter of the balls and the dimensions of the box will return the number of balls that will fit into the box. You can assume that all balls for a particular box will be the same diameter.

This is fairly illustrative of the types of programming problems that you are likely to see, except that normally the problem statement will also include an example of how the input is to be formatted and how the output is to be displayed. We will consider this aspect of the problem somewhat arbitrary for now, as long as it looks reasonable when we are done.

Solution Feasibility

The question that one must ask oneself before embarking on this task is: can it even be done? This is called a question of **feasibility**. Clearly, it makes sense that it could be done, as long as we can figure out the volume of the box and the volume for each ball, because we can then divide one by the other to get the number of balls. Almost. Balls will actually take up more volume than their own volume, so we have to have the *actual* volume that the ball requires. Now, can we do this? The answer is yes! The next step is to identify the mechanism whereby the problem solution will be brought about. We have written our potential approach in English, but we need to translate this into an **algorithm**, a formalized description of how to solve the problem. In order to do so, we must identify the knowledge domain needed to solve the problem, and then show how we can use it to get from the program inputs to the desired program outputs. In this example, the domain knowledge is algebraic, so designing the algorithm is not really a problem:

```
volume of box   = length x width x height
volume of ball = 4/3 x pi x radius-cubed
actual volume of ball = (2 x radius)-cubed
number of actual volumes along length = length / (2 x radius)       (1)
number of actual volumes along width  = width  / (2 x radius)       (2)
number of actual volumes along height = height / (2 x radius)       (3)
number of actual volumes that will fit into box nicely = (1) x (2) x (3)
```

As you can see, we do not really need the volumes for the balls to solve the problem, but it is better to write down extra information and come to this conclusion than to leave it out and wonder why you cannot solve the problem. This description already needs some refinement in how we name things, so lets decide on a few variable names now:

```
boxvol      = blength x bwidth x bheight
ballvol     = 4/3 x PI x ballrad x ballrad x ballrad
actvol      = 8 x ballrad x ballrad x ballrad
numvlength  = blength / (2 x ballrad)
numvwidth   = bwidth / (2 x ballrad)
numvheight  = bheight / (2 x ballrad)
numvols     = numvlength x numvwidth x numvheight
numballvols = boxvol / ballvol
numacts     = boxvol / actvol
```

As you can see, we have kept the ball volume and actual volume for comparison purposes, and that there are really only 4 input variables (`blength`, `bwidth`, `bheight`, `brad`) and one constant (`PI`) that are used in this process. All the other variable values can be calculated from these.

Subtask Refinement

Now that we have some faith in the eventual success of developing a program to solve the Balls and Boxes problem, we need to organize the program by subtasks. Here is a first cut at an algorithm (the algebraic tasks have already been defined).

- display instructions
- obtain values for 4 variables
- perform volume calculations for box and ball
- perform comparison calculations
- display information

In the modular programming approach, each of these subtasks will either be statement in the **main** function or they will be handled by functions. Since we have already seen two functions in this chapter that perform similar tasks as items labeled (**1**), (**2**) and (**3**), lets assume that we can modify them to suit our needs accordingly. This is where modular programming satisfies the need for code reusability.

Framework Construction

Often the most difficult task in writing a program is to write that first level of functions and the **main** program. It requires a committment to the variable names, their types, and the function types, even if you think they might change later on. Lets give it a try. Lets modify the program `FirstModIO.c`, because it has a similar structure. Here is what I have done prior to displaying the program below:

- Copy the file and rename it.
- Edit the banner comments for the main program and the functions.
- Add known variable names to protocols, calls, and headers.
- Modify the functions that we already have to do the right thing.
- Leave stubs for the functions we haven't written yet.

Granted this is a number of steps, but we do not want to print this thing out many times. The intermediate file, named `"BallsAndBoxes.c,"` is shown in Fig. 9.14. The three functions that were similar to `PrintVals` and `GetArgs` should be very straightforward to understand, as the the same functionality is invoked from them and only the names and number of variables, and literal strings, are being changed. Item (**1**) notes that we have to add the math library functions if we are going to use the **pow** function. If you do not add this **include** statement, the program will still compile, and it will not complain during execution, but you will get junk for the values associated with the function which was never used. Item (**2**) notes that we have to add a constant for `PI` for the true ball volume calculation. Item (**3**), notes the function protocols for the program. This is really a very good way to keep track of all the variables you have chosen, especially if you have the **main** program located at the top of the file, since your function calls will all be close to the protocol definitions and it will be easier for you to perform type and argument position check-ing. Item (**4**) notes that sometimes some inline comments serve to remind the programmer of what these odd identifiers refer to. For my own programming, I never place variable descriptions inline, but, rather, in the program or func-tion banner. I have placed them inline in this example for conservation of space. Item (**5**) tells the novice C programmer that functions without argu-ments must use parentheses or the function will not be invoked. You will not get an error, but nothing related to the function will happen. Item (**6**) is proba-bly the one interesting thing in this first series of changes. We have not mixed input and output variables in previous examples; however, in `CalcVols` some variables, such as `blen` are being passed in but are not changed by the function, whereas others, such as `boxvolp` are being modified in the func-tion. Hence you see both call by value and call by reference in the function call, and you will also see it in the protocols (item **3**) and headers (item **7**).

Figure 9.14: Main program and function calls for `BallsAndBoxes.c`

```
/***************************************************************/
/* FILE:        BallsAndBoxes.c                                */
/*                                                             */
/* AUTHOR:      J.B. Hodges                                    */
/* DATE:        August, 1993                                   */
/* FUNCTION:    Reads information about boxes and balls        */
/*              and returns information about how many         */
/*              balls will fit into the box.                   */
/* APPROACH:    Uses stdio.h function library. Uses the        */
/*              algorithms for box volume and sphere           */
/*              volume.                                        */
/* FUNCTIONS:   GetDims: reads the object dimensions           */
/*              PrintNums: displays the number of balls        */
/*              CalcVols: calculates object volume             */
/*              CompVols: compares object volumes              */
/* COMMENTS:    Demonstrates modular program design            */
/***************************************************************/

#include <stdio.h>
#include <math.h>                                                    ①

#define PI 3.14159                                                   ②

void PrintDirs(void);                                               ③
void GetDims(double *blenp, double *bwidp, double *bdepp, double *bradp);
            int *numvlengthp, int *numvwidthp, int *numvheightp);
void CalcVols(double blen, double bwid, double bdep, double brad,
              double *boxvolp, double *ballvolp, double *actvolp,
void CompVols(double boxvol, double ballvol, double actvol,
              int *numvolsp, int *numballvolsp, int *numactsp,
              int numvlength, int numvwidth, int numvheight);
void PrintNums(int nact, int nballs, int nvols);

int
main(void)
{
  double blength, bwidth, bheight,        /* box dimensions    */
         ballrad,                         /* ball dimensions   */
         boxvol, ballvol, actvol;         /* volume variables */    ④
  int    numvols, numballvols, numacts,   /* output variables */
         numvlength, numvwidth, numvheight;

  PrintDirs();                                                      ⑤
  GetDims(&blength, &bwidth, &bheight, &ballrad);
  CalcVols(blength, bwidth, bheight, ballrad, &boxvol, &ballvol,    ⑥
           &actvol, &numvlength, &numvwidth, &numvheight);
  CompVols(boxvol, ballvol, actvol, &numvols, &numballvols,
           &numacts, numvlength, numvwidth, numvheight);
  PrintNums(numvols, numballvols, numacts);
  return (0);
}
```

Figure 9.14: `PrintDirs` function for `BallsAndBoxes.c` (cont.)

```c
/******************************************************************/
/* PrintDirs: Prints instructions to user                        */
/*                                                                */
/* INPUT:    None                                                 */
/* OUTPUT:   None                                                 */
/* RETURN:   None                                                 */
/* USAGE:    [main] PrintDirs();                                  */
/******************************************************************/

void
PrintDirs(void)
{
  printf("\n*****************************************\n" \
         " ***             BALLS AND BOXES          ***\n" \
         " ***                                      ***\n" \
         " *** This program calculates the number   ***\n" \
         " *** of balls of radius 'R' that will     ***\n" \
         " *** fit into a box of dimensions 'L',    ***\n" \
         " *** 'W', and 'H'.                        ***\n" \
         " ***                                      ***\n" \
         " *** The user enters the box dimensions   ***\n" \
         " *** and the ball radius.                 ***\n" \
         " ***                                      ***\n" \
         " *** The program displays the number of   ***\n" \
         " *** balls that will fit based on three   ***\n" \
         " *** measures:                            ***\n" \
         " ***                                      ***\n" \
         " ***       (1) cubic volume displaced     ***\n" \
         " ***       (2) true volume displaced      ***\n" \
         " ***       (3) actual volume displaced    ***\n" \
         " ***                                      ***\n" \
         "*****************************************\n\n");

  return;
}
```

Figure 9.14: `GetDims` function and function stub for `CalcVols` function (cont.)

```
/*****************************************************************/
/* GetDims:   Reads box and ball dimensions variables          */
/*                                                             */
/* INPUT:     None                                             */
/* OUTPUT:    blenp, bwidp, bdepp, bradp                       */
/* RETURN:    None                                             */
/* USAGE:     [main]                                           */
/*                                                             */
/*            GetDims(&blength, &bwidth, &bheight, &ballrad)    */
/*                                                             */
/*****************************************************************/

void
GetDims(double *blenp, double *bwidp, double *bdepp, double *bradp)
{
  printf("\nPlease type the box dimensions, separated by spaces: ");
  scanf("%f%f%f", blenp, bwidp, bdepp);
  printf("\nPlease type the ball radius: ");
  scanf("%f", bradp);

  return;
}


/*****************************************************************/
/* CalcVols: Calculates object volume                          */
/*                                                             */
/* INPUT:     blength, bwid, bdep, brad                        */
/* OUTPUT:    boxvolp, ballvolp, actvolp, numvlengthp,         */
/*            numvwidthp, numvheightp                          */
/* RETURN:    None                                             */
/* USAGE:     [main]                                           */
/*                                                             */
/* CalcVols(blength, bwidth, bheight, ballrad, &boxvol, &ballvol, */
/*          &actvol, &numvlength, &numvwidth, &numvheight);    */
/*                                                             */
/*****************************************************************/

void
CalcVols(double blen, double bwid, double bdep, double brad,
         double *boxvolp, double *ballvolp, double *actvolp,
         int *numvlengthp, int *numvwidthp, int *numvheightp)
{

  return;
}
```

(7)

Figure 9.14: `CompVols` function stub and `PrintNums` function (cont.)

```
/****************************************************************/
/* CompVols: Compares object volumes                            */
/*                                                              */
/* INPUT:     boxvol, ballvol, actvol, numvlength,              */
/*            numvwidth, numvheight                             */
/* OUTPUT:    numvolsp, numballvolsp, numactsp                  */
/* RETURN:    None                                              */
/* USAGE:     [main]                                            */
/*                                                              */
/*    CompVols(boxvol, ballvol, actvol, &numvols, &numballvols, */
/*             &numacts, numvlength, numvwidth, numvheight);    */
/*                                                              */
/****************************************************************/

void
CompVols(double boxvol, double ballvol, double actvol,
         int *numvolsp, int *numballvolsp, int *numactsp,
         int numvlength, int numvwidth, int numvheight)
{

  return;

}


/****************************************************************/
/* PrintNums: Prints output variables                           */
/*                                                              */
/* INPUT:     numvols, numballvols, numacts                     */
/* OUTPUT:    None                                              */
/* RETURN:    None                                              */
/* USAGE:     [main] PrintNums(numvols, numballvols, numacts);  */
/****************************************************************/

void
PrintNums(int numvols, int numballvols, int numacts)
{
  printf("\nCUBIC DISPLACEMENT:  %3d balls will fit into the box\n"  \
         "TRUE DISPLACEMENT:   %3d balls will fit into the box\n"    \
         "ACTUAL DISPLACEMENT: %3d balls will fit into the box\n\n", \
         numvols, numballvols, numacts);

  return;
}
```

What we have in this first attempt is a program which will compile but will not function properly simply because some of the guts are missing. Let us now complete the phase with one of the functions, and leave the other as an exercise. We decided earlier that the calculations that we wanted to perform, given that we could calculate the object volumes and the number of ball volumes along any particular box dimension, would be as follows.

```
numvols      = numvlength x numvwidth x numvheight
numballvols = boxvol / ballvol
numacts      = boxvol / actvol
```

so all we need to do is convert this **pseudocode**[1] into source code and dump it into the function statement block. This has been done below:

Figure 9.14: Pseudocode conversion in `CompVols` (cont.)

```
/****************************************************************/
/* CompVols: Compares object volumes                           */
/*                                                             */
/* INPUT:    boxvol, ballvol, actvol, numvlength,             */
/*           numvwidth, numvheight                            */
/* OUTPUT:   numvolsp, numballvolsp, numactsp                 */
/* RETURN:   None                                             */
/* USAGE:    [main]                                           */
/*                                                             */
/*    CompVols(boxvol, ballvol, actvol, &numvols, &numballvols, */
/*             &numacts, numvlength, numvwidth, numvheight);   */
/*                                                             */
/****************************************************************/

void
CompVols(double boxvol, double ballvol, double actvol,
         int *numvolsp, int *numballvolsp, int *numactsp,
         int numvlength, int numvwidth, int numvheight)
{
  *numvolsp      = numvlength * numvwidth * numvheight;
  *numballvolsp = boxvol / ballvol;
  *numactsp      = boxvol / actvol;

  return;
}
```

①

②

Notice that those variables which are being called by reference use what is called the **indirection operator**, and those that are called by value are used directly. The indirection operator takes as an argument a pointer and returns the associated variable. Hence, if we want to assign a value to a variable which we only have access to through a pointer, we must dereference it with the indirection operator. As a final illustration of functions in C, I am including a sample run from the program we just developed.

---

1. Pseudocode means an English version of the algorithm that is so close to source code that it is one step away. It is often easier to write source code on paper as pseudocode and translate it when editing.

```
localhost> gcc BallsAndBoxes.c
localhost> a.out
    ********************************************
    ***            BALLS AND BOXES          ***
    ***                                     ***
    *** This program calculates the number  ***
    *** of balls of radius 'R' that will    ***
    *** fit into a box of dimensions 'L',   ***
    *** 'W', and 'H'.                       ***
    ***                                     ***
    *** The user enters the box dimensions  ***
    *** and the ball radius.                ***
    ***                                     ***
    *** The program displays the number of  ***
    *** balls that will fit based on three  ***
    *** measures:                           ***
    ***                                     ***
    ***          (1) cubic volume displaced ***
    ***          (2) true volume displaced  ***
    ***          (3) actual volume displaced***
    ***                                     ***
    ********************************************

Please type the box dimensions, separated by spaces: 12.5 24.1 10.5
Please type the ball radius: 2.25

CUBIC DISPLACEMENT:    20 balls will fit into the box
TRUE DISPLACEMENT:     66 balls will fit into the box
ACTUAL DISPLACEMENT:   34 balls will fit into the box
```

9.5 Exercises and Sample Quiz Questions

9.5.1 Exercises

Exercise 1 Complete the last function in `BallsAndBoxes` and run the entire program to make sure it works properly with your function.

Exercise 2 Write a program that starts with the integer 1000 and repeatedly adds 5000 to it. After each addition, print the resulting sum. What happens after the sum exceeds 2,147,483,649?

Exercise 3 Write a program that accepts as input an integer "n" and then adds "`1.0/n`" to itself "n" times. For example, if the input is 5, then the sum is the real number "`1.0/5 + 1.0/5 + 1.0/5 + 1.0/5 + 1.0/5`." After computing this sum, the program should compare it to 1.0 and output the word "equal" if the "`sum = 1.0`" and "not equal" otherwise. Run your program with different values of "n" and try to determine the smallest integer for which the sum does not equal 1.0. This type of error is called a round-off error.

9.5.2   Sample Quiz Questions

Problem 1   Which relational operator(s) can be used to identify if data which is read into a C program is correct? Assuming that the data is assigned to a variable named "foo," and that its value should be from 0 to 9, inclusive, provide a set of expressions that perform the test.

Problem 2   Write a C program that reads values into an integer variable "foo." When the value is within range, print the name of the variable and its value. When the value is out of range, print an error message and the name of the variable. The range is shown below:

- $0 \leq foo \leq 9$

Problem 3   The logical connective operators (`&&`, `||`, `!=`) are used to construct combinations of logical expressions. Provide an expression which performs the same function as the one provided in the latter part of Problem 1.

Problem 4   Rewrite the program in Problem 2 to use two variables: `"foo"` and `"bar"` and compound logical expressions. Use the ranges of values below.

- $10 \leq foo \leq 99$
- $0 \leq bar \leq 9$

Problem 5   What are the components to a general iteration construct? What component does an entry/exit condition fit into, and what is the relationship between an entry condition and an exit condition?

Problem 6   Write a C program to read in 10 numbers from the keyboard and to count the number of values which are less than 25.

Problem 7   Which arithmetic operator can be used to determine even multiples of a number? Which assignment operator can be used to exponentially decrement a number?

Problem 8   Wrote a C program to read in 10 numbers from the keyboard and to count the number which are multiples of 3. Print the number 3 raised to a power equal to the number found.

Problem 9   What is the importance of the function call/function header relationship?

Problem 10   Write a C program which iteratively reads 10 values, accumulates their values, and prints the result. Implement each functional segment with a function.

Chapter 10
Arrays, Structures, and Files

10.1 Introduction and Scope

In this chapter, we will extend your C programming skills to include the use of arrays and structures. In Chapter 9, you extended your ability to write simple programs, enabling you to direct execution, repeat code segments, and develop your own functions. In order to take full advantage of the power of these constructs, particularly iteration, you must be able to use them to locate and compare data as well as to use the data generated. Simple variables can be used as long as they are being used right away, but otherwise a structured variable, one that keeps track of many variables and their values, is needed. Once the need for variable organization is recognized, a logical extension is to use the organization in data files, so you will then learn how to read data from a file into a structure and write it out to a file from a structure. Finally, often the data you want to compare requires access to different variable types, in which case new structured data types are necessary. We will introduce these concepts and their application in small examples, the source code for which can be found in the `"UNIX/Ch10"` directories. The following topics wil be addressed in this chapter:

Ch10

- Comparing results of many iterations
- Reading data from a file into an array variable
- Writing data out to a file
- Structured variables for unlike data types
- More on memory addresses

When you have completed this chapter, you should understand how array and structure data types are defined, declared, accessed, and used in simple programs and functions. You should be able to read values into array and structure types, and you should be able to read information from text files into program variables or write information from program variables to text files.

10.2 Comparing Iterations Using Arrays

One of the most useful functions of iteration is to compare values of variables which are indexed to a loop counter. So far, we have not been able to use this feature because we did not have any way of organizing variables in such a way that they could be **indexed** (related) to one another and, so, compared by their order.

10.2.1 The Array as Structured Variable

An **array** is a **structured variable** in that it organizes many variables of the same type. An array is actually a collection of variables, and an indexing scheme for accessing the values of those variables. An array variable has an identifier and a type like any other variable, as shown below:

```
char     obj_type;
double   obj_sizes[20];
```

In this example, `obj_type` is a regular variable, often called a **scalar variable** because it can only have one value at a time. On the other hand, `obj_sizes` is an array variable. Its identifier `obj_sizes` refers to all of the variables it organizes, and its `double` type is the type of all of the variables it organizes. An array is declared when the identifier is associated with more than a single value by square brackets and a value. `obj_sizes` actually declares up to `20` `double` variables, since its type is `double` and the value in brackets is `20`. Although the value is `20`, the value is only used to define the largest number of variables which can be associated with the array variable.

10.2.2 Using Array Variables

A programmer can do with array variables anything that can be done with scalar variables. They can be accessed, assigned values, reassigned values, and they can be used as arguments in functions. Moreover, the array index (the number inside the brackets, e.g., 20 in [20]) can also be manipulated in the same ways. The array index *always* starts at 0 and goes to n − 1, and the index must *always* be an integer or a character. Let's look at an example program, "`SimpleArr.c`" (Fig. 10.1) and see how arrays work in C.

Figure 10.1: Array Usage in `SimpleArr.c`

```
/*********************************************************/
/* FILE:       SimpleArr.C                       */
/*                                               */
/* AUTHOR:     J.B. Hodges                       */
/* DATE:       August, 1993                      */
/* FUNCTION:   Calculates an addition table of integers */
/*             and then determines how many of them are */
/*             multiples of a user input value.  */
/* APPROACH:   Uses stdio.h function library. Uses array */
/*********************************************************/

#include <stdio.h>
#define  MXSZ1 100
#define  MXSZ2 200

int
main(void)
{
  int   start1, start2,        /* starting addend values  */
        max1, max2,            /* limits of each addend   */
        add[MXSZ1][MXSZ1],     /* storage array           */     (1)
        counter1, counter2,    /* loop counters           */
        incr,                  /* the search increment    */
        vals[MXSZ2],           /* values matching search  */     (2)
        numincr;               /* the number of incr found */

  printf("Input starting and ending integers for addend1: ");
  scanf("%d%d", &start1, &max1);
  printf("Input starting and ending integers for addend2: ");
  scanf("%d%d", &start2, &max2);
  printf("Input the search increment: ");
  scanf("%d", &incr);

  numincr = 0;

  for ( counter2 = start2; counter2 <= max2; ++counter2 )           (3)
    for ( counter1 = start1; counter1 <= max1; ++counter1 )
      add[counter1][counter2] = counter1 + counter2;                (4)
  for ( counter2 = start2; counter2 <= max2; ++counter2 )
    for ( counter1 = start1; counter1 <= max1; ++counter1 )
      if ( ( add[counter1][counter2] % incr ) == 0 ) {              (5)
        ++numincr;                                                  (6)
        vals[numincr] = add[counter1][counter2];                   (7)
      }
  printf("\n%d numbers were divisible by %d in the range\n\n", \
          numincr, incr);
  return (0);
}
```

Although this is a simple, perhaps redundant, program, it illustrates some interesting aspects of array usage. First, we have used both a single-subscripted array and a double-subscripted array in this program. A **single-subscripted** array is one which has a single index (i.e., one set of square brackets). The array vals is a single-subscripted array (item **2**), often referred to as a **vector**. Each variable element of vals can be accessed and modified with a single index value by naming the array variable with a set of square brackets and the index value, as shown on the lefthand side of the assignment statement below:

```
vals[numincr] = add[counter1][counter2];
```

A **double-subscripted** array has two **indices**, and access or modification of any array element requires two index values. The array add is a double-subscripted array (item **1**), and an element in the array is accessed and manipulated with two sets of square brackets and index values, as shown on the righthand side of the assignment statement above. The array index can itself be a variable, as shown, or a constant, or an expression that evaluates to an integer or a character. Item (**3**) identifies a nested for loop, which was mentioned in Chapter 9 but not illustrated. The two loops both work on the same expression as noted at item (**4**), which performs the addition and assigns the value to the add array. Notice that the array element identifier is a combination of the array variable identifier and the specific indices. This first loop combination is intended simply to create the array which will serve as a basis for the comparison in the second loop. The second loop is virtually identical to the first, except that the executable statement (at item **5**) is an if, which tests to see if the remainder of (%) dividing the addition table value by the user defined increment (incr) is zero. If so, then the addition table value is an even multiple of the increment, the number of successful tests is incremented (numincr at item **6**), and the value is written to an unused array vals, at item (**7**). The array was used to check and validate the program results, which are shown below:

```
localhost> gcc SimpleArr.c
localhost> a.out
Input the starting and ending integers for addend1: 23 35
Input the starting and ending integers for addend2: 62 81
Input the search increment: 12
21 numbers were divisible by 12 in the range
```

Caution should be taken to avoid trying to address an array component whose index is larger than one less than the maximum size stated in the variable declaration. In the current example, 19 is the largest index that can be referenced. This is because the compiler reserves memory addresses for the number of array elements defined in the declaration, but no more. If the programmer mistakenly references a location which is beyond the number allocated, then that address may be associated with a value, but it will certainly not be the one intended by the programmer and may result in a run-time error. One way to avoid this problem is mentioned above, and that is to define constants which represent the maximum sizes of arrays and use those constants as checks and looping limits in constructs which manipulate arrays.

10.2.3 Operations with Arrays

Arrays can be used in three ways: (1) to compare values of array elements, (2) to locate elements in an array, and (3) to compare elements at the same index in different arrays. We have illustrated an example of the the first application.

The second application is called **search**. Search can be performed in many ways. In its simplest incarnation, search involves an exhaustive comparison of the desired, or **target**, value, with each element in the array. This is achieved by cycling through the array element indices. Because every element is potentially tested, this approach is called **linear** search.

An efficient search strategy is the **binary** search, but requires that the array first be sorted. **Sorting** an array means to order it by some metric, for example from smallest to largest using a > or < operator. There are different mechanisms for sorting an array, but they all involve transposition of elements until an ordering is achieved. A search on a sorted array is binary when you select the middle array element and compare it to the target value, because all of the elements with indices larger than the middle element will either be larger than the target or smaller than the target. So half the elements are eliminated the first time you choose a value to compare, and will be halved again each time a value is tested. This elimination of values that must be considered is called **pruning**. Examples illustrating the use of arrays for sorting and searching are not presented in this book, but can be found in any introduction to C programming text, such as [Hanly et al 1993; Kernighan and Ritchie 1981].

The third application makes use of two or more arrays of the same size but of different types. For example, five arrays may be used to represent the characteristics of an employee: (1) their name, (2) their employee identification number, (3) their salary grade, (4) their salary, and (5) their email addresses. If we want to find out something about a particular employee, then we need to search for their name in the first array and return the index to the array element whse value is the name we seek. After that, assuming that all of the arrays are indexed the same way, the index found can be used to access the desired information in the other arrays. This arrangement of arrays is called **parallel arrays**, because each array has the same number of arguments that are semantically related.

10.2.4 Command-Line Arguments

So far whenever we have presented a program, the program has executed interactively, meaning that any data which was required by the program was explicitly requested by keyboard input. When a program is executed, it is possible to include command-line arguments that will effect the operation of the program. For example, suppose we wish to write a program to sum two numbers. We may choose to enter the two numbers as arguments to the program when it is called at the UNIX command line. Suppose the source code for the program is in file "`CmdArgSum.c`." We can compile and run it as follows:

```
localhost> gcc -o CmdArgSum CmdArgSum.c
localhost> CmdArgSum 3 4
```

The 3 and 4 here are called **command line arguments**. To do this we include in the main block of CmdArgSum.c the following:

```
void
main(int argc, char *argv[])
```

The operating system knows to assign to `argc` the number of arguments that are included on the command line, and to assign each of these arguments (as strings) to the array `argv` as elements `argv[0]`, `argv[1]`, `argv[2]`, etc. Note that `argv` is an array of unspecified length, where each element is a pointer to a string. In the example:

```
localhost> CmdArgSum 3 4 5
```

`argc` gets the value 3, meaning that there are 4 arguments. The first argument `argv[0]` is always the command name, so the value assigned to `argv[0]` is the string "`CmdArgSum`." All of the values are shown in Table 10.1.

Table 10.1: `argv` values in command line arguments

Element		Value
`argv[0]`	$\Rightarrow$	"CmdArgSum"
`argv[1]`	$\Rightarrow$	"3"
`argv[2]`	$\Rightarrow$	"4"
`argv[3]`	$\Rightarrow$	"5"

10.3 Array Variables in File Operations

Our last program had a special nested loop to generate the values which we used to show how arrays are used. We could have written a single nested loop to generate and test the values, but that would have been less fun and wouldn't have set us up for this example. It would be nice if we could read the addition table into an array variable from a UNIX file and then analyze it. If we can do this, then we can read large data files into local arrays and perform bulk analysis. We can let someone else worry about how to generate the data file. Reading data from a file into a local data structure requires the completion of three subtasks: (1) declaration of a file variable, (2) open the file for reading, and, when finished, (3) close the local file. These will be the topics of this section.

There are two types of files that can be read in C: (1) text files, and (2) binary files. Most files which are read into programs are text files, and most of the files you have seen in this book are text files. A **text** file is an ASCII, or editable, file. In a text file, each *viewable* line ends with a special character called an **end-of-line character**. The end-of-line character is also known as a **newline** character. The end of line character is usually a control character which cannot be seen under normal editing. After the last end-of-line character in the file is another special character, called an **end-of-file** (EOF) character. All of the information in the file: the characters for every line, the end-of-line characters at the end of each line, and the end-of-file character, are organized as a single set, or string, of characters. When the file is viewed, the end-of-line characters are interpreted, and you 'see' lines on a screen. The set of characters which makes up the file is associated with a name, which is the **filename**. The filename is referenced in the operating system just as a variable is in a program.

10.3.1 File Declaration

To read from a file (instead of the keyboard or standard input), a variable must be declared in the program which will represent the file in the operating system. This will be called a **file variable**. Since the local variable and the real file are different, we refer to them by making use of the file's address in memory. Thus the file available in the program must be declared as a pointer associated with the file which can be referenced in the program. Until now, we have referred to pointers as the memory addresses of variables, and that is what they are, but it is easier to call them pointers, so we will do so henceforth. The file variable is declared as follows:

```
FILE *infilep, *outfilep;
```

where `infile` might represent the name of a file that data will be read *from*, and `outfile` might represent the name of a file that data will be written *to*. There need not be any correlation between the file name and the pointer variable, I have done this as an example only. The notation of using a "p" after a pointer variable (or ptr, or some other notational mechanism) makes it easier to identify pointers in source code. The "FILE *" type is associated with file pointers and is required.

10.3.2 Opening a Local File for Read or Write

A file is **open**ed for use with the fopen function. fopen requires two arguments: (1) a string that represents the local file name in the operating system, and (2) a character that designates whether the file is to be used for reading ("r") or writing ("w"). The return value of a call to fopen is a pointer to the file, and it is the pointer which is used in subsequent operations (i.e., read and write). Consider the program "SimpleFileIO.c" shown in Fig. 10.2, which illustrates the use of files for reading values into arrays and writing them back to files when done. The first portion of the figure is documentation the way I like to prepare it, as opposed to other examples in this text.

Figure 10.2: Array Usage in `SimpleFileIO.c`

```
/*****************************************************************/
/* FILE:       SimpleFileIO.C                                  */
/*                                                             */
/* AUTHOR:     J.B. Hodges                                     */
/* DATE:       August, 1993                                    */
/* FUNCTION:   Reads values from the UNIX file system a local  */
/*             array, select values within a user defined range, */
/*             and writes those to another file in the UNIX file */
/*             system.                                         */
/* APPROACH:   Uses arrays to store the file contents.         */
/* LIBRARIES:  Uses the string function library.               */
/*                                                             */
/* CONSTANTS:  STRSZ  20 -  Maximum string size                */
/*             MAX   100 -  Number of allowable successes       */
/*                                                             */
/* VARIABLES:  FILE  *infilep        - input file pointer      */
/*             FILE  *outfilep       - output file pointer     */
/*             char  infilen[STRSZ]  - input filename          */
/*             char  outfilen[STRSZ] - output filename         */
/*             int   val             - value from infilen      */
/*             int   lower           - limits of age range     */
/*             int   upper           - limits of age range     */
/*             int   vals[MAX]       - storage array           */
/*             int   succ[MAX]       - ages in range           */
/*             int   counter, counter1 - loop counters         */
/*             int   nsucc           - number of successes     */
/*             int   status          - number args fscanf read */
/*                                                             */
/*****************************************************************/
```

Figure 10.2: Array Usage in `SimpleFileIO.c` (cont.)

```c
#include <stdio.h>
#include <string.h>

#define STRSZ   20
#define MAX    100

int
main(int argc, char *argv[])
{
  FILE  *infilep, *outfilep;                                    (1)
  char  infilen[STRSZ],                                         (2)
        outfilen[STRSZ];
  int   val,
        lower, upper,
        vals[MAX],
        succ[MAX],
        counter, counter1,
        nsucc,
        status;

  strcpy(infilen, argv[1]);                                     (3)
  strcpy(outfilen, argv[2]);
  infilep  = fopen(infilen, "r");                               (4)
  outfilep = fopen(outfilen, "w");

  printf("Input the youngest/oldest ages in search range: ");
  scanf("%d%d", &lower, &upper);

  counter = 0;
  nsucc   = 0;

  for ( status = fscanf(infilep, "%d", &val);                   (5)
        status == 1 && counter < MAX;
        status = fscanf(infilep, "%d", &val) )
    vals[counter++] = val;

  for ( counter1 = 0; counter1 <= counter; counter1++ )
    if ( ( vals[counter1] >= lower ) &&
         ( vals[counter1] <= upper ) )
      succ[nsucc++] = vals[counter1];

  fclose(infilep);                                              (6)
  counter = 1;

  for ( fprintf(outfilep, "%d\n", succ[counter++]);             (7)
        counter <= nsucc;
        fprintf(outfilep, "%d\n", succ[counter++]) );

  fclose(outfilep);

  return (0);
}
```

This program reads some values from a file, does a single test, and writes the items which succeed at the test to another file. The input file is shown below, and consists of a number of items, one per line.

```
localhost> cat foo
10
21
24
8
12
29
43
99
63
48
31
```

In order to function as described, `SimpleFileIO.c` must declare the input and output file variables, open the files, read the values from "foo," test to see if each one falls in the desired range and, if so, write it out to another file. Item (**1**) in the listing above shows that the input and output file pointers are being declared. In this program, I have chosen to demonstrate the use of command line arguments to provide the input and output filenames. These are declared at item (**2**) with a maximum length of `STRSZ`, which is defined as a constant of `20`.

Although we have not discussed strings to any extent in this book, `SimpleFileIO.c` needs them since the functions **fopen** and **fclose** need string arguments for the file names. The **strcpy** string library function (note that the string library, `string.h`, has been included) is used (item **3**) to assign string variables to the input arguments. Then, at item (**4**), **fopen** is used to produce the file pointers needed to reference and close the files, one call for each pointer.

With the files opened for read and write, the data from the input file can be read. A **for** loop is used to read the data using the **fscanf** function, noted at item (**5**). **fscanf** is a more general form of **scanf** that can read data using the file pointer passed in as an argument. As such, **fscanf** can also read from the standard input (i.e., keyboard, using the standard input file pointer **stdin**). The **for** loop at item (**5**) reads a value from the input file as long as the value returned from **fscanf** is equal to `1`, and as long as the number of items read doesn't exceed the maximum size for the array. Like **scanf**, **fscanf** returns an integer value which holds the number of items it has read, so if the variable `status` is not equal to `1`, the number of values which are supposed to be read, we do not want to read a value. For example, if the end of information is found, a negative integer associated with the end-of-file character is returned. Nothing is wrong, but there is no more information. As mentioned in the previous section, "MAX" is used to make sure that an array index outside the declared range is not used, which would result in an address error. The body of the loop is to store the values read into an array called vals.

The second loop peforms the test on each value of vals, updates the number of matches when one is found, and writes the success to another array variable, succ. These in-between steps are purposefully redundant for the example.

10.3.3 Closing a Local File

When all of the data has been read, the input file is closed (item **6**). All open files must be closed before the program is done executing. The fclose function closes a file pointer, and is invoked at item (**6**) in SimpleFileIO.c. fclose takes an output file pointer as its argument.

10.3.4 Using Array Variables to Write Data

Another loop, at item (**7**), and almost identical in form to the one at item (**5**), is used to write the values of the new array to the output file using the function fprintf. fprintf has the same relationship with printf that fscanf has with scanf.[1] The program execution is shown below:

```
localhost> gcc SimpleFileIO.c
localhost> a.out foo baz
Input the youngest/oldest ages in the search range: 20 70
localhost> cat baz
21
24
29
43
63
48
31
```

10.4 Structured Variables for Unlike Data Types

In Section 10.2.3 we mentioned parallel arrays and the comparison and use of different types of information. Although the array can be used in this awkward fashion, C provides a data structure, called a **structure** (type struct), which allows the programmer to represent/implement dissimilar variable types in a sin-

---

1. To use fprintf with the standard output device, use the standard output file descriptor stdout.

gle structured variable. Unlike the array, in which element variable names are identified by the array variable name and the index to the element, a structure is a user-defined variable, so the user defines the names of the variables which it organizes. The example below, called "`SimpleStruct.c`" will illustrate the syntax and use of structures.

10.4.1 The `struct` as Structured Variable

The C struct variable type is not organized in as straightforward a manner as an array, so it cannot be declared without first defining how the elements will be organized. Thus the structure requires the programmer to define a new **structure type** for the structure which they are going to use. Consider a structure variable to hold data about the current date, shown below:

```
#define STRSZ 20

typedef struct date_s {                                               (1)
    char    month[STRSZ];                                             (2)
    int     day,
            year;
} date_t;                                                            (3)
```

The term "`typedef`" is used in C to define a new structure type and, in this example, is being used to define a new "`struct`" **class** of data. The format is pretty straightforward: the reserved word `typedef` must appear first, followed by the reserved word `struct`. `struct` is an environment in which the various variables, called **field variables**, which comprise the new structure class are declared. A **field variable** is semantically identical to an array element, insomuch as having a type, an access mechanism, and an identifier. The field variable type, unlike the array element, can be *any* data type defined. The field variable access mechanism is basically the same as its identifier.

The identifier following the close of the `typedef struct` environment is called the **structure type** of the structure, and is used in declaring new variables of this type. The structure type is required; however, if a **structure tag** is provided, at the beginning of the structure definition, it can also be used to declare new stucture variables of this kind. "`date_s`" (Item **1**) is a structure tag for the 'date' structure we are defining above, and "`date_t`" (item **3**) is the structure type. `date_t` is comprised of three field variables: a string variable, `month`, and two integer variables, `day` and `year`.

10.4.2 Declaring a Structure Variable

Once a structure class is defined, a variable of that structure type can be declared and used. For example, given the date_t class defined above, a variable called "current_date" can be declared as follows:

```
date_t   current_date;
```

as though date_t was provided as a standard C type. An array of dates can similarly be declared as shown below:

```
date_t   current_date[MAXDATES];
```

where the constant "MAXDATES" would have to be declared. This variable would then declare an array of structures, each of which is of type date_t, and each of those of which has a month, day, and year element.

10.4.3 Accessing Elements of a Structure Variable

An array's elements are accessed by referencing their location, or order, in the array. This can be done because all of the elements of an array variable are the same data type. A structure's field variables are not necessarily the same data type, and they are not organized by any particular ordering. So how do we reference them, and how are they uniquely identified? The elements of a structure are referenced, accessed, by their names, and are kept distinct by separating the names with periods, as shown below:[1]

```
structure_name[.structure_field]*
```

Using this mechanism, no two references are identical. Consider the current_date variable illustrated above. To assign the value of "January 5, 1992" to its field variables, we would do the following:

```
strcpy(current_date.month, "January");
current_date.day    = 5;
current_date.year   = 1992;
```

---

1. We are adopting the UNIX nomenclature, [foo]*, to represent an arbitrary number of optional items (in brackets), where the asterisk is a wildcard which allows 0 or more of the item.

In this example, the `month`, `day`, and `year` field variables for `current_date` are assigned values by referencing them with the period notation (e.g., `current_date.day`). Using the same mechanism, structures and field variables can be compared and modified.

10.4.4 Structures within Structures: Hierarchical Organization

When one data type is defined 'inside' of another data type, whether an array, a structure, or some other structured data type, the organization is called **hierarchical**. A structure variable is hierarchically organized if one of its field variables is declared to be another structure variable type. That is, a structure within a structure. The access mechanism of using the field names then gets propagated through the structures, using periods, as before. When referencing and accessing hierarchical structure components, you do not need to refer to the name of the embedded structures, only their field variables, because the embedded structures *are* the field variables for the structure which references them. Consider a hierarchical structure for describing the purchase of an item:

```
typedef struct purc_s {
   char      where[STRSZ];
   date_t    when;                                             ①
   double    cost;
   date_t    warr;                                             ②
} purc_t;
```

"purc_t" has four field variables, of which `when` and `warr` are themselves of type `date_t`. To assign values to the purchase date of a variable called `current_purchase`, we would do the following:

```
strcpy(current_purchase.when.month,  "August");
current_purchase.when.day    = 21;
current_purchase.when.year   = 1993;
```

10.4.5 Example with Structure Variables

With some understanding of the basic mechanics of structures, a simple example is useful to bring these ideas into sharper focus. The program included in Fig. 10.3, called "`SimpleStructure.c`," illustrates the use of hierarchically defined structure variables that are read from a file and manipulated locally. The file entries are items in a person's collection of objects and can be thought of as records in a kind of simple database. The program is used to obtain information about a user-selected object in the database.

Figure 10.3: Struct definition and usage in `SimpleStruct.c`

```
/***********************************************************/
/* FILE:        SimpleStruct.C                           */
/*                                                        */
/* AUTHOR:      J.B. Hodges                              */
/* DATE:        August, 1993                            */
/* FUNCTION:    Reads values from the UNIX file system   */
/*              into a structure variable, finds a record */
/*              in a user selected field, and displays    */
/*              other desired fields for that record.     */
/* CONSTANTS:   STRSZ 20 - Maximum string length          */
/*              MAX   10 - Maximum items analyzed         */
/* VARIABLES:   FILE   *infilep       - file pointer      */
/*              char   infilen[STRSZ] - input filename    */
/*              int    cntr           - loop counter      */
/*              int    status         - number args read  */
/*              toy_t  current_toy    - present item       */
/*              toy_t  target_toy     - search item        */
/*                                                        */
/***********************************************************/

#include <stdio.h>
#include <string.h>

#define STRSZ 20
#define MAX    10

typedef struct date_s {                                    ①
  char     month[STRSZ];
  int      day,
           year;
} date_t;

typedef struct purc_s {                                    ②
  char     where[STRSZ];
  date_t   when;
  double   cost;
  date_t   warr;
} purc_t;

typedef struct toy_s {                                     ③
  char     name[STRSZ];
  char     type[STRSZ];
  char     loc[STRSZ];
  purc_t   purc;
} toy_t;

int Print_Toy(toy_t toy);                                  ④
```

Figure 10.3: Struct definition and usage in `SimpleStruct.c` (cont.)

```
int
main(int argc, char *argv[])
{
  FILE   *infilep;
  char   infilen[STRSZ];
  int    cntr,
         status;
  toy_t  current_toy,                                              (5)
         target_toy;

  strcpy(infilen, argv[1]);
  infilep  = fopen(infilen, "r");

  printf("Input the toy name you want information for: ");
  scanf("%s", &target_toy.name);

  cntr   = 0;
  status = 0;

  while ( (status == 10 || status != EOF) && cntr <= MAX )        (6)
    status = fscanf(infilep, "%s", current_toy.name);
    if ( status == 1 ) {
      status = fscanf(infilep, "%s%s%s%s%d%d%f%s%d%d",            (7)
                               current_toy.type,
                               current_toy.loc,
                               current_toy.purc.where,
                               current_toy.purc.when.month,
                               &current_toy.purc.when.day,
                               &current_toy.purc.when.year,
                               &current_toy.purc.cost,
                               current_toy.purc.warr.month,
                               &current_toy.purc.warr.day
                               &current_toy.purc.warr.year);
    }
    cntr++;
    if ( strcmp(target_toy.name, current_toy.name) == 0 ) {       (8)
      print_toy(current_toy);
    }
  }

  fclose(infilep);

  return (0);
}
```

Figure 10.3: Struct definition and usage in `SimpleStruct.c` (cont.)

```
/**********************************************************/
/* Print_Toy: displays object characteristics            */
/*                                                        */
/* INPUT: toy_t toy - An item to print                   */
/**********************************************************/

void
Print_Toy(toy_t toy)
{
  printf("\n********* %s ***********\n\n", toy.name);
  printf("   NAME:    %s\n"                                       (9)
         "   TYPE:    %s\n"
         "   LOC:     %s\n"
         "   WHERE:   %s\n"
         "   DATE:    %s %d, %d\n"
         "   COST:    $%6.2f\n"
         "   WARR:    %s %d, %d\n\n",
         toy.name, toy.type,  toy.loc, toy.purc.where,
         toy.purc.when.month, toy.purc.when.day,
         toy.purc.when.year,  toy.purc.cost,
         toy.purc.warr.month, toy.purc.warr.day,
         toy.purc.warr.year);

  return;
}
```

Three structure data types are defined for this program: (item **1**) `date_t`, (item **2**) `purc_t`, and (item **3**) `toy_t`. At item (**2**), you should note that two of the field variables for `purc_t` are type `date_t` variables, `when` and `warr`. Also, the `toy_t` structure has a `purc` field variable, declared as a `purc_t` type structure. Both `purc_t` and `toy_t` are hierarchically defined structures.

Typedef and Prototypes

When a new struct type is defined, such as with a `typedef` statement, in order for the new type to be accessible by other user-defined functions, it must appear before any function definitions. This means that function prototypes must appear *after* the `typedef`s, as at item (**4**) for the function `Print_Toy`. If the `typedef`s are put inside `main`, then they cannot be used by functions like `Print_Toy` and an error will be flagged at compile time.

Structure Variable Declarations

The prototype declaration for `Print_Toy` includes a structure parameter of type `toy_t`. When a structure is used as a function parameter, then its data type must be used. In the sample program, the `typedef` for toys is `toy_t`, for *toy-type*. Every time a new structure variable of this type is declared, this type must be included. For example, item (**5**) notes the declaration of two locally used structures of type `toy_t`, `current_toy`, for the object which is read from the UNIX file, and `target_toy` for the toy which the user is seeking information about. Item (**6**) is noted to show a more appropriate while approach to reading from the input file than the example using arrays would suggest. Although a for loop is an efficient approach for reading items from a file, the while is used more often and is easier to read.

Access and Reference to Record Fields

To reference an element in an array, one must know what its index in the variable is. Although the index scheme may not be very intuitive for some, it is consistent and easy to remember. The indexing scheme for accessing structure record fields is very mnemonic, because the field names are user-selected, but it can be tedious and space consuming for hierarchical structures such as those in the sample program. Items (**7**) and (**8**) illustrate the structure field access mechanism. You simply separate the structure name and field name with a period (.). Because the combination of structure name and field name can only be associated with a particular value, this mechanism does not lead to confusion. The mechanism also works fine for hierarchical structures, as done at item (**8**). Some of the examples are quite long. Notice that we are referencing, at once, the top-level toy_t structure, the mid-level purc_t structure, and the low-level date_t structure.

Searching for the Target

At item (**8**) we once again introduce the use of string functions. One cannot simply compare two strings for equivalence with the == operator, because the string is an array and the operator doesn't have the smarts to know which item to compare. Because an array is represented by its starting address in memory, the use of == would result in comparing address values. Not very meaningful. So the string function strcmp performs an item-by-item comparison, and returns 0 if all elements are equivalent.[1] To use `strcmp`, or any other string function, the `string.h` library must be included in the file.

Structure Output

The last point to be made, at item (**9**), is about how the data is printed in this sample program. I originally wanted to have the user select fields of the chosen structure to display instead of having the entire record displayed. However, it turned out that to add that one change made the program much longer than I wanted for the example. One way to implement field selectability would be to

---

1. strcmp can also be used to determine lexical ordering of strings. If the first string is lexically greater than the second, then strcmp will return a positive integer. Likewise, if the first string is lexically less than the second string, strcmp will return a negative integer.

write separate statements, or functions, to display the different fields, and then prompt the user for the fields to print. A switch construct that could then select the statement or function for displaying the field.

Data Format for Structures

A simple data base of three "toys," stored in a local file called "foo2," is shown below. Notice the organization of entries on different lines. The function fscanf will ignore end-of-line characters when it reads the file, so it doesn't matter if the data is all on one line, or whether each item is on a separate line 5 lines from the next item. It is best that you create data files which are easy to read by you and not be overly concerned about C reading them.

```
localhost> cat foo2
Delta_14_bandsaw woodworking_tool garage
tooland_burlingame August 12 1993 600
August 12 1995

Jive_26_paraglider aircraft living_room
Airtime_SF August 1 1993 2000
September 12 1993

5HP_compressor tool garage
Sears_SM April 8 1993 400
April 8 1995
```

A sample run of SimpleStruct.c using foo2 as the input file is shown below:

```
localhost> gcc SimpleStruct.c
localhost> a.out foo2
What toy do you want information for: Jive_26_paraglider

********** Jive_26_paraglider ************
   NAME:   Jive_26_paraglider
   TYPE:   aircraft
   LOC:    living_room
   WHERE:  Airtime_SF
   DATE:   August 1, 1993
   COST:   $2000.00
   WARR:   September 12, 1993
```

where the output shows how the various fields are formatted by Print_Toy.

10.5 Exercises and Sample Quiz Questions

10.5.1 Exercises

Exercise 1   The program "SimpleStruct.c," while functional as shown, has a bug in it. See if you can locate the bug and fix it without running the program (Hint: what other test cases could be run?).

Exercise 2   The program "SimpleStruct.c" can be modified, with some effort, to allow user-selected field printing instead of the entire record. One must first write functions to print selected fields. One must then write a function which will print a field given a user-provided input. Finally, one must gather the input. Write sample functions to extend the program in this way. You can use a two dimensional array to store character choices and use switch-case if you want.

10.5.2 Sample Quiz Questions

Problem 1   An array is a called a structured variable. What is the structure and what is the naming convention for the components of the structure? What is the purpose of the array index, and what are the requirements, if any, for its use in expressions?

Problem 2   Write a C program which will read in 5 values from the keyboard and store them into an array named "foo." Perform the following analysis on foo and display the resulting array. Compare two items at a time. If the first is larger than the second, do nothing. If it is smaller than the second, then swap the positions of the two elements in the array. This is an ordering/sorting procedure.

Problem 3   What is the mechanism for bringing input values into a C program from the UNIX command line? Define a header for main which will suffice for providing two command line arguments.

Problem 4   Write a C program which takes two command line arguments: one for a number, and one for an exponent, and returns the first number raised to the second (this may require use of the math library).

Problem 5   C programs often obtain input from a file in the UNIX file system. What steps must be taken to access a file for use in a C program, and what objects are needed within the program?

Problem 6   Write a C program which takes its input from a file named "P10.6Dat" and displays the multiplication of all its values. The first value in the file will be an integer specifying the number of items to be analyzed.

Problem 7   Define a hierarchical structure variable for a student or employee that has the following fields:

- Name
- Social security number
- Date of birth
- Age
- Address

Problem 8   Write a C program that reads information from a file of student or employee records and displays them. The first value in the file will be the number of records (students or employees) in the file.

Chapter 11
Programming Tools

11.1 Introduction and Scope

Learning how to program is not without its perils. A general axiom is that your programs will rarely if ever compile and run the first time. If you can develop good design, development, and testing habits, then you can reduce the amount of time it takes to get your programs to compile and execute as intended. This chapter is intended to present a few techniques which may become useful to you. They are introduced last simply because they are not necessary to a basic understanding of programming and program development, but they are invaluable for any real (i.e., useful) programming. Four topics are presented in this chapter.

- Debugging a C program
- Program testing techniques
- Developing program libraries
- Organizing complex programs

At the conclusion of this chapter, you should have a better idea of how to develop, debug, and test programs. When you encounter an error, you should be able to recognize what kind of error it is and know how to locate it. You should be able to develop and include function libraries into your programs so that you do not have to have all the code you need provided by system libraries or in one file. You should be able to invoke a debugger to assist in finding and correcting problems in your code. Finally, you should understand the value of using the `make` utility for organizing complex programs. Examples shown in this chapter can be found in the "UNIX/Ch11" directory subtree.

Ch11

11.2 Debugging a C Program

Programming errors can be divided into two categories: (1) compile-time errors and (2) run-time errors. Although most debugging will at first appear to be compilation errors, the worst errors are run-time errors, because the program runs but the error is not flagged in any direct way.

11.2.1 Compile-Time errors

Compilation errors are tedious but they can usually be corrected easily because the compiler will inform you of approximately where the error is and what type of error it is.

Compile-time errors are errors which are picked up by the compiler. These can be further divided into lexical errors and syntax errors. **Lexical errors** are spelling (or case) errors in the keywords of the programming language, or identifiers in the program. For example, if you misspell the reserved word "while," then the compiler will note this error and report it to you at compile time. Similarly, if you declare a variable with one spelling of the identifier and then reference the identifier with a different spelling, you will most likely be shown an "undeclared identifier" message.

Syntax errors are errors in the order or structure of elements of the program. For example, it is a rule of syntax that left and right parentheses must be matched. Similarly, a missing semicolon or a "{" without a matching "}" will cause the compiler to **flag** (i.e., note or identify) an error.

Error Propagation

One phenomenon to be aware of, with respect to compiler errors is called **error propagation**. This occurs when one error causes others to be detected further along in the program. For example, suppose you are missing a semicolon in a variable declaration, such as

```
double x,y                                              no semicolon
int    z;
```

The missing semicolon may cause "x" and "y" to be undeclared. A later reference to "x" in the body of the program will generate an error of an undeclared variable. That is, the compiler reports two errors instead of just one. As a rule of thumb, always fix the first error that was reported by the compiler first, and determine if correcting that error will correct other errors. Sometimes the compiler will report the wrong error. This commonly occurs when a comment is left open. That is, if at some point in your program you open a comment and then neglect to close it, many lines of the program may be considered as part of the comment. The compiler may consider the comment closed only after finding the closing point of a later comment. Consequently, an error may be reported that would not be there if the original comment had been closed properly. The point to keep in mind is that the actual error may have occurred above the line in which the compiler reports it (see the previous example). The most effective way to obviate this kind of error is to enclose every comment line in both opening and closing comment characters. Then, if you uncomment a line, you have not adversely affected program compilation with other unterminated comments. All examples in this text have used this approach.

11.2.2 Run-Time Errors

In general, non algorithm-related **run-time** errors result from misusing the C language semantics rather than making a lexical or syntactic error. The program will compile but may crash or not produce the correct results when executed. Run-time errors are very different from compile-time errors. An algorithm-based run-time error can be more devastating that a syntax error or a language semantics error, because the program will compiles correctly but may not produce the correct results on a given data set. Four run-time error types will be addressed here:

- Memory reference errors
- Double vs. int number representation
- Number imprecision
- Logical/algorithm errors

Memory Reference

A commonly made error in C is to forget to properly reference a variable pointer. The most common instance of this is forgetting an ampersand (&) in a scanf. The program will compile, and will begin to run, and will even try to read the variables. However, as soon as it tries to use the variable values it will not have a pointer to their address in memory, and possibly a **bus error** will result. A bus error can also result from trying to use an address which doesn't exist, such as when manipulating array locations. The best thing to do is to see if you can identify what type of function is being executed when the error occurs. If you have scanfs, then check to make sure that you have included the location reference in the function call. If you are using arrays, make sure that you are not writing to a nonexistent location. You can use a debugger like gdb to help find the location in your source code where the failure is occuring, and that should be a value.

Another confusing error is a **segmentation fault**. Segmentation faults occur when you try to write into a memory address which doesn't exist. For example, if you declare an array to be of size 100, and somehow you try to assign a value to the index 121, then you will get a segmentation violation, usually with an illegal address comment. This type of error can be avoided with the use of constants. For example, if a programmer is performing an array assignment inside a loop, then by using a constant to describe the maximum limits of the array, and using that constant throughout the program, the programmer eliminates the need to have to consciously remember what the array size is in every segment. Segmentation violations can also result from confusing a pointer for a simple variable and vice versa. If the programmer identifies pointers with some kind of naming convention, this kind of error can also be reduced if not eliminated.

Double vs. Int Number Representation

One type of run-time error occurs because of the way the computer represents integers. The computer uses a binary system (base 2) to represent numbers. In the decimal system we use the digits "0,1,2, . . . ,9" to count, but in the binary system only 0 and 1 are used.[1] Each symbol in a decimal number is called a **digit**. Each symbol in a binary number is called a **bit** (i.e., a binary digit). Each place in a decimal number represents a power of 10. For example, the number in the string "3456" represents:

$$3 \times 1000 + 4 \times 100 + 5 \times 10 + 6 \times 1 = 3 \times 10^3 + 4 \times 10^2 + 5 \times 10^1 + 6 \times 10^0$$

Each place in a binary number represents a power of 2. For example, the string "1011" represents:

$$1 \times 8 + 0 \times 4 + 1 \times 2 + 1 \times 1 = 1 \times 2^3 + 0 \times 2^2 + 1 \times 2^1 + 1 \times 2^0$$

To convert a binary number to decimal, expand it in terms of powers of 2 and sum the terms. There are two methods for converting decimal to binary: (1) the most significant bit method, and (2) the least significant bit method.

In the first method, determine the largest power of 2 less than or equal to the number. Subtract this power of 2 from the number and repeat the process until the difference is 0. Record a 1 for each power of two subtracted from the number.

---

1. Physically, in the hardware of the computer, 0 and 1 represent the direction of a magnetic field or the flow of an electric current. In the old days, when decimal numbers were represented in the computer, there was a need for calibrating 10 different values of some physical parameter to represent each digit. With binary, off and on are represented with 0 and 1.

Table 11.1: Most Significant Bit Example: Convert 46 to binary

$2^5 = 32$	is largest power of $2 \leq 46$	$46 - 32 = 14$
$2^3 = 8$	is largest power of $2 \leq 14$	$14 - 8 = 6$
$2^2 = 4$	is largest power of $2 \leq 6$	$6 - 4 = 2$
$2^1 = 2$	is largest power of $2 \leq 2$	$2 - 2 = 0$

$$46 = 1 \times 2^5 + 0 \times 2^4 + 1 \times 2^3 + 1 \times 2^2 + 1 \times 2^1 + 0 \times 2^0 = 101110$$

With the second method, if the number is even, then record a 0; if odd, then record a 1. Divide the number by 2, drop any remainder, and repeat the process until the quotient is 0.

Table 11.2: Least Significant Bit Example: Convert 46 to binary

Step 1	46 is even	record a 0	$46 / 2 = 23$
Step 2	23 is odd	record a 1	$23 / 2 = 11$
Step 3	11 is odd	record a 1	$11 / 2 = 5$
Step 4	5 is odd	record a 1	$5 / 2 = 2$
Step 5	2 is even	record a 0	$2 / 2 = 1$
Step 6	1 is odd	record a 1	$1 / 2 = 0$

Step6	Step 5	Step4	Step3	Step2	Step1
1	0	1	1	1	0

In computer memory, there is a limit to the size of integers. Typically, integers are represented as 32-bit words, where the first bit is the sign bit (0 for positive, 1 for negative) and the remaining bits represent the magnitude of the number. The largest integer that can be represented this way is:

$$01111111111111111111111111111111 = 1 \times 2^{30} + 1 \times 2^{29} + \ldots + 1 \times 2^1 + 1 \times 2^0 \quad \textit{binary}$$
$$= 2147483649 \longleftarrow \textit{decimal}$$

An error will occur if the result of an arithmetic operation is greater than this maximum integer, or if the programmer tries to read or print a larger number of items than this number. This type of error is called an **overflow error**.

If your program is producing unusual values, it may be because of this type of error. C actually has standard objects which represent [architecture dependent] minimum and maximum values (e.g., INT_MIN and INT_MAX, found in <limits.h>), and they can be used to check for overflows.

Number Imprecision

Another type of error occurs because of the imprecision in representing real numbers. In C, real numbers are represented with type double, where the mantissa is represented with one integer and the exponent is represented with a second integer. As a result, there can be a precision error for the number, and is generally architecture dependent. Consider the decimal representation of 1/3. This is an infinite string (.33333...). Real numbers can only be approximated by a fixed number of bits in the computer. The round-off may cause an error in a computation.

Logical Errors

The largest class of run-time errors are logical errors, which cause the program to produce incorrect results. Below is a list of some typical logical errors for which you should be constantly on the look out:

- Failure to initialize a variable
- Nonterminating loops
- Mistake in operator precedence
- Off-by-one errors

Failure to Initialize a Variable If variables are not given an initial value, there is no telling what value they will have when it comes time to use them. This problem becomes most apparent in looping constructs, where the loop is incremented on values which change throughout the iteration, and values affected by the loop are also modified. If variables are not initialized, then odd behavior can ensue. The following program segment:

```
for ( i = 1; i <= 10; ++i ) {
  printf ("enter an integer: ");
  scanf ("%d", &x);
  sum = sum + x;    ◄──────────────────────── error here
}
```

is in error unless the variable "sum" is initialized to 0 before entering the loop. If not, the first time the commented line starting is executed, the value in sum will be unpredictable. A related error occurs if initialization of sum occurs inside of, instead of before entering, the loop. In this case, sum will be reset to 0 with each iteration of the loop.

```
/* example of initialization error */

   for ( i = 1; i <= 10; ++i ) {
      sum = 0;           ◄───────────────────────
      printf ("enter an integer: ");
      scanf ("%d", &x);
      sum = sum + x;
   }
```

This line should appear before the for statement

Nonterminating Loops Although the errors shown above will produce incorrect results, they do not make the program **blow up**. If a loop exit condition cannot be met, then the loop will continue until someone comes along and stops execution. This is called an **infinite loop** and should be avoided at all cost. All "while" and "do..while" loops should contain an instruction that eventually causes the loop to terminate. For example:

```
   while ( y > 0 )
      x++;
```

may go on forever, since the value of "y" never changes in the body of the loop. The simple way to avoid this kind of error is to make sure that all of the variables used in a loop condition can change within the loop body, and that there is a method whereby they can be assigned the necessary value to satisfy the exit condition.

Mistake in Operator Precedence A prominent error in logic occurs when the programmer has mistaken the order in which operators (arithmetic or relational) are evaluated. In the arithmetic expression:

```
x = 3 + y / z + 2;
```

the first operation computed is the division of "y" by "z," because division has precedence over addition. If the programmer expects the addition to be computed before the division, then there is a logical error. In the expression:

```
if ( y == 5 ) || ( z == 3 ) && ( x > 2 )
```

the "&&" will be computed before the "||." The truth of the expression may depend on the order of computation. In both cases, a change in the order of computation can be controlled by the use of parentheses.

Off-by-One Errors A frequent error in a loop is for the loop index to be off by one when the loop terminations. Consider the loop below, which sums the numbers from 1 to 10:

```
sum = 0;
x   = 1;
while ( x <= 10 ) {
   sum = sum + x;
   x++;
}
```

Upon exit from the loop, the value of "x" is 11. If "x" is used in a subsequent computation, then it will be off by one if the programmer expects its value to be 10. This brief list only touches the surface of possible programming errors. The remainder of this chapter will discuss ways in which programs may be tested in order to locate and correct the source of errors.

11.3 Program Debugging

Before looking at some debugging techniques, we must emphasize the importance of program testing. In assignments for programming courses, you may find your programs are short, and their correctness can be ascertained by reading through them. Research has shown that less than 30% of time spent on large programming applications is actual program coding. The majority of the time is spent in program design and program testing. Good programmers use these tools along with the technique of **modular design** to make the debugging phase more efficient. With this caveat, four approaches to debugging programs will be presented in this section:

- Print debugging
- Interrupt debugging
- Tracing functions
- Program stubbing

11.3.1 Print Debugging

Often the fastest mechanism for locating errors in a program is the printf statement. Suppose that you have an error occurring somewhere in your code and you suspect that it has something to do with a particular looping construct. You can insert a printf statement that prints the values of the affected variables before the loop is begun, and after it is complete, and then compare the values to what they should be (say, from a desk trace of the same mechanism). If the values agree, then your error is somewhere else. Otherwise you can focus your attention on finding the code in the looping expressions.

Although the printf statement is a valuable debugging tool, it is painful to use because it requires the programmer to remember where it was put, and to eliminate it when debugging is complete. It is of much greater value to have a debugging statement which is easily found, and much better, yet, to have one that can be turned on and off at one location in the source code. The first case is actually fairly easy to implement, as you can simply add a constant phrase to each printf used for debugging, and then perform a global search-and-replace to comment them out when you are done debugging. One such approach is shown below:

```
sum = 0;
x   = 1;

while ( x <= 10 ) {
  sum = sum + x;
  x++;
}
/*dbg*/ printf ("line 105:, x = %d, sum = %f", x, sum);    ←————————  (1)
/*dbg*/ scanf ("%c" &dummy);    ←————————  (2)
```

When the program executes, it will report the value of "x" and "sum" in the first /*dbg*/ lines (item **1**). The 105 is a number that will tell at what point in the program the printf is located. During execution the output will look like:

```
line 105: x = ... sum = ...
```

By placing the comment /*dbg*/ to the left of this line, you can easily find it later when you want to remove this line from the program. Sometimes it is good practice to put an entire line inside the comment so that it is not executed. In the future, if the program is altered somewhat, it may be helpful to uncomment the line so that it can be used for debugging again. If it is "commented out," restoring it is a simple matter.

11.3.2 Interrupt Debugging

Another mechanism is the interactive abort or breakpoint. You can place a scanf statement into your code (at items **1** and **2** in the next example), so that when the line is evaluated, execution will stop and await your input. You can write a scanf statement which doesn't require any input, as above, so you are effectively telling the program to stop while you look it over. If you choose to abort the execution, you can type <Cntl-C> at this point, otherwise you can type a <CR> and continue processing. Of course, this approach would be problematic if you were reading values by redirection from a file, or from a file directly, so caution must be used so that the debug statements do not interfere with other I/O.

```
/* [main] */
  char dummy;
    .
    .

  My_Fun1(z, w);
/*dbg*/ printf ("\nReturn from My_Fun: z = %d, w = %d\n", z, w);
/*dbg*/ scanf ("%c", &dummy);  ◄──────────────────────────  ①

void
My_Fun1(int x, int y)
{
  char dummy;

  /*dbg*/ printf ("\nEntering My_Fun: x = %d, y = %d\n", x, y);
  /*dbg*/ scanf ("%c", &dummy);  ◄──────────────────────────  ②
    .
    .

  return (x);
}
```

A good debugging habit is to use print statements in all programs you write. That way, when you need to use them they are available.

11.3.3 Trace Functions

Another method of debugging which makes use of printf is to write a function that is invoked only during debugging, and is ignored at all other times. The use of such a function requires that you initially write the function and make it available for use in all your programs. The time spent developing such a function can pay off in reducing the number of printf statements you have to write, and the contents of the function can be changed without changing the contents of programs which use it. Below is an example of one such function, which makes use of a global debugging **flag** constant, TRACE (items **2**, and **5**).

Figure 11.1: Using a trace function for debugging

```
/* Trace: Prints values of arguments of function named     */
/*                                                          */
/* APPROACH:   Uses if with a TRACE flag variable          */
/* INPUT:      inout variable, name of function            */
/* OUTPUT:     NONE                                         */
/* RETURN:     NONE                                         */
/************************************************************/

void
Trace(const char inout[], const char tracename[])           ①
{
  if ( TRACE )                                              ②
    if ( strcmp(inout, "in") == 0 )                         ③
      printf("\nEntering function: %s\n\t", tracename)
    else
      printf("\nExiting function: %s\n\t", tracename);

  return;
}
```

The use of an array variable in an input function has not been demonstrated but is used in this function. Since the string is not being modified in the function, it can be called by value. The "const" declaration simply states this fact. The empty array index [ ] (item **1**) identifies the first element as the variable pointer. The function **strcmp** (item **3**) is used by this function to determine whether the function is being used on the way into a function or on the way out. The application of "Trace" is shown on the next page in the continuation of Fig. 11.1.

Figure 11.1: Using a trace function for debugging (cont.)

```
#include "My_Trace_Functions.h"                             ④
#define TRACE 1                                             ⑤

void TestFun(void);

int
main(void)
{
  ...
  Trace("in", "Test_Fun");
  TestFun(q, r);                                            ⑥
  Trace("out", "Test_Fun");

  return (0);
}
```

that would simply write out statements when the function "TestFun" is entered and exited (item **6**). Similar functions can be written to display values of variables associated with a function.

This type of debugging can be extended by using **conditional compilation**, in which the C preprocessing directives #if and #endif are wrapped around the calls to "Trace" so that they are not even compiled in the code if the TRACE constant isn't defined. The next continuation of Fig. 11.1 is a modified example showing how these are used.

Figure 11.1: Using a trace function for debugging (cont.)

```
#include "My_Trace_Functions.h"                                  ④
#define TRACE 1                                                   ⑤

void Test_Fun(void);

int
main(void)
{
   ...
#if ( TRACE )
  Trace("in", "Test_Fun");
#endif
  Test_Fun(q, r);                                                ⑥
#if ( TRACE )
  Trace("out", "Test_Fun");
#endif

  return (0);
}
```

In this example, the #if and #endif directives (at item **6**) mean that if "TRACE" is defined, then compile the program with the "Trace" calls included. Otherwise the program is compiled without them. In this way, large amounts of code are potentially ignored in the object file when debugging is over. Of course, these directives can be used with inline printf statements as well. In both examples, we have included a user-defined header file (at item **4**) which directs inclusion of tracing functions, so that they need not be included directly into every source program which uses them.

11.3.4 Program Stubbing

The printf method of debugging is probably the most often used, because, regardless of its implementation, it is quickly coded and is very portable (it can be added and removed relatively easily). In general, the latter print method of writing a 'Trace' function may take some extra time to develop the debugging functions, but is faster to use and remove later on. The next level of program debugging tools uses the structure of modular programming and the anonymity of procedural abstraction to isolate portions of the code and test them independently of the rest of the program. This can be looked at in two ways: (1) from the overall execution of the program, in which case you want to use a *stub* approach; and (2) from the execution of each function, in which case you want to use dummy functions and function drivers. Each approach will be presented.

11.3.5 Overall Program Execution and Program Stubs

Large programs that have many functions are difficult to debug without a careful analysis of the flow of control through the program. When testing a large program, it is not a good idea to test all of the code at once. A much more efficient approach is to test each module, in turn, to make sure that it is logically correct and executing properly. One way to do this is to create program **stubs**. That is, by placing segments of the program in comments, it is possible to test other pieces to make sure control is flowing properly. Consider the program "StubTest.c" in Fig. 11.2.

Figure 11.2: Using function stubs to bypass function execution

```
/**********************************************************/
/* FILE:      StubTest.c                                  */
/*                                                        */
/* AUTHOR:    J.B. Hodges                                 */
/* DATE:      August, 1993                                */
/* FUNCTION:  Tests the main program and provides dummy   */
/*            input for the GetArgs and PrintVals         */
/*            functions.                                  */
/**********************************************************/
#include <stdio.h>

void PrintVals(char arg1, char arg2, char arg3, int arg4);          (1)
void GetArgs(char *first, char *middle, char *last, int *ndogs);

int
main(void)
{
   char fi, mi, la;
   int  nd;

/*stub*/   /* GetArgs(&fi, &mi, &la, &nd); */    ◄──────────       (2)
/*stub*/   fi = 'j';
/*stub*/   mi = 'b';
/*stub*/   la = 'h';
/*stub*/   nd = 3;
/*stub*/   /* PrintVals(fi, mi, la, nd); */      ◄──────────       (3)
/*stub*/   printf("\nHello, %c %c %c, you own %d dogs," \
/*stub*/           "right?\n\n", fi, mi, la, nd);

   return (0);
}
```

Figure 11.2: Using function stubs to bypass function evaluation (cont.)

```
/***********************************************************/
/* PrintVals: Prints output variables                      */
/*                                                         */
/* INPUT:     first, middle, last, ndogs                   */
/* OUTPUT:    None                                         */
/* RETURN:    None                                         */
/* USAGE:     Called by main                               */
/***********************************************************/

void
PrintVals(char arg1, char arg2, char arg3, int arg4)
{
  return;
}
```
(4)

```
/***********************************************************/
/* GetArgs: Reads input variables                          */
/*                                                         */
/* INPUT:     None                                         */
/* OUTPUT:    first, middle, last, ndogs                   */
/* RETURN:    None                                         */
/* USAGE:     Called by main                               */
/***********************************************************/

void
GetArgs(char *first, char *middle, char *last, int *ndogs)
{
  return;
}
```
(4)

Assuming that the programmer is developing the two functions (i.e., GetArgs and PrintVals) to read arguments and display results of some computation, the function prototypes and headers must be defined. In StubTest.c the prototypes are shown at item (1) and the function headers (with empty bodies) are shown at item (4). When the main body of the program reaches the location where the GetArgs function would normally be called (item 2), the function call itself has been commented out, and it has been replaced by statements which produce the same local effect of assigning appropriate values to the variables fi, mi, la, and nd. The same is true for the call to PrintVals (item 3). By putting the procedure calls in comments, the program will not enter either procedure. By letting the user set the value of local variables, we can guarantee that main will have valid values at the location in the program where the functions will be, and we can test the main statement block without ever entering the functions. If the main block can be shown to work correctly, then we can go on to test GetArgs and PrintVals by removing the comments and allowing the program to enter the functions.

11.3.6 Dummy Functions

The flip side of program stubbing is a stub for the function. When you first develop a program, you write the function calls in the main statement block, you write the function prototypes, and you write the function headers with empty statement blocks. The header and empty statement block is an effective function stub, because it allows overall execution of the program, which tests the organization of functions and their parameters, but doesn't actually *do* anything.

The next step in function stubs is to have the function return some value to its calling module. If the programmer returns a legal value, one which will make the calling program work correctly, then the programmer will be able to ascertain correct function as with the previous program stub, but the program will have actually entered the function and returned. There are different *flavors* to this approach. Below is one example of how this can be done using a program called "DummyTest.c" which is a modification of the program FirstModIO.c (see Fig. 11.3).

Figure 11.3: Using dummy functions to return known values to function calls

```
/*******************************************************/
/* FILE:       DummyTest.C                          */
/*                                                   */
/* AUTHOR:     J.B. Hodges                          */
/* DATE:       August, 1993                         */
/* FUNCTION:   Tests the GetArgs function with a dummy */
/* APPROACH:   Uses stdio.h function library.       */
/* FUNCTIONS:  GetArgs: returns sample data         */
/*******************************************************/

#include <stdio.h>

void PrintVals(char arg1, char arg2, char arg3, int arg4);
void GetArgs(char *firstp, char *middlep, char *lastp, int *ndogsp);

int
main(void)
{
  char fi, mi, la;
  int  nd;
  GetArgs(&fi, &mi, &la, &nd);                          ①
  PrintVals(fi, mi, la, nd);

  return (0);
}
```

Figure 11.3: Using dummy functions to return known values to function calls (cont)

```
/*********************************************************/
/* PrintVals: Prints output variables                   */
/*                                                       */
/* INPUT:     first, middle, last, ndogs                */
/* OUTPUT:    None                                       */
/* USAGE:     Called by main                             */
/*********************************************************/
```

```
void
PrintVals(char arg1, char arg2, char arg3, int arg4)
{
  printf("\nHello %c %c %c, you own %d dogs, right?\n\n", \
         arg1, arg2, arg3, arg4);

  return;
}
```

②

```
/*********************************************************/
/* NAME:      GetArgs                                    */
/* FUNCTION: Reads input variables                       */
/* INPUT:     None                                       */
/* OUTPUT:    first, middle, last, ndogs                */
/* USAGE:     [main] GetArgs();                          */
/*********************************************************/
```

```
void
GetArgs(char *firstp, char *middlep, char *lastp, int *ndogsp)
{
  *firstp  = 'j';
  *middlep = 'b';
  *lastp   = 'h';
  *ndogsp  = 3;

  return;
}
```

③

In DummyTest.c the functions are actually called from main (at item **1**), but the values returned from them are preset (items **2** above and **3** below).

Notice that the innards of the GetArgs function (item **3**) have been changed, and that the variable values returned are forced to be values which should make the main program work. When you are writing dummy function contents in this way, you can also modify the contents in more meaningful ways. For example, you can have the program prompt you for values and have the effects of those values propagate from the test function. This particular approach doesn't make sense in a function like GetArgs, which is supposed to read values, but in other functions it can be helpful. A sample run of the dummy program is shown below:

```
localhost> gcc DummyTest.c
localhost> a.out
Hello j b h, you own 3 dogs, right?
```

11.3.7 Function Drivers

A **function driver** is similar to a dummy function except that the `main` function is now effectively the dummy. In a driver, the main function consists of the minimum code needed to call the function being tested or debugged. You can slowly build up a function using a driver, and when it finally performs the way that you want it to, you can strip away the dummy "`main`" function and insert the function into the larger program body. Here is an example driver for the `GetArgs` function presented in Chapter 9.

Figure 11.4: Dummy main functions serve to test-drive a function

```
/********************************************************/
/* FILE:       GetArgsDriver.C                          */
/*                                                      */
/* AUTHOR:     J.B. Hodges                              */
/* DATE:       August, 1993                             */
/* FUNCTION:   Test vehicle for the GetArgs function.   */
/* FUNCTIONS:  GetArgs: reads the input data            */
/********************************************************/

#include <stdio.h>

void GetArgs(char *firstp, char *middlep, char *lastp, int *ndogsp);

int
main(void)
{
  char fi, mi, la;
  int  nd;

  GetArgs(&fi, &mi, &la, &nd)                                    (1)
  printf("\nValues input: %c, %c, %c, and %d\n", fi, mi, la, nd);

  return (0);
}
```

Figure 11.4: Dummy main functions serve to test-drive a function (cont)

```
/****************************************************/
/* GetArgs: Reads input variables                   */
/*                                                  */
/* INPUT:     None                                  */
/* OUTPUT:    first, middle, last, ndogs            */
/* RETURN:    None                                  */
/* USAGE:     Called by main                        */
/****************************************************/

void
GetArgs(char *firstp, char *middlep, char *lastp, int *ndogsp)
{
  printf("\nPlease type your initials, separated by no spaces: ");
  scanf("%c%c%c", first, middle, last);
  printf("\nPlease type how many dogs you own: ");            ②
  scanf("%d", ndogs);

  return;
}
```

I have included more detail in this driver than you might want to use, simply to illustrate that you could develop an entire function, including its documentation, separate from the program in which it will be called, and later dump the whole thing into the partially completed program. The statement at item (**1**) is the one statement which has been added for testing purposes and simply prints out the values returned by the function. Although the program from which this function was originally taken is only slightly more complex than the driver (item **2**), in most programs a driver can be very worth the time it takes to write it. Below is a listing of the driver being executed:

```
localhost> gcc GetArgsDriver.c
localhost> a.out
Please type your initials, separated by no spaces: jbh
Please type how many dogs you own:3
Values input: j, b, h, and 3
```

11.4 Debuggers

Many compilers have debuggers that allow you to **step** through the program at run time and take a look at the value of any variable during the execution of any statement. The GNU C compiler has a debugger called *gdb* that can be used in this manner. In general, a debugger is used in the following ways:

- Stop the program at specified locations during execution.
- Examine the values of variables.
- Modify the values of variables.

11.4.1 GNU Debugger

To use gdb, you must specify to the compiler that you want debugging information when you compile the source code. To request debugging information, use the '-g' option when you invoke the compiler. You can invoke the debugger in a number of ways. One way is to run it on a program which has produced a core dump and to use the core dump to debug the program. A **core dump** is an object version of the program in the state it was in when the failure occurred. Unless you are using a debugger, you should generally remove core files. Another way to use a debugger is to evaluate the program while it is running. The syntax for invoking the GNU debugger is shown below.

```
gdb [-help][-c cfile][-e pfile][-s sfile][-se pfile][-q][-x cmdfile]
```

where the options are listed below, "name" is the name of your object code program, and "core" is the name of the core file. The default core file name is simply "core." If you plan on debugging the executing program, you will not need a core file.

Table 11.3: gdb Options

-help	⟹	Displays a listing of options but doesn't enter the debugger
-c CFILE	⟹	Use CFILE as the core dump to examine
-e PFILE	⟹	Use PFILE as the executable file
-s SFILE	⟹	Read the symbol table from SFILE
-se PFILE	⟹	Read the symbol table from PFILE and use it as the executable file
-q	⟹	Don't print introductory banners (quiet option)
-x CMDFILE	⟹	Execute gdb commands from CMDFILE

Once started, gdb takes and evaluates one command at a time. The commands can be of any length, and their names can be abbreviated up to the point where they cease to be unambiguous. Other than exiting the debugger, there are three types of commands in a debugger: (1) execute, (2) stop, and (3) observe. The **step, next, run,** and **continue** commands are execute commands.

The break commands tell the debugger when and where to stop execution. The backtrace, list, info, and print commands are used to locate and observe variable values and code.

Table 11.4: gdb Command options

`quit`	⟹	Exits gdb
`blank line`	⟹	Repeat the last command
`help [name]`	⟹	Show information about gdb command name, or general information about using gdb
`break FUN`	⟹	Set a breakpoint at the entry to function FUN
`break LIN`	⟹	Set a breakpoint at line number LIN
`break FIL:FUN`	⟹	Set a breakpoint at function FUN in file FIL
`break *address`	⟹	Set a breakpoint at address (asterisk is required)
`enable BNUM`	⟹	Enable the breakpoint(s) specified by BNUM
`disable BNUM`	⟹	Disable the breakpoint(s) specified by BNUM
`clear FUN`	⟹	Remove any breakpoints for function FUN
`condition BNUM EXPR`	⟹	Break for break number BNUM when expression EXPR evaluates nonzero
`backtrace FRM`	⟹	Show stack frames for frames FRM
`frame FRM`	⟹	Examine the stack for frame FRM
`up N`	⟹	Select and print the frame N frames up from the current frame
`down N`	⟹	Select and print the frame N frames down from the current frame
`info frame`	⟹	Displays information about the current frame
`list LIN`	⟹	Displays ten lines centered around line number LIN
`list`	⟹	Displays ten more lines
`list-`	⟹	Displays ten lines before the lines last printed
`print expr`	⟹	Display the value of an expression
`step`	⟹	Execute each statement one at a time
`run [arglist]`	⟹	Start your program, with arglist, if specified
`c`	⟹	Continue running your program after a breakpoint

11.4.2 Using `gdb` - A Sample Session

A sample run using a debugger can quickly show the merit of using gdb during program development and testing. Consider the bus error that was discussed in section 11.2.2. The error was in the scanf function, where the programmer had forgotten to use an ampersand (&) to reference the input variable. To use gdb with this program, the following sequence could be followed:

```
localhost> gcc -g CountByN.c
localhost> gdb -q
(gdb) add-file a.out                                                    ①
Reading symbols from /Users/hodges/a.out...done.
Reading symbols from /usr/shlib/libsys_s.B.shlib...done.
(gdb) run                                                               ②
Starting program: /Users/hodges/a.out
Input the starting/ending integers, and the step: 1 100 10              ③
Program generated(1): Memory access exception on address 0x50242fc (pro-
tection failure).
0x501564e in _sys_nerr ()
(gdb) bt                                                                ④
Reading in symbols for countbyn.c...done.
#0  0x501564e in _sys_nerr ()
#1  0x64 in ?? ()
#2  0x501514e in _sys_nerr ()
#3  0x504d5b2 in _sys_nerr ()
#4  0x3e36 in main () at countbynbug.c:22                               ⑤
(gdb) list 22
17      main(void)
18      {
19          int     first, last, incr, counter, current;
20
21          printf("Input the starting/ending integers, ...
22          scanf("%d%d%d", &first, &last, incr);
23
24          current = first;                    Error Here
25          counter = 1;
26
```

continued...

In this sample session, an error was introduced into the program "Count-ByN.c" in the scanf call, by removing the required ampersand address-of operator from the variable incr (see 'Error Here' line). The program was compiled with the '-g' option, which sets up the executable file for debugging. The debugger was then started with the *quiet* option, '-q.' The first command issued by the user from within gdb, (item **1**), was to load the executable file "a.out" into the debugger. The response from the debugger is to display the path to the executable and some other information. The next command (item **2**) was to run the program. Although this sample session will only show the actual commands and responses from a debugging session, the user can issue commands for assistance at any (gdb) prompt. Simply type "help<CR>" to get a list of top-level topics, or "help topic" to get a list of lower-level topics for a specific top-level topic. You can then see what alternatives and options there are.

The result of running the program (a.out) is the request for input which is displayed by the program. This is noted at item (**3**), where the values 1, 100, and 10 were input to correspond to the variables "first," "last," and "incr." The debugger then notes a memory address exception and provides the address where the error occured. At this point, it is often useful to find out where in the execution trace the error occured, so I type "bt" (for backtrace, at item **4**). This provides a full listing of the trace by **stack frames**, which are basically function call environments, along with associated address entry points. Most useful is the address in main and the line on which the error was flagged. If the program had had many functions, instead of just one, then the backtrace would have shown the function calling sequence all the way back to main. The frames lower than scanf in the backtrace are calls from scanf, so the actual error was detected inside of scanf. The line number next to main helps to locate *which* scanf produced the error.

Item (**5**) notes a command to list the source code at line 22, because we now know to look there for a problem. The debugger will then list lines on either side of line 22 to show context.

```
(gdb) list *0x3e36                                                         (6)
0x3e36 is in main (countbyn.c:22).
17      main(void)
18      {
19          int     first, last, incr, counter, current;
20
21          printf("Input the starting integer/ending ...
22          scanf("%d%d%d", &first, &last, incr);
23
24          current = first;
25          counter = 1;
26
(gdb) continue                                                             (7)
Continuing.
Program generated(1): Memory access exception on address 0x50242fc (pro-
tection failure).
0x501564e in _sys_nerr ()
(gdb) step                                                                 (8)
Current function has no line number information.
Single stepping until function exit.
    1     1

Program exited normally.
(gdb) quit                                                                 (9)
```

Another listing command, by address, is shown at item (**6**). The user must type the asterisk *and* the address, not just the address. Note that the listing is identical.

From this point it becomes necessary that the programmer be able to identify the error, and this is not always easily done, and requires more familiarity with the debugger. This session is only intended to provide the novice with enough clout to use the debugger and to experiment further on your own with the available commands. The command at item (**7**) tells the debugger to resume execution of the program, after which the execution is stepped (item **8**) until termination, which happens to be a single step. Normally, stepping allows the user to 'walk' through program execution and view the environment, but in this case the error occurred right away so stepping was of little value. Item (**9**) shows the exit from the debugger.

11.5 Developing Program Libraries

11.5.1 Header Files

Large C programs are often divided into several components which are combined with the use of #include statements. We have used #include statments to provide access in a program to library functions. The #include statement includes what is called a **header file**, which is a listing of the function prototypes for the function names, and corresponds to a C source file by the same root (i.e., it has a ".c" suffix) name. Programmers can define their own libraries by creating the appropriate header and C files, and then including them in whatever programs require the library.

When creating a library of functions from a source file, two new files are created: (1) a header file with the name of the library followed by ".h" and (2) a source code file with the name of the library followed by ".c." The header file consists of the constant definitions and prototypes for each function in the library, and should have a general banner describing the library: its use, its contents, and any suitable comments. The declaration for each function prototype in the header file should be preceded by "extern," which declares the prototype to be exportable to other files.

The primary requirement of using user-defined libraries is that, in the include statement, double quotes (" ") are used to delimit the name of the header file instead of the normal angle braces (< >). Consider the inclusion of a user-defined library called "My_Functions.c." The inclusion of this library into a program would appear as shown below.

```
#include "My_Functions.h"
```

Figure 11.5: A header file template

```
/********************************************************/
/* My_Functions.h - header file                        */
/*                                                      */
/* Library of functions intended to support some task   */
/*                                                      */
/* Included functions:    func1                         */
/*                        func2                         */
/*                        ...                           */
/*                        funcn                         */
/*                                                      */
/********************************************************/

#define XYZ                                                    (1)

/********************************************************/
/* func1 banner from source code file                  */
/********************************************************/

extern type1 func1 (parameters);                               (2)

/********************************************************/
/* func2 banner from source code file                  */
/********************************************************/

extern type2 func2 (parameters);
```

The creation of the source code library "My_Functions.c" may require some changes to the source code for the functions. The functions should be re-written to make them as general as possible. This may include changing constant and function names, and possibly moving constants into the function parameter list. In addition, the header file must be included, as shown above, for both the program which uses the library and the library **implementation file** (i.e., source code file), My_Functions.c. Of course, the function prototypes must be removed from My_Functions.c first.

Figure 11.6: Use of a user-defined header file in the implementation file.

```
#include "My_Functions.h"

/********************************************************/
/* Complete definitions of the functions listed in     */
/* My_Functions.h                                       */
/********************************************************/
```

When the header file and source file are created for the library, the source file needs to be compiled so that you have an object code file for it. This is done by using the '-c' compiler option on the library source code file, as shown below:

```
localhost> gcc -c My_Functions.c
```

After this step is complete, you can use the function library by loading the object file for the library (and including the header file in the new program source file of course) when you compile a program which uses the library:

```
localhost> gcc -o My_Prog My_Functions.o My_Prog.c
```

11.6 Organizing and Maintaining Complex Programs

The student has been introduced to basic programming and programming skills with the C programming language. These skills will only be useful as a stepping stone to improving your skills, and will only provide you with enough knowledge to read and experiment further on your own. The programs you have seen and written in this part of the text are single file programs, meaning that all of the source code resides in one file in the operating system, and all libraries are included in that file. Most application programs make use of many system and user-defined libraries, source files, and object files. When developing large programs, you will frequently find yourself needing to edit one segment of the overall program. There is no need for you to manually recompile and link all of the programs which depend on the modified module(s). A utility called *make* allows you to define, beforehand, how all of the components of the program fit together, and will then determine, when make is invoked, which files have to be recompiled and compile them. This way the programmer is freed from having to think carefully about what program segments must be recompiled, and it makes certain that the recompilation is done correctly. This section will introduce you to make and show you how to create a simple makefile. After that you should look in the reference section for more information on make, what it can do for you (which goes beyond compilation and simple tasks), and how to use it.

11.6.1 The Makefile

make organizes the tasks that need to be performed to maintain a complex program. Some tasks involve changes to source code and recompilation. Others involve installing new executables in the proper directories. Others involve building archives or installing the program from archives. Still others require construction and installation of online man pages for the application. make takes as an argument a file, called a **makefile**, which is typically named "Makefile" or "makefile." A makefile identifies each organizational task by what actions need to be performed, and by the dependencies between actions and the components of the program.

A **dependency** describes a relationship between files. For example, every executable program has at least one source file and at least one object file. When you modify the source file, in order to get the new executable you must recompile the source file and produce a new object file. We say that the executable *depends* on the object file, and the object file *depends* on the source file. If that object file is needed by another program in order to compile, then you can begin to see that the executable file may depend on many source files and object files whose dependencies are sequentially and hierarchically defined. When you create a makefile, you define the dependencies for the different components of your program and its associated organizational tasks. When you want to perform any of these tasks, you simply invoke the makefile with an argument which is associated with the task you want performed. This procedure is illustrated below for six different organizational tasks.

```
% make
% make program
% make clean
% make man
% make install
% make archive
```

In this example, the make utility will, by default, use the makefile for the project and, if given an argument, such as 'program,' 'clean,' 'man,' 'install,' or 'archive,' will search for that task in the makefile and perform the associated actions. When no argument is provided, make generally defaults to the first task in the makefile.

11.6.2 Constructing a Makefile

Consider the construction of a simple makefile to perform the organizational tasks mentioned above for a simple program. The makefile has three distinct section types, as illustrated below:

- Macros
- Dependencies
- Actions

Figure 11.7: A template makefile

```
CC       - compiler_version
PROG     = program_executable_name
SRC      = primary_source_code
OBJS     = list_of_objectfile_dependencies
LIBS     = list_of_libraries_used
CFLAGS   = list_of_compiler_options
BINDIR   = location_to_put_executable
MANLIB   = location_to_put_manpage
ARCHIVE  = ${PROG}.tar
```
① (with arrows to macro lines)

```
#PROGRAM                                                          ②
program: ${OBJS} ${LIBS}                                          ③
    ${CC} -o ${PROG} ${CFLAGS} ${OBJS} ${LIBS} ${SRC}            ④

#OBJECTS
objects: ${LIBS}
    ${CC} -c ${LIBS}                                             ⑤

#CLEAN
clean:
    /bin/rm -f core ${OBJS}

#MAN
man:
    cp ${PROG}.l ${MANLIB}                                       ⑥

#INSTALL
install: ${OBJS} ${LIBS}
    /bin/uncompress ${ARCHIVE} | tar xvf ${ARCHIVE}              ⑦
    ${CC} -o ${PROG} ${CFLAGS} ${OBJS} ${LIBS} ${SRC}           ⑧
    mv ${PROG} ${BINDIR}
    cp -r ${LIB} ${MANLIB}                                       ⑨
    cp ${PROG}.l ${MANLIB}                                       ⑩

#ARCHIVE
archive:
    /bin/tar cvf ${ARCHIVE} | /bin/compress ${ARCHIVE}          ⑪
```

The lines labeled item (**1**) are called **macros**, and represent local variables for the makefile. Macros can be referenced anywhere in the makefile by preceding them with a dollar sign ($), as with shell variables, and embedding the macro name in either a set of curly braces ({ })or a set of parentheses (( )). The use of macros makes the makefile easier to read and reduces typing. In this example, macros have been defined as noted at (item **1**), and would be replaced as necessary by the appropriate items when referenced in either a dependency expression or an action expression. Item (**2**) is a comment, which is ignored by make, and follows the convention of shell comments. Anytime a pound sign (#) is used it denotes a comment. If a pound sign is seen anywhere on a line, then nothing after it will be interpreted by make.

Item (**3**) is a **dependency relation**. It has three components: (1) a target identifier, which is on the left side of the colon, (2) a colon, which separates/ delimits the target from its dependencies, and (3) a list of dependencies, which is on the right side of the colon. The relation *means* that the target is dependent on the dependencies. The target identifier is what the programmer uses as an argument to make during invocation.

Items (**4** to **10**) define the **actions** taken for various tasks associated with various targets. The action **must** begin with a <TAB> character in column 1. Any use of tabs after column 1 are ignored (except for readability) by make, but the tab in column 1 is used by make to determine that what follows is an action. As a result, any number of lines can follow the dependency relation and be counted as associated actions as long as they begin with a tab character. Item (**4**) is the action to perform when code is modified, and defines the dependencies between the various objects and libraries that are necessary to recompile the program. In this example, only the template has been shown; however, in any real example, each object file would have its own dependency relation. Some tasks do not have source/binary code dependencies, such as the "clean" task. clean removes any core files which are leftover from code development, and is simply a UNIX script.

Item (**5**) defines the dependencies and action necessary to compile the libraries to produce the object files need for program compilation. Item (**6**) is the action associated with placing the manpage in the appropriate location, and requires that the macro for MANLIB be defined.

Items (**7** to **10**) are the actions to perform all the tasks associated with installation, in which the library is unarchived using uncompress and tar (item **6**), the source code is compiled as before, the executable is placed in the appropriate directory (item **7**), the appropriate libraries are placed in the correct directory (item **8**), and the man page is moved (item **9**).

Item (**11**) defines actions to perform to archive the files associated with the program. The archival requires a name of the directory in which all of the program files can be found, and then the directory is archived using tar and compress.

Let us now consider a more realistic example, by converting the program for the Balls and Boxes problem so that it has a source code library, separately compiling that library, and writing a makefile to organize the program segments. The following items describe the procedure we will use.

- Create the header file for the Balls and Boxes functions

- Create the function library for the Balls and Boxes program
- Modify the original BallsAndBoxes.c source code file
- Create the makefile file for the program
- Test the makefile

Recalling the Balls and Boxes problem, we will begin by moving all the functions except main into a new 'library.[1]' We will call it "BandBF.c". The associated header file will be called "BandBF.h":

Figure 11.8: A sample header file for `BandBF.c`

```
/******************************************************************/
/************** Balls and Boxes Function Library ****************/
/**************                              ****************/
/*********************** header file ***********************/
/******************************************************************/


/******************************************************************/
/* PrintDirs: Prints instructions to user                      */
/******************************************************************/

extern void PrintDirs(void);                                    ①

/******************************************************************/
/* GetDims: Reads box and ball dimensions variables            */
/******************************************************************/

extern void GetDims(double *blenp, double *bwidp, double *bdepp,
                    double *bradp);

/******************************************************************/
/* CalcVols: Calculates object volume                          */
/******************************************************************/

extern void CalcVols(double blen, double bwid, double bdep,
                double brad, double *boxvolp, double *ballvolp,
              double *actvolp, int *numvlengthp, int *numvwidthp,
                int *numvheightp);

/******************************************************************/
/* CompVols: Compares object volumes                           */
/******************************************************************/

extern void CompVols(double boxvol, double ballvol, double actvol,
                int *numvolsp, int *numballvolsp, int *numactsp,
                int numvlength, int numvwidth, int numvheight);

/******************************************************************/
/* PrintNums: Prints output variables                          */
/******************************************************************/

extern void PrintNums(int numvols, int numballvols, int numacts);
```

---

1. This is not actually a library, since we will move all the functions for the program into this file. Normally, a library would consist of those functions which have a common function, or the functions which operate on a common data type.

Each of the function prototypes is declared as 'extern' in the header file, as noted at item (**1**), so that it will be available by functions defined elsewhere. The associated BandBF.c implementation file is partially shown in Fig. 11.9.

Figure 11.9: Implementation file `BandBF.c` for new `BallsAndBoxes.c`.

```
/*****************************************************************/
/*************** Balls and Boxes Function Library ***************/
/***************                              ***************/
/********************** source code file ***********************/
/*****************************************************************/

#include <stdio.h>
#include <math.h>                                              ①
#include "BandBF.h"

#define PI 3.14159                                             ②

/* Normal Function Definitions Here                        */
```

Note that the header file is included at item (**1**), along with the other libraries used by the functions in this library. It is also important to locally define any constants (item **2**) that are used by the functions in the library. As such, it is often unnecessary to include/define these items in the main program segment. In this example, PI has been defined for the use of the functions for the Balls and Boxes problem, but these functions comprise the entire procedural component of the program (outside of main), so this may not be indicative of all programs.

Next we will modify the original Balls and Boxes source file. In this particular case, we have only included in the program the main function segment. In general, however; we might have many segments with many functions in each. In this particular example, once the function prototypes are replaced by the inclusion of the header file, little is left in main (as shown in Fig. 11.10).

Figure 11.10: Main program modifications for `BallsAndBoxes.c`

```
/***********************************************************/
/* FILE:       BallsAndBoxes.c                           */
/*                                                        */
/* AUTHOR:     J.B. Hodges                                */
/* DATE:       August, 1993                               */
/* FUNCTION:   Reads information about boxes and balls    */
/*             and returns information about how many      */
/*             balls will fit into the box.               */
/* APPROACH:   Uses stdio.h function library. Uses the    */
/*             algorithms for box volume and sphere       */
/*             volume.                                    */
/* FUNCTIONS:  GetDims: reads the object dimensions       */
/*             PrintNums: displays the number of balls    */
/*             CalcVols: calculates object volume         */
/*             CompVols: compares object volumes          */
/* COMMENTS:   Demonstrates modular program design        */
/***********************************************************/

#include <stdio.h>
#include <math.h>
#include "BandBF.h"                                        ①

#define PI 3.14159

int
main(void)
{
  double blength, bwidth,  bheight, ballrad,
         boxvol,  ballvol, actvol;
  int    numvols,     numballvols, numacts,
         numvlength, numvwidth,   numvheight;

  PrintDirs();
  GetDims(&blength, &bwidth, &bheight, &ballrad);
  CalcVols(blength, bwidth, bheight, ballrad, &boxvol, &ballvol,
           &actvol, &numvlength, &numvwidth, &numvheight);
  CompVols(boxvol, ballvol, actvol, &numvols, &numballvols,
           &numacts, numvlength, numvwidth, numvheight);
  PrintNums(numvols, numballvols, numacts);

  return (0);
}
```

The final task is to create the macros which will be used in the sample makefile. In this case, we will name the makefile "`Makefile`," and we will use the names of the files we have generated for this example. When the program is complete, we will call it "BAB," for Balls and Boxes (item **1** in Fig. 11.10). The only personal library used in this example is the "`BandBF.c`" source code file, so it will become the single component of the `${LIBS}` macro (item **2**). Likewise, the result of compiling "BandBF.c" is the object file "BandBF.o," which is the only object component in the ${objs} macro. We will also include the main function file in this component (also at item **2**). The result is shown below:

Figure 11.11: Makefile for new `BallsAndBoxes.c` program

```
PROG     = BAB                                              ①
OBJS     = BandBF.o
SRC      = BallsAndBoxes.c                                  ②
LIBS     = BandBF.c
CC       = cc
CFLAGS   =
BINDIR   = ~/bin
MANLIB   = ~/lib
ARCHIVE  = ${PROG}.tar

#PROGRAM
program: ${OBJS} ${LIBS}
        ${CC} -c ${LIBS}
        ${CC} -o ${PROG} ${CFLAGS} ${OBJS} ${SRC}

# rest of makefile is the same as the template
```

Note that the original template, for this particular example, has not been modified at all! The definition of the macros takes care of the idiosyncrasies of this particular program. Now let's test the file to see if it lives up to its promise. First we will recompile an executable as shown at item (**1**) below. In this case,

```
localhost> make                                            ①
cc -o BAB BandBF.o BallsAndBoxes.c
localhost> ls *.o
BandBF.o
localhost> make clean                                      ②
/bin/rm -f core *.o
localhost> !ls
ls *.o
No match.
localhost> make                                            ③
cc  -c BandBF.c
cc -c BandBF.c
cc -o BAB  BandBF.o BallsAndBoxes.c
localhost> make archive                                    ④
/bin/tar cvf BAB.tar | /usr/ucb/compress BAB.tar
humpback[127] ls BAB*
BAB*        BAB.tar.Z
```

we already had a copy of "BandBF.o" from a previous test, so only the overall compilation was performed. As proof that make will recompile the necessary components, we then remove the object file for the function library using the 'clean' option that we implemented (at item **2**). Then we re-make the file (at item **3**) and note that both passes (the library compilation and the final compilation) are performed. Finally (item **4**), we execute the 'archive' option, which tars and compresses the source code tree for the project.

11.7 Recommended Reading

Learning to Program in C

Kernighan, B. and Ritchie, K. [1991]. *The C Programming Language*, Prentice Hall, Englewood Cliffs, NJ.

Hanly, J. and Koffman, E. and Friedman, F. [1993]. *Problem Solving and Program Design in C*, Addison Wesley, Reading, MA.

Oram, A. and Talbott, S. [1991]. *Practical C*, O'Reilly Associates, Sebastapol, CA.

C Programming and UNIX

Advanced C Programming

Kernighan, B. and Pike, R. [1984]. *The UNIX Programming Environment*, Prentice Hall, Englewood Cliffs, NJ.

Rochkind, Marc J. [1985]. *Advanced UNIX Programming*, Prentice Hall, Englewood Cliffs, NJ.

Make

Oram, A. and Talbott, S. [1991]. *Managing Projects with Make*, O'Reilly Associates, Sebastapol, CA.

PART III
UNIX Shell Programming

This final part of the text combines the concepts and utilities in UNIX with those in the C programming language. A programming language can be extremely useful for manipulating UNIX files, commands, arguments, and responses. Each command shell has its own programming language, and a program written for a particular shell is generally called a **shell script**. Unlike an executable C program, an executable shell script is not a binary file. The shell command interpreter reads each line of the program and evaluates it. This part of the course introduces you to the tools you will need for shell programming in the C Shell and the Bourne Shell. You are not expected to become fluent in writing shell scripts, nor are you expected to become a good programmer by writing a few simple scripts. However, you *are* expected to learn how to write a shell program in each environment, which includes the use of general programming functionality applied to UNIX system commands and responses. No aspect of either command shell's programming language is presented in much detail. Generally, a topic is introduced that covers a broad range of programming situations. An example is discussed that illustrates how that topic fits into the UNIX programming environment and how it is used. By the end of each chapter, you should have a few template examples that enable you to construct simple working scripts that exhibit behavior commensurate with the topics leading up to and including those introduced in the chapter.

Chapter 12
Regular Expressions
and Scripts

12.1 Introduction and Scope

A **shell script** is an executable file comprised of expressions which can be evaluated in a UNIX command shell by the UNIX command interpreter. The language used to control the evaluation of command expressions is called a **shell programming language**. Much of shell programming consists of **matching** a desired pattern with a list of potential patterns, and executing a UNIX , or UNIX utility, command on the patterns which succeed the match. The matching process requires an understanding of regular expressions, because a regular expression is the means for comparing, or matching patterns. The following topics will be presented in this chapter:

- Regular expressions
- egrep
- awk
- sed

When you have completed this chapter, you should be able to tell when a language is regular, how to make a language regular, why regular expressions are helpful in UNIX and when they are used. You should be able to provide examples of different uses of regular expressions in UNIX commands, and you should be able to use regular expressions in `egrep`, `awk`, and `sed` scripts. You should be able to describe what `egrep`, `awk`, and `sed` are, when they are useful, what their differences are, and you should be able to write simple to

Ch12

moderate `awk` and `sed` scripts. The examples illustrated in this chapter can be found in the "`UNIX/Ch12`" directory and can be executed and modified to help you learn the material.

Before discussing regular expressions and their uses in shell programming, it is informative to know that a shell script need not be complicated at all. You can create a file of UNIX commands and execute all of them by executing the file in the shell environment. For example, create a file called "`LatexAPaper`" that contains the following six lines:

```
latex paperfile;
bibtex paperfile;
makeindex paperfile;
latex paperfile;
dvi2ps paperfile > paperout.ps
```

You can now execute all of these processes by entering the single command:

```
localhost> /bin/csh LatexAPaper &
```

where "`paperfile.tex`" is the name of a latex source file. `LatexAPaper` is a simple shell script. Note that the commands are known UNIX commands and utilities, and that the file, `paperfile.tex` would have to exist. All the script does is sequentially execute a number of commands so that you can continue doing something else. The commands are executed in the background so that the user can perform other tasks. In this example, however, the debugging output is displayed to the standard output anyway. This simple example is the essence of shell programming. A shell script can be a one line file that has a command sequence that you have a difficult time remembering, or it can be an extremely complex program. Start small and work your way up.

12.2 Regular Expressions

An expression defines a relationship between operations and the objects they operate on. A **regular expression** is one in which the operations are those which are legal on regular languages, and the objects are the words in the regular language. The result of a regular expression is a set of words which would match the original expression, and forms the basis for pattern matching in UNIX. Regular languages form the basis for all computer programming languages, so their scope extends beyond that of UNIX. For that reason, a shallow discussion of the mathematical basis of regular languages and expressions precede our discussion of their use in shell programming. The UNIX utilities `awk`, `sed`, and `egrep` are introduced at the end of the chapter. You have already

Ch12

regular

been using regular expressions in many commands, so try to view the following discussion in terms of examples you have seen or can look up. Regular expressions are used in utilities like vi, egrep, and find for pattern matching while searching for strings.

12.2.1 Mathematical Background

Let A be a finite set of characters called an **alphabet**.[1] A **word** is a string of characters from A. For example, "aab," "abc," "ccc," and "babbc" are all words in the standard alphabet, because they are all comprised of strings of characters from the standard alphabet. There is also a special word called the **empty word** which has no characters. This word will be designated with an "e."

A **language** is a set or collection of words. For example:

```
L1 = {a, bb, acab},
L2 = {a, aa, aaa, ...} and
L3 = {e, ab}
```

are all languages. Notice that some languages are **finite** (e.g., L1 and L3, which have exactly 3 and 2 elements, respectively) and some are **infinite** (e.g., L2).

12.2.2 Language Construction Operators

Given a collection of languages, there are ways to construct other languages from them using the following set operations:

- **Union** ($\cup$)
- **Intersection** ($\cap$)
- **Difference** ($-$)
- **Concatenation**
- **Star closure** (*)

---

1. We will use A = {a, b, c} for set examples in this section. In UNIX, the character set includes all characters—upper and lowercase alphabetic characters, digits, the blank character, punctuation, and math symbols,—except for the newline character.

Union

The union of languages is the same as the union of sets that you are familiar with. That is, the union is the combination of all non-repeated elements of both languages. For example, suppose that L1 and L2 are defined as follows:

```
L1 = {urchin, starfish, nudibranch}
L2 = {dolphin, otter, starfish}
```

then the union of L1 and L2 is:

```
L1 ∪ L2 = {urchin, starfish, nudibranch, dolphin, otter}
```

where the ∪ symbol is normally used to denote the union operator.

Intersection

Similarly, the intersection of languages is the collection of elements repeated in both languages. For example, suppose that L1 and L2 are defined as follows:

```
L1 = {pumpkin, zucchini}
L2 = {tomato, potato, pumpkin}
```

then the intersection of L1 and L2 is:

```
L1 ∩ L2 = {pumpkin}
```

Again, the ∩ is the standard symbol for the intersection operator.

Difference

Given two sets, the *difference* between the sets is arrived at by taking the members of one set which are not members of the other set. For example, suppose that L1 and L2 are defined as follows:

```
L1 = {school, pool, dog, snail}
L2 = {pool, snail, tree, stone}
```

then the difference between L1 and L2 is:

```
L1 - L2 = {school, dog}
```

and the difference between L2 and L1 is:

```
L2 - L1 = {tree, stone}
```

Notice that set difference is directional, since L1 – L2 is different than L2 – L1.

Concatenation

Given two words, we *concatenate* them by placing them together to make a longer word. For example, the concatenation of "school" and "house" is "schoolhouse." The concatenation of "aab" and "cbbba" is "aabcbbba." Note that the concatenation of any word with "e" is the word itself (e.g., "aab" concatenated with "e" is "aab"). We can concatenate two languages by taking all possible combinations of concatenations of words in the first language with words in the second. For example, if L1 and L2 are defined as follows:

```
L1 = {school, pool, dog}
L2 = {house, hall}
```

---

then the concatenation of L1 and L2 is:

```
L1L2 = {schoolhouse, poolhouse, doghouse,
        schoolhall, poolhall, doghall}
```

The concatenation of two languages is written like an arithmetic product (i.e., L1L2).

Star Closure

New languages can be constructed by repeating the concatenation operation any number of times. This operation is called ***-closure (star closure)**. For example, a language can be concatenated with itself:

```
L2L2 = L22 = {househouse, househall,
             hallhouse, hallhall}
```

---

where the notation L22 means that the language L2 is concatenated with itself (i.e., twice) This can be done three times:

```
L2L2L2 = L23 = {househousehouse, househousehall,
                househallhouse, househallhall,
                hallhousehouse, hallhousehall,
                hallhallhouse, hallhallhall}
```

And so on. For any language L, let `L0 = {e}`, then, the *-closure of language L, denoted `L*`, is the union of `L0, L1, L2, ...` Basically, a word is *in* (i.e., a member of) `L*` if it is the concatenation of zero or more words from L (The zero condition, `L0`, pertains to `{e}`).

We are now ready for the definition of regular languages. A language is **regular** if it contains only a finite number of words *or* it can be constructed from other regular languages using unions, concatenations, or *-closures. For example, if:

```
L1 = {aa, bb}
L2 = {c}
```

are languages then:

- `L1` and `L2` are regular because they are finite
- `L3 = L1* = {e,aa,bb,aaaa,aabb,bbaa,bbbb, aaaaaa,aaaabb,...}`
  is regular since it is the *-closure of regular language L1
- `L4= L2L3 = {c,caa,cbb,caaaa,caabb,cbbaa cbbbb,caaaaaa,...}`
  is regular since it is the concatenation of L2 and L3
- `L5 = L3 ∪ L4 = {e,c,aa,caa,bb,cbb,aaaa,caaaa, aabb,caabb,..}`
  is regular since it is the union of regular languages.
- `L6 = (L2*L1)*` is also a regular language. It is the *-closure of the concatenation of the *-closure of L2 with L1. Note in this example, that there is an 'embedding' of one *-closure within another.

12.2.3 Regular Expressions in Unix

In UNIX, regular expressions are used by many utilities to define/identify appropriate sets of words. The basic idea is that a regular expression is used as a **pattern** which is compared to a large number of character/word strings. When a string is found to be equivalent to the pattern, then it has "matched," or "pattern matched" the expression. The set of strings that matches the pattern is a regular language. For example, in the `vi` editor,[1] there is a **substitute** command for making a change in a line. The syntax for the substitution is:

```
:s/old_text/new_text
```

Given the ': s' command, the editor searches the current line for a string matching the "old_text" and replaces it with the "new_text." The "old_text" is the pattern to compare against sample strings. Notice that the two strings are separated by a slash (/). The slash is called a **pattern** *delimiter*. The pattern delimiter need not be a slash, but can often be any special symbol as long as the symbol is not a part of either the original pattern string or the replacement string. For example, if the line:

```
John's car is rad
```

exists in a file and the vi command

```
:s/ra/re
```

is issued while editing the file, then the result will be

```
John's car is red
```

In this example, the search command could be modified as follows without any affect on the result

```
:s#ra#re
```

More generally, the specification of the "old_text" can be a regular expression. For example, the **kleene star** (*) can be used to match zero or more occurrences of the single character regular expression that precedes it. Note that this is a different usage than the asterisk as a wildcard. It only matches a single character. The pattern "we*k" matches "wk," "wek," "week," "weeek," etc. Suppose the line of text is:

```
This wk is the last wek in which to purchase a weeek's supply.
```

---

1. We will use vi and pattern search to illustrate some applications of regular expressions, however, it should be remembered that the regular expression is the statement portion demarked by delimiters and is not the search command itself.

Then the command:

```
:s/we*k/week/g
```

will produce:

```
This week is the last week in which to purchase a week's supply.
```

The "e" must precede the "*" or it will match the "w" instead. The "g" on the end of the command means make the replacements globally, i.e., everywhere in the current line. Without the "g," the substitution will only be made on the first string that matches the pattern. Besides the *, there are several other special symbols used in regular expressions, some of which are tabulated below.

Table 12.1: Symbols used in matching regular expressions

[]	⇔	Any characters within the brackets will be matched, e.g. [a-z, A-Z] matches all alphabetic characters in both lower and upper cases
.	⇔	Matches any single character

One important note: Sometimes the pattern to be matched contains a special symbol as one of its characters. For example, suppose the line of text is:

```
Replace the notion of * with the star closure in this line.
```

and you wish to substitute the "*" with "*-closure." The command:

```
:s/*/*-closure
```

will not work, because the * is a special symbol. To remove its special symbol status, called **escaping** the symbol, precede it with a backslash (\). The correct command is:

```
:s/\*/\*-closure
```

The backslash preceding the asterisk means "ignore the normal meaning" of the next character.

12.2.4 Bracketing Regular Expressions

In the UNIX commands ed and grep, there is also the ability to refer to a collection of symbols as a unit. The reference is then called a **tag** of the collection and can be used in place of the collection. To tag part of an expression, enclose it within parentheses. The parentheses will have to be escaped, so precede each with a backslash, (\). Once a part of an expression is tagged it may be referred to by number based on its ordinal position: 1 refers to the first tagged expression, 2 refers to the second, and so on. The position should be preceded with a backslash (\). For example, consider the text in the file "regular/ taggedtest" below:

```
I feel good.
John loves Mary.
```

Positioning on the first line in vi, the following command can be issued:

```
:s/\(good\)/\1 \1 \1/
```

which produces

```
I feel good good good.
```

As another example, by positioning vi on the third line and issuing the following search and replace command:

```
:s/\(John\)loves \(Mary\)/\2 loves \1/
```

replaces

```
John loves Mary.
```

with

```
Mary loves John.
```

12.2.5 Full Regular Expressions

Note that not all regular expressions are possible with the special symbols above. It is not possible to embed one * within another such as (ab*c)*. However, with some UNIX utilities, such as awk and egrep, "full regular expressions" are possible. The additional special symbols used in full expressions are.

Table 12.2: Symbols used in full regular expressions

( )	⇔	Parentheses can be used to group part of an expression; for example, `a(dog)*` matches a, adog, adogdog, etc
+	⇔	Matches one or more occurrences of the regular expression that precedes it
.	⇔	Matches any character
^	⇔	Matches the first character on a line
$	⇔	Matches the last character on a line
|	⇔	Matches either of two patterns separated by `|`; for example, `red|rad` matches red or rad
?	⇔	Matches zero or one occurrence of the preceding regular expression

Parentheses have precedence over the other symbols, then `*  +  ?`, concatenation, and, finally, `|`.

12.3 egrep

The command `egrep` is a pattern matcher like `grep` and `fgrep`, but it allows the use of full regular expressions, allows you to specify several patterns, and permits pattern input from a file. The way to specify pattern input from a file is to use the '`-f`' option. For example:

```
egrep -f patfile searchfile
```

will search the "`searchfile`" using patterns in the "`patfile`." As another example:

```
localhost> egrep -c 'A[0-9]+Q' *.c
```

will provide a count (`-c` option) of the number of lines in each "`.c`" file which contain the pattern "`A`" followed by any number of digits (`[0-9]+`) followed by a "`Q`." Each file will be reported independently. See the command reference for the `grep` family in Chapter 3, page 86.

12.4 awk

The *awk* utility is an extremely important and useful method for locating and manipulating information in highly stylized/ordered data, such as the output from UNIX commands. Data which is highly structured is often referred to in terms of fields and records, so awk is really a **field matcher**. awk can be used to scan the lines of a file (or many files) looking for a particular pattern and perform an action on those lines that contain a match (or don't contain a match) of the pattern. The output from awk is sent to standard output but can be redirected to a file. There are two formats for awk: the first takes an **awk script/ program** on the command line, while the second takes it from a file. We address the command-line version, because understanding one will be enough to understand and use the other.

`awk script [file-list]`

The "`script`" above refers to an awk script. An awk script is a sequence of pattern/action pairs:

`pattern {action}`

The pattern is used to select lines to analyze, and the action is used to analyze the line. Both patterns and actions are optional. If a pattern is missing from this generic form, then awk selects all lines of the input file. If an action is missing, then awk performs the default action of print, which copies the line to standard output (most often the display). Each "`pattern`" is a regular expression enclosed in slashes (/). Actions can be quite complex, and entire books are devoted to awk script writing (see Section 14.8). A large subset of C instructions can be used as actions. Actions are always enclosed in curly braces ({ }). **Note**: It is a good idea to place the entire script in single quotes (' ') so that it is not confused with shell commands. Here are some examples which use a long listing as input. First let's look at the long directory listing, which I have redirected to a file called "`foo`" using tee.

```
localhost> ls - | tee foo
total 361
-rwxr-xr-x  1 jhodges      5731 Mar 23   1989 aaai.sty
-rwxr-xr-x  1 jhodges     15826 Mar 21   1989 alpha4.bst
-rwxr-xr-x  1 jhodges     21794 Jan  6   1990 apalike.bst
-rwxr-xr-x  1 jhodges      2303 Jan  6   1990 apalike.sty
-rwxr-xr-x  1 jhodges     40798 Mar 23   1989 cite.bst
-rwxr-xr-x  1 jhodges       689 Mar 23   1989 cite.sty
-rw-r--r--  1 jhodges     12723 Aug 12 12:15 csuletter.sty
-rwxr-xr-x  1 jhodges     14287 Aug 12 12:15 csuseal.ps
-rwxr-xr-x  1 jhodges     15017 May 16   1990 diss.bst
-rwxr-xr-x  1 jhodges     23280 May 16   1990 diss.doc
-rwxr-xr-x  1 jhodges      7693 May 16   1990 diss.sty
-rwxr-xr-x  1 jhodges     15947 May 16   1990 diss12.doc
-rwxr-xr-x  1 jhodges      5369 May 16   1990 diss12.sty
-rwxr-xr-x  1 jhodges      2233 Oct 19   1990 disstitle.doc
-rwxr-xr-x  1 jhodges      1685 Oct 19   1990 disstitle.sty
-rwxr-xr-x  1 jhodges      5521 Sep 11   1990 doublespace.sty
-rw-r--r--  1 jhodges         0 Jan 29 18:15 foo
-rwxr-xr-x  1 jhodges      5437 Apr 30   1989 jack.sty
-rwxr-xr-x  1 jhodges      6326 Jun 21   1991 mitthesis.sty
-rw-r--r--  1 jhodges     12726 Aug 12 12:13 sfsuletter.sty
-rwxr-xr-x  1 jhodges     14287 Aug 12 12:15 sfsuseal.ps
-rwxr-xr-x  1 jhodges      7224 Jun 21   1991 sfsuthesis.sty
-rwxr-xr-x  1 jhodges     63235 Jun  4   1990 texinfo.tex
-rw-r--r--  1 jhodges     12722 Aug 12 12:10 uclaletter.sty
-rwxr-xr-x  1 jhodges     14287 Feb  1   1990 ucseal.ps
-rwxr-xr-x  1 jhodges     30639 Jun 21   1991 ucthesis.sty
```

Note that `tee` reserved a name and location (at item **1**) in the current directory before completing the command. Also recall that the long directory listing is extremely structured. Every line follows the same format, so you can always expect to find similar information in a similar location. This is the kind of information which is ideal for `awk`, as you will see. Now we can issue a simple `awk` script on this file.

```
localhost> awk '{print}' foo
total 361
-rwxr-xr-x  1 jhodges      5731 Mar 23  1989 aaai.sty
-rwxr-xr-x  1 jhodges     15826 Mar 21  1989 alpha4.bst
-rwxr-xr-x  1 jhodges     21794 Jan  6  1990 apalike.bst
-rwxr-xr-x  1 jhodges      2303 Jan  6  1990 apalike.sty
-rwxr-xr-x  1 jhodges     40798 Mar 23  1989 cite.bst
-rwxr-xr-x  1 jhodges       689 Mar 23  1989 cite.sty
-rw-r--r--  1 jhodges     12723 Aug 12 12:15 csuletter.sty
-rwxr-xr-x  1 jhodges     14287 Aug 12 12:15 csuseal.ps
-rwxr-xr-x  1 jhodges     15017 May 16  1990 diss.bst
-rwxr-xr-x  1 jhodges     23280 May 16  1990 diss.doc
-rwxr-xr-x  1 jhodges      7693 May 16  1990 diss.sty
-rwxr-xr-x  1 jhodges     15947 May 16  1990 diss12.doc
-rwxr-xr-x  1 jhodges      5369 May 16  1990 diss12.sty
-rwxr-xr-x  1 jhodges      2233 Oct 19  1990 disstitle.doc
-rwxr-xr-x  1 jhodges      1685 Oct 19  1990 disstitle.sty
-rwxr-xr-x  1 jhodges      5521 Sep 11  1990 doublespace.sty
-rw-r--r--  1 jhodges         0 Jan 29 18:15 foo
-rwxr-xr-x  1 jhodges      5437 Apr 30  1989 jack.sty
-rwxr-xr-x  1 jhodges      6326 Jun 21  1991 mitthesis.sty
-rw-r--r--  1 jhodges     12726 Aug 12 12:13 sfsuletter.sty
-rwxr-xr-x  1 jhodges     14287 Aug 12 12:15 sfsuseal.ps
-rwxr-xr-x  1 jhodges      7224 Jun 21  1991 sfsuthesis.sty
-rwxr-xr-x  1 jhodges     63235 Jun  4  1990 texinfo.tex
-rw-r--r--  1 jhodges     12722 Aug 12 12:10 uclaletter.sty
-rwxr-xr-x  1 jhodges     14287 Feb  1  1990 ucseal.ps
-rwxr-xr-x  1 jhodges     30639 Jun 21  1991 ucthesis.sty
```

This *ultra* simple script has no pattern and only the simplest of actions, it reads and prints the entire file, one line at a time. The next most simple awk script does almost the same thing, but has a simple pattern match test and an action to print the result

```
localhost> awk ' /cite.bst/ {print} ' foo
-rwxr-xr-x  1 jhodges     40798 Mar 23  1989 cite.bst
```

The pattern matches all lines in the file "foo" which contain the string "cite.bst" (note the use of slash delimiters, which are used to bound a string), and sends these lines to standard output. Because the contents of foo is a directory listing, and since there is only one item in this directory with that name, the script output is comprised of a single line.

12.4.1 awk **and Field Variables**

The real strength of awk is how it works with structured data. A data file called "data" is shown below. Each of the columns is separated by empty space, so it is fairly easy to look at and compare each column. awk has a facility for looking at these columns, or **fields**, by identifying the column separator and the column number the item is associated with. As a default, awk denotes fields as items separated by spaces. Each column, or field, is associated with a number, and is referenced with a leading dollar sign ($). For example, wherever the notation $3 is seen in the awk script below, the third field is being referenced. Below are the contents of a file that has five rows of four numbers, called data:

237	19	85	48	◄───────────	37 embedded in field #1 of line #1
422	28	16	8	◄───────────	22 embedded in field #1 of line #2
371	12	8	7	◄───────────	37 embedded in field #1 of line #3
345	67	89	0		
323	19	37	8	◄───────────	37 is field #3 of line #5

Below is an awk script which matches '37' and '22.' If a '37' is found anywhere in a row, then the script will print the first field in that row. If a '22' is found in a row, then the script will print the third field in that row:

```
localhost> awk ' /37/ {print $1} /22/ {print $3} ' data
```
237	◄───────────	field #1 of line #1
16	◄───────────	field #3 of line #2
371	◄───────────	field #1 of line #3
323	◄───────────	field #1 of line #5

In the example above, the field where the match occurs is not specified, so if the pattern occurs in any field, the action will be executed. In addition, if both patterns are matched, then both actions will be executed. Now let's return to a UNIX example using fields in the action part of our "ls -l" example.

```
localhost> awk ' /.ps/{print $4} /.doc/{print $4, $8} ' foo
23280 diss.doc
14287
15947 diss12.doc
2233disstitle.doc
14287
14287
```

The input file for this example is again "foo." The first pattern matches all lines which contain ".ps,"[1] and the second pattern matches all lines which

---

1. Note that the '.' is not a special character unless it is escaped. Because it is not, it is interpreted by awk as a period.

contain ".doc." If the line matches either pattern, then the action `print $4` says to print the fourth field in the line. If the test is true for ".doc," then `awk` also prints the eighth field. As a result, `awk` is extremely useful for manipulating the results of UNIX commands, because they are always very structured. The use of fields in `awk` scripts can also be applied to files with different field delimiters (separators). `awk` has an optional argument, '-Fc,'[1] that allows the user to define which character "c" will be treated as the field separator. If, for example, you are trying to analyze a file, "test," whose fields are separated by colons, as follows:

```
localhost> cat test
bob:ted:mary:alice:baz:bar:dog:fish:snail:cloud
```

then your **awk** script could identify each field as follows:

```
localhost> awk -F: ' /mary/{print $5} /ted/{print $6} ' test
baz
bar
```
                  ↑
        field separator

In this example, when `awk` finds a "mary," it prints out the fifth field, which happens, in this case, to be "baz." Likewise, when it finds a "ted," it prints out the sixth field, which, in this case, is "bar." It doesn't matter that they are on the same line in the file.

12.4.2 `awk` and Logical Tests

Often one will want to have `awk` make decisions about what to do based on the values of fields. A logical test may take the form of conjunction, a disjunction, or a negation. Returning to the "foo" example, we could easily have tied the two tests together by adding a logical test to the conditional:

```
localhost> awk ' /.ps/ || /.doc/ {print $4, $8} ' foo
14287 csuseal.ps
23280 diss.doc
15947 diss12.doc
2233 disstitle.doc
14287 sfsuseal.ps
14287 ucseal.ps
```

In this example, the two vertical bars (| |) represent the logical OR operator, so the conditional is true if *either* ".ps" or ".doc" is on a line of "foo."

---

1. The 'F' need not be capitalized to work.

Notice that I have changed the action slightly, but the intent was to show how the logical operator works. The other logical operator you might use is the AND, or conjunction, operator, which is the double-ampersand (&&).

12.4.3 Formatted Output

awk allows the programmer to make use of commands other than print. One extension is to control the format of output using the C programming function printf (see Section 8.3.4, page 278). We can apply the same example using printf, as follows:

```
localhost> awk ' /.ps/ || /.doc/ {printf "The file size is: %d,
                                  the file name is %15s", $4, $8} ' fo
The file size is: 14287, the file name is csuseal.ps
The file size is: 23280, the file name isdiss.doc
The file size is: 15947, the file name isdiss12.doc
The file size is: 2233, the file name is disstitle.doc
The file size is: 14287, the file name is sfsuseal.ps
The file size is: 14287, the file name is ucseal.ps
```

The printf command requires that the user identify both the field type (integer, string, etc.) and the size of the space allocated for printing the field value. In this example, the '%d' means to print the value in decimal (integer) format, and by not specifying its size the entire number is printed. The '%15s' means to print a string of 15 characters, where 15 is the specified size.

In this case, we have formatted the output and specified the form of that output. That is, the eighth field will be written as an integer. To make matters slightly more palatable, we might want to send the output to a file instead of the standard output. For that we must add some redirection, as described next.

12.4.4 awk Process I/O - Redirection and Piping

awk need not display to the screen or take data from a file anymore than any other UNIX utility. Below we demonstrate the creation of files from awk and piping UNIX command responses into awk.

```
localhost> awk '/.ps/ || /.doc/ {printf "The file size is: %d,
                                 the file name is %15s", $4, $8>"footmp"}' foo
localhost> more footmp
The file size is: 14287, the file name is csuseal.ps
The file size is: 23280, the file name isdiss.doc
The file size is: 15947, the file name isdiss12.doc
The file size is: 2233, the file name is disstitle.doc
The file size is: 14287, the file name is sfsuseal.ps
The file size is: 14287, the file name is ucseal.ps
```

The component of the `awk` script associated with the redirection has been bolded. Notice that the redirection is performed within the action part of the `awk` statement and that the filename is quoted. Finally, what if we would rather not create the long directory listing first, with the `ls -l` command, but wanted, instead, to pipe it directly into the `awk` script. This can also be done easily, as follows:

```
localhost> ls -l | awk '/.ps/ || /.doc/ {printf "The file size is: %d,
                        the file name is %15s", $4, $8
                        >"footmp1"}'
localhost> more footmp1
The file size is: 14287, the file name is csuseal.ps
The file size is: 23280, the file name isdiss.doc
The file size is: 15947, the file name isdiss12.doc
The file size is: 2233, the file name is disstitle.doc
The file size is: 14287, the file name is sfsuseal.ps
The file size is: 14287, the file name is ucseal.ps
```

Again, the component of the `awk` script associated with the pipe is bolded. `awk` doesn't know the difference between a single file as input and a list of files, so you can perform the same tasks on many files sequentially. Of course, if you are sending the output to a temp file, as above, you have to modify the script to append, rather than write, using `>>`, or some other creative method.

12.4.5 Field Variables in the `awk` Test

Field variables can be used in the test part of an `awk` script as well as they are in the action part of the script. In the next example, we will look at field number 4. In a long directory listing, the fourth field represents the size of the file. In this instance, we want to flag any file with a size between 20 and 100 kilobytes. We use the test called **is a member of**, which is the tilde symbol (~).

```
localhost> ls -l | awk '$4 ~ [2-9][0-9][0-9][0-9][0-9]
                  {printf "The file size is: %d, the file name is
                  %15s", $4, $8>"tmp1rg"} '
localhost> more tmp1rg
The file size is: 21794, the file name is apalike.bst
The file size is: 40798, the file name cite.bst
The file size is: 23280, the file name diss.doc
The file size is: 63235, the file name is texinfo.tex
The file size is: 30639, the file name is ucthesis.sty
```

In this example, those lines from the listing `ls -l` in which the fourth (size) field matches the pattern (a digit between 2 and 9 followed by four digits between 0 and 9, or a file wholse size is between 20 and 100 Kilobytes) are selected. The action is to print the same size and name as before. The same example can also be performed with inequalities, as shown below.

```
localhost> ls -l | awk '$4 >= 20000 && $4 < 100000
                        {printf "The file size is: %d, the file name is
                              %15s", $4, $8>"tmp1rg"} '
localhost> more tmp1rg
The file size is: 21794, the file name is apalike.bst
The file size is: 40798, the file name cite.bst
The file size is: 23280, the file name diss.doc
The file size is: 63235, the file name is texinfo.tex
The file size is: 30639, the file name is ucthesis.sty
```

In this example, we used both inequalities for greater than or equal to (>=) and less than (<), as well as the **AND** operator (&&).

12.4.6 Shell Variables and awk

As a final illustration of the strength of awk, it is possible to evaluate shell variables from outside an awk script inside the script despite the fact that awk has its own idea of what a field is and how to designate/reference one. That is, a shell variable named $1 could be understood by awk, even though awk understands that $1 is the first field in a given record. In order to do so, you must think in terms of what awk is expecting to see. Consider first a case where you want to input a string which awk will use to match against, but the string will be input as the value of a shell variable. If two shell arguments specify (1) the file which will be read and (2) the item to match, then the awk script to find the field and print its characteristics is shown below.

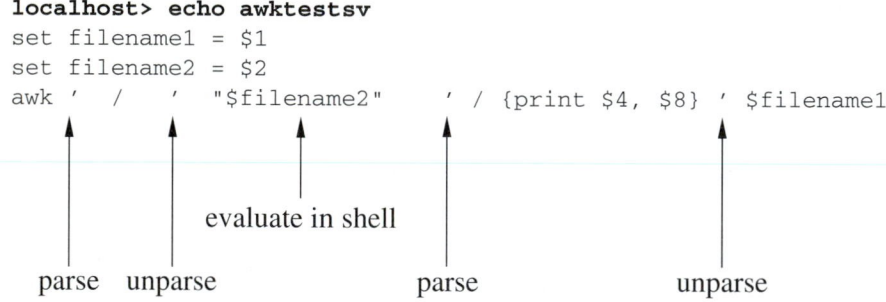

```
localhost> echo awktestsv
set filename1 = $1
set filename2 = $2
awk '  /  '  "$filename2"     '  / {print $4, $8} ' $filename1
```

parse   unparse   evaluate in shell   parse   unparse

If $filename1 has the value "foo," and $filename2 has the value "diss.bst," then this print produces the following:

```
localhost> awktestsv foo diss.bst
15017 diss.bst
```

where the first column of the output is the file size and the second is the file name, as expected. This example can be confusing, because, as a beginner, you do not really know how the single quote is being used by awk, nor what the double quote is for. The single quote is used to identify to awk what will be interpreted as part of the script and what will not. The balanced quotes indicate the script to be **parsed** (interpreted) by awk. The first quote tells to start parsing the script, and the second means to stop parsing (*un*parse) and go back to interpreting in the shell environment. So, you can start and stop quoting anywhere within the script, depending on what you are trying to accomplish. The double quote tells the shell's command interpreter to evaluate the associated argument and return its value. Thus, the effect of the single and then double quotes surrounding the shell variable $filename2 is to tell awk to not try to interpret the variable as a field, and then to evaluate the variable and return the value to this location in the script.

Sometimes you find yourself in a position of wondering if you could concatenate a field from the awk test with the value of a shell variable. In such a case, you can use a similar tactic as above. Consider a case where you want to concatenate the name of a file with the value of the **HOME** shell variable. This can be done as follows:

```
localhost> awk '/.tex/ {print " ' "$HOME" '/"$8} ' foo
/usr/f1/jhodges/texinfo.tex
```

Now awk is being told to print a string, but just after the string argument is started, the script is unparsed. Then **$HOME** is ignored by awk and evaluated by the shell, before starting the script parsing again. Finally, the string argument is ended with a '/' which is followed by the name of the file in field 8. The interesting thing going on is the string conversion in awk. Note that the last slash is located inside the string double quotes, just prior to concatenating with the field variable. Also note that spacing has been provided, around "$HOME," for clarity, but should not be used to produce the desired output.

12.5 sed

sed is called a **stream editor** and is an important and useful tool in selecting patterns and manipulating them. It is different than awk because it doesn't operate on fields but, rather, allows editing commands to be used on general patterns. What sed does is to take a list of patterns line by line, much as does awk, and executes a set of actions on them. The editing actions which sed uses are the same as the global editing commands in vi. They work with regular expressions and allow offline (i.e., not using an editor) editing of files. sed will edit lines of a file according to a specified script. By default, sed sends the results to the standard output. sed has two formats, like awk. The first is to take the script on the command line as follows.

```
sed script [file-list]
```

where the editing commands in the script are applied to all lines in the each of the files in the "file-list." The second format uses an option '-f' to locate the script in a file:

```
sed -f scriptfile [file-list]
```

in which the editing commands are stored in the file "scriptfile." A "script" or "scriptfile" contains one or more lines in the following form:

```
[address [,address]] instruction {argument-list}
```

The "address" may be line numbers in the file. In general, any global command you would use in vi to find a line can be used to specify an address in sed. Addresses in sed are optional. If only one is specified, then that line is edited. If two addresses are specified (separated by a comma), then that *range* of lines is edited. The address may also be regular expressions, in which case those lines which match the pattern are selected. If addresses are not specified, then sed edits all lines. As a simple example using sed, consider the following file:

```
localhost> more test
When I was a boy we had a dog named Greta. I have no idea how we were
supposed to spell that dog's name, I was really quite young. Dogonit,
you'd think I would have learned something about dogs by now. I think
I've owned a dog almost my entire adult life.
```

Suppose you want to replace all occurrences of a particular string, like "dog," regardless of case, with "Llama," for a specified range of lines in a file. You could do so as follows:

```
localhost> sed '1,$ s/[dD][oO][gG]/Llama/g' test
When I was a boy we had a Llama named Greta. I have no idea how we were
supposed to spell that Llama's name, I was really quite young. Llamaonit,
you'd think I would have learned something about Llamas by now. I think
I've owned a Llama almost my entire adult life.
```

Note that the script, as in awk, is enclosed in single quotes. The first component of the script is used to identify the pertinent range of lines in the file. In this case, the lines from the first (1) to the last ($) inclusive are included, so the entire file is analyzed. The second component of the script is the action to perform. In this case the global search and replace command is used. Notice also the 'g' at the end which tells sed to replace all occurrences on a line. It is just as easy to input the script from a file.

```
localhost> sed -f sedfile *.cl
```

where the sample "sedfile" contains the line shown below:

```
localhost> cat sedfile
s/^;/%;/
```

Note first that the file-list is all files with a '.cl' extension. The sed script uses the instruction '^' to replace each semicolon *at the beginning of a line* with a percent-sign (%). As an illustration, consider the sample lisp file below:

```
localhost> more shortlispfile2.cl
;;; lst is nil, return lst
;;; lst is single atom, return lst
;;; car lst is atom, return car lst cons'ed to flatten of cdr lst
;;; car lst is list, return flatten car lst appended to flatten cdr lst

(defun fltn (lst)
  (cond                            ; start conditional
    ((null lst) lst)               ; end conditional
    ((atom (car lst))
     (cons (car lst) (fltn (cdr lst))))
    (t (append (fltn (car lst)) (fltn (cdr lst)))))))

(defun bob (x) (+ x 3))
```

We can use the template and the file, or list of files, on "shortlispfile2.cl" as follows.

```
localhost> sed -f sedfile *.cl
%;; lst is nil, return lst
%;; lst is single atom, return lst
%;; car lst is atom, return car lst cons'ed to flatten of cdr lst
%;; car lst is list, return flatten car lst appended to flatten cdr lst

(defun fltn (lst)
  (cond                                    ; start conditional
    ((null lst) lst)                       ; end conditional
    ((atom (car lst))
     (cons (car lst) (fltn (cdr lst))))
    (t (append (fltn (car lst)) (fltn (cdr lst))))))

(defun bob (x) (+ x 3))
```

Note that semicolons in other locations would not be affected by this script because the test only mentioned the first column of every line.

12.5.1 Selection of Line Ranges in sed

In the first sed example we selected the entire file for output. Often when working with the output of UNIX commands you will be working with a subset of the total number of lines in the command response. For example, a ps command will display a heading before listing the processes and their attributes. If you want to perform some analysis on the response to the ps command, then in order to use awk you need to eliminate that first line. The script below performs that function for you using sed.

```
localhost> ps uxa | sed -n '2,$ p' | awk '{print $1, $10}'
```

In the example above, a number of new tools are introduced. Most importantly, the '-n' option is used, which means "do not print anything which does not meet the criterion of the match". Then, in the script, anything we want returned must be explicitly printed. This is why the 'p' is used. Finally, the result of the script is piped into awk, which prints the process owner userid and the process name (fields 1 and 10). Below is a sample run of this script.

```
localhost> ps uxa | sed -n '2,$ p' | awk '{print $1, $10}'
jhodges ps
jorge rtin
geisman /usr/local/lib/mocka/sys/Mc
jhodges -
azhao pine-exe
vcsc3081 vi
jhodges sed
```

12.5.2 Regular Expressions in `sed` Tests

`sed` will allow the use of regular expressions in the selection of string patterns. The script below looks for a number in the first column of the input file and illustrates the use of bracket ([ ]) in `sed` scripts.

```
localhost> sed -n '[0-9] p'
```

12.5.3 Shell Variables in `sed` Scripts

As with `awk`, it will often be important to use a shell variable to select a pattern for analysis in `sed`. The script below shows that, to perform this kind of task, the same mechanism that was used in `awk` also works for `sed`. Particularly, one doesn't quote that portion of the script used to identify the shell variable, and then the quote is again begun, or restarted. This example selects patterns which include the value of the shell variable 'third'.

```
localhost> sed -n $third' p'
```

Unlike `awk`, `sed` does not work with field variables, so there is no confusion in referencing the shell variable in the script, but the parsing of the script must still be turned off while the shell variable is interpreted.

12.5.4 `sed` Option Reference

Table 12.3 is an abridged table of `sed` options which may be useful in learning how to use `sed` effectively.

Table 12.3: **sed Command options reference**

`N`	⇔	Append the next line of input to the selected patterns with an embedded new line
`p`	⇔	Print the selected patterns to the standard output
`q`	⇔	Go to the end of the script
`r RFILE`	⇔	Read the contents of file `RFILE`
`s/test_pat/new_string/options`	⇔	Search and replace. Any character may be used instead of '/'; options are zero or more of:

		`g`	⇔	Global change on a line
		`p`	⇔	Print the selected patterns if a replacement was made
		`w WFILE`	⇔	Append the selected patterns to `WFILE` if a replacement was made
		`w FNAME`	⇔	Append the selected patterns to `FNAME`

`y/string1/string2`	⇔	Replace the characters in `string1` with the corresponding characters in `string2`; the lengths of `string1` and `string2` must be equal
`!-function`	⇔	Apply the `function` only to lines not selected by the addresses
`=`	⇔	Place the current line number on the standard output as a line

12.6 Exercises and Sample Quiz Questions

12.6.1 Exercises

Exercise 1   Let `L1 = {aa,bbb}` and `L2 = {cc}`.

- What is the union of `L1` and `L2` (L1 ∪ L2)?
- What is the intersection of `L1` and `L2` (L1 ∩ L2)?
- What is the concatenation of `L1` and `L2` (L1L2)?
- What is `L2*`?

Exercise 2   Practice with each of the special symbols, '.,' '[ ],' '*,' '\,' and '$' in different UNIX commands and regular expressions. Some examples are the `grep` family, `find`, `ls`, `cp` and `rm`.

Exercise 3   Create a file with three columns of numbers. Write an `awk` command which prints the third number on each line in which the first number is larger than the second.

Exercise 4   Write a combination `sed/awk` script that takes the output from the UNIX w command and prints out only the first 10 users (alphabetically) and what processes they are running. You can use the `head` command for this exercise.

Exercise 5   Copy the lines below into a file. Use `sed` to change all lines containing the word "know" into a line that reads "Why not?" You will need a scriptfile.

```
I stayed up late.
I know I shouldn't have.
I ate too much.
I know this is bad for me.
I will be better in the future.
I don't know if this is possible.
```

12.6.2 Sample Quiz Questions

Problem 1   Why are regular expressions a useful tool for UNIX users? Give two examples which illustrate your answer.

Problem 2   Use a regular expression and the `find` command to locate all files below your current directory which end with some extension, like '.c,' and print them.

Problem 3   You have to transfer a number of files from a Macintosh to the local host. The Macintosh file system separates directories with colons, as shown on the first line below. You want to convert the Macintosh file system into your UNIX file system, so that your files are organized the same way on both machines. What utility is most useful for this task, and why? Write the line of code which will translate a file called "filein" with file paths of exactly four directories to the form shown on line 2 below. Write the output to a file called "fileout."

Documents:Classes:UNIX:Manual:Man2.tex
Documents/Classes/UNIX/Manual/Man2.tex

Problem 4   Write a sed program that looks through every file in the current directory and replaces every occurrence of "got a fair trial" with "got an unfair trial."

Problem 5   Explain what "escaping" a character means, and when its use is necessary. Give an example.

Problem 6   Write an **awk** script that takes the output of the command ls -l and returns a file named "foo" which contains the names and sizes of those files whose size exceeds 100 kilobytes. Sample input is shown below:

```
% ls -l
-rw-r--r--  1 hodges      613633 May 14 13:44 All.ps
-rw-r--r--  1 hodges         463 May 14 13:43 Module11ABCD.aux
-rw-r--r--  1 hodges       13374 Apr 30  1992 Module11ABCD.tex
-rw-r--r--  1 hodges         463 May 14 13:43 Module12ABCD.aux
```

Problem 7   Consider the two regular languages, L1 and L2, below. Present an example of concatenation.

- L1: { ant,spider,beetle }
- L2: { hill,web,juice }

Problem 8   Write an **awk** script which takes as input the output from the w command and returns the list of users and what they are doing (fields #1 and #8).

Chapter 13
C Shell Scripts

13.1 Introduction and Scope

When a user issues commands or command sequences in the C shell, they are executing programs, and the arguments they give at the keyboard are the arguments to the program. In the case of interactive dialog in the command shell, this sort of program execution is similar to interpreter-based programming languages such as Lisp. In interpreter-based programming languages, expressions are typed at the keyboard, evaluated by an expression interpreter, and responses are returned on the display. The C shell and Bourne shell can be used as high-level programming interpreters. As with most programming languages, the expressions which can be evaluated by the shell environment are potentially more complex than a user might wish to type at a keyboard; certainly more so than they would want to type repetitively. For this reason, commands can be written into a file and executed in the shell environment. The resulting file is called a **shell script**. Also similar to a computer program, a shell script can be as simple as a single command that a user doesn't wish to type over and over, and it can be as complex as any program in any programming language.

A shell script can take many forms. The most simple form is typing a command sequence directly at the shell prompt. A shell script can also be a file with a sequence of commands that is executed like a program. You have already been introduced to many shell scripts in the form of initialization (dot) files. In Chapter 5, the special login scripts, ".login" and ".cshrc," were introduced and discussed. Both files are C shell scripts. In addition, many other dot files (e.g., ".logout," ".vacation," ".mailrc," ".newsrc," ".exrc," ".profile," etc.) are also shell scripts which are executed along

425

with their own special environments. A dot file is a script which is called to initiate a utility, and is where a user defines variable values and customizes a utility's functionality. For example, the file ".newsrc" file is where the user defines which newsgroups will be read.

Each command shell that a user creates has a command interpreter. Often, the default login shell is the C shell, as has been assumed in this text. Sometimes it is the Bourne shell. There are many different kinds of shell interpreters, and each is optimized for different kinds of tasks. In this chapter, you will be introduced to writing scripts for execution in the C shell (/bin/csh). Scripts executed in the Bourne shell are introduced in Chapter 14. One advantage the C shell has over the Bourne shell is that it can work with digit strings as if they were numbers. Another is that the command syntax is more similar to the C programming language. The notions of shell variables and scripts are common to any shell environment; however, each environment is slightly different and has its own syntax, so the C shell and Bourne shell envinronments will be presented independently. The following topics will be covered in this chapter:

- Script execution
- Script variables
- Script arguments
- Script creation
- Script control structures

Ch13

On completion of this chapter, you should be comfortable with the notion of scripts, how they are created, how they are made executable, how they are executed, how variables are defined and accessed, how to perform different kinds of operations, and how to perform iteration. You should be able to write simple C shell scripts which manipulate and execute simple UNIX commands, and you should be able to incorporate the use of the sed and awk utilities in your scripts. If you need to see the source code for examples shown in this chapter, they can be found in the "UNIX/Ch13" directory.

13.2 C Shell Script Execution

When you write a shell script, it must be executed in the shell environment for which it was written. You can invoke a C shell script at the command line. Of course, if you are currently executing commands in a C shell this is obvious. But if you are currently executing commands in a Bourne shell, you could tell the shell to execute following commands in the C shell. To know what to do, you must be able to recognize the prompt that signifies one shell over another. The prompt that is used by your computer system indicates which shell is operating. Almost always the default prompt for the Bourne shell is a dollar sign, $, and the default prompt for the C shell involves either a percent sign, %, or a greater than sign >. If you modify your login shell prompt, then you should make sure that you can still recognize the difference between different shell environments. Suppose that you are normally working in the Bourne shell and want to execute a set of commands in thc C shcll, you would invoke the shell with the `csh` command as follows:

```
/bin/csh command  ◄────────────────────────
```
                                            initiates the C shell on "command"

This command will create a **subshell** in which the commands will be executed. The process of creating a subshell is called **forking a shell**, and the new shell is a **child process** of the current, or **parent**, **shell**. When the command execution is completed, control returns to the parent shell. You can also fork a new shell which will execute all commands in the new environment until you exit the shell. This is done as follows:

```
/bin/csh
```

When this command is issued, the dot-file associated with the C shell (.cshrc) is executed. To return to the **parent** or calling shell, type `<Cntl-d>`.

13.3 C Shell Script Variables

One of the most important notions of a shell script is the **shell variable**. As in any program, the arguments which are provided by the user, and the values used within the script, must be associated with variables which can be addressed and manipulated by the user. There are two variable *types* used in shell scripts: (1) **string variables**, and (2) **numeric variables**. In addition, variables can be defined three ways: (1) within the shell, (2) automatically as shell command line arguments, or (3) as environment variables.

13.3.1 Assigning and Referencing String Variables

In the C shell, string variables are assigned a value with the `set` command. For example, the shell variable named "`filen`," below, is a string variable:

```
set filen = Unix-Man.tex
```

Note that the syntax allows spaces between the variable name, `filen`, the assignment character, =, and the variable value, "`Unix-Man.tex`." They aren't required. The name "`set`" *is* required. Variables in both the C and Bourne shell environments are referenced by preceding the variable name with a dollar sign, $. For example, the variable `filen` has been defined and can now be echoed or displayed.

```
localhost> echo $filen
Unix-Man.tex
localhost> tail $filen
%\appendix{answtoexs}
%\include{answtoexs}
%\appendix{\latex Examples}
%\include{LatexExamples}
%\printindex
%\bibliographystyle{apalike}
%\bibliography{unixmanual}
%\end{document}
```

13.3.2 Assigning and Referencing Numeric Variables

Numeric variables are assigned values with the '@' command. For example, you might be looping through a command sequence, and the looping may continue until a shell variable called "total" reaches some value. The total variable can be incremented as follows:

```
@ total = ( $total + 1 )
```

or

```
@ total++
```

The latter example (++ after the variable name total) is called the C postfix increment operator (see Table 9.3, "Assignment operators in C," on page 315). In either case, it is important to keep a space between the at sign (@) and the variable name. It is equally important to remember that numeric variables are integers, so the @ cannot be used to perform operations on double type variables.

13.3.3 Command Line Arguments as Shell Variables

Many shell variables will be defined implicitly through the script invocation. When a script is called, any command line arguments are automatically defined as local variables, with names $1, $2, ..., $9. They can be redefined inside the shell to be called something different, and they can be referenced within the shell like any other shell variable. For example, suppose you want to write a script which takes two arguments at the command line. Each argument will automatically be assigned a numeric variable name associated with its order in the argument list. The following script echos the values assigned to two command line arguments, regardless of what they are

```
#!/bin/csh  ◄─────────────────────────────────────  ①
# A script that takes two command line arguments and echos them

echo $1
echo $2
```

The line labeled item (**1**) has significance worth mentioning now. Normally, a pound sign denotes a comment line. However, when the pound sign is followed by an exclamation point and a shell path, on line 1, it forces the script to be evaluated in that shell. Thus, item (**1**) is telling the shell to evaluate this script in the C shell. Assuming that we have called this script "echoargs," an example of how this simple script is used follows:

```
localhost> echoargs pink elephants
pink
elephants
```

13.3.4 Environment Shell Variables

There are many shell variables that take on special values from the environment, or can be set by the user. For example, the variables HOME, USER, MAIL, HOST and TERM are all global **environment variables**, which can be referred to in any shell script.

13.4 C Shell Script Arguments

Many shell scripts get their input from the user at the shell prompt, while others may get it from the user at execution time. When a script is invoked with arguments it looks as follows:

```
script args
```

where "args" are the required arguments of the script. Internally, the user-provided arguments are ordered by their appearance at the command line, as mentioned above, and referenced with a dollar sign ($) and their ordinate position. For example, suppose we write a script called "phones.csh," which searches a file named "addresses" for a "name" and returns the telephone number. Simple enough. The script keeps track of the variable by calling "name" $1

```
localhost> cat phones.csh
#!/bin/csh
#look up a name in a phone directory

fgrep $1 $HOME/addresses
```

Consider a sample piece of an "addresses" file below.

```
localhost> more addresses
    .

    .

USHGA: P.O. Box 8300 Colorado Springs, CO 80933 (719) 632-8300
APA: 25 Goller Place Staten Island, NY 10314 (718) 698-5738
    .

    .
```

When the script is executed at the command line, the user provides the "name" argument, such as "APA," which is defined within the script as $1:

```
localhost> phones.csh APA
APA: 25 Goller Place Staten Island, NY 10314 (718) 698-5738
```

13.4.1 Prompting the User for Arguments

A script might also obtain information from the user by prompting for it. The most prevalent instance where one uses interrogated input is when you do not want to remember the number of arguments or their order, or when you are writing the script but others will be the predominant users. In such cases, the user assigns a variable name with the value $<, and the script expects input from the standard input. Below is an example of how one might use the "echo" command and variable assignment to interrogate the user for someone's name:

```
echo "Enter the person's name:"
set answer = $<
```

in which case whatever the user responds will then be the value of the script variable "answer." Now consider a modified version of "phones.csh," called "phonesp.csh," which prompts the user for the directory and name of the the "addresses" file, and for the "name" to look up:

```
localhost> cat phonesp.csh
#!/bin/csh
# look up a name in a phone directory

echo what is the directory path for the addresses file:
set dir = $<
echo what is the name of the address file:
set address = $<
echo what is the name to look up:
set name = $<

fgrep $name $dir/$address
```

and a sample usage of the script:

```
localhost> phonesp.csh
what is the directory path for the addresses file:
/usr/f1/jhodges
what is the name of the address file:
addresses
echo what is the name to look up:
USHGA
USHGA: P.O. Box 8300 Colorado Springs, CO 80933 (719) 632-8300
```

where the bolded items are those entered at the keyboard.

13.5 C Shell Script Creation and Execution

There are two steps in writing a script: (1) the script has to be written and tested, and (2) the script has to be made executable. A script is created with an editor. In the following example, the vi editor will be used, but it doesn't matter which editor is used. What does matter is that you write scripts which are clear and readable, just as you should when you write other programs. For example, type the lines below into a file and call it "helloyou.csh." This example will demonstrate how the ($<) variable is used to read user input.

```
localhost> vi helloyou.csh
#!/bin/csh
# This simple script tests user input

echo Please enter your name:
set name = $<
echo Hello $name!
~
~
~
~
~
~
~
~
~
~
~
~
~
~
~
~
~
~
~
"helloyou.csh" [New file] 6 lines, 111 characters
```

Two items of note in this file are the first two lines. The pound sign (#) is generally a comment character, except when followed by the exclamation point. Then it forces execution in the environment following, so the first line forces the script to be executed in the **csh** (C shell) environment. The second line is a comment telling what the script does.

Generally, the default file creation mask is 022. This means that you, as owner, should have full access privileges. If you do, then you can execute the script directly. If you do not, it is easy enough to check, by requesting the "long" file listing for the file:

```
localhost> ls -l hell*
-rw-r--r-- 1 jhodges 64 Aug 25 23:54 helloyou.csh
```

Note the use of the asterisk wildcard (*) to list out any file starting with "hell." Also notice that the file is created with 'read' and 'write' privileges, but not with execute privileges. So the next thing you must do, before you can test the script, is to make the file executable. Use the chmod command to give yourself execute permission for "`helloyou:`"

```
localhost> chmod 755 helloyou.csh
localhost> ls -l hell*
-rwxr--r-- 1 jhodges 64 Aug 25 23:54 helloyou.csh
```

which retains the earlier permissions, but adds the execute permission for you. Now execute the script in the C shell:

```
localhost> helloyou.csh
Please enter your name:
jack
Hello jack!
localhost>
```

This simple example illustrates two of the essential features of all shell scripts: (1) the use of variables and (2) the execute permissions.

Once the script is running properly, you will want to name it something memorable and move it into your default execution path. Normally, users put their executables, whether binary or not, in the directory "`~/bin:`"

```
localhost> mv helloyou.csh ~/bin; ls ~/bin/hell*
-rwxr--r-- 1 jhodges 64 Aug 25 23:54 helloyou.csh
```

As you begin to add more complexity to your shell scripts, it may be difficult to find errors in how the script executes. Two methods which are commonly used in locating errors are (1) to *trace* the script execution and (2) to insert echo statements to display variable values in strategic places.

13.5.1 Tracing a C Shell Script

A C shell script can be traced by modifying the first line of the script as follows:

```
localhost> cat helloyoudebug.csh
#!/bin/csh -x   ◄──────────────────────  debugging mode is on
# This simple script tests user input
# and traces the script at execution time
echo Please enter your name:
set name = $<
echo Hello $name!
```

When executed, this script produces an echo for each line evaluated in addition to whatever behavior would normally occur. The output from "helloyoudebug.csh" is shown below.

```
localhost> helloyoudebug.csh
Please enter your name:
Jack Hodges
set name = Jack Hodges
echo Hello Jack Hodges!
Hello Jack Hodges!
```

13.5.2 Using Echo Statement to Follow Script Execution

One of the most effective programming tools for debugging is to insert a print statement in a strategic position within a program. When the program executes the statement, the selected values are displayed and the user can determine whether the program is functioning properly (at that location) by comparing what is displayed to what is expected/desired. This tactic is also very useful in writing shell scripts, and is done by inserting an echo statement with the desired variable(s) before or after the statement of interest. Often a programmer will display the variable value both before and after to make sure that the expression is performing the task as desired.

The echo command can be used with or without quoting its arguments, and this can sometimes be a source of confusion for new users. By quoting the arguments to echo, the programmer bypasses the shell convention of ignoring extra spaces between arguments, because anything between quotes identifies that thing as a single argument, called **a string**. Within a string arguments can be spaced in any way desired, and they will be displayed exactly as typed. Without the quotes, they will be displayed one space apart. By strategically using quotes with the echo command, the programmer can format the output in their scripts nicely. For example, consider the following six words and two echo commands:

```
localhost> echo Column 1          Second Column          Column          3
Column 1 Second Column Column 3
```

Notice how the extra spaces are ignored. Now we will quote the arguments and make them a single string argument:

```
localhost> echo "Column 1          Second Column          Column          3"
Column 1          Second Column          Column          3
```

Note that the spacing between items in the string is maintained by echo.

13.6 C Shell Script Control Structures

A **control structure** is a mechanism for conditionally executing a set of expressions. The essence is to provide a test criterion, as in sed and awk, and one or more actions to be taken as a result of matching or not matching some value against the the criterion. C Shell scripts have control structures and syntax which are similar to the C programming language (hence the name of the shell). Numerical, relational and logical operators are the same as in C. The use of the common control structures will be illustrated here.

- if-then-else-endif
- foreach-end
- while-end
- goto
- switch-endsw

13.6.1 if-then-else-endif

If-then-else is a standard conditional branching expression in programming. A **branching statement** simply takes an expression and evaluates it. Depending on the value, it either executes one series of expressions or another. The semantics of if-then-else is simple. An expression which can evaluate to 'true' or 'false' is given after the "if." Such an expression is called a **logical expression**. If the expression evaluates to true, then the expressions following "then" are evaluated. If not, then the expressions following "else" are evaluated. The else part can give rise to new, embedded, if-then-elses. The structure is terminated with the statement "endif." When one series of expressions is executed, or if none of the expressions is executed, control falls to the endif. The syntax for the if-then-else statement can take two forms, as shown below. In both cases, the test expression must be enclosed in parentheses:

```
if ( test-expression ) command
```

This first case is for a simple test, such as "does this variable have a value" or "is the value of this variable blah?" If the logical expression, "test-expression," evaluates to "true," then the "command" is executed. Otherwise control is passed to the first statement after the if. The second case is the more general form.

```
if ( test-expression ) then
    then-commands
else
    else-commands
endif
```

The "else" clause is optional. It is important to place the if, else, and endif statement on new lines, at the beginning of the line, regardless of where the beginning is indented. Consider a simple example, "simpleif.csh," which considers two shell arguments and makes a simple decision based on their values:

```
localhost> cat simpleif.csh
#!/bin/csh
# a simple if-then-else script

if ( $1 == 5 ) then
   du $2
else
   ls $2
endif
```

This script takes two arguments at the command line. If the first argument's value is 5, then a disk usage command (du) is executed on the directory named in the second argument. If the first argument's value is not 5 (i.e., anything but 5), then a listing is executed on the directory named in the second argument. The C logical equivalence operator (==) is used to test the pattern. After the script has been made executable, it can be tested as follows:

```
localhost> simpleif.csh 5 Texmacros
371 Texmacros
localhost> simpleif.csh 0 Texmacros
aaai.sty        diss.doc        footmp1         tmplrg2endif
alpha4.bst      diss.sty        jack.sty        tmplrg3
apalike.bst     diss12.doc      mitthesis.sty   uclaletter.sty
apalike.sty     diss12.sty      sfsuletter.sty  ucseal.ps
cite.bst        disstitle.doc   sfsuseal.ps     ucthesis.sty
cite.sty        disstitle.sty   sfsuthesis.sty
csuletter.sty   doublespace.sty texinfo.tex
csuseal.ps      foo             tmplrg
diss.bst        footmp          tmplrg1
```

The types of tests which can be performed in the C shell conditional are not related to simple variable and value tests. One can refer to status of files in the operating system, or even to the number and values input arguments, within the script. Tables 13.1 and 13.2 show some of the available options.

Table 13.1: File system logical tests in the C shell

-r FILE	$\Rightarrow$	returns 1 if the file named FILE is readable by the user
-w FILE	$\Rightarrow$	returns 1 if the file named FILE is writable by the user
-x FILE	$\Rightarrow$	returns 1 if the file named FILE is executable by the user
-o FILE	$\Rightarrow$	returns 1 if the user owns the file named FILE
-e FILE	$\Rightarrow$	returns 1 if the file named FILE exists
-f FILE	$\Rightarrow$	returns 1 if the file named FILE exists and is a regular file
-d FILE	$\Rightarrow$	returns 1 if the file named FILE exists and is a directory

Table 13.2: Standard variables in the C shell

$0	$\Rightarrow$	calling function name
$N	$\Rightarrow$	Nth command line argument value
$*	$\Rightarrow$	all the command line arguments
$@	$\Rightarrow$	all the command line arguments
$#	$\Rightarrow$	the number of command line arguments
$$	$\Rightarrow$	process number (PID) of the current process
$!	$\Rightarrow$	process number (PID) of the last background process
$?	$\Rightarrow$	exit status of the last task

13.6.2 foreach-end

Probably the most powerful control structure in programming is the loop. **Loops** perform the task of iteration, by executing a series of commands repeatedly. Each time the command sequence is executed is called a **cycle** or **pass**.

In order to make use of the loop, the programmer must be able to enter it and exit it at will. The loop is begun (entered) when some condition is met, and the loop is ended (exited) when that criterion is no longer met. *foreach* is a looping mechanism which performs an iteration a specific number of times. foreach is useful in shell programming because it performs a set of operations once for each of a set of arguments. For example, if you want to write a script which performs the same task on every element in a directory, or for every process in a ps list, then foreach is the loop mechanism to use for the C shell. foreach has a simple syntax, as outlined below.

```
foreach item ( listofitems )
    commands
end
```

where "item" will be associated with each element in "listofitems" for each loop pass (or cycle). Within the loop, "item" is referred to as a shell variable. For example, consider the loop for the script "onsince.csh," below. "onsince.csh" looks at all the users in a list and checks to see if they are currently working on the local host. If so, "onsince.csh" prints out their current status. The script is shown below:

```
localhost> cat onsince.csh
#!/bin/csh
# a simple foreach script

echo -n "Enter a list of userids please (without quotes): "        (1)
foreach user ( $< )
  echo ""
  finger $user | fgrep "On since"                                   (2)
end
echo ""
```

The first item of interest in this script is the optional '-n' argument with the echo command (at item **1**). This option instructs echo to not print a line feed (i.e., a carriage return) after the echo. This is particularly useful for having the displayed command and the user response on the same line. Unfortunately, this mechanism requires the user to insert another echo " " somewhere after the initial echo to print a carriage return. In the script called onsince.csh, the user inputs the userids of users he or she wants to check up on. For each user name input, onsince.csh executes finger on user. The userids are entered at the command line and read with the $< format inside the foreach item list. Notice (at item **2**) that **user** is actually a shell variable which is iteratively assigned a new value from the list on each pass through the loop. In C, **user** would be consider a **loop control variable**.

When a user is currently logged on, there is a line in the `finger` output with the line "On since" in it, so if the user is logged on, running `finger` and piping it into `fgrep "On since"` will return that line if the user is currently logged on. There are other ways to perform this task, but it illustrates the notion of `foreach`. The script is executed as follows:

```
localhost> onsince.csh
Enter a list of userids please (without quotes): jhodges susan
On since Feb 1 08:01:21 on ttyp1 from huckleberry.sfsu
On since Feb 1 09:26:06 on ttyp4 from modem11.sfsu.edu
```

`foreach` is particularly useful for performing the same action on a number of items returned from a UNIX command. For example, suppose that you want to rename all of the files in a directory with a new extension. First you would want to list all of the files in the directory, and for each item, you want to use the `mv` command to rename it. You can use `foreach` to perform this task using "`ch-ext.csh`" as follows:

```
localhost> cat ch-ext.csh
#!/bin/csh
# this script changes extensions in a directory
# exto - original extension
# extn - new extension

set exto = $1
set extn = $2

foreach item ( `ls *.$exto` )                                    ①
    mv $item $item:r.$extn                                        ②
end
```

In this example, the list of items is defined by executing a UNIX command (at item **1**). The UNIX command must be enclosed in single back quotes in order to execute, and the user should pay close attention to select backquotes instead of regular single quotes, as they look very similar on most keyboards. The balanced backquotes tell the command interpreter to evaluate the expression.

The script has two variables: (1) "`exto`," which is the original extension[1] on files, and (2) "`extn`," which is the new extension for the files. The `ls` command lists all files in the current directory which have the original extension, so these are the items which will be flagged in the `foreach`. The `mv` com-

---

1. The `:r` terminology is part of the edit global search command syntax. See Table 5.9, "Command modification reference," on page 168.

mand operates on each of these items, replacing the ".xxx" extension with the new extension.

13.6.3 while-end

while is a **looping** mechanism which performs iteration as long as the entry criterion is met. Often the criterion includes what is called a **counter variable** which is incremented within the loop. The while takes an expression or condition, which serves as an entry condition, and loops on the embedded commands as long as the entry condition is true. The while loop is terminated with an end statement. When the entry condition is false, control **falls through**[1] to the end statement. Both the while and end statement must be on their own lines, and at the beginning of those lines. The syntax for the while loop is shown below:

```
while ( test-expression )
    commands
end
```

while loops can be used for **count-control loops** as in the following script called "looptest.csh." Count control means that a counter is given an initial value, and then the looping mechanism will increment and evaluate the counter value during each loop pass.

```
localhost> cat looptest.csh
#!/bin/csh
# a simple while script

set count = 0        ◄──────────────────  initialize counter variable
set limit = 7        ◄──────────────────  set exit variable value

while ( $count != $limit )
    echo hello JBH
    @ count++
end
```

In this example, the "!=" C relational operator, which means "not equal," is used, as well as the "count++" postfix increment operator, which increments the "count" numeric shell variable by one. The while loop then iterates the same set of "commands" seven times. The script output is straightforward.

---

1. This is a programming terminology which refers to the fact that no other statements are executed and control is directed to the last statement in the loop.

```
localhost> looptest.csh
hello JBH
hello JBH
hello JBH
hello JBH
hello JBH
hello JBH
hello JBH
```

The `while` loop construct hides a potentially serious problem for the unsuspecting programmer. If the loop is successfully entered, but there is no means to exit it, then the programmer has created an **infinite loop**, which will continue to execute until some form of intervention is manifested. Often this form of intervention is a `<Cntl-z>` (i.e., stop the job) or a `<Cntl-c>` (i.e., interrupt the job). An infinite loop will *not* correct itself. The most common error in generating an infinite loop is not updating a counter which is needed to exit the loop.[1] Another is not having a valid test criterion, so the test is never successfully evaluated after the initial pass. More important than identifying all of the mechanisms for creating infinite loops, because this is a situation to be avoided, there are a few ways which, if invoked religiously, will virtually guarantee against the possibility of an infinite loop.

- Always initialize looping variables before entering a loop. If a variable is not initialized, then there is a possibility that it will take on a value which can have deleterious effects.
- Always increment counter variables within the loop body. The body is that series of expressions which are executed repeatedly.
- Test the loop test condition with the expected entry and exit values, on paper, to make sure that they will work before executing the loop.

In addition, it is always a good idea when learning how to write loops to test the loop with an expression which will allow the programmer to exit the loop without killing the associated process. This expression could be a branch statement such as described in the next section.

13.6.4 Goto

The `goto` construct is used to switch the flow of execution to a different statement. The `goto` is generally used with a conditional operator to exit from a loop without explicit reference to the loop's own exit condition. The syntax for the `goto` statement follows.

---

1. Usually called an **exit criterion**, which is the logical complement of the entry condition or test expression.

```
goto label
    .
    .
    .
label:
   commands
```

where "label" can be any string. When the goto is encountered, control jumps to "label" and the commands below "label" are executed. Consider an example script called "simplegoto.csh," which modifies looptest.csh to exit after 3 iterations:

```
localhost> cat simplegoto.csh
#!/bin/csh
# a simple while-goto script

set count = 0          ◄───────────────────── counter initialization
set limit = 10

while ($count != $limit)
   echo hello JBH
   @ count++
   if ($count == 3) goto foo
end
foo:   ◄─────────────────────────────  foo is the label
ls                                       control is shifted to here
```

Executing the script does the obvious.

```
localhost> simplegoto.csh
hello JBH
hello JBH
hello JBH
AKCL             MH-Stuff       Texinputs     latex
AKCL-MANUAL-PS   MX-TESTS       Texmacros     lib
Archive-TEX      Mail           UnixManual    mail-elsewhere
Code             Misc           akcl          manpages
Documents        News           bin           temp
F90              OracleProject  dvi2ps        tmac
LATEX-TESTS      TeX3.0         filterfile
```

In the last section, it was mentioned that a programmer learning to use loops might want to insert a goto/label statement which would allow a graceful exit from a loop. The above script is modified, below, to show one way this could be done. The other difference is that this script has an error in it, so that an infinite loop is generated which the `goto` will catch.

```
localhost> cat badgoto.csh
#!/bin/csh
# a simple while-goto script with a costly error
# embedded in it

set count = 11          ◄───────────────────────  bad counter value
set limit = 10

while ($count != $limit)
    echo hello JBH
    @ count++
    echo "counter is: $count"
    echo ""
    echo -n "Is it alright to continue? (y/n): " ◄─┐
    set test = $<                                   ├─ test exit block
    if ($test != "y") goto stop                   ◄─┘
    endif
end
stop:              ◄───────────────────  control is shifted to here
ls
```

This script illustrates a previously unmentioned means of creating an infinite loop: a poor choice of counter initialization values. In this case, a value which exceeds the limit variable will allow the loop to begin, but doesn't allow an exit. The test sequence inserted allows the programmer to view the value of the counter variable and to exit without outside assistance, as shown below while executing "badwhile.csh."

```
localhost> badwhile.csh
hello JBH
count is: 12
is it alright to continue (y/n): y
hello JBH
count is: 13
Is it alright to continue (y/n): y
hello JBH
count is: 14
Is it alright to continue (y/n): y
count is: 15
Is it alright to continue (y/n): n
AKCL            MH-Stuff       Texinputs    latex
AKCL-MANUAL-PS  MX-TESTS       Texmacros    lib
Archive-TEX     Mail           UnixManual   mail-elsewhere
Code            Misc           akcl         manpages
Documents       News           bin          temp
F90             OracleProject  dvi2ps       tmac
LATEX-TESTS     TeX3.0         filterfile
```

As you can see, the script was allowed to cycle several times, to illustrate that the counter variable value was incrementing properly, but that the exit test was not succeeding and wasn't going to. At that point, the script was instructed to exit the loop.

13.6.5 switch and case

Often a programmer will encounter a situation in which a decision must be made but more than two possibilities exist for branching. In such cases, one can employ **nested** `if-then-else` constructs, or one can use the *switch* **and** *case* construct.

The `switch` construct is used to test a pattern against a number of possibilities and to redirect execution based on the value of the pattern. The syntax for the switch statement is shown on the next page.

```
switch ( test-string )
   case pattern1:
      commands
      breaksw
   case pattern2:
      commands
      breaksw

      .

      .

   default:
      commands
      breaksw
endsw
```

where "`default`" is used as an "otherwise" clause. The "`test-string`" is evaluated and compared to "`pattern1`," "`pattern2`," etc. If it matches one of the values, then control is shifted to the associated set of commands that are then evaluated. When execution reaches the "`breaksw`" statement, control is switched to the first statement following "`endsw`." If none of the case patterns match, then the "`default`" commands are executed.

`switch` is used when a number of different possibilities must be considered, since it is easier to program than many `if-else` sequences. Consider the "`simpleswitch.csh`" script below, which decides what to do based on what type of input it gets.

```
localhost> cat simpleswitch.csh
#!/bin/csh
# A simple switch and case script

switch ($1)
    case dog:
        echo The lazy brown dog crawls under the rickety fence
        breaksw
    case cat:
        echo The spunky cat plays with catnip
        breaksw
    case fish:
        echo The slippery fish swims all day
        breaksw
    default:
        echo "The lazy typist cannot think of anything"
        breaksw
endsw
```

Several points should be made with respect to this example. First, the script doesn't do much. Second, the test variable *must* have a colon (:) immediately following it. Third, there must be a default case to catch errors (a catch-all in the event that cases are left out of the options). Like the other control structures, switch and endsw must be on separate lines, and at the beginning of their respective lines. The simpleswitch.csh script produces the following output when executed:

```
localhost> simpleswitch.csh dog
The lazy brown dog crawls under the rickety fence
localhost> simpleswitch.csh fish
The slippery fish swims all day
```

13.7 Exercises and Sample Quiz Questions

13.7.1 Exercises

Exercise 1   Write a C shell script that does the following. It accepts three arguments on the command line, each of which is a file name, and it uses `cat` to copy the contents of the first two onto the third.

Exercise 2   Write a C shell script that documents programs using **man** format. It prompts the user for the information associated with standard manual headings, and it uses an editor to have the user write the text associated with the heading. When all of the headings have been completed, then the script writes the document file. This may seem very complicated, but it is within your capabilities if you have understood the material up to and including this chapter.

Exercise 3   Write a C shell script that reads the program document written in Exercise 2. It prompts the user for the name of the program and the directory in which it is located, and it displays the appropriate manual page using `more`. Both of these questions are associated with the material in Chapter 6.

13.7.2 Sample Quiz Questions

Problem 1   How are variables identified in C shell scripts? Give an example of a valid C shell variable. Given an example of a C shell variable you have seen used in this manual.

Problem 2   What steps must be taken to make a shell script executable?

Problem 3   Suppose that you are about to write a C shell script that will take two arguments at the command line and set one variable, `"pathname,"` in the script. Suppose that `"pathname"` is the concatenation of the second argument with the suffix `".tex."` How would you assign the variable in the script? How would you refer to the first command-line argument from within the script?

Problem 4   You are about to write a C shell script that will take a user name and list of machine names which will vary but will never be smaller than eleven. What are the considerations for deciding how to input these arguments into the script, and how are they assigned and referenced within the script?

Problem 5   What are the differences between C shell scripts and Bourne shell scripts for the following constructs. You can answer this after reviewing the next chapter.

- Variable assignment
- Numeric variable increments
- Reading arguments interactively

Problem 6   Write a C shell segment that uses the 'while' syntax and semantics to execute an input command n times, where the command and its arguments, and the number of times to execute the command, are input

Problem 7   Write a C shell script that takes a directory path and a file type as command line arguments and recursively descends the file system from the directory path given, finds and prints all files of file type or size greater than 1 Megabyte to a file named "large-files."

Problem 8   Write or describe how to write a C shell segment that asks the user to select among two choices on a fast food menu, each of which has a different number that will be printed and some way to identify the item. The script will read the response, increment the value associated with the response by itself multiplied by California sales tax (you can assume 8%), and print the result "your total comes to RESULT cents" where RESULT is the amount in pennies. You cannot use real numbers to increment variable values with the @ operator.

Chapter 14
Bourne Shell Scripts

14.1 Introduction and Scope

The last chapter mentioned that the C shell and Bourne shell are both command interpreters. Each environment has its own programming language that can be used to write scripts which are executable in its environment. This chapter presents the programming language associated with the Bourne shell. We address similar issues as to those that were presented in the last chapter but apply them to the syntax and semantics of the Bourne shell. The following topics are covered in this chapter:

- Invoking a Bourne shell script
- Shell variables
- Shell arguments
- Shell creation
- Shell control structures
- Script functions and subscripts

When you have completed this chapter, you should be comfortable with the notion of Bourne shell scripts: how they differ from C shell scripts, how they are executed, how they are created, how they are made executable, how variables are defined and accessed, how to perform different kinds of operations, and how to perform iteration. Like the C shell, you should be able to write simple Bourne shell scripts which execute simple UNIX command sequences, and you should be able to incorporate the use of the `sed` and `awk` utilities in your scripts. If you need to see the source code for the script examples in this chapter, you will find them in the `"UNIX/Ch14"` directory.

Ch14

449

To help clarify the similarities and differences between C shell scripts and Bourne shell scripts, many of the examples provided in this chapter will be the same ones implemented in Chapter 13 on C shell scripts. Pay close attention to the differences, as they can slip you up when you forget.

14.2 Invoking a Bourne Shell Script

When you write a shell script, it must be executed in the shell environment for which it was written. In Chapter 13 we introduced the notion of the (#!) special characters on the first line of a script. When the command interpreter sees these characters, it expects the next characters to identify what shell environment to execute the following script in. In the C shell, the path following #! would be "`/bin/csh`."[1] In the Bourne shell, that path is "`/bin/sh`," and the first lines of the script would appear as follows:

```
#!/bin/sh
# This is a bourrne shell script
```

You can also invoke a Bourne shell script at the command line. Of course, if you are currently executing commands in a Bourne shell this is obvious. But if you are currently executing commands in a C shell, you could tell the shell to execute the following commands in the Bourne shell. To know what to do, you must be able to recognize the prompt that signifies one shell from another. The prompt that is used by your computer system often indicate which shell is operating. Almost always the default prompt for the Bourne shell is a dollar sign, $. If you modify your login shell prompt, as you were shown how to do in Chapter 5, then you should make sure that you can still recognize the difference between different shells. Suppose that you are normally working in the C shell and want to execute a set of commands in the Bourne shell. You would invoke the shell with the *sh* command as follows:

`/bin/sh command` ◄—————————————————— *initiates a Bourne shell on "command"*

This command will create a **subshell** in which the commands will be executed. The process of creating a subshell is called **forking a shell**, and the new shell is a **child process** of the current shell or **parent shell**. When the command execution is completed, control returns to the parent shell. You can also fork a new shell which will execute all commands in the new environment until you exit the shell. This is done as follows.

---

1. On most systems, your default path will probably include the "`bin`" directory. I am including the path to be explicit.

`/bin/sh`

When this command is issued, the dot-file ".profile" will be executed. To return to the **parent** or calling shell, type a <Cntl-d> to exit the shell. You may have used the mechanism of forking shells with the "*script*" command, which sends everything typed to standard input or displayed on standard output to a file. When done with the script session, one must exit the shell with <Cntl-d>. The default file name for the session is "typescript."

14.3 Bourne Shell Variables

Besides being a command interpreter, the shell is also a high level programming language. The language includes variables and control structures much like any programming language. We will first look at variables, how they are declared, how they are assigned values, and how they are used. One of the most important notions of a shell script is the **shell variable**. As in any program, the arguments which are provided by the user, and the values used within the script must be associated with variables which can be addressed and manipulated by the user. The Bourne shell does not distinguish between string and numeric variable types, as does the C shell. Variables can be defined within the shell, they may be defined automatically as shell command line arguments, or they may be defined globally as environment variables. Bourne shell variables can also be exported to the calling environment.

In the Bourne shell, variables are assigned by following the variable name with an equals sign and then the the value, without spaces:

`filen=Unix-Man.tex`

Note that the syntax does *not* allow spaces between the variable name, "filen," the assignment character, =, and the variable value, "Unix-man.-tex." Variables in the Bourne shell environments are referenced by preceding the variable name with a dollar sign, $, as in the C shell. For example, the variable filen has been defined and can now be echoed or displayed.

```
localhost> echo $filen
Unix-Man.tex
localhost> tail $filen
%\appendix{answtoexs}
%\include{answtoexs}
%\appendix{\latex Examples}
%\include{LatexExamples}
%\printindex
%\bibliographystyle{apalike}
%\bibliography{unixmanual}
%\end{document}
```

14.3.1 Numeric Variables

The Bourne shell treats numeric and non-numeric variable similarly. So any numeric variable which must be manipulated must be considered an expression which should be evaluated. The *expr* command can be used in either shell environment, but because the Bourne shell doesn't have a specific mechanism for numeric variable evaluation it is often used in the Bourne shell. The syntax for using expr is shown below, along with an example.

expr argument*

where "argument*" means that zero or more arguments can be used, depending on the task. expr evaluates each argument separately, and is defined to work on string comparisons as well as numeric and logical operators. Remember to leave no space between the shell variable name, the assignment operator, and the expression. See the man page for more information on its use. Below is an example of incrementing a numeric variable for a Bourne shell script:

```
myvar=3
myvar=`expr $myvar + 1`
```

where the entire expression is backquoted to inform the Bourne shell to evaluate the expression.

14.4 Bourne Shell Arguments

Like the C shell, Bourne shell shell scripts can get their input from the user at the shell prompt or interactively within the shell. The use of command-line arguments is identical to the C shell, but will be repeated here for completeness.

14.4.1 Command-Line Arguments

When a script is invoked with arguments on the command line it appears as follows:

`script_name [args]`

---

where "`args`" are the required arguments of the script. Internally, the user-provided arguments are ordered by their appearance at the command line, and referenced with a dollar sign ($) and their ordinal position. For example, suppose we rewrite the script called `phones.csh` for the Bourne shell, which searches a file named "`addresses`" for a "`name`" and returns the phone number. Simple enough. The script keeps track of the variable by calling `name` $1:

```
localhost> cat phones.sh
#!/bin/sh
#look up a name in a phone directory

fgrep $1 $HOME/addresses
```
ONLY difference
with C shell

The "`addresses`" file, below, is unchanged from the previous example:

```
localhost> more addresses
 .
 .
USHGA: P.O. Box 8300 Colorado Springs, CO 80933 (719) 632-8300
APA: 25 Goller Place Staten Island, NY 10314 (718) 698-5738
 .
 .
```

When the script is executed at the command line, the user provides the name argument, such as "APA," which is defined within the script as $1:

```
localhost> phones.sh APA
APA: 25 Goller Place Staten Island, NY 10314 (718) 698-5738
```

---

where the script has been executed with the argument APA, and the result of `fgrep` on this value, in the file `addresses`, is shown. In this script, there is only one occurance of APA. Had there been others, `fgrep` would have listed them all in order.

14.4.2 Prompting the User for Arguments

A script might also obtain information from the user by prompting for it. The most prevalent instance where one uses interrogated input is when you do not want to remember the number of arguments or their order, or when you are writing the script but others will be the predominant users. In such cases, the user assigns a variable name with the command *read*, and the script takes the variable value from the standard input. A simple example of this type of input is shown below.

```
echo "Enter the person's name:"
read answer
```

Now consider a modified version of `phonesp.csh`, called "`phonesp.sh`," which prompts the user for the directory and name of the the `addresses` file, and for the `name` to look up. The response typed by the user is assigned to the shell variable "`answer`" as shown below for the variables "`dir`," "`address`," and "`name:`"

```
localhost> cat phonesp.sh
#!/bin/sh
# look up a name in a phone directory

echo what is the directory path for the addresses file?
read dir
echo what is the name of the address file?
read address
echo what is the name to look up?
read name

fgrep $name $dir/$address
```

and a sample usage of the script:

```
localhost> phonesp.sh
what is the directory path for the addresses file:
/usr/f1/jhodges
what is the name of the address file:
addresses
echo what is the name to look up:
USHGA
USHGA: P.O. Box 8300 Colorado Springs, CO 80933 (719) 632-8300
```

where the bolded items are those entered at the keyboard. A Bourne shell variable can be made available to other shells and scripts with the use of `export`. Its use follows.

```
export filename
     .
     .
     .
filename=$1
```

14.5 Bourne Shell Creation

There are two steps in writing any script. First, the script has to be written and tested. Second, the script has to be made executable. Depending on who will be using the script, this latter step may require you to place the script into a directory in your execution path or into a directory which you make public, as for linking. A script is created with an editor like any other program. In the following example, the `vi` editor will be used, but it doesn't matter which editor is used. What does matter is that you write scripts which are clear and readable, just as you should when you write other programs. For example, invoke an editor and type the lines below into a new file. Save the file as "`helloyou.sh`." This example will demonstrate how the `read` command is used to assign variables from the standard input.

```
localhost> vi helloyou.sh
#!/bin/sh
# This simple script tests user input

echo Please enter your name:
read name
echo Hello $name!
~
~
~
~
~
~
~
~
~
~
~
~
~
~
~
~
~
"helloyou.sh" [New file] 6 lines, 106 characters
```

Two items of note in this file are the first two lines, because they indicate that the only initial difference between the Bourne shell and the C shell is the path to the shell environment (i.e., /bin/sh). Also, the pound sign (#) is still the comment character. As before, #! is a special comman that forces execution of the script in the environment following it, so the first line forces the script to be executed in the sh (Bourne shell) environment. As with the C shell, when you have created the file for the shell script, you will want to make sure that it is executable, and you will do so in the same way:

```
localhost> ls -l hell*
-rwxr-xr-x 1 jhodges 64 Aug 25 23:54 helloyou.csh
-rw-r--r-- 1 jhodges 59 Feb 1  11:26 helloyou.sh
```

Note the use of the asterisk wildcard to list out any file starting with "hell." This way I get both the C shell version and the Bourne shell version. Note that "helloyou.csh" is executable but that "helloyou.sh" is not. So the next thing you must do, before you can test the script, is to make the file executable. Use the chmod command to give yourself execute permission for "helloyou.sh:"

```
localhost> chmod 755 helloyou.sh
localhost> !ls -l hell*
ls -l hell*
-rwxr-xr-x 1 jhodges 64 Aug 25 23:54 helloyou.csh
-rwxr-xr-x 1 jhodges 59 Feb 1  11:26 helloyou.sh
```

which retains the earlier permissions, but also gives you, and others, execute permissions. Note the difference in permissions between the two scripts. Now execute the script in the Bourne shell:

```
localhost> helloyou.sh
Please enter your name:
jack
Hello jack!
localhost>
```

This example peforms exactly the same function as did helloyou.csh, and does so so that the difference between the two environments can be easily demonstrated. As before, this example is presented to illustrate the use of prompted variable assignment and variable reference. Once the script is running properly, you will want to name it something memorable and move it into your default execution path. Normally, users put their executables, whether binary or not, in the directory "~/bin:"

```
localhost> mv helloyou.sh ~/bin; ls ~/bin/hell*
-rwxr-xr-x 1 jhodges 64 Aug 25 23:54 helloyou.csh
-rwxr-xr-x 1 jhodges 59 Feb 1  11:26 helloyou.sh
```

In future examples, the mode change will be assumed for brevity. When you move a file from one directory to a directory in your default execution path, the shell will not know that the file is now in that directory. You can reset the pointers to the default path by invoking *rehash* at the command line.

```
localhost> rehash
```

You can now type the script file name directly at the command line. The rehash command works the same for both the C shell and the Bourne shell.

14.6 Bourne Shell Control Structures

We now turn to the important topic of **flow control** in shell scripts. Flow control means to control which UNIX expressions are executed, and when. A **control structure** is a programming mechanism or construct for conditionally executing a set of expressions. The essence is to provide a test criterion, as in sed and awk, and one or more actions to be taken as a result of matching or not matching. The use of the common Bourne shell control structures will be illustrated here.

- if-then-else-fi
- for-in-done
- while-do-done
- until-do-done
- case-esac

14.6.1 if-then-else-fi

if-then-else construct in the Bourne shell is similar to that in the C shell. A test-expression is given, and, if true, the "then-commands" following then are executed. If not, then the "else-commands" following else are executed. The structure is terminated with an fi statement instead of an endif as for the C shell. The syntax for the if-then-else construct follows.

```
if [ test-expression ]
then
    then-commands
else
    else-commands
fi
```

Two notes should be made regarding Bourne shell syntax as compared to C shell syntax for the if-then-else construct. First, the conditional (i.e., test-commands) is bounded by square brackets ([ ]). Remember that, in the C shell, the conditional was bounded by parentheses. Second, the construct is closed by a mandatory fi that matches the if. The else clause is not necessary unless the alternate path statements (i.e., else-commands) are included. if-then-else-fi constructs can be nested. "Commands" here means any list of Bourne shell commands. Consider a simple example, "simpleif.sh," which considers two shell arguments and makes a simple decision based on their values.

```
localhost> cat simpleif.sh
#!/bin/sh
# a simple if-then-else script

if [ "$1" = "5" ]
then
  du $2
else
  ls $2
fi
```

This script takes two arguments at the command line. If the first argument's value is 5, then a disk usage command (du) is executed on the second argument. If the first argument's value is not 5, then a listing is executed on the second argument. The logical equivalence relational operator (=, unlike the C shell == operator) is used to test the pattern. Since there is a difference between the equality test operator for C shell and Bourne shell, a table is presented below of all the logical operators for the Bourne shell.

Table 14.1: Relational operators in the Bourne shell

`x -lt y`	$\Longrightarrow$	returns 1 if x is **less than** y
`x -le y`	$\Longrightarrow$	returns 1 if x is **less than or equal to** y
`x -eq y`	$\Longrightarrow$	returns 1 if x is **equal** to y and both (x, y) are numbers
`x = y`	$\Longrightarrow$	returns 1 if x is **equal to** y and both (x, y) are strings
`x -ne y`	$\Longrightarrow$	returns 1 if x is **not equal** to y and both (x, y) are numbers
`x != y`	$\Longrightarrow$	returns 1 if x is **not equal to** y and both (x, y) are strings
`x -gt y`	$\Longrightarrow$	returns 1 if x is **greater than or equal to** y
`x -ge y`	$\Longrightarrow$	returns 1 if x is **greater than** y
`A -a B`	$\Longrightarrow$	returns 1 if expression A **and** expression B are true (i.e., return 1)
`A -o B`	$\Longrightarrow$	returns 1 if expression A **or** expression B is true (i.e., return 1)

Table 14.2: File system logical tests in the Bourne shell

`-r FILE`	$\Longrightarrow$	returns 1 if the file named `FILE` is readable by the user
`-w FILE`	$\Longrightarrow$	returns 1 if the file named `FILE` is writable by the user
`-x FILE`	$\Longrightarrow$	returns 1 if the file named `FILE` is executable by the user
`-e FILE`	$\Longrightarrow$	returns 1 if the file named `FILE` exists
`-f FILE`	$\Longrightarrow$	returns 1 if the file named `FILE` exists and is a regular file
`-d FILE`	$\Longrightarrow$	returns 1 if the file named `FILE` exists and is a directory

Note that the shell variable $1 is quoted in the conditional of the example above. This is how the Bourne shell evaluates expressions. Remember that, in the C shell, expressions evaluated by the shell had to be placed in single backquotes. After the script has been made executable, it can be tested as follows.

```
localhost> simpleif.sh 5 Texmacros
371 Texmacros
localhost> simpleif.sh 0 Texmacros
aaai.sty        diss.doc        footmp1          tmplrg2endif
alpha4.bst      diss.sty        jack.sty         tmplrg3
apalike.bst     diss12.doc      mitthesis.sty   uclaletter.sty
apalike.sty     diss12.sty      sfsuletter.sty  ucseal.ps
cite.bst        disstitle.doc   sfsuseal.ps      ucthesis.sty
cite.sty        disstitle.sty   sfsuthesis.sty
csuletter.sty doublespace.sty texinfo.tex
csuseal.ps      foo             tmplrg
diss.bst        footmp          tmplrg1
```

The student should modify this example, as an exercise, so that the numerical logical operators are used for comparison instead of the string operators.

The types of tests which can be performed in the Bourne shell conditional are not related to simple variable and value tests. One can refer to status of files in the operating system, or even to the number and values input arguments, within the script. Tables 14.2 and 14.3 show some of the available options.

Table 14.3: Standard variables in the Bourne shell

$0	⟹	calling function name
$N	⟹	Nth command line argument value
$*	⟹	all the command line arguments (if quoted, quotes all the arguments in one string)
$@	⟹	all the command line arguments (if quoted, quotes each argument individually)
$#	⟹	the number of command line arguments
$$	⟹	process number (PID) of the current process
$!	⟹	process number (PID) of the last background process
$?	⟹	exit status of the last task

14.6.2 for-in-done

As with the C shell, the Bourne shell has looping constructs. As a reminder, a loop is an expression which performs a number of commands repeatedly until some exit condition is matched. *for* is a looping mechanism which is used often in Bourne shell programming, because it performs a set of operations once for each of a set of arguments. The C shell equivalent is `foreach`. Since, in many cases, the set of arguments can be the result of a directory listing, or the items in a process status listing, etc., `for` can be a very powerful mechanism. `for` has a simple syntax, as outlined below.

```
for index in listofitems
    commands
done
```

The "`index`" here defines a local variable called a **loop control variable**. `index` is assigned the first element of the list as a value and the **loop body** (i.e., the command sequence which is repeated, here "`commands`") is executed. Then `index` is assigned the second element of the list and the body of the loop is executed again, and so on. The "`in`" is a required component of the for loop. Also note that the closing statement is "`done`," whereas in `foreach` it was "`end`."

```
localhost> cat onsince2.sh
#!/bin/sh
# a simple for script

users='hodges hodges hodges'

for user in $users
  do
    finger $user | fgrep "On since"
done
```

It should be noted that the single quote on the users list, above, could just as easily be a double quote, as long as the programmer is consistent in the expression. The script is executed below.

```
localhost> onsince2.sh
On since Aug 6 07:51:05 on console 10 days Idle Time
On since Aug 6 07:51:05 on console 10 days Idle Time
On since Aug 6 07:51:05 on console 10 days Idle Time
```

One can also write a `for` loop without a list such as:

```
for index
  do
    commands
done
```

In this case, the list is assumed to be the command line arguments. As an example of the `for` loop, consider the loop for the script "onsince.csh" presented in Chapter 13, rewritten for the Bourne shell. `onsince.sh` looks at all the users in a list and checks to see if they are currently working on the local host. If so, `onsince.sh` prints out their current status. The script is shown below.

```
localhost> cat onsince.sh
#!/bin/sh
# a simple for script

for user
  do
    finger $user | fgrep "On since"
done
```

In this script, the user inputs the userids of users he or she wants to check up on when the script is invoked. For each user name input, `onsince.sh` `fingers` the user. When a user is currently logged on, there is a line in the `finger` output with the line "On since" in it, so if the user is logged on, running **finger** and piping it into `fgrep`[1] will tell. The script is executed as follows:

```
localhost> onsince.sh jhodges csalmon
On since Feb 1 08:01:21 on ttyp1 from huckleberry.sfsu
On since Feb 1 12:26:08 on ttyp4 from oad-8cs1d.sfsu.edu
```

14.6.3 while-do-done

while is a second Bourne shell looping mechanism which takes an expression or condition which serves as an entry condition, and loops on the embedded commands *while* the entry condition is true. The `while` loop is semantically identical to the `while` loop in the C shell. The only differences are the square brackets (`[  ]`)around the entry condition, as for the `if-then-else-`

---

1. There is no particular need for `fgrep` here. Any of the grep family would work, but `fgrep` is faster for simple string searches than `grep` or `egrep`.

fi construct, and the "done" which closes the construct, like the for loop. The Bourne shell while execution loop is described with a do clause, and it is terminated with a done statement. The while, do, and done statements should be on their own lines, and at the beginning of those lines. The syntax for the while loop is shown on the next page:

```
while [ entry-test-expression ]
   do
      commands
done
```

while loops can be used for counting events, often called **count-control loops,** as in the following script called "looptest.sh."

```
localhost> cat looptest.sh
#!/bin/sh
# a simple while script

count=0    ◄─────────────────────────────   initialize counter variable
limit=7    ◄─────────────────────────────   set exit variable value

while [ "$count" != "$limit" ]
   do
     echo hello JBH
     count=`expr $count + 1`
done
```

In this example, the "!=" C operator, which means "not equal," is used because variables are being referenced. As in previous Bourne shell scripts, the use of shell variables in the test condition must be double quoted, and the variable assignment spacing must be paid attention to throughout. Of course, literals, such as numbers, need not be quoted, but the logical operators are different. In the Bourne shell, the incrementing of numeric arguments is performed by explicitly evaluating an expression with *expr.* In the do part of the loop the *expr* expression must be backquoted. Other than these differences, the script is very similar to looptest.csh. The script output is obvious.

```
localhost> looptest.sh
hello JBH
hello JBH
hello JBH
hello JBH
hello JBH
hello JBH
hello JBH
```

14.6.4 until-do-done

The final Bourne shell looping construct is the *until* loop. There is no syntactic difference between the while and until loops, and the only semantic difference between while and until is the test condition. In the former, the loop is executed *as long as* the condition is satisfied, while in the latter the loop is executed *until* the condition is satisfied. The syntax of the until loop is as follows.

```
until [ exit-test-expression ]
   do
      commands
done
```

To demonstrate the use of until in a script, we will modify looptest.sh to work with until ("untiltest.sh"):

```
localhost> cat untiltest.sh
#!/bin/sh
# a simple until script

count=0
limit=7

until [ "$count" = "$limit" ]          ←———————     exit condition is the
   do                                                logical complement
      echo hello JBH                                 of while entry condition
      count=`expr $count + 1`
done
```

which executes predictably:

```
localhost> untiltest.sh
hello JBH
hello JBH
hello JBH
hello JBH
hello JBH
hello JBH
hello JBH
```

14.6.5 case-esac

The Bourne shell *case* construct is the analog to the C shell switch construct. A case takes a "test-string" and matches it against a number of "patterns." If one of the patterns matches the string, then the associated commands are executed until a double semicolon (; ;) is encountered. The syntax for the `case` command is shown below.

```
case [ test-string ] in
   pattern1)
      commands
      ;;
   pattern2)
      commands
      ;;
   .

   .
   *)
      commands
      ;;
esac
```

The "in" is again used (similar to the for construct) and is again required. Also, each pattern must be terminated with a closing parenthesis (). Finally, the `case` is closed with `esac`. Unlike the patterns in the C shell `switch`, the `case` patterns can include wildcards. For example, a * can be used as one of the patterns. * matches any string, so * will frequently be the last pattern used in the list, as a default/otherwise case (which is required). If `test-string` doesn't match any of the other patterns, it will definitely match the *. A simple script illustrating basic use of the Bourne shell case is shown in "simple-case.sh" below:

```
localhost> cat simplecase.sh
#!/bin/sh
# A simple case script

case $1 in
    dog)
        echo The lazy brown dog crawls under the rickety fence
    ;;
    cat)
        echo The spunky cat plays with catnip
    ;;
    fish)
        echo The slippery fish swims all day
    ;;
    *)
        echo "No item of that type in case list"
    ;;
esac
```

The execution of this script is straightforward. The user inputs an item and, depending on which item is input, echos a string associated with that item. If the item doesn't match any of those in the case list, then an amorphous statement is printed:

```
localhost> simplecase.sh dog
The lazy brown dog crawls under the rickety fence
localhost> simplecase.sh fish
The slippery fish swims all day
localhost> simplecase.sh octopus
No item of that type in case list
```

14.7 Exercises and Sample Quiz Questions

14.7.1 Exercises

Exercise 1   Write a simple shell script. Try to execute your script. You may want to review Section 3.6.2 on access permissions.

Exercise 2   What does it mean to **fork** a process?

Exercise 3   Project: In this project you will create a shell script to customize your programming environment. With this script, you will need to enter only one character in order to edit, compile, or run the program you are currently working on. When executed the script will present the menu of choices below and prompt the user for a single character to direct its execution.

Menu

Table P.4:

E	--	edit
C	--	compile
L	--	list
R	--	run
Q	--	quit

Enter your selection (E, C, L, R, or Q):

Each choice will correspond to another script that will be executed as a child process. When the process is complete, the menu will be presented again and a new choice will be prompted for. This will continue until the user chooses quit.

14.7.2 Sample Quiz Questions

Problem 1   How are variables identified (referenced) in Bourne shell scripts? Give an example of a valid Bourne shell variable. Given an example of a Bourne shell variable you have seen in this manual.

Problem 2   What [minimal] step must be taken to make a Bourne shell script useable? What additional consideration for general use of the script would be wise?

Problem 3   Suppose that you are about to write a Bourne shell script that will take two arguments at the command line and set one variable, `"path-name,"` in the script. Suppose that `"pathname"` is the concatenation of the second argument with the suffix `".tex."` How would you assign the variable in the script? How would you refer to the first command-line argument from within the script?

Problem 4   You are about to write a Bourne shell script that will take a user name and list of machine names which will vary but will never be smaller than eleven. What are the considerations for deciding how to input these arguments into the script, and how are they assigned and referenced within the script?

Problem 5   What are the differences between Bourne shell scripts and C shell scripts for the following constructs:

- "if" conditionals
- numeric variable increments
- "for" looping

Problem 6   Write a Bourne shell segment that uses the `while` syntax and semantics to execute an input command N times, where the command and its arguments, and the number of times to execute the command, are command line input variables.

Problem 7   Write a Bourne shell script that takes a directory path and a file type as command line arguments and recursively descends the file system from the directory path given, finds and prints all files of file type or size greater than 1 Megabyte to a file named `"large-files."`

Problem 8   Write or describe how to write a Bourne shell script that asks the user to select among two choices on a fast food menu, each of which has a different number that will be printed and some way to identify the item. The script will read the response, increment the value associated with the response by itself multiplied by California sales tax (you can assume 8%), and print the result "your total comes to **RESULT** cents" where **RESULT** is the amount in pennies. From a logical viewpoint, do you see any problems with this script?

14.8 Recommended Reading

sed and awk

Dougherty, D. [1990]. *sed & awk*, O'Reilly Associates, Sebastapol, CA.

UNIX Programming

Kernighan, B. and Pike, R. [1984]. *The UNIX Programming Environment*, Prentice Hall, Englewood Cliffs, NJ.

Rochkind, Marc J. [1985]. *Advanced UNIX Programming*, Prentice Hall, Englewood Cliffs, NJ.

Chapter 1 – The Login Session

Problem 1

- **length** ⇒ Short passwords are easier to break.
- **familiarity** ⇒ Too close and it is easier to break, too distant and you cannot remember it.
- **simplicity** ⇒ Too simple is easily broken, and too complex is hard to type.

Problem 2   When the fewest users are logged on, and when the fewest disk-hogs are logged on. Mornings are good, and *very* late.

Problem 3

- **slow** ⇒ baud (transmission) rates are much slwer with dialin modems.
- **reliability** ⇒ Long telephone lines are not designed for high speed, high quality data transmission.
- **demand** ⇒ too many people trying to use a finite number of ports.

Problem 4   A user ID is associated with an account, and can be the same on different hosts (machines) with different directories. The directory is simply a location in the file system where other directories and files can be organized. A home directory need not be named the same as the user ID.

Problem 5   You somehow entered the mail utility. Type "q" to exit and return to the shell prompt.

Problem 6

- **whoami** ⇒ returns your login ID
- **who am i** ⇒ returns your login ID and some information about your current login session.

Problem 7

- A prompt is the systems character for requesting input and changes with the type of input requested. Each utility has its own prompt and accepts specific response types at that prompt.
- During any session, a user will see a terminal-server prompt, a login prompt, a password prompt, a shell prompt, and perhaps a mail prompt.
- terminal-server prompt; `13_FOGNet>`, login prompt; `login:`, password prompt; `password:`, shell prompt; `;sfsuvax1>`, mail prompt, `&`.

Problem 8

- Login ID and password.
- No and yes.
- The user ID can only be changed by the superuser; however, the user can change the name associated with the ID with chfn. The password can be changed by the user and by the superuser.

Problem 9

- **sfsuvax1> passwd** ⇒ issue the command at the shell prompt without arguments
- **Changing password for jhodges**
- **Old password:** ⇒ type your old password, to verify who you are
- **Enter new password:** ⇒ type the new password
- **Verify:** ⇒ type the new password again, to make sure you know what you typed
- **sfsuvax1>**

Problem 10   Hayes command for "ATtention Dial Telephone number 338-1200, for use with a modem to dial in remotely.

Chapter 2 – Electronic Communications

Problem 1

- Advantages:
- **SPEED**: You can receive and respond to information much faster than through other media.
- **RELIABILITY**: You know the message has been sent and that the recipient will receive it.
- **CONVENIENCE**: You can do it without leaving your work area or even your keyboard.
- Disadvantages:
- **NETWORK**: You are at the whims of network reliability/unreliability.
- **MISUNDERSTANDINGS**: It is difficult to express your ideas and understand those of others.

- **SOLICITATION**: There is no easy way to stop junk mail.

Problem 2

- must know how to **address** the mail
- `mail` $\Rightarrow$ must be able to **invoke** the application at the shell prompt
- mail commands $\Rightarrow$ must know how to interpret and **use** the commands: how to read mail, how to compose, send, and respond to mail
- `q`, `x`, or `ex` $\Rightarrow$ you must know how to **exit** the application

Problem 3

- The > symbol tells which message is current
- The MH equivalent to the > is the + symbol
- Examples:
- Mail: `>U  1 schulz-dieterich@vax  Mon  Mar  2  06:18  19/772 "Pl..."`
- MH: `1+ 03/02 93 vcsc190 <<`

Problem 4

- Get new messages into MH: **inc**
- List all messages in your working mail folder: **scan**
- Respond to message number 32: **repl 32**
- Put message number 32 into your "Personal" mail folder: **refile 32 +Personal**
- Exit MH $\Rightarrow$ There is no need to exit MH because you are not in a separate environment.

Problem 5

- c
- Slash, as in vi.

Problem 6

- *SPEED*: One can respond to a posting so rapidly that it is easy to say something you would later regret.
- *ANONYMITY*: Because you are rarely close to the person with whom you are communicating, it is easy to say something you might never say openly.
- *EXPRESSION*: The receiver has no way to guage your expression, your inflection, your pauses, each keys to understanding what a person means.

Problem 7   A flame is an electronic insult or criticism. Flames are usually sent when a person is responding to a flame, when a person is acting before thinking, when a person has a mean streak, or when a user has said something, publicly, which is both incorrect and the way it was said shows inconsideration. Oftentimes this will draw flames from people who are knowledgeble and insulted by the poster's ignorance.

Problem 8

- =
- g newsgroupname
- f or F

Problem 9   The name address convention is given below. The first item is the local host name, such as SFSUVAX1. The second term is the institution, such as SFSU, and the third term is the institution-type, such as EDU: HOST.INSTITUTION.INSTITUTION-TYPE

- .COM
- .EDU
- .GOV
- .MIL
- .UUCP
- Country Codes (such as CA for Canada, FR for france, etc.

Problem 10   The file is called "etc/hosts," which contains a list of hosts which the present host knows about. This table is used for internetwork communications, in particular electronic mail.

- **ENTRY #1** ⇒ Internet Protocol (IP) Address, which is used like a telephone number for host-to-host communications
- **ENTRY #2** ⇒ Symbolic or Name address for the machine
- **ENTRY #3. . .** ⇒ Name aliases for the host

Chapter 3 – The UNIX File System

Problem 1   `find ~ -name \*foobar\* -print`

Problem 2

```
mkdir ~/Docs/Letters/TeX-Old;cp -r ~/Docs/Letters/TeX ~/Docs/Letters/TeX-Old
```

Problem 3   `ls -aF`

Problem 4   **which** tells where to find an executable and **whereis** is used to additionally find source and man pages. Whereis is more versatile and may produce the same answer as which. Then again it may not. Consider the example below. The user wants to know what will happen when he or she types mail, and finds out that `/usr/ucb/Mail` will be executed. A major difference between which and whereis is that the former looks for the executable that is invoked when you type what you typed, but the latter looks for exact references to what you typed.

- **which** (e.g., which mail)
  `/usr/ucb/Mail`
- **whereis** (e.g., whereis mail)
  `mail: /bin/mail /usr/ucb/mail /usr/man/man1/mail.1`

Problem 5   cp -r dir

Problem 6   Any of the following is acceptable:

- `cd`
- `cd ~`
- `cd ..`
- `cd $home`
- `cd /usr/f1/vcsc1999`

Problem 7

    % chmod 755 *.tex

Problem 8

    % rm ~/sub1/sub2/*.dvi

Problem 9   The following are illustrative of directories off root on UNIX systems:

- **bin** $\Rightarrow$ system binaries
- **usr** $\Rightarrow$ local files, user directories, man pages, etc.
- **dev** $\Rightarrow$ device files such as ttys, disk drives, printers
- **lib** $\Rightarrow$ system libraries
- **etc** $\Rightarrow$ system commands such as chown, chmod, mount

Chapter 4 – File Editing

Problem 1

- access/open/create the file
- insert/append text
- move around the file in comfortable sized chunks
- modify text on comfortable sized chunks
- perform global manipulations/modifications
- exit in different ways save the file
- include other files or parts of files
- cutting and pasting between files

Problem 2

- **vi** $\Rightarrow$ `:57`
- **emacs** $\Rightarrow$ `<Meta-x> gotoline` (prompts for line: 57)

Problem 3

- **vi** $\Rightarrow$ ZZ and :q or :q!, or :wq or :wq!
- **emacs** $\Rightarrow$ \<Cntl-x\> \<Cntl-s\>, \<Cntl-x\> \<Cntl-c\>

Problem 4   ZZ or :wq!

Problem 5   \<Cntl-x\> \<Cntl-f\> filename

Problem 6   /beezlebub (slash)

Problem 7   Line and screen editors. A line editor displays and works on one line of a file at a time. A screen editor displays blocks of a file and may manipulate and modify blocks of text.

Problem 8

:1,$ s/coconut/pineapple/g

Problem 9

- **vi** $\Rightarrow$ $, :1
- **emacs** $\Rightarrow$ \<Cntl-e\>, \<Meta-\<\>

Problem 10

:25,26 s/ZZZ /

Chapter 5 – The Command Shell

Problem 1

- Do one modification at a time so that you can identify the changes and make corrections for singles changes, as necessary.
- Test all changes at the command line first.
- Make a copy of the original file – just in case (self preservation) or if you want to retrieve/use it later.
- If you do not follow these, common sense, guidelines (for any file you edit), then the likelihood of disaster (file loss or loss of session) increases substantially.

Problem 2   Semicolons are used to run commands sequentially, but to input the commands on a single line. The semicolons simply separate the commands, which are run one after the other. If one command fails, the next will execute.

Problem 3

- 2630
- The "S" means that the process is sleeping, the "blank" means that the process is in core, and the "N" means that the process is running with reduced priority.
- No, you cannot tell from this listing. Using the options "lga" would work.

Problem 4

- **I/O REDIRECTION**: Is most useful when the program expects data from the standard input (SI) and the amount of data would be tedious to provide at the command line.

- **I/O REDIRECTION EXAMPLE**: A command that takes a number of inputs, like the contents of a directory or the names of many machines, which could just as easily be put into a file. A computer program designed to take input from the SI would also benefit this way.

- **PIPING**: Most useful when you do not have the space or inclination to send the output to a device and you do not need the intermediate result.

- **PIPING EXAMPLE**: A good example is the device independent files produced by latex, which are only of value to latex and not to the user.

Problem 5   Backgrounding embodies the notion of multitasking. When you put a job into the background, you are *forking* a new shell to process the job while you go on working with the current one. Many jobs can be running in the background at once. You can invoke multi-tasking at the command line using the ampersand (&), or you can stop a job and put it into the background after it has begun executing.

- **<Cntl z>** ⇒ Stops the job without killing it.
- **bg** ⇒ Puts the job into the background.
- **jobs** ⇒ Reports the status of all jobs.
- **fg jobid** ⇒ Brings the job into the foreground.

Problem 6   The `history` command displays the commands issued at the shell prompt in sequential order. The user can refer to the history to reevaluate a command or to make modifications to a command, instead of retyping it in entirety. This is most fruitfull when long path names are used in a command and simple changes can be made.

- **REPETITION** ⇒ !! (repeat last command)
- **REPETITION** ⇒ !23 (repeat 23rd command)
- **MODIFICATION** ⇒ !!:s/string1/string2 (use history and string search and modification to execute next command)

Problem 7   When you first log on, the ".login" script is executed. The ".login" tells the host machine who you are and sets a number of variables which are associated with you and your directory. Then the "cshrc" script is executed. The ".cshrc" is used to initialize every c shell process or subprocess. The order of execution is important if you have a Bourne shell as the default login environment and a C shell or Korn shell as the normal working environment. If you only have one shell, then only one login script will be executed.

Problem 8   Environment variables hold values that the operating system associates with each user's shells.

- **USER** $\Rightarrow$ tells the OS who you are . . . result of whoami.
- **HOME** $\Rightarrow$ tells the OS where your home directory is.
- **MAIL** $\Rightarrow$ tells the OS where to look for your mail.

Problem 9   A command alias allows the user to provide a new name to one or
more commands. It is basically a lookup table entry for what comes afterward. Another way to look at it is that the **alias** command is used to
collapse long or often used commands to easily remembered command
names, but directory paths can be collapsed this way as well.

Problem 10   The problem is most likely an incorrect terminal type, since that controls the definition of keyboard equivalents. \example

- `% echo $term`
- `% set term=vt100`
- `% rehash`
- Try **vi** again. If these did not work, then go look in `"/etc/termcap"` for
  a potentially suitable replacement term type.
- try looking at **stty** for ways to manually set the keyboard characteristics.
- talk to a guru or a system_administrator

Problem 11

```
!!:s/755/700
```

Problem 12

```
(a) process 215, 210, 206, 217 are sleeping
(b) % kill -9 214
```

Chapter 6 – File Formatting and Printing

Problem 1   **wc** counts lines, words, and characters.

Problem 2   PostScript figures can take up a lot of space, and even one page may
be a large printing job. The easiest way to reduce the affect on other
users is to print pages with PostScript figures one at a time. Always use
a previewer to reduce the number of print cycles you require, not to
mention saving trees.

Problem 3

- HEADINGS:

  NAME
  SYNOPSIS or SYNTAX
  DESCRIPTION

EXAMPLES
BUGS
FILES

- REFERENCE FORMAT:

  .TH ⇒ Multipart title
  .SH ⇒ Subject header
  .EX, .EE ⇒ Examples
  .nf, .fi ⇒ Verbatim Examples

- DISPLAY METHOD:

  ```
  tbl file | nroff -man - | col | more
  ```

  The file has to be formatted in manpage format. There is a special macro package (the man package) for doing this. This command takes input from the SI. Output must go through more for paging. The TBl and COL commands are OK, but I do not even know what they do yet, so do not worry about them.

Problem 4

- **nroff** ⇒ .in +NUNIT ... .in -NUNITS, where N is a number and units is a unit of choice, inches, cm, mm, etc
- **latex** ⇒ begin{quote} ... end{quote}

Problem 5

- **nroff**-1 ⇒ .ps +2 increase the point size of text by two steps
- **nroff**-2 ⇒ \f2 over \f1 does local italics
- **latex**-1 ⇒ \Large increases the point size of text by two steps
- **latex**-2 ⇒ {\em over} does local italics

Problem 6

- **nroff/troff**: The macros ".ll 1" starts the list, ".ls" begins each list item, and ".el" ends the list.
- **latex**: begin{enumerate} starts the list, each item is begun with item, and end{enumerate} ends the list.
- **nroff/troff**:

```
.ll 1
.ls
less student support
.ls
increased tuitions and fees
.ls
lower motivation
.el
```

- **latex**:

```
\begin{enumerate}
\item{less student support}
\item{increased tuitions and fees}
\item{lower motivation}
\end{enumerate}
```

Problem 7   It prints the file `"code.c"` on 8 1/2" x 11" pages with the header `"my-file"` on each page using the vgrind program.

Problem 8

- `latex filename` (assumes filename.tex)
- `bibtex filename` (assumes filename.aux)
- `latex filename` (assumes filename.tex)
- `latex filename` (assumes filename.tex)
- `dvi2ps filename` (assumes filename.dvi)
- `lpr -Plaser -J BINN filename` (assumes filename.ps)

```
A full set of passes in latex may be all of these passes,
depending on what you are doing. The minimum is a latex
pass, a dvi2ps pass, and maybe an lpr pass, depending on
how dvi2ps is interpreted by the system
```

Problem 9

- **nroff title1**:

```
.ce 1 "Mating Habits of Computer Generated Amoebas"
```

- **nroff title2**:

```
.sc 0 "Mating Habits of Computer Generated Amoebas"
```

- **nroff title3**:

```
.su "Mating Habits of Computer Generated Amoebas" 0
```

- **latex title**:

```
\title{Mating Habits of Computer Generated Amoebas}
```

- **nroff heading**:

```
.su "Introduction" 1
```

- **latex heading**:

```
\section{Introduction}
```

Problem 10

- **nroff** ⇒ The no-fill command is `.nf` and the fill command is `.fi`. These commands would be placed at the beginning of a new line, the first before the text and the second after the text.

- **latex** ⇒ The no-fill command is `begin{verbatim}` and the fill command is `end{verbatim}`. These commands would be placed at the beginning of a new line, the first before the text and the second after the text.

Chapter 7 – Networking

Problem 1   The idea here is that you do not know what the person's userid is, so first you must find that out and then you use the userid to find out what the person is up to.

- `finger foobar`
- `rwho -a | fgrep foobar-ID`
- `who | fgrep foobar-ID`
- `users | fgrep foobar-ID`
- `rusers | fgrep foobar-ID`

Problem 2   `tar` is used to take many files and concatenate them into a single file. By so doing, the minimum block size is forgone, resulting in a small savings in size. `compress` removes unused/unecessary space in a file, and usually results in 50% savings in size, depending on file type.

- create an archive ⇒ `c`
- view the contents of an archive ⇒ `t`
- extract an archive ⇒ `x`

Problem 3

- login sequence ⇒ `ftp sumex-aim.stanford.edu` (ID anonymous, the password is generally your userid and domain address)
- find file ⇒ `cd pub`, `ls`, `cd` to directory, etc.
- change retrieve mode ⇒ `binary`
- retrieve mode ⇒ `get file`, `mget files` (this latter supports wildcards)
- exit mode ⇒ `exit` or `bye`

Problem 4   Approximately 50% of the file's original size is saved.

Problem 5

`tar tvf cl.3.1.2.tar`

Problem 6   The optimal choice is to use rcp, since the alternative is a combination of telnet or rlogin, cd, ls, tar, compress, and ftp.

```
rcp -r fuzz.cs.blowtorch.edu:/usr/lib/tex/inputs texinputs
```

Problem 7

- **who** ⇒ Fastest for login.
- **rwho** ⇒ Same for remote hosts as well.
- **users** ⇒ Fastest for login.
- **rusers** ⇒ OK as fastest.
- **w** ⇒ Most specific for idle time and current processing.
- **finger** ⇒ The most personal. Shows login time.
- **last** ⇒ Most specific for idle time. Not fast if machine has been up long.

Problem 8   File system management refers to the organization, distribution, and allocation of resources within your personal directory. You should keep your directories clean and organized at all times, and they should be organized similarly to the UNIX file system as a whole. That is, the names of binary directories inside your directory should be bin, and so on. You should make sure that you are not wasting space by eliminating unnecessary files regularly, and by archiving or at least compressing those used infrequently. du, df, tar, and compress are used a lot for filesystem management.

Problem 9   The listings were produced by the df command. Filesystem A does not have enough free space on any filesystem to support the uncompressed directories, so we cannot use any of those disks. The "/" disk on filesystem A, associated with the device "/dev/raom," has the least space (~6.5 Meg); so it would be the least likely candidate to support the port.

Problem 10

- Because the problem is intermittent, one would suspect someone running a large process, or a number of different people running large processed, perhaps for a class.
- To check out this theory, or any theory, you could see who is on the system and what they are doing. This is most expeditiously accomplished with the 'w' command, since it also provides system load information. You could use this in concert with 'finger' to find out more about the user(s) in question.
- The issue here is one of responsibility. If a user knowingly slows an entire host and the work of all its users, then someone is violating basic common sense. The machine is not their own personal toy; it is not a PC, and they should respect other user's right to do work too. The best thing to do would be to ask them to nice their jobs, so that they took a low priority in processing. Another thing they might do would be to run their job(s) on an isolated

part of the network where their work would not adversely affect anyone. If this was the problem, then the user should also be spoken to, so that they realize their impact and seek ways to reduce it.

Chapter 8 – C Programming I

Problem 1

- **syntax** $\Rightarrow$ The structure/order associated with symbols and expressions which comprise legal expressions in the language. Examples are the use of parentheses to define a function, or the use of a semicolon to terminate an expression.

- **semantics** $\Rightarrow$ The meaning of expressions in the language...what they are used for. Examples are the concepts associated with the definition of a function and the termination of an expression (not the symbols or how it is implemented).

Problem 2   C is a high-level programming language. The strengths of a high-level language are that they are somewhat hardware independent (portability), they are easier to read because they appear more like a natural language such as English, and they are easier to compose into procedural units.

- **low level** $\Rightarrow$ The programmer is writing expressions which will manipulate hardware components almost directly. There is almost no abstraction of the expressions.

- **high level** $\Rightarrow$ The programmer writes expressions which appear more English-like and effect many lower level operations. The actual tasks which are performed by the hardware are abstracted so that the programmer need not be aware of how they are done.

Problem 3   Portability means that a program which is implemented in a programming language on one hardware platform can be taken in source-code version to another platform with a similar/same compiler, recompiled, and it will run without modifications or affect on functionality. ANSI C is a good language to learn because it is a standardized version of the language. It is not currently the most portable dialect of C, but it has the potential to be.

Problem 4   Programming style is important for you, the programmer, in terms of re-reading/modifying your programs in the future, or for other programmers to read/understand your programs. We find it easier to read any kind of text if it follows certain grammatical, organizational , and style conventions. The same is true for a program. The opposite is also true; if a program doesn't comply with certain conventions, it is painful to read.

- **Banner** ⇒ program name, file name, author, version, purpose, local variables, implementation notes, formulas, credits for borrowed algorithms, etc.
- **Readability** ⇒ veritcal and horizontal spacing of functional segments, spacing between operators and variables/arguments, location of curly braces, lining up of assignment statements, and so forth.

Problem 5   There are three component blocks in a C program: (1) headers, (2) delcarations, and (3) statements. The header block defines the interfaces between functional components. The declaration block defines variable and function types. The statement block defines the expressions that will be evaluated during execution.

Problem 6   The { and } (open and close curly braces) define a functional context in a C program. They can be used around any expression, but, according to convention, should only be used to surround compound (more than one) expressions.

Problem 7   Two standard functions are `scanf` and `printf`. They both reside in the stdio library, which is accessed with the `#include <stdio.h>` precompiler directive, where `stdio.h` is the name of a function header file.

Problem 8

```
scanf("%d", &foo);

printf("The annual rainfall in Springfield, MA is %d inches\n", foo);
```

Problem 9   It is often the case that one error propagates and creates other errors. If you remove the first error, you will [very] often serendipidously correct other errors as well. If you try to correct the other errors, you may well inject new errors.

Problem 10   A function prototype is simply a duplicate of a function's type and header, terminated with a semicolon. A prototype is placed before the first procedural component in a program as a check on the types and order of functions and parameters. After that, the actual definition of a function can occur in any location in the file. One reason why it is important to use function prototypes is that it allows the programmer to place functions where they semantically make the most sense. Another reason is that it sets the programmer up for later using the functions defined in the file in a library.

Chapter 9 – C Programming II

Problem 1   The >= and <= operators are used to compare variable values for the greater-than-or-equal-to and less-than-or-equal-to relations, respectively. The == operator is used to check equality.

```
if ( foo >= 0 )
  if ( foo <= 9 )
    ...
```

Problem 2

```
#include <stdio.h>

int
main(void)
{
  int foo, bar;

  printf("Input a value for the integer foo: ");
  scanf("%d", &foo);

  if ( foo >= 0 )
    if ( foo <= 9 )
      printf("The value of foo is: %d\n", foo);
    else
      printf("You input an invalid value for foo\n");
  else
    printf("You input an invalid value for foo\n");

  return (1);
}
```

Problem 3

```
if ( foo >= 0 && foo <= 9 )
```

Problem 4

```
#include <stdio.h>

int
main(void)
{
  int foo, bar;

  printf("Input a value for the integer foo: ");
  scanf("%d", &foo);
  printf("Input a value for the integer bar: ");
  scanf("%d", &bar);

  if ( foo >= 10 && foo <= 99 )
      printf("The value of foo is: %d\n", foo);
  else
      printf("You input an invalid value for foo\n");
```

```
    if ( bar >= 1 && bar <= 9 )
        printf("The value of bar is: %d\n", bar);
    else
        printf("You input an invalid value for bar\n");

    return (1);
}
```

Problem 5   The are primarily two components to a general looping construct: (1) a condition and (2) a body. Within the condition is a test called an entry/exit condition. The entry condition is a logical relation, which, when true, signals that the loop body should be executed. The entry condition is the logical complement of the exit condition.

Problem 6

```
#include <stdio.h>

int
main(void)
{
    int foo, count, successes;

    successes = 0;

    for ( count = 1; count <= 10; count = count + 1 ) {
        printf("Input a value for the integer foo: ");
        scanf("%d", &foo);
        if ( foo < 25 )
            successes = successes + 1;
    }

    printf("%d values less than 25\n", successes);

    return (1);
}
```

Problem 7   The % operator can be used to determin multiples. For example, to find multiples of 7, one cound use the expression (foo % 7 == 0), which states that when the remainder of dividing some number foo by 7 is zero, the relation will return true.

Problem 8

```
#include <stdio.h>

int
main(void)
{
    int foo, count, succ, pow3;

    succ = 0;
    pow3 = 1;

    for ( count = 1; count <= 10; count++ ) {
        printf("Input a value for the integer foo: ");
        scanf("%d", &foo);
```

```
        if ( foo % 3 == 0 ) {
            succ++;
            pow3 *= 3;
        }
    }

    printf("3 raised to the power %d is %d\n", succ, pow3);

    return (1);
}
```

Problem 9   The function call and the function header make up an interface between two functions. C only requires that the arguments to the function
call and the parameters of the function header have the same type and
order, so the variable names in the calling function and the parameter
names in the local function can be different, thus supporting the notion
of procedural abstraction.

Problem 10

```
#include <stdio.h>

void getvalue(int *myinvalue);
void dispvalue(int myoutvalue);

int
main(void)
{
    int foo, count, accum;

    accum = 0;

    for ( count = 1; count <= 10; count++ ) {
        getvalue(&foo);
        accum += foo;
    }

    dispvalue(accum);

    return (1);
}

void
getvalue(int *myinvalue)
{
    printf("Input an integer: ");
    scanf("%d", myinvalue);

    return;
}

void
dispvalues(int myvalue)
{
    printf("\nThe accumulated sum is: %d\n", myvalue);

    return;
}
```

Chapter 10 – C Programming III

Problem 1   The array is a compound variable that has a name and organizes multiple elements, each of which is a scalar variable (i.e., can only take on one value at a time). The element variables are accessed through an indexing scheme, and the identifier for each element variable is the name of the array variable concatenated with the index for the element. For example, the third element of an array variable named `"foo"` is `foo[2]`.

Problem 2

```
#include <stdio.h>

void getvalue(int *myinvalue);
void swap(int *myvalue1, int *myvalue2);

int
main(void)
{
  int foo[5], count;

  for ( count = 0; count < 5; count++ )
    getvalue(&foo[count]);

  for ( swapped = 4; swapped >= 0; swapped-- )
    for ( count = 0; count < swapped; count++ )
      if ( foo[count] < foo[count + 1] )
        swap(&foo[count], &foo[count + 1]);

  for ( count = 0; count < 5; count++ )
    printf("%3d", foo[count]);

  printf("\n");

  return (1);
}

void
getvalue(int *myinvalue)
{
  printf("Input an integer: ");
  scanf("%d", myinvalue);

  return;
}

void
swap(int *myvalue1, int *myvalue2)
{
  int temp;

  temp      = *myvalue1;
  *myvalue1 = *myvalue2;
  *myvalue2 = temp;

  return;
}
```

Problem 3   The two parameters, argc and argv are used in the main header to read values from the command line. The following header would suffice for an arbitrary number of command line arguments:

```
int
main(int argc, char *argv[])
```

Problem 4

```c
#include <stdio.h>
#include <math.h>
#include <string.h>

int
main(int argc, char *argv[])
{
  int base, exp;

  sscanf(argv[1], "%f", &base);
  sscanf(argv[2], "%f", &exp);
  printf("\n%f raised to the power %f is: %4.2f\n", base, exp, pow(base, exp));

  return (1);
}
```

Problem 5   To use a UNIX file in a C program, the programmer must have an object which represents the address of the file in memory (i.e. a pointer, or a file pointer). To make a correspondence between the file pointer and the file, a function named fopen is called, which returns the address of the real file. This address is used in all file operations. When the use of the file is complete, a second function, fclose, is called to relinquish control of the file.

Problem 6

```c
#include <stdio.h>

int
main(void)
{
  FILE    *infilep;
  int     numvals, count;
  double fval, maccum;

  infilep = fopen("P10.6Dat", "r");

  fscanf(infilep, "%d", &numvals);

  maccum = 1;

  for ( count = 1; count <= numvals; count++ ) {
    fscanf(infilep, "%lf", &fval);
    maccum *= fval;
  }

  fclose(infilep);
  printf("\nThe multiplication of %d values is %4.2f\n", numvals, maccum);

  return (1);
}
```

Problem 7   There are 5 field variables and two embedded structures in the person record information:

```
name      string
social    string
dob       date_t
age       integer
add       address_t

typedef struct person_s {
  char        name[50];
  char        social[9];
  date_t      dob;
  int         age;
  address_t   add;
} person_t;

typedef struct date_s {
  int         day;
  char        month[9];
  int         year;
} date_t;

typedef struct address_s {
  int         number;
  char        street[12];
  char        city[15];
  char        state[10];
  int         zip;
} address_t;
```

Problem 8

```c
#include <stdio.h>
#define  MAXPERS 10

typedef struct date_s {
  int       day;
  char      month[9];
  int       year;
} date_t;

typedef struct address_s {
  int       number;
  char      street[12];
  char      city[15];
  char      state[10];
  int       zip;
} address_t;

typedef struct person_s {
  char      name[50];
  char      social[9];
  date_t    dob;
  int       age;
  address_t add;
} person_t;

int
main(void)
{
  FILE *infilep;
  int  numrecs, count;
  person_t aperson[MAXPERS];

  infilep = fopen("P10.8Dat", "r");
  fscanf(infilep, "%d", &numrecs);
  printf("\n");

  for ( count = 1; count <= numrecs; count++ ) {
    fscanf(infilep, "%s", aperson[count].name);
    fscanf(infilep, "%s", aperson[count].social);
    fscanf(infilep, "%d%s%d", &aperson[count].dob.day,
                              aperson[count].dob.month,
                              &aperson[count].dob.year);
    fscanf(infilep, "%d", &aperson[count].age);
    fscanf(infilep, "%d%s%s%s%d", &aperson[count].add.number,
                              aperson[count].add.street,
                              aperson[count].add.city,
                              aperson[count].add.state,
                              &aperson[count].add.zip);

    printf("NAM: %s\n", aperson[count].name);
    printf("SOC: %s\n", aperson[count].social);
    printf("DOB: %s %d, %d\n", aperson[count].dob.month,
                              aperson[count].dob.day,
```

```
                                        aperson[count].dob.year);
        printf("AGE: %d\n", aperson[count].age);
        printf("ADD: %d %s\n", aperson[count].add.number,
                              aperson[count].add.street);
        printf("    %s, %s  %d\n\n", aperson[count].add.city,
                                     aperson[count].add.state,
                                     aperson[count].add.zip);
    }

    fclose(infilep);

    return (1);
}
```

Chapter 12 – UNIX **Programming Tools**

Problem 1   They allow users to collapse long commands into shorter versions of
the same commands, and to sometimes eliminate them completely. I
use regular expressions constantly in C and Bourne shell scripts, and
for listing or changing directories.

Problem 2

```
localhost> find . -name \*.eps -print
```

Problem 3

```
 awk -F: '{print $1 "/" $2 "/" $3 "/" $4 "/" $5 >"fileout"}'
```

Problem 4

```
sed -f sedfile *
```

sedfile:

```
s/got a fair trial/got an unfair trial/g
```

Problem 5   Whenever a reserved character, such as a dollar sign, a backslash, or
an asterisk is used in a regular expression, it must be escaped by preceding it with a backslash. For example, the use of an asterisk in a regular expression could be done as follows:

```
localhost> find . -name \*UnixProject\* -print
```

where the asterisk is escaped because the find command has a special
meaning for it otherwise, so you must disable that meaning.

Problem 6

```
localhost> ls -l | awk '$4 > 100000 {print $4, $8 >"foo"}'
```

Problem 7

```
L1 L2  => {anthill, spiderweb, beetlejuice}
```

Problem 8

```
localhost> w | awk '$1 /[a-z]*/ {print $1 $8}' or
localhost> w | awk '{print $1, $8}'
```

Chapter 13 – C Shell Programming

Problem 1   Shell variables are identified with a leading dollar sign ($). A valid example would be $1, where 1 refers to the first user-provided argument. Instances of C shell variables that we have seen are $term and $editor.

Problem 2

- Change the permissions on the script so that it is executable
- Put the script into a [bin] directory with other scripts
- Otherwise add the directory where the script resides to your search path

Problem 3

```
(a) set pathname = $2.tex
(b) $1
```

Problem 4   The number of command-line arguments is not limited to 9, but the user is not sure what number of arguments will be required, so the script cannot be written to take a fixed number of arguments. The best thing to do is to somehow get a list of machines from some other process (ruptime for machines which are currently up, etc.) and input them as a single argument and then use foreach to cycle through each machine and evaluate it in whatever way the user intends.

```
set user = $1
set machines = 2
foreach machine in machines
...
```

Problem 5

- Variable assignment:

C shell ⇒ uses **set** and spaces between variable, equals sign, and value

Bourne shell ⇒ doesn't have to use set and no spaces between variable, equals sign, and value

- Numeric variable increments:

C shell ⇒ use the @ sign to assign and increment variable values

Bourne shell ⇒ uses standard notation to assign and uses **expr** to increment variables

- Reading arguments interactively:

C shell $\Rightarrow$ uses the echo and $< notation to read arguments

Bourne shell $\Rightarrow$ uses the echo and **read** notation to read arguments

Problem 6

```
#!/bin/csh

set count   = 0
set limit   = $2
set command = $1

while ( $count != $limit )
    $command
    @ count++
end
```

Problem 7

```
#!/bin/csh

set dir = $1
set ext = $2

find $dir \( -name \*.$2 -o -size 100 \) -print
```

Problem 8

```
#!/bin/csh

echo "What would you like to order from the menu below?"
echo ""
echo "  Enter 1 for.....Big Mac - 150"
echo "  Enter 2 for.....Fries - 125"
echo ""
set answer = $<

if ( $answer == 1 ) then
  @ price = 150
else
  @ price = 125
endif

@ price = ( $price + (( $price * 8 ) / 100 ))

echo ""
echo "Your total comes to $price cents"
```

Chapter 14 – Bourne Shell Programming

Problem 1 Shell variables are identified with a leading dollar sign ($), just like C shell variables. A valid example would be $1, where 1 refers to the first user-provided argument. We have not seen instances of variables specific to the Bourne shell because the default shell we have worked with is the C shell; however, the same variables, such as $term, would be defined for the Bourne shell.

Problem 2 Also identical to the C shell:

- **Change the permissions on the script so that it is executable**
- Put the script into a [bin] directory with other scripts.
- Otherwise add the directory where the script resides to your search path.

Problem 3 Reference is the same as for the C shell:

```
(a1) pathname=$2.tex or
(a2) set pathname=$2.tex
(b) $1
```

Problem 4 The number of command-line arguments is not limited to 9, but the user is not sure what number of arguments will be required, so the script cannot be written to take a fixed number of arguments. The best thing to do is to somehow get a list of machines from some other process (ruptime for machines which are currently up, etc.) and input them as a single argument and then use for to cycle through each machine and evaluate it in whatever way the user intends.

```
user=$1
machines=$2

for machine in machines
do ...
done
```

Problem 5

- "if" conditionals:

Bourne shell ⇒ uses brackets around the conditional and ends with "fi."

C shell ⇒ uses parentheses around the conditional and ends with "endif."

- Numeric variable increments:

Bourne shell ⇒ uses standard notation to assign and uses **expr** to increment variables

C shell ⇒ use the @ sign to assign and increment variable values

- "for" looping:

Bourne shell $\Rightarrow$ uses "for" and "done."

C shell $\Rightarrow$ uses "foreach" and "end."

Problem 6

```
#!/bin/sh

count=0
limit=$2
command=$1

while [ "$count" != "$limit" ]
do
    $command
    count=`expr $count + 1`
done
```

Problem 7

```
#!/bin/sh

dir=$1
ext=$2

find $dir \( -name \*.$2 -o -size 100 \) -print
```

Problem 8

```
#!/bin/sh

echo "What would you like to order from the menu below?"
echo ""
echo "  Enter 1 for.....Big Mac - 150"
echo "  Enter 2 for.....Fries - 125"
echo ""
read answer

if [ "$answer" = 1 ]
then
  price=150
else
  price=125
fi

price=`expr \( $price + \( \( $price \* 8 \) / 100 \) \)`

echo ""
echo "Your total comes to $price cents"
```

- The file system is comprised of directories and files

- A **directory** (●) is a branch point and is used to *organize* files and other directories

  - ROOT directory: The top of the file system

    - ROOT organizes all files and directories

    - ROOT is the access point for any file or directory in the file system

    - ROOT is not organized by any other directory

- A **file** (▭) contains or organizes information

  - A file cannot organize any other files or directories

  - A file is always a terminal (end) of a branch in the file system

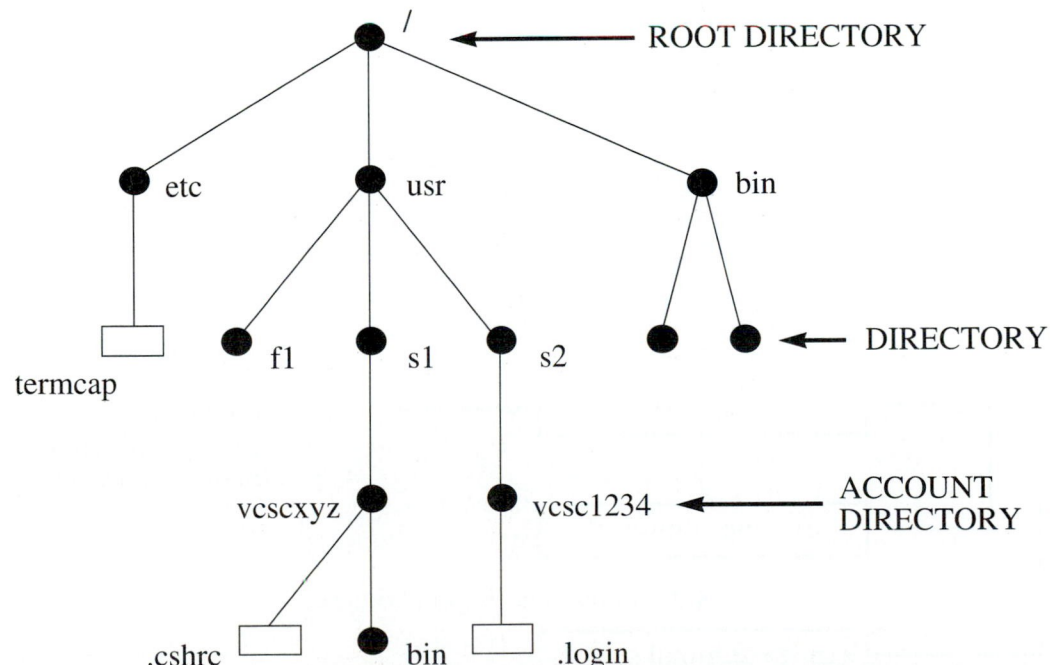

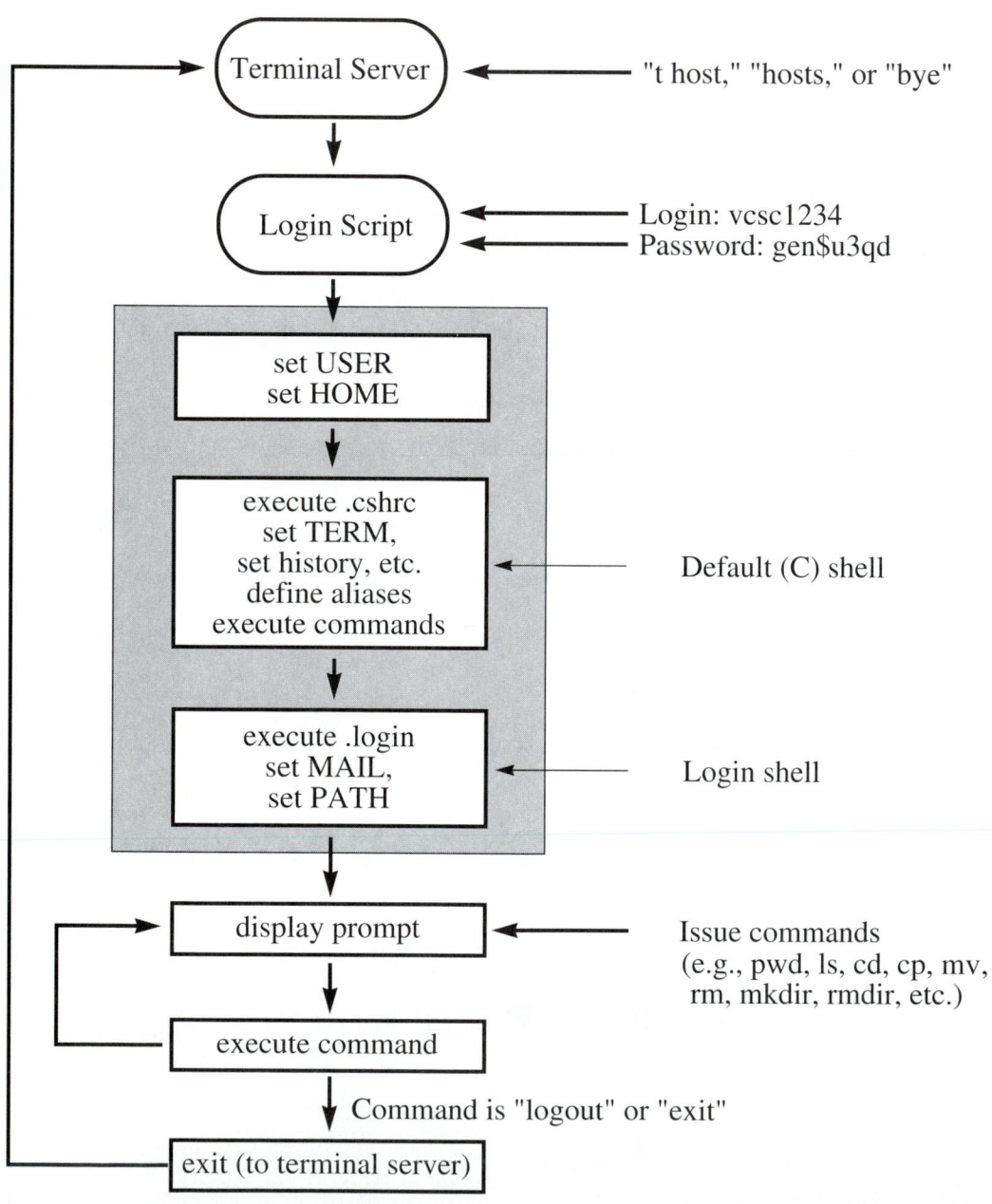

Terminal Server ← "t host," "hosts," or "bye"

Login Script ← Login: vcsc1234
Password: gen$u3qd

set USER
set HOME

execute .cshrc
set TERM,
set history, etc.
define aliases
execute commands
← Default (C) shell

execute .login
set MAIL,
set PATH
← Login shell

display prompt ← Issue commands
(e.g., pwd, ls, cd, cp, mv,
rm, mkdir, rmdir, etc.)

execute command

Command is "logout" or "exit"

exit (to terminal server)

- NAVIGATION
  - **whoami**:   what USERID is associated with this session?
  - **pwd**:   what is the path to this directory?
  - **cd** DIR: relocate me to the directory DIR

- DIRECTORIES
  - **mkdir** DIR: create a new directory named DIR
  - **mv** DIR DIR2:   change the name of directory DIR to DIR2
  - **rmdir** DIR: delete empty directory DIR
  - **chmod** XXX DIR: change permissions on directory DIR to XXX

- FILES
  - **cp** FILE FILE1:   create a copy of FILE and name it FILE1
  - **mv** FILE FILE2:   change the name of the file FILE to FILE2
  - **rm** FILE: delete the file FILE
  - **chmod** XXX FILE: change permissions on file FILE to XXX
  - **cat** FILE: display a file named FILE (scrolls)
  - **more** FILE: display a file named FILE (pages)
  - **file** FILE: identifies file type of FILE

- ARGUMENT TYPES
  - File and directory arguments can be explicit **OR** path, as required
  - **Example**:

    cp foo mynewfoo

    cp /usr/f2/jhodges/UNIX/MOD5/DOTFILES/host   bin

- SHORTCUTS and WILDCARDS
  - $home: home/login directory
  - ~[userid]:   account directory path for userid (defaults to $home)
  - .:   current directory
  - ..:   parent directory (one up from current)
  - *:   matches any number/kind of characters

Appendix E
A Generic Utility

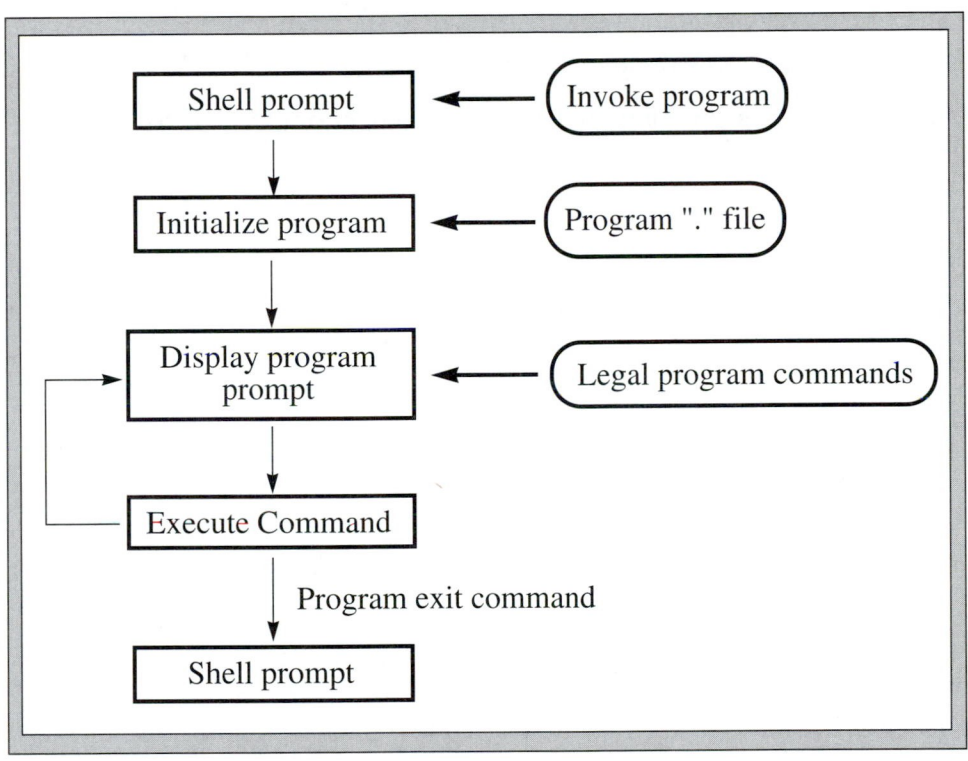

- **ELECTRONIC MAIL (EMAIL)**
    - A method for communicating with other computer users
    - A method for submitting assignments
    - A method for requesting assistance
    - A method for seeing when someone is around, when they are busy

- **MAILER or MAIL HANDLER**
    - A program that allows you to compose, send, and read email

- **MAIL MESSAGE**
    - Text that you create or compose (and edit)
    - When someone sends you email, you can read and respond to it, save it, and delete it as you would with any file

- **REQUIREMENTS**
    - you must have access to a mailer
    - you must know how a mailer works
    - you must know the "address" of the user you are sending mail to

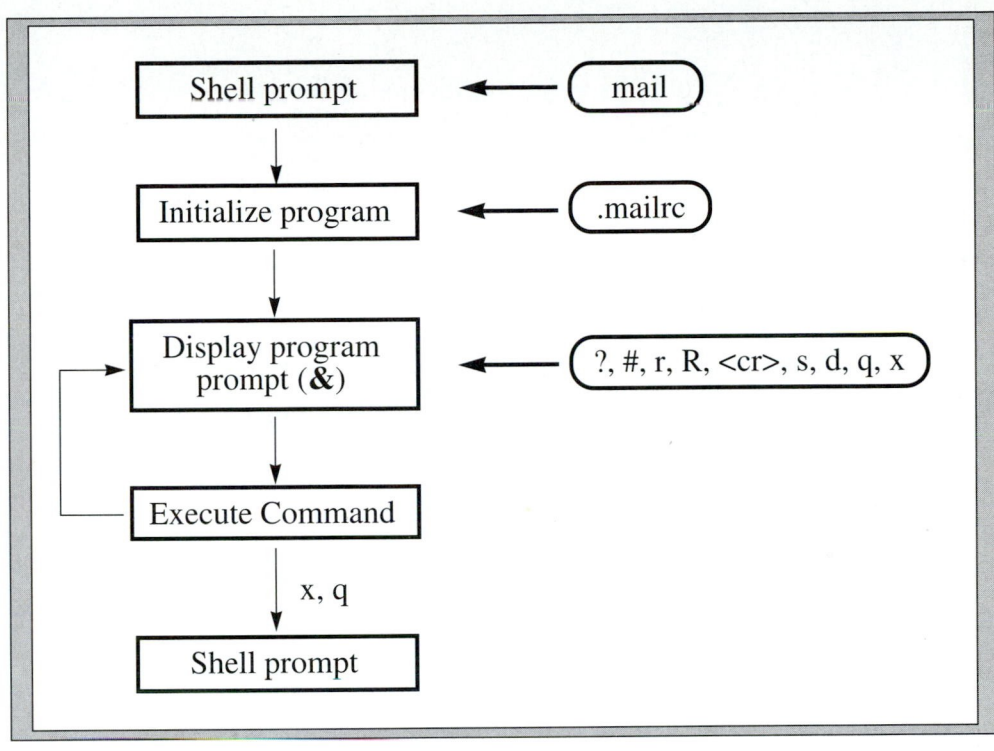

1. mail <cr> ————————► **READ** mail

2. mail foo ————————► **COMPOSE** mail to userid foo

3. mail foo < FILE ————► **SEND** file FILE to userid foo

4. ~v ————————► **EDIT** mail message (on a blank line, insert with 'i', stop insert with <ESC>, exit with ZZ)

5. ~r FILE ————————► **INCLUDE** file FILE into mail message (on a blank line)

6. s FILE ————————► **SAVE** mail message to FILE (after reading a msg)

7. # ————————► **READ MESSAGE** number # (e.g., 3)

8. r, R ————————► **RESPOND** to mail message (r replies to all recipients)

9. d # ————————► **DELETE** mail message number # (e.g., d3)

10. . ————————► **SEND** composed mail message (or <Cntl-d>)

11. ? ————————► **HELP** (info on commands/syntax)

12. x, q ————————► **EXIT, QUIT** the mailer

Appendix G
File Editing as a Generic Utility

- A **file**: What you create or modify when you use an editor
    - **Contents:** Data or information
        - A word processor creates and saves **documents** into files
        - A graphics application creates and saves **figures** into files
        - An editor creates and saves **text** into files (i.e., the two above are editors)
    - **Operations**: Ways to manipulate files
        - Create, copy, rename, delete
        - File operations take file names as arguments
    - **Types**: Text and binary
        - **Text** refers to [human] readable characters and numbers

            Text is coded according to a convention, called ASCII (American Standard for Coded Information Interchange)

            If you can read a file, then it is a text file

            Any readable file (text file) is editable

            Source refers to the text version of a program
        - **Binary** refers to a machine readable file

            Binary files are not human readable

            Binary files are not, in general, editable
- File **editing**: Creation, insertion into and modification of file content
    - **Requirements**:
        - You must have access to an editor, **AND**
        - You must know how to use the editor, **AND**
        - The file must not exist, **OR**
        - The file must exist and be editable, **AND**
        - You must have read/write permission on the file

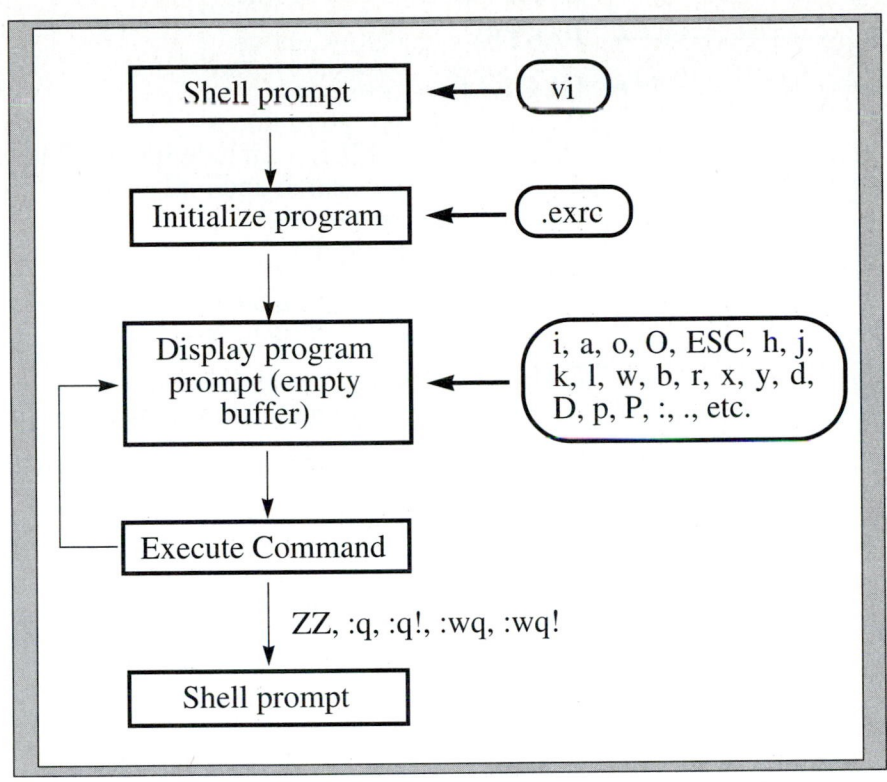

1. vi ⟶ **INVOKE** vi EDITOR

2. vi FILE ⟶ **INVOKE** vi on FILE

3. i, a, A, o, O ⟶ **INSERT** characters(here, right, end of sentence, below, above)

4. ESC ⟶ **TOGGLE** to command mode

5. h, j, k, l ⟶ **MOVE** cursor BY CHARACTER; (left, down, up, right)

6. w, b ⟶ **MOVE** cursor BY WORD; (forward, backward)

7. rCh ⟶ **REPLACE** character where cursor points with Ch

8. x ⟶ **DELETE** character under cursor

9. yy, yNy ⟶ **YANK** sometimes called **COPY**; (one line, N lines)

10. dd, dNd ⟶ **DELETE** sometimes called **CUT**; (one line, N lines)

11. d$, D ———————▶ **DELETE**   to end of line

12. p, P ———————▶ **PASTE**   below, above

13. : ———————▶ **GLOBAL**   command
                                        :# - go to line #
                                        :r FILE - include file FILE at cursor
                                        :s - search and replace
                                        :w - write
                                        :q - quit

14. . ———————▶ **REPEAT**   last command
                                        (in command mode only)

15. ZZ, ... ———————▶ **EXIT**   vi (some save, some don't,
                                            some write to new file)

16. nG ———————▶ **GO**   to line n. If n is omitted, then go to
                                        end of file.

Appendix H
Execution Path

- Program/command **EXECUTION**
  - Running the program on data
  - Invoking the command on arguments

- **REQUIREMENTS**
  - The program must be executable, **AND**
  - The program/command must be located in the directory in which you are currently located, **OR**
  - The program/command must be located in a directory in your execution path, **OR**
  - The user must provide a path to the command

- **FILE SYSTEM PATH**
  - A method of organizing and locating files and directories
  - Full path: Starts with the root directory, /
  - Directories are separated with slashes, /
    - **Example**: /usr/local/bin

- **EXECUTION PATH**
  - A list of directories
  - When you issue a command, each directory in the list is searched for the command
  - If found, and if it is executable, it is executed
    - **Example**: mail and vi

      these clearly do not reside in the user's home directory, but they are executed nonetheless
  - Most commands are in the default (already provided) path, so is the bin directory in each account directory.

- If you EVER see the response "Command not found" when you know the command exists, then you are not using the proper path to the command

- Each directory and file can be secured by the owner.

- There are three **LEVELS** of security:
    - **Owner** (permissions for the owner: YOU in your directory)
    - **Group** (permissions for a specific and predefined group)
    - **Other** (permissions for anyone else)

- There are three **TYPES** of permission:
    - **Read** (allows users in level to read a file or directory)
    - **Write** (allows users in level to modify a file or directory)
    - **Execute** (allows users in level to execute a file or search a directory)

- Each permission type is defined with a binary flag (0 is off, 1 is on).

- The permissions are concatenated into a single 9-bit string:

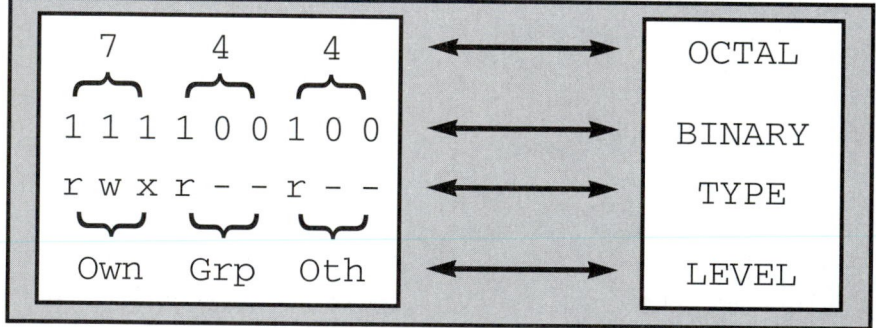

- When a long directory listing command (ls -l) is issued, the binary permissions are displayed.

- When a user wants to change permissions (chmod), they can use the octal code.

- The execute bit must be **ON** for a user for a program to be executable by the user.

Appendix J
ASCII Characters

ASCII (American Standard Code for Information Interchange) is a protocol for standardizing character sets for use in different computers. The usable set consists of the integer equivalents in the table below. For example, the blank character, represented as 'bl' in the table, is represented with the integer '32' (row 3, column 2). The capital 'A' is represented with the integer '65,' and the lower case 'a' is represented with the integer '97.' Because the standard alphabets, for either case, are represented with sequential integers, the conversion from uppercase to lowercase (or vice versa) can be accomplished through simple addition or subtraction (e.g., A = a - 32, a = A + 32)

	0	**1**	**2**	**3**	**4**	**5**	**6**	**7**	**8**	**9**
3			bl	!	"	#	$	%	&	'
4	(	)	*	+	,	-	.	/	0	1
5	2	3	4	5	6	7	8	9	:	;
6	<	=	>	?	@	A	B	C	D	E
7	F	G	H	I	J	K	L	M	N	O
8	P	Q	R	S	T	U	V	W	X	Y
9	Z	[	/	]	^	_	'	a	b	c
10	d	e	f	g	h	i	j	k	l	m
11	n	o	p	q	r	s	t	u	v	w
12	x	y	z	{	|	}				

ASCII Character Set

This text has introduced the basic concepts associated with programming in ANSI C. The novice programmer may wish to extent his or her skills by making use of function calls which have not been discussed in the text. For that purpose, the followng table is included. The table presents standard functions available with ANSI C, their use, their library, their argument types, and their function tyoes. Specific implementations may differ in location or explicit invocation.

Function Name	Description	Library	Argument Types	Function Type
abs	integer absolute value	math.h	int	int
acos	arc cosine	math.h	double	double
asin	arc sine	math.h	double	double
atan	arc tangent	math.h	double	double
atan2	arc tangent	math.h	double, double	double
ceil	ceiling (lowest whole number not less than arg)	math.h	double	double
cos	cosine	math.h	double	double
cosh	hyperbolic cosine	math.h	double	double
exp	exponential function (e^x)	math.h	double	double
fabs	double absolute value	math.h	double	double
floor	largest whole number not greater than argument	math.h	double	double

MATHEMATICAL

Function Name		Description	Library	Argument Types	Function Type
MATHEMATICAL	**log**	natural logarithm (base-e)	math.h	double	double
	log10	base-10 logarithm	math.h	double	double
	pow	exponentiation	math.h	double, double	double
	sin	sine	math.h	double	double
	sinh	hyperbolic sine	math.h	double	double
	sqrt	square root	math.h	double	double
	tan	tangent	math.h	double	double
	tanh	hyperbolic tangent	math.h	double	double
INPUT / OUTPUT	**fclose**	file close	stdio.h	FILE *	int
	fgets	string input from file	stdio.h	char *, int, FILE *	char *
	fopen	file open	stdio.h	char *, char *	FILE *
	fprintf	text file formatted output	stdio.h	FILE *, const char * types that match output arguments	int
	fread	binary file input	stdio.h	void *, size_t, size_t FILE *	size_t
	fscanf	text file input	stdio.h	FILE *,const char * types that match input arguments	int
	fwrite	binary file output	stdio.h	void *, size_t, size_t FILE *	size_t
	getc	character input from text file	stdio.h	FILE *	int
	getchar	character input from keyboard (stdin)	stdio.h	no arguments	int
	gets	string input from keyboard (stdin)	stdio.h	char *, int	char *

Function Name		Description	Library	Argument Types	Function Type
I N P U T / O U T P U T	**printf**	formatted output to screen (stdout)	stdio.h	const char *, types that match output arguments	int
	putc	character output to text file	stdio.h	int, FILE *	int
	putchar	character output to screen (stdout)	stdio.h	int	int
	scanf	input from keyboard (stdin)	stdio.h	const char *, types that match input arguments	int
	sprintf	formatted conversion to a string	stdio.h	char *, const char *, types that match output arguments	int
	sscanf	formatted conversion from a string	stdio.h	const char *, const char *, types that match input arguments	int
C H A R A C T E R S	**isalpha**	logical function for alphabetic character	ctype.h	int	int
	isdigit	logical function for base-10 digit character	ctype.h	int	int
	islower	logical function for lower case letter	ctype.h	int	int
	ispunct	logical function for punctuation character	ctype.h	int	int
	isspace	logical function for whitespace character	ctype.h	int	int
	isupper	logical function for uppercase character	ctype.h	int	int
	tolower	converts uppercase letter to lowercase	ctype.h	int	int

	Function Name	Description	Library	Argument Types	Function Type
	toupper	converts lowercase letter to uppercase	ctype.h	int	int
	memmove	copies given number of characters into string	string.h	void *, const void *, size_t	void *
STRINGS	**strcat**	string concatenation	string.h	char *, const char *	char *
	strcmp	lexical string comparison	string.h	const char *, const char *	int
	strcpy	string copy	string.h	char *, const char *	char *
	strlen	string length (doesn't include null string, \0)	string.h	const char *	size_t
	strncat	string concatenation up to a maximum number of characters	string.h	char *, const char *, size_t	char *
	strncpy	string copy up to maximum number of characters	string.h	char *, const char *, size_t	char *
GENERAL	**calloc**	dynamic array allocation	stdlib.h	size_t, size_t	void *
	exit	program termination	stdlib.h	int	void
	free	deallocates dynamically allocated memory	stdlib.h	void *	void
	malloc	dynamic memory allocation	stdlib.h	size_t	void *
	rand	pseudorandom number	stdlib.h	int	int
	system	calls to the operating system	stdlib.h	const char *	int

Appendix L
L^AT_EX Templates

This appendix includes extended samples for latex. In particular, we have included detailed examples for producing a resumé, an article (e.g., for a class term project), and a personal letter. The appendix also includes discussions of the use of bibliographies and indexes in latex. By copying and modifying these files, which can be found in the "UNIX/Ch6" directories, you should be on your way to producing complex documents with this text formatters. Following the examples, a synopsis of how to generate and use bibliographic databases and indexes with latex are presented.

Ch6

- latex resumé example
- latex article command file example
- latex article example
- latex letter example
- latex bibliography examples
- latex index examples
- latex to HTML comparisons

L.1 The L^AT_EX Resumé Template

Below is a sample resumé document, named "resume.tex," using the LaTeX text formatter. The commands of interest are annotated on the right border and explained below.

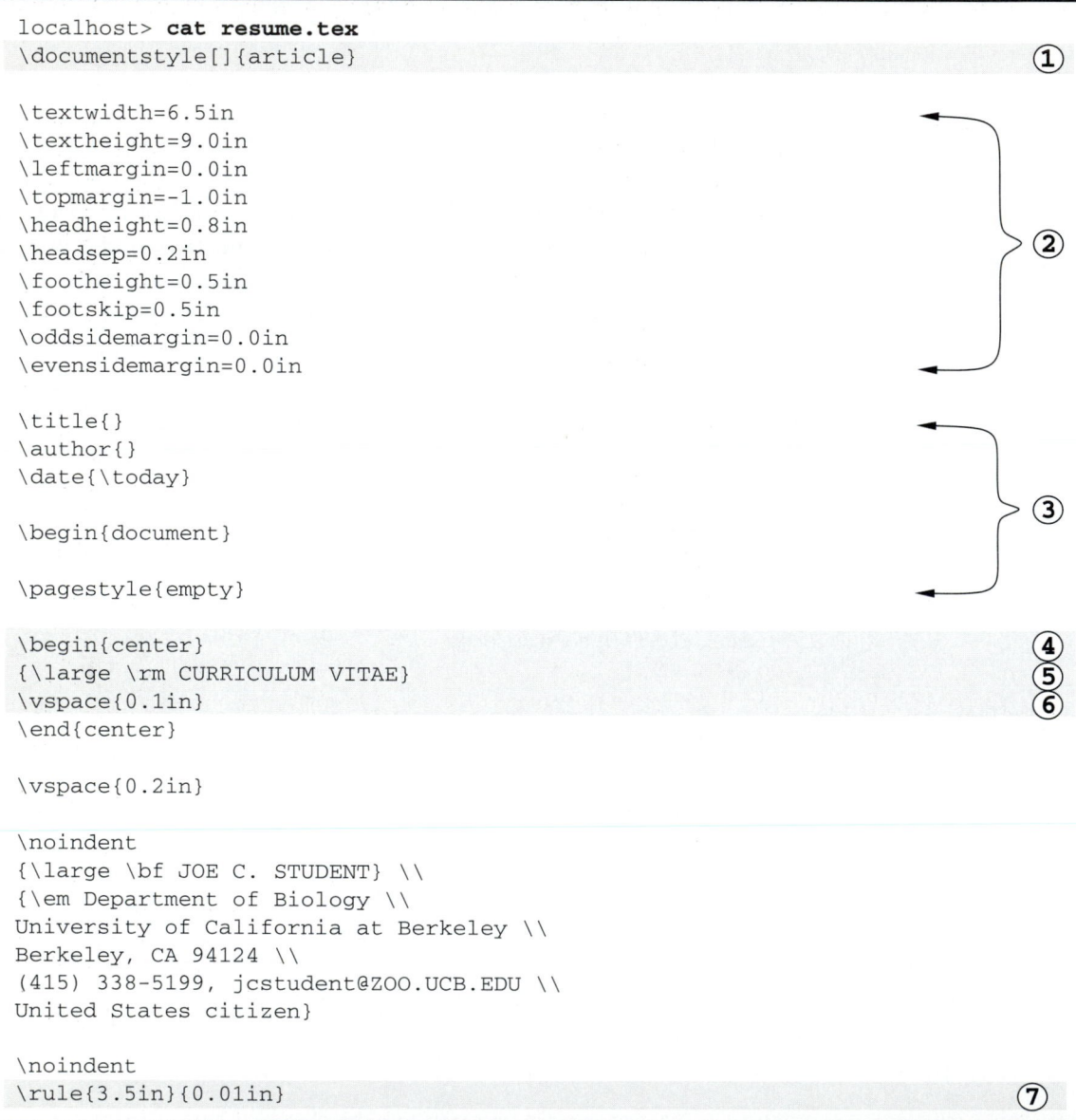

```
localhost> cat resume.tex
\documentstyle[]{article}                                      ①

\textwidth=6.5in
\textheight=9.0in
\leftmargin=0.0in
\topmargin=-1.0in
\headheight=0.8in                                              ②
\headsep=0.2in
\footheight=0.5in
\footskip=0.5in
\oddsidemargin=0.0in
\evensidemargin=0.0in

\title{}
\author{}
\date{\today}
                                                               ③
\begin{document}

\pagestyle{empty}

\begin{center}                                                 ④
{\large \rm CURRICULUM VITAE}                                  ⑤
\vspace{0.1in}                                                 ⑥
\end{center}

\vspace{0.2in}

\noindent
{\large \bf JOE C. STUDENT} \\
{\em Department of Biology \\
University of California at Berkeley \\
Berkeley, CA 94124 \\
(415) 338-5199, jcstudent@ZOO.UCB.EDU \\
United States citizen}

\noindent
\rule{3.5in}{0.01in}                                           ⑦
```

It should be noted that this document does not have the end document line which would be associated with the file. This is because to insert that line would end the document I am writint, so it has been omitted. The items below should help understand how this document is prepared. Some of the items, such as the double spaces at the ends of lines, have to be experimented with.

Item (**1**) The document style is defined as an article format with no options (empty square brackets).

Item (**2**) The article documentstyle has a predefined page layout (as do all document styles. These commands redefine the page, and doing this kind of thing is difficult so be careful if you try to modify these numbers.

Item (**3**) The article style also has author, date, and other fields. This portion simply sets the arguments which will be printed to null strings, so that they are ignored. The empty pagestyle simply defines the first page as an unnumbered page.

Item (**4**) The center paragraph style is used to center the lines that it encompasses, in this case the title "CURRICULUM VITAE."

Item (**5**) The "CURRICULUM VITAE" is boldened and set in the roman font.

Item (**6**) The smallskip command is used to create vertical space between paragraphs. You can also use medskip and bigskip commands, but the more versatile command is vspace, which takes an argument and argument type.

Item (**7**) A horizontal line is created under the name information using the rule environment. The two numbers refer to the length and thickness of the line.

Item (**8**) The beginning of a description paragraph style, which is a form of enumeration in which the item description is an indented paragraph, or hanging indent, from the item name, which is boldened.

Item (**9**) Each item in a description paragraph style must have the item defined in brackets and the text identified outside the brackets. Curly braces are not required, but serve to identify the scope of the text. Notice that the description items identify the primary headers in the resume.

```
\begin{description}                                                    (8)
\item[{\bf EDUCATION}]                                                 (9)
\item[University of California, Berkeley,]
{\bf Department of Biology} \\
{\em 9/89 -- present.} {Ph.D. expected 1996.} \\
{Major: Marine Mammal Physiology.  Minors: Bio-Engineering
and Pharmacology.}
{Current research:}
{\em ESHRAD: A program to study elephant seal heart rate and blood
flow in dive metabolism and efficiency.} \\
{\small The goal of this project is to understand the metabolic
factors leading to dive performance in elephant seals. Three key
issues exist in this research:

\begin{enumerate}
\item{The role of seal metabolism in deep dive}
\item{The relationship between heart rate and blood flow and dive
physiology}                                                            (10)
\item{The design of experiments and the associated apparatus for
observing seal metabolism during deep dives.}
\end{enumerate}

\item[San Francisco State University,]
{\bf Department of Zoology} \\
{8/86 -- 6/88.  Master of Science in Biology, 6/88. \\
Graduate work in marine mammal physiology. \\
Partial MSE in bio-engineering.}

\item[San Francisco State University,]
{\bf Department of Engineering} \\
{8/82 -- 6/66.  Bachelor of Science in Engineering, 6/86.}

\bigskip                                                               (11)
\item[{\bf RESEARCH EXPERIENCE}]
\item[University of California, Berkeley, Department of Biology:] \\ \\
{Research Assistant, UCB Marine Mammal Laboratory, 1/91 -- present.} \\
{Support from the Naional Science Foundation for the ESHRAD project,
three year
term from 8/90 -- 6/92.}

\item[San Francisco State University, Department of Zoology.] \\ \\
{Research Assistant, 6/86 -- 5/88.}
```

L.2 A L^A_TEX Command File for Articles

Every student and faculty member will write a paper from time to time. latex provides documentstyles to suit most paper types; however, to include many commands in the text file can be confusing and, sometimes, unruly. A paper command file allows the author to separate the paper, to some extent, from the rest of latex. Any paper that is read using the command file will be formatted with the same template. A command template can be designed for a particular class or journal.

"com.tex" is a command file for use in preparing articles. Included in "com.tex" are locally written macros which may be used in the article. For example, in com.tex two command macros are provided, one for incorporating externally-created PostScript files, and the other for labelling and including figure and table captions so they can be cross referenced in text.

```
localhost> cat com.tex
\documentstyle{article}                                                     ①

\newcommand{\figcap}[2]{                                                    ②
  \small
  \rm
  \caption{#2\label{f:#1}}
  }

\newcommand{\putfigure}[2]{                                                 ③
  \begin{figure}[ht]
  \input{#1}
  \centerline{\box\graph}
  \rm
  \small
  \caption{#2\label{f:#1}}
  \end{figure}
  }

\newcommand{\macputhv}[5]{                                                  ④
  \special{macfile="#1"                                                     ⑤
          hscale=#2
          vscale=#2                                                        ⑥
          hoffset=#4
          voffset=#5}                                                      ⑦
  \vspace{#3in}                                                            ⑧
  }
```

The file com.tex has been broken into two pieces, the one above, and another below, to aid the discussion.

Item (**1**) The the documentstyle "article" is determined. In this example, note that there aren't even any square brackets for documentstyle options. Items (**2 to 4**) are commands associated with figures.

Item (**2**) A macro for including figure captions. The item in the square brackets is the number of arguments to the macro, while the item in the curly braces is the macro itself. The syntax has a flavor of a shell script. Once inside the text of a macro, reference to arguments is by their number preceded by a pound sign (#). In the "figcap" macro, the latex command caption is used; however, it has been wrapped inside a call to small and rm. These make the caption small and roman. Inside the caption command is the text of the caption, argument #2, and the label for cross-referencing purposes, #1.

Item (**3**) The second macro, "putfigure," begins a figure environment and includes a captioning argument so that they do not have to be written inline for every figure.

Item (**4**) The "macputhv" macro is used to incorporate externally created PostScript files into documents. That is, an end to "cutting-and-pasting" pictures into documents! The macro takes five arguments:

Item (**5**) The name of the file to be included.

Item (**6**) The horizontal and vertical scaling for the figure.

Item (**7**) The horizontal and vertical offset.

Item (**8**) The vertical space reserved for the figure between paragraphs.

Scale values are given in percentage of the original figure. If you want to reduce the picture to 50% of its original, then argument #2 is {0.5}. Offsets are given in pixel units, 1/72 of an inch. Thus, if you want to give the figure a 2-inch horizontal offset, then argument #4 will have a value of {144}. The vertical space reserved for the figure is given as argument #3, in inches.

The remainder of the file com.tex is included below:

```
\textheight 9.00in
\textwidth 6.70in
\headheight -.85in
\footheight 0.5in
\oddsidemargin -.11in
\headsep 0.0in
\begin{document}
\include{paper}
\bibliography{paperbib}
\bibliographystyle{unsrt}
\end{document}
\end
```

The final part of `com.tex` is the page layout portion of the preamble.

Item (**1**) notes the inclusion of the data file, an example of which is included below.

Item (**2**) tells latex where to look for the bibliographic entries. The file should be called "`paperbib.bib`," i.e., with a "`.bib`" suffix.

Item (**3**) defines the bibliographic style that will be used for inline cite references and for the reference list.

It should be noted that bibliographic references can be included in the text and need not be in a separate file. However, latex will only use bibliographic references actually mentioned in text, so one huge bibliographic reference file can be used for all papers.

L.3 Executing latex on a Command File

To use latex on a large document, a number of phases must be executed, as follows:

- Run `latex` on the document file
  ("file.tex" $\Rightarrow$ "file.aux," "file.dvi")
- Run `makeindex` on the document file
  ("file.idx" $\Rightarrow$ "file.ind")
- Run `bibtex` on the document file
  ("file.aux," "file.bib" $\Rightarrow$ "file.bbl")
- Run `latex` on the document to include the new files
  ("file.aux," "file.bbl," "file.ind" $\Rightarrow$ "file.aux," "file.dvi")
- Run `latex` on the document to resolve references
  ("file.aux," "file.bbl," "file.ind" $\Rightarrow$ "file.aux," "file.dvi")
- Run `dvi2ps` on the document
  ("file.dvi" $\Rightarrow$ "file.ps")

Other intermediate and debugging files are constructed along the way of compiling all these files, namely "file.log" and "file.blg." For example, below is a trace of the commands run for compiling and printing the latex version of the manual you are reading:

- latex Unix-Man
- makeindex Unix-Man
- bibtex Unix-Man
- latex Unix-Man
- latex Unix-Man
- dvi2ps Unix-Man

Oftentimes you will have to run `latex` a number of times after running `bibtex` to get the cross-references correct. This is especially true if you are using a table of contents, because it lags the references by one compilation cycle.

L.4 A L^A^T~E~X **Sample Article or Research Paper**

```
localhost> cat paper.tex
\title{The Mating Rituals of Computer-Generated Rabbits          ①
\thanks{The research reported in this paper was funded in part     ②
by a grant from the Food and Drug Administration (contract no.
P00032-95-7615).}}

\author{Foo B. Baz \\ Zip Z. Zappo \\                              ③
Artificial Reality Laboratory \\ 3290 Bunko Hall \\
University of Cachaphony, Los Alamos \\ Los Babbaloey, AC  09002}

\date{}                                                           ④
\maketitle                                                        ⑤
\vspace{0.5in}
\centerline{\Large\bf Abstract}                                   ⑥
\bigskip

This paper briefly reports on the computational mating habits of
computer-generated rabbits.  This work is part of a research project
at the University of Cachaphony, department of Surrealism, and has
been supported by the FDA for 23 years...

\section{Introduction}                                            ⑦

The computational model of rabbit mating patterns has been widely
talked about since the discovery that computer-generated rabbits have
unusual behavior traits, such as...

\vspace{0.2in}
```

This example is fairly typical of latex papers:

Item (**1**) The paper title.

Item (**2**) Embedded in the title reference is an acknowledgement for financial support, which is printed in footnote format at the bottom of the page.

Item (**3**) The author list, separated by double backslashes to produce unique lines, and the address of the authors.

Item (**4**) The current date, which is printed below the author/address list, and can be eliminated if desired.

Item (**5**) Tells latex to print the title.

Item (**6**) Begins the paper abstract. Note that the abstract in this document is on the same page with the title.

Item (**7**) The one item of note in the generic paper is the *section* command, with its text argument. In latex, all numbered sequences are performed during the compilation, so the author need not worry about section numbering. If sections are moved, latex reorders the numbering the next time the document is compiled.

Much of the detail is missing in this example, because none of the list paragraph styles, such as itemize or enumerate are used. A copy of one of the manual chapters is also kept in the "manual" directory so that interested users can look at something a bit more complex.

L.5 A L^A_TEX Letter Command File

"tletter.tex" is a simple version of a letter format that takes a standard document, "newletter.tex," as input, and produces a letter with a technical letterhead. You can place a PostScript letterhead on the page easily. You can do this by modifying the command file below so that a PostScript figure is included, but that no space is allocated for it between paragraphs, in which case the letter is written on top of the figure.

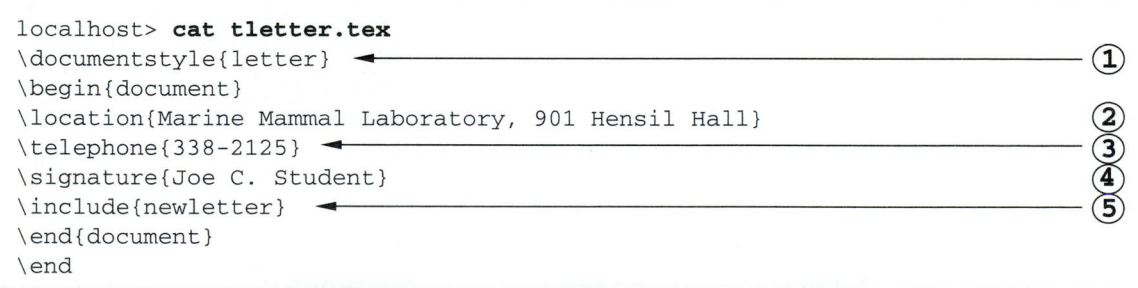

```
localhost> cat tletter.tex
\documentstyle{letter}  ─────────────────────────────── ①
\begin{document}
\location{Marine Mammal Laboratory, 901 Hensil Hall}  ─── ②
\telephone{338-2125}  ─────────────────────────────────── ③
\signature{Joe C. Student}  ───────────────────────────── ④
\include{newletter}  ──────────────────────────────────── ⑤
\end{document}
\end
```

The command file, above, remains the same all the time. When you run latex, this is the file you run it on, as with other command files. For example, a sample command would appear as follows.

```
localhost> latex tletter
This is TeX, C Version 3.0
(tletter.tex
LaTeX Version 2.09 <7 Dec 1989>
(/usr/f1/jhodges/TeX3.0/usr/local/lib/tex/inputs/letter.sty
Document Style 'letter' <20 Sep 88>.) (newletter.tex [1]) )
Output written on tletter.dvi (1 page, 220 bytes).
Transcript written on tletter.log.
```

The source letter can be called anything. When you are done, simple save it as "newletter." This will overwrite your previous newletter, but is OK as long as the letters, or whatever, are saved under separate names. A sample source letter newletter is shown below:

```
localhost> cat newletter.tex
\begin{letter}{Foo B. Baz \\ 123 Xyz St. \\ Anywhere USA 03246}    ①

\opening{Mr. Baz,}                                                 ②

Regarding our phone conversation on Tuesday, May 23 I would like to
order a ...

\closing{best regards,}                                            ③
\end{letter}
```

Item (**1**) in the example is the address which you are sending the letter to. This is usually printed on the left, just prior to the opening statement. Also, latex will print today's date above the address in the same location. Item (**2**) is the opening, which could be *Dear*, *To whom it may concern, Shirley,* etc., as you choose. Similarly, item (**3**) is a closing statement, and will be indented to near the middle of the page, below the last bit of text. Other letter commands are used similarly to other latex commands: enclose arguments in curly braces. The commands available for letters are

Table L.1: `latex` Letter options reference

`\opening{item}`	⇔	Your opening gratuity
`\closing{item}`	⇔	Your closing gratuity
`\cc{item}`	⇔	A carbon copy line
`\encl{item}`	⇔	Enclosures

All other latex formatting commands can be used in letters, such as enumerate, itemize, and quote.

L.6 L^AT_EX Bibliography Examples

Bibliographies are very important in academic reports. latex has a special processor, called bibtex, which pulls cites out of a latex document, takes these references from a reference database, formats them according to the author's desires, and places them back into the document. The following two sections illustrate the use of cites in this manual, and the format of cite references in the reference database. The use of bibliographies in the preamble and closing segments has already been discussed.

L.6.1 Bibliographic Entries in the L^AT_EX Document

```
examples\cite{pc87}. The example at (2) is the most straight forward of
```

There isn't much to it, really.

L.6.2 Bibliographic Reference Templates

The following are templates for various document types. I will explain the format of one, and let that serve as a basis for their use. With this and the documentation, you should be able to incorporate cites in your documents. The first thing you will notice is that there is a broad range of text types that are referenced in the templates subsequently.

- Manual
- Techreport
- Book
- Article
- Inproceedings
- Incollection
- Phdthesis
- Unpublished
- Inbook

Ch6

bib

The samples below are included in a file named "bibtemplates.bib" in the "bib" directory.

```
localhost> cat bibtemplates.bib
% Sample Bibliography Templates
%
% The percent sign is a comment character in TeX and LaTeX. Anything
% appearing after a percent sign will not be compiled.
%
% Each entry in one reference will be described:
%
% @techreport{joy:80a,                          <== (1)
%    title       = "An introduction to ...",    <== (2)
%    author      = "Joy, W.",                    <== (3)
%    institution = "Computer Science ...",       <== (4)
%    year        = "1980",                       <== (5)
%    type        = "Manual",                     <== (6)
%    month       = "September"                   <== (7)
% }                                              <== (8)
%
% (1) All reference types are preceded by an @ sign and an open
%     curly brace. This is followed by your label/key for the
%     cite. This is what you will type in the text when you refer
%     to the cite.
% (2) Each reference type (in this case, techreport) has fields
%     which are required and fields which are optional. Spacing
%     is unimportant, but the text of the field must be enclosed
%     in double quotes, and the field must be followed by a comma.
% (3) Authors are usually written last name first. Multiple authors
%     are demarked with "and."
% (4)
% (5)
% (6)
% (7) May be required and may be optional fields. When you run
%     BibTeX, you will be told if a required field is missing from
%     the reference. The last field does *not* end with a comma.
% (8) The reference must end with a closing curly brace.
%
% It should be mentioned that the fields provided in these templates
% need not come in any particular order.
```

```
@Article{              @Inbook{               @InProceedings{
  Author  =              Author   =             Author     =
  Title   =              Title    =             Title      =
  Journal =              BookTitle =            BookTitle  =
  Volume  =              Chapter  =             Organization =
  Number  =              Pages    =             Editor     =
  Month   =              Editors  =             Publisher  =
  Pages   =              Publisher =            Volume     =
  Year    =              Address  =             Month      =
  Note    =              Note     =             Pages      =
  }                      Year     =             Year       =
                         }                      Note       =
                                                }


@Techreport{           @Unpublished{          @PhdThesis{
  Title       =          Author   =             Author =
  Author      =          Title    =             Title   =
  Institution =          Publisher =            School  =
  Year        =          Address  =             Note    =
  Type        =          Month    =             Year    =
  Month       =          Year     =             }
  Note        =          Note     =
}                        }

@Book{                 @InCollection{         @Manual{
  Title     =            Author   =             Author    =
  Publisher =            Title    =             Title     =
  Edition   =            Booktitle =            Publisher =
  Year      =            Publisher =            Address   =
  Author    =            Year     =             Number    =
  Address   =            Editor   =             Year      =
  Note      =            Note     =             }
}                        }
                                               @Misc{
                                                 Title     =
                                                 Publisher =
                                                 Address   =
                                                 Year      =
                                                 Note      =
                                                 }
```

L.7 L^AT_EX **Index Examples**

When you write a longer document, such as a masters thesis, it is often a good idea to include a glossary or index. In latex, you can include index entries very simply, and generate an index at the end of your document. Your institution must have a copy of *makeindex* in order to construct the index entries. The program is written in C and can be found on the internet using archie. It was written at UC Berkeley in 1987. The following segments illustrate the use of index entries in the document and in the preamble and closing segments.

L.7.1 Index Entries in the Document

Below is an example of index entries in the current manual. Notice that, for readability, they are separated from other line items. This makes it easier to find them later on when you need to modify or otherwise upgrade them.

```
Using the on-line manual is simple. The command is {\em man}, which
you type at the shell prompt. The general usage is shown below:

\index{man@{\bf man}|ii}                          <== (1)
\index{man page}                                  <== (2)
\index{shell!prompt}                              <== (3)
\unixcom{man command}                             <== (4)
\noindent

where ``\%'' is the C shell prompt, ``man'' is the command name, and
``command'' is the name of some command you wish information about. For
```

To insert an index entry into the document, use "\index{item}" anywhere in the text. As mentioned, I like to keep them separate. In the example above, three index types are illustrated. There are other types, and the interested reader is encouraged to read latex documentation for more examples [Chen 1987]. Item (**2**) is the most straight forward of the examples. This will simply print out an entry in the index with the item labeled and the page reference on which it occured. Item, (**3**) is a slight modification, which indents "prompt" as a subitem under the index entry for "shell." Both will have page number references. Item (**1**) has two features in it. The first is the use of the at sign (@). This symbol tells the formatter to print the index item as shown afterward. In this case, "man" will be printed in bold in the index. The second part of the entry is the use of the vertical bar and the "ii." This does exactly what one would think, and pipes the index entry into a tex macro named "ii" which italicizes the page number. This is used, in this manual to indicate that this is the page on which the command was first introduced and the macro is shown in the next section.

L.7.2   Index Entries in the Preamble

```
\documentstyle[apalike,bk11,makeidx]{book}                          ①

%Italic and Index Entry and Range commands (from the makeindex
%documentation file)
\newcommand{\ii}[1]{{\it #1}}                                       ②

\author{Jack Hodges \\ Computer Science Department \\ San
Francisco State University \\ San Francisco, CA  94132}

\date{}
\makeindex                                                          ③

\begin{document}
\include{Unix-AppB}
\printindex                                                         ④
\bibliographystyle{apalike}
\bibliography{unixmanual}
\end{document}
```

The portion of this manual's command file is shown above (severely chopped up for brevity). Item (**1**), of course, is the documentstyle command. Notice that "makeidx" is a secondary, or modifying option to the primary style. The command for italicizing index entries described above is shown in item (**2**). This is part of the preamble for the document. Item (**3**) is where the index is generated, also in the preamble. Note that it precedes the document beginning statement. Finally, in the document body segment (item **4**) the index is printed.

Beware when you create these lists that their generation lags the latex compilation by at least one cycle, depending on other options you are invoking. Once the "paper.ind" file is generated, you can edit out any problems you do not like. You can also do this with .toc files, .lof files, etc.

L.8 Other Features of TEX

Ch6

texmacros

Although difficult, it is possible to write your own documentstyles for latex. As examples of what can be done, I have included a few homegrown styles in the "UNIX/Ch6/texmacros" directory. The first is "apa-like.sty," which will produce an APA formatted bibliographic reference list and cites. The second is "jack.sty," which is a paper drafting style. "jack.sty" will print text double-spaced, but everything else (e.g., quotes, figure captions, abstract, title, references, etc.) is single spaced. In every other respect it follows the "article" document style and is used to draft journal articles. The third is an "sfsuthesis.sty" can be used to format according to the SFSU master's thesis guidelines. The fourth style is "sfsuletter.sty" which is a template for writing letters but uses a letterhead file.

L.9 Comparison to HTML

LaTeX is similar to a current popular markup language called HyperText Markup Language (HTML) which is used to describe documents for network display on the World Wide Web. HTML is also a **tag-based** language, where the items we have been using to identify and interpret a portion of text, such as \title{foo} are called tags. In both languages some commands have single tags, which are called opening/closing tags. This means that they perform a function and nothing else need be done. In LaTeX two examples are \noindent or \newpage. In HTML two examples are <img> and <p>. Both languages also have commands which have both opening and closing tags. These tags are used when the scope of text over which the tag applies might be confused if not explicitly delimited at both ends. In LaTeX two such examples are \begin{document} . . . \end{document} and \begin{enumerate} . . . \item{} . . . \end{enumerate}. In HTML two such examples are <body> . . . </body> and <ol> . . . <li> . . . </ol>. The two languages are also similar in that they are both subsets of other languages. LaTeX is a subset of the TeX language, and HTML is a subset of the SGML language. Finally, documents written in both languages cannot be displayed directly, but must be interpreted locally and then displayed. This supports efficient transfer of documents and local interpretation of their formatting commands. The vehicle for displaying HTML documents is generally called a **browser**.

Below is a tabulation of some commands in HTML and their equivalents in LaTeX, and an example document illustrating HTML, called a home page. To find out more about the World Wide Web, browsers, HTML, and home pages at your location speak to your system administrator.

Table L.2: HTML and latex comparative document control options

HTML		LaTeX
<title>TITLE</title>	⇔	\title{TITLE}
<head> ... </head> <body> ... </body>	⇔	\begin{document}... \end{document}

The comparison between HTML head/body and LaTeX document is loose. In LaTeX, the document begin/end commands are required, whereas in HTML neither head nor body is explictly required, but they both identify the same elements of a document.

HTML ignores horizontal spaces like LaTeX and ignores vertical spacing between paragraphs even more than LaTeX. In LaTeX, two carriage returns will signify a paragraph, but in HTML it must be done explicitly with a `<p>` or `<br>` command, or one of the heading or listing commands which control their own vertical spacing.

Table L.3: `HTML` and `latex` comparative section header options

HTML		LaTeX
`<h1>text</h1>`	⇔	`\part{text}`
`<h2>text</h2>`	⇔	`\chapter{text}`
`<h3>text</h3>`	⇔	`\section{text}`
`<h4>text</h4>`	⇔	`\subsection{text}`
`<h5>text</h5>`	⇔	`\subsubsection{text}`
`<h6>text</h6>`	⇔	`\paragraph{text}`

There isn't a direct comparison between HTML and LaTeX for headings, because there is less agreement on how headings 1—6 are to be displayed in various Web browsers than for LaTeX, but the concept is the same. Each of the six headers can potentially refer to more specialized heading type.

Table L.4: `HTML` and `latex` comparative font type options

HTML		LaTeX
`<b>item</b>`	⇔	`{\bf item}`
`<i>item</i>`	⇔	`{\em item}`
`<code>item</code>`	⇔	`{\tt item}`

Table L.5: HTML **and** latex **comparative paragraph style options**

HTML		LaTeX
`<ol>`	⇔	`\begin{enumerate}`
`...`		`...`
`<li>`		`\item{}`
`...`		`...`
`</ol>`		`\end{enumerate}`
`<ul>`	⇔	`\begin{itemize}`
`...`		`...`
`<li>`		`\item{}`
`...`		`...`
`</ul>`		`\end{itemize}`
`<dl>`	⇔	`\begin{description}`
`...`		`...`
`<dt>text1<dd>text2`		`\item[text1]{text2}`
`...`		`...`
`</dl>`		`\end{description}`
`<pre>`	⇔	`\begin{verbatim}`
`...`		`...`
`text`		`text`
`...`		`...`
`</pre>`		`\end{verbatim}`

In LaTeX all listing paragraph styles use the `\item` tag to identify a list item. In HTML the `<li>` tag performs the same task.

LaTeX allows the user to insert figures and tables in much the same fashion. In HTML figures can be located anywhere in the network, so a URL (which stands for Uniform Resource Locator) is needed to identify the network path to a figure. All images in HTML are called inline images, because they are placed inline with text as though they were part of the text. This is similar to normal LaTeX, though there are ways to control where on the page figures will appear with LaTeX.

Table L.6: `HTML` and `latex` comparative figure control options

IITML		LaTeX

`<img align=ALIGN src="URL" alt="ALT">`	⇔	`\begin{figure}[htbc]`
		`..stuff..`
		`\end{figure}`

The HTML figure also has alignment characteristic which is similar to the La-TeX `[htbc]` characteristics. The `align` characteristic refers to the orientation of the figure w.r.t. the surrounding text, whereas the LaTeX designation specifies where on the page (vertically) to place the figure. In HTML there is no notion of a page, so the comparison is loose. The HTML `alt` characteristic is used to specify what will be displayed if the figure cannot be displayed.

The one thing that HTML does that page formatting languages cannot do at all is to refer and display documents which are located on other computers around the world. This is done through what is called a hypertext reference anchor. The anchor has two parts: (1) the item which is being referenced and (2) the item which is displayed. The displayed item, if text, will have some identifying characteristic (such as color or uderline) so that the user knows that it refers to another item. The item being referenced is identified by a URL.

Table L.7: `HTML` hypertext reference anchors

HTML
`<a href="URL">display-item</a>`

In this case the opening tag is `<a>` and the closing tag is `</a>`, but the `href` characteristic is used to identify the hypertext reference URL. The document being referenced or the display-item can be any type of document (e.g., picture, sound, text, movie).

A **home page** is simply a welcome message (and is often named "Welcome.html") to be displayed by a WWW browser. It is written in HTML. An example home page is shown below which illustrates some of the features of HTML which have been discussed and tabulated above. A URL for a complete home page is "`http://futon.sfsu.edu/~hodges`".

```
<title>Your Name</title>                                                    ①

<h1>Your Name
<a href="TIFFS/you.tiff"><img align=center src="GIFS/smiley-icon.gif"></a②
</h1>
<hr>


For contact information click <a href="#contact">here</a><p>              ③

<h4>A significant person in the world.</h4>

<ul>
<li> B.S.E. in Cyberspace Engineering, University of Babalooey, 1916
<li> M.A in Rabbit Sociology, Planetary Technical University, 1998          ④
</ul>


<h2>Areas of Interest</h2>

Virtual reality and cyber rabbits. <p>

<h2>Summary of Research</h2>

I have been looking into how cyber rabbits socialize and procreate in the
virtual network. I have developed an environment for tracking the whereabouts
and watching cyber rabbit behavior. This environment is extensible to other
cyber creatures.

See the <a href="pus-vrcr-group.html">CyberRabbit home page</a> for more info.

<h2><a name="contact"</a>Contact Information</h2>                           ⑤

<b>Office:</b><i> 020 Washington Hall</i> <p>
<b>Email address:</b><i> yourname@yourdomain</i><p>
<b>Postal address:</b><p>
<i> CyberRabbit VR Laboratory <br>
    Planetary Technical University <br>                                    ⑥
    Some Address <br>
    Some Place </i><p>
<b>Office Phone:</b><i> your phone </i><p>

<hr>
```

Item (**1**) illustrates the syntax for a title. Titles are not displayed in a viewer. Often the title is very similar or identical to the text of the first heading, as it is i this example.

Item (**2**) shows a fun thing to do. This is a hypertext anchor which is embedded inside of heading 1. The refenced document has a URL without a network address, so it is a local file. Note that the referenced file is a TIFF image. The item which is displayed is also an image, but this one happens to be a small image of a smiley face. When clicked on, the referenced document is loaded.

Item (**3**) shows how to reference a location within a document (the current one or another one). The same format is used, but the reference (#contact) refers to a label in the document, so when the document is loaded by the browser the location within the document where the label occurs will be visible on the screen. The associated location where the label is defined is shown at item (**5**). Notice that instead of a `href` characteristic a `name` characteristic is used instead.

Item (**4**) illustrates the use of a bulleted list. Lists can be nested as in LaTeX and in general where listing is used. The horizontal spacing used in the example will be ignored by the browser.

Item (**6**) shows another way to format a group of items, by changing fonts, breaking lines, etc.

The last item in the example, `<hr>`, which appears in other locations as well, displays a horizontal line across the page.

The appearance of this document in the X Mosaic browser is shown below:

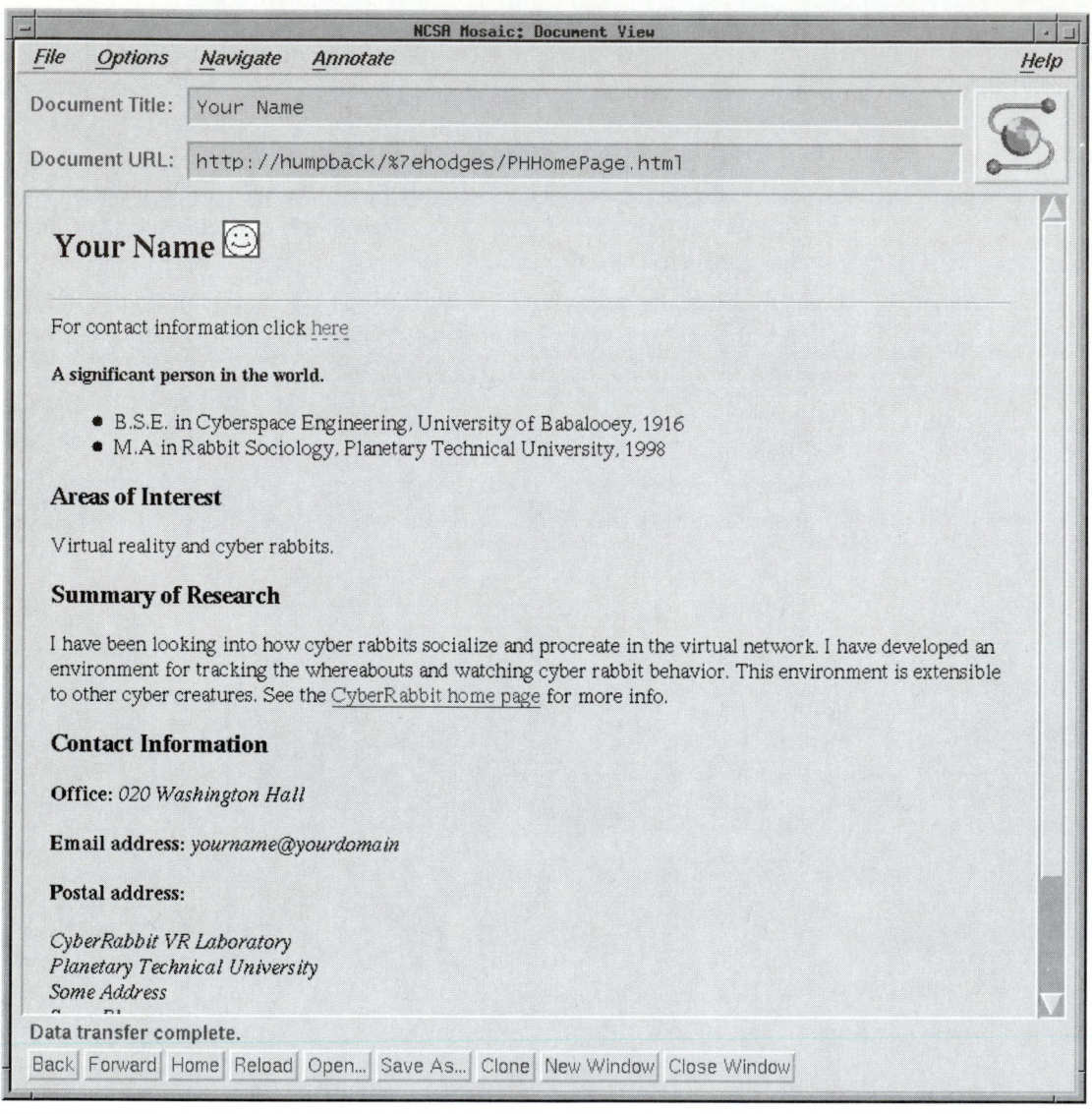

Index

Symbols

!
    in `.newsrc` file 50
    in command repetition 164

!=
    in C shell 440

\#
    comment character in Bourne shell 456
    comment character in C shell 432
    comment character in shell 137
    in C programming 273

\#!
    in Bourne shell 450, 456
    in C shell 429

\#define
    C preprocessor directive 288

\#endif
    C preprocessor directive 374

\#if
    C preprocessor directive 374

\#include
    C preprocessor directive 385
    personal libraries 385

$
    default Bourne shell prompt 450
    shell variable reference 146
    variable reference in Bourne shell 451
    variable reference in C shell 427

$<
    read shell variable from command line 430

$HOME variable 68

%
    comment character in `latex` 204
    in job reference 163
    integer remainder in C 291

%=
    modulo assignment operator 315

&
    address-of operator in `scanf` 280
    execute process in background 162

&&
    conjunction operator (AND) in C 310
    in `awk` 414, 416

*
    command wildcard 73
    executable file suffix in `ls -F` listing 70
    in case-esac 465
    kleene star 405
    multiplication operator in C 290

*/
    close comment character in C 269

*=
    multiplication assignment operator 315

*-closure 403

+
    addition operator in C 291
    in **folder, refile, scan** 38
    in MH 35

++
    increment operator 313

+=
    addition assignment operator 315

.
    access mechanism for C structs 353
    current or working directory 71
    in **nroff** 188
    repeat last command in `vi` 111
    to send email 25

..
    parent directory 71

.cshrc 9, 134, 135
    customizing 149

.login 9, 134, 142
    customizing 149

.mailrc
    mail aliases 31

.mh_profile 35

.newsrc 46, 47, 50

.plan 232

.profile
    Bourne shell initialization file 451

.project 232

.rhosts file 247

.so
    load source file in **nroff** 190

.Z
    compressed file suffix 260

/
    directory separator 60
    directory type in listing 70
    division operator in C 291
    in **more** 90
    root directory designation 60
    search command 66

/*
    open comment character in C 269

/=
    division assignment operator 315

/bin directory 59

/etc directory 59

535

A

B

D

N

S